ROBERT M. STAMP is co-ordinator of the Canadian Studies Program at the University of Calgary.

In the late nineteenth and throughout much of the twentieth century, the image of Ontario education has been one of extreme centralization and of a supposedly superior system. This study presents both the illusion and the reality, documenting the accomplishments and shortcomings of a massive provincial educational enterprise that sought to balance the perceived needs of its juvenile clients with those of the wider adult society.

Following Egerton Ryerson's retirement as Chief Superintendent of Schools in 1876, Ontario's elementary and secondary schools were controlled at the local level by school-boards and boards of education, and at the provincial level by a Department of Education (later Ministry of Education) headed by a cabinet minister. Within such a political environment, educational decisions were influenced continually by what was regarded as appropriate policy at both the community and provincial levels. Public policies, in turn, were shaped by a combination of economic, social, and cultural influences and occasionally by the outlook and determination of individual policy makers.

While the image grew of centralization, with all-powerful ministers of education and departmental officials controlling both provincial and local developments from their offices in Queen's Park, in reality a strong reservoir of community power shaped local and even provincial action for the full century after Ryerson's retirement.

On questions of pedagogy, curriculum, and educational programs, Robert Stamp takes an ideological position emphasizing the periods of innovation that challenged traditional class-room approaches, including the New Education reforms of 1890–1910, the progressivist thrust of the 1937 Ontario curriculum, and the Hall-Dennis Report of 1968.

This comprehensive study of the post-Ryerson period in Ontario education will be of importance and interest to historians, educators, and educational administrators.

THE ONTARIO HISTORICAL STUDIES SERIES

The Ontario Historical Studies Series is a comprehensive history of Ontario from 1791 to the present, which will include several biographies of former premiers, numerous volumes on the economic, social, political, and cultural development of the province, and a general history incorporating the insights and conclusions of the other works in the series. The purpose of the series is to enable the general reader and the scholar to understand better the distinctive features of Ontario as one of the principal regions within Canada.

Published

Olga B. Bishop, Barbara I. Irwin, Clara G. Miller, eds *Bibliography of Ontario History, 1867–1976: Cultural, Economic, Political, Social,* 2 volumes (1980)

J.M.S. Careless, ed *The Pre-Confederation Premiers: Ontario Government Leaders, 1841–1867* (1980)

Peter Oliver *G. Howard Ferguson: Ontario Tory* (1977)

Christopher Armstrong *The Politics of Federalism: Ontario's Relations with the Federal Government, 1867–1942* (1981)

David Gagan *Hopeful Travellers: Families, Land and Social Change in Mid-Victorian Peel County, Canada West* (1981)

Robert M. Stamp *The Schools of Ontario, 1876–1976* (1982)

Forthcoming

Roger Graham *Hon. Leslie M. Frost* (Premier, 1949–1961)

A.K. McDougall *Hon. John P. Robarts* (Premier, 1961–1971)

E.S. Rogers, ed *A History of the Indians of Ontario, 1550–1980*

ROBERT M. STAMP

The Schools of Ontario, 1876–1976

A PROJECT OF THE BOARD OF TRUSTEES
OF THE ONTARIO HISTORICAL STUDIES SERIES
FOR THE GOVERNMENT OF ONTARIO
PUBLISHED BY UNIVERSITY OF TORONTO PRESS
TORONTO BUFFALO LONDON

ISBN 0-8020-2437-8

Canadian Cataloguing in Publication Data

Stamp, Robert M., 1937–
  The schools of Ontario, 1876–1976
  (Ontario historical studies series, ISSN 0380–9188)
  "A project of the Board of Trustees of the Ontario
  Historical Studies Series for the Government of
  Ontario."
  Includes index.
  ISBN 0-8020-2437-8
  1. Education – Ontario – History.   I. Title.
  II. Series.
  LA418.06S72   371'.009713   C81-095006-5

This book has been published with the assistance of funds provided by the
Government of Ontario through the Ministry of Culture and Recreation.

FOR MY PARENTS:
THOMAS CARSON STAMP
CLARICE EDITH MILES

Contents

The Ontario Historical Studies Series

When discussions about this series of books first arose, it was immediately apparent that very little work had been done on the history of Ontario. Ontario has many fine historians, but much of their work has been focused on national themes, despite the fact that the locus of many of the important developments in the history of Canada – as recent events remind us – was, and is, in the provinces. While other provinces have recognized this reality and have recorded their histories in permanent form, Ontario is singularly lacking in definitive works about its own distinctive history.

Thus, when the Ontario Historical Studies Series was formally established by Order-in-Council on 14 April 1971, the Board of Trustees was instructed not only to produce authoritative and readable biographies of Ontario premiers but also 'to ensure that a comprehensive program of research and writing in Ontario history is carried out.'

From the outset the Board has included both professional historians and interested and knowledgeable citizens. The present members are: Margaret Angus, Kingston; J.M.S. Careless, Toronto; Floyd S. Chalmers, Toronto; R.E.G. Davis, Toronto; Gaetan Gervais, Sudbury; D.F. McOuat, Toronto; Jacqueline Neatby, Ottawa; J. Keith Reynolds, Toronto; and J.J. Talman, London. E.E. Stewart and Raymond Labarge served as valued members of the Board in its formative period. The combination of varied interests and skills of Board members has proven useful. A consensus was soon reached on the need for research in neglected areas of Ontario history and for scholarly and well-written works that would be of interest and value to the people of Ontario. We trust our work will satisfy these criteria.

After much careful deliberation the Board settled on six major areas in which to pursue its objectives: biographies of premiers; a bibliography; a historical atlas; a group of theme studies on major developments (social, economic, and cultural, as well as political) in the province; the recording on tape of the attitudes, opinions, and memories of many important leaders in Ontario; and, as a culmination of these studies, a definitive history of Ontario.

The first edition of the bibliography was published in 1973. Since it was well received, the Board sponsored the preparation of a second, comprehensive edition prepared by Olga Bishop, Barbara Irwin, and Clara Miller, entitled *Bibliography of Ontario History, 1867–1976*. This volume was published in 1980. Our first major publication was *G. Howard Ferguson* by Peter N. Oliver (1977), followed in 1978 by *Ontario since 1867*, a general history of the province, by Joseph Schull. *The Pre-Confederation Premiers: Ontario Government Leaders, 1841–1867*, edited by J.M.S. Careless, the second volume in the biographies series, was published in 1980. The first of the theme studies, *The Politics of Federalism: Ontario's Relations with the Federal Government, 1867–1942*, by Christopher Armstrong was published in 1981. David Gagan's *Hopeful Travellers: Families, Land and Social Change in Mid-Victorian Peel County, Canada West*, the second of the theme studies, was published also in 1981. *The Schools of Ontario, 1876–1976* by Robert Stamp is the third of the theme studies. We hope it will find a large and interested reading audience and that it will be followed each year by one or more equally interesting books, the total of which will inform and illuminate Ontario history in a new and lasting way.

The Board is greatly indebted to its editors, Goldwin French, Editor-in-Chief, Peter Oliver, Associate Editor, and Jeanne Beck, Assistant Editor, for their assistance in the selection of subjects and authors and for their supervision of the preparation, editing, and publication of works in the Series.

MURRAY G. ROSS
Chairman, Board of Trustees
Ontario Historical Studies Series

22 September 1981

For many years the principal theme in English-Canadian historical writing has been the emergence and the consolidation of the Canadian nation. This theme has been developed in uneasy awareness of the persistence and importance of regional interests and identities, but because of the central role of Ontario in the growth of Canada, Ontario has not been seen as a region. Almost unconsciously, historians have equated the history of the province with that of the nation and have depicted the interests of other regions as obstacles to the unity and welfare of Canada.

The creation of the province of Ontario in 1867 was the visible embodiment of a formidable reality, the existence at the core of the new nation of a powerful if disjointed society whose traditions and characteristics differed in many respects from those of the other British North American colonies. The intervening century has not witnessed the assimilation of Ontario into the other regions in Canada; on the contrary, it has become a more clearly articulated entity. Within the formal geographical and institutional framework defined so assiduously by Ontario's political leaders, an increasingly intricate web of economic and social interests has been woven and shaped by the dynamic interplay between Toronto and its hinterland. The character of this regional community has been formed in the tension between a rapid adaptation to the processes of modernization and industrialization in western society and a reluctance to modify or discard traditional attitudes and values. Not surprisingly, the Ontario outlook is a compound of aggressiveness, conservatism, and the conviction that its values should be the model for the rest of Canada.

The purpose of the Ontario Historical Studies Series is to describe and analyse the historical development of Ontario as a distinct region within Canada. The series as planned will include approximately thirty-five volumes covering many aspects of the life and work of the province from its original establishment in 1791 as Upper Canada to our own time. Among these will be biographies of several prominent political figures, a three-volume economic history, numerous works on topics such as social structure, education, minority groups, labour, political and administrative institutions, literature, theatre, and the arts, and a comprehensive synthesis of the history of Ontario, based upon the detailed contributions of the biographies and thematic studies.

In planning this project, the Board and its editors have endeavoured to maintain a reasonable balance between different kinds and areas of historical research, and to appoint authors ready to ask new kinds of questions about the past and to answer them in accordance with the canons of contemporary scholarship. Ten biographical studies have been included, if only because through biography the past comes alive most readily for the general reader as well as the historian. The historian must be sensitive to today's concerns and standards as he engages in the imaginative recreation of the interplay between human beings and circumstances in time. He should seek to be the mediator between all the dead and the living, but in the end the humanity and the artistry of his account will determine the extent of its usefulness.

The Schools of Ontario, 1876–1976, the third theme study to be published, is a detailed account of the development of primary and secondary education in Ontario since the retirement of Egerton Ryerson. The author has described frankly the 'accomplishments and the shortcomings' of the schools, and the complex relationships between the Department (later Ministry) of Education, the teachers, the students, and the community. He has analysed critically the growth of the widespread belief that Ontario has a highly centralized and markedly superior educational system and has assessed the impact of successive periods of innovation on the objectives and effectiveness of the schools. We hope that this work will enlarge our understanding of this important aspect of the social history of Ontario and that it will stimulate extensive research on this subject.

GOLDWIN FRENCH
Editor-in-Chief
PETER OLIVER
Associate Editor
JEANNE BECK
Assistant Editor

Toronto
22 September 1981

Preface

The purpose of this book is to describe and analyse the development of the school system of the province of Ontario in the first century following Egerton Ryerson's retirement as chief superintendent of schools in 1876. During this period, Ontario's elementary and secondary schools were part of the public domain, controlled at the local level by school-boards and boards of education, and at the provincial level by a Department of Education (later a Ministry of Education) headed by a cabinet minister. Within the political environment, educational decisions were influenced continually by what was regarded as appropriate public policy at both the community and provincial levels. Public policies, in turn, were shaped by economic, social, and cultural influences, as well as by the outlook and determination of individual policy makers.

The image of Ontario education in the late nineteenth century and throughout much of the twentieth century is one of extreme centralization, with all-powerful ministers of education and departmental officials controlling both provincial and local developments from their offices in Queen's Park. In reality, there existed a strong reservoir of community power that shaped local and even provincial action for the full century after Ryerson's retirement. A second image that needs re-evaluation – and one that was widely held both at home and abroad during this hundred-year period – is the supposed superiority of the Ontario educational system. This study seeks to present both the illusion and the reality. It endeavours to document the accomplishments and the shortcomings of a massive provincial educational enterprise that sought to balance the perceived needs of its juvenile clients with those of the wider adult society.

Much of the traditional writing on Ontario educational history has perpetuated the twin myths of centralization and superiority. During the past ten years, however, a number of historians working in several areas of educational history have begun to question these premises. The late Donald Kerr supervised my doctoral thesis, and first challenged me to question the traditional perspective in one field: the campaign for technical education. The work of Donald Wilson,

Susan Houston, and Alison Prentice in early nineteenth-century Ontario school-ing, of Robert Gidney and the late Douglas Lawr in local/provincial relations, and of Peter Oliver and David Cameron on individual themes of the twentieth century has been most helpful.

Some readers may detect that I have an ideological position on questions of pedagogy, curriculum, and educational programs. Periods of innovation in which traditional class-room approaches were challenged are emphasized in this account. Thus the New Education reforms of the 1890–1910 period, the progres-sivist thrust of the 1937 Ontario curriculum, and the Hall-Dennis Report of 1968 are all presented in a sympathetic light. In this regard I must thank the editorial team of the Ontario Historical Studies Series. The editor, Goldwin French, and the associate editor, Peter Oliver, provided generous moral support and con-structive editorial criticism of the entire manuscript over a five-year period. Jeanne Beck, the assistant editor, gave me very valuable advice and information, particularly on the final chapters. For those sections in which my attitude is most evident, the editors provided two additional invaluable services: an insistence on historical perspective and the freedom to reach my own conclusions. I thank them on both counts.

The reader will find relatively few references to educational developments in other parts of Canada and the North Atlantic world. There are two reasons for this. First, the educational system of the province of Ontario tended to evolve in comparative isolation, with little reference to conditions elsewhere. Such fea-tures as grade 13 and the provisions for Catholic separate schools and French-language bilingual schools are without precise parallels elsewhere. In the few instances where outside influences were prevalent – generally in the New Educa-tion movement of the early twentieth century, and specifically in the enterprise curriculum of 1937 – such borrowing is acknowledged. But this leads to the second consideration. For most of the century under review, Ontario educators were convinced of the superiority of their school system. They sincerely believed that they had little to learn from the rest of the world. Consequently, they paid amazingly little attention to changes and innovations elsewhere. Only in the post-1960 years did this attitude begin to change.

The decision to follow the development of Ontario education to the year 1976 creates two major problems. First, it becomes increasingly difficult to view the more recent past with the same depth of historical perspective that can be applied to earlier periods. Second, the traditional kinds of primary and secon-dary source material – the manuscript collections, theses, journal articles, and monographs – are scanty. These two problems influence the chapters dealing with the years following the Second World War, particularly the final chapter on the late 1960s and early 1970s. The reader will note in these chapters both the results of the writer's own involvement in educational issues and a heavy reliance on daily newspapers as sources of information. One hopes that these short-comings are balanced by the benefits of carrying the narrative to 1976.

This work could not have been accomplished without assistance in gaining access to primary source materials. I wish to thank Dr Edward Stewart, deputy minister, office of the premier, for permission to consult the John Robarts files, prime minister's office papers, Provincial Archives of Ontario. I also thank G.H. Waldrum, former deputy minister of education, for permission to consult the education department records for the years 1946–68, also in the Provincial Archives of Ontario. The entire staff of the Provincial Archives has been most helpful during my hurried visits to Toronto over the past few years; I owe special thanks to Robert Tapscott and Dorothy Kealey in this regard. Archivist Donald Nethery of the Historical Collection, Toronto Board of Education, has been equally helpful and generous with his time, as have the staffs of the Public Archives of Canada and a number of other local school-boards. John McDonald of the Ontario School Trustees' Association and Margaret Wilson and James Forster of the Ontario Secondary School Teachers' Federation gave me good counsel and much helpful information, for which I am very grateful.

Research costs have been met through a grant from the Ontario Historical Studies Series. Much helpful advice and constructive criticism have come from fellow educational historians at the University of Calgary – Nancy Sheehan, David Jones, and Catherine Littlejohn – who read earlier versions of this manuscript. Thanks are also due to the staff of the Interlibrary Loans Office, University of Calgary Library, for assistance in locating and securing obscure secondary sources not available in Calgary. Portions of the manuscript have been typed with skill and courtesy by Ruth Smith and Marian Burke of Calgary.

This book is dedicated formally to my parents, Tom and Clarice Stamp, both of whom attended the schools of Ontario during the second and third decades of the twentieth century. It is dedicated informally to my wife, Arlene Stamp, who like myself attended Ontario schools in the 1940s and 1950s and returned to teach in those schools in the 1960s; and to our children, Shelly and David Stamp, who were prevented from attending the schools of Ontario during the 1970s because of my decision to gain a spatial perspective on my native province by moving two thousand miles away.

RMS
Calgary, Alberta
May 1981

Photographic Credits

Archives, Toronto Board of Education   10, 29, 30, 31, 33
Canadian National Railways   21
City of Toronto Archives   6, 14, 15
Ontario Ministry of Education   1, 4, 22, 32, 34, 35, 38
Provincial Archives of Ontario   2, 5, 7, 8, 12, 16, 17, 18, 19, 23, 26, 27, 36, 37
Public Archives of Canada   9, 11, 13, 20, 25, 28
Robert M. Stamp   3, 24

1 Education department display at Philadelphia Centennial Exposition, 1876

2 Port Perry High School, Intermediate class, June 1876

3 Presenting the external world to the nineteenth-century pupil: the Ontario Readers, Second Reader, 1884

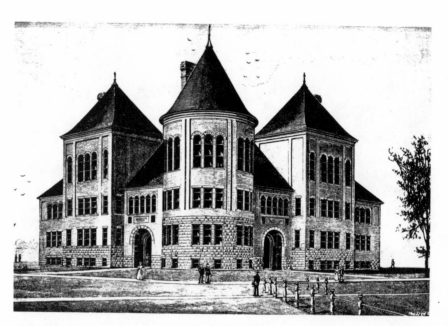

4 The physical presence of the school: Chatham's Central School, 1898

5 The child in the free urban environment: a Toronto newsboy, late nineteenth century

6 Children in a controlled urban environment: Cherry Street Playground, Toronto, 1913

7 Adam Crooks

8 George Ross

9 Teachers in training at Woodstock Model School, c. 1887

10 Kindergarten class in Toronto, 1893

11 A girls' class at the Ottawa Model School, 1899

12 Manual training class, Givens Street School, Toronto, 1901

13 Teachers in training at the Ontario Normal School of Domestic Science and Art, Hamilton, early 1900s

14 A 'Little Mothers' class in a Toronto school, 1913

15 Nose-blowing exercise in Toronto school, 1913

16 James Hughes

17 Adelaide Hoodless

18 John Seath

19 Richard Harcourt

20 Northern children come to the school: a camp school at Dane on the Timiskaming and Northern Ontario Railway, 1907–8

21 The school comes to northern children: teacher Fred Sloman in a railway car school

22 A unique response to the 'rural school problem': Rittenhouse School, Jordan Station, 1914

23 A provincial response to the 'rural school problem': Millbrook Continuation School, 1920s

24 Snap-shot memories: Mr Scott and Miss Wilcocks, teachers of the 'Senior Fourth' class at Homewood Public School, Toronto, 1923

25 A special occasion: school children welcome HRH The Prince of Wales, Toronto, 1919

26 Henry Cody

27 Howard Ferguson

28 Home and School Association, Burford, September 1921

29 Girls' basketball team, Oakwood Collegiate Institute, Toronto, 1926

30 Boys' softball team, Bowmore Road Public School, Toronto, 1938

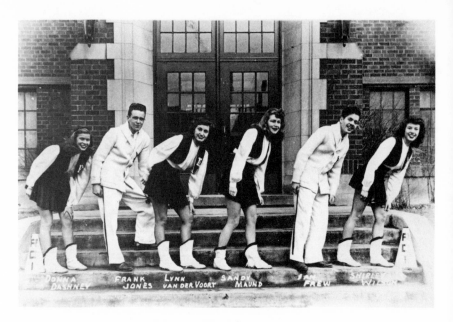

31 Cheerleaders at Runnymede Collegiate Institute, York Township, 1944–5

32 School buses loading at Brampton High School, 1947

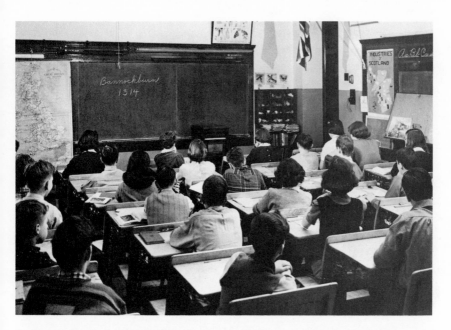

33 The elementary school of the 1950s: listening to a radio broadcast, Oriole Park Public School, Toronto

34 The secondary school of the 1950s: working in the library, Listowel District High School, 1954

35 William Dunlop

36 George Drew

37 John Robarts

38 William Davis

Abbreviations

ACFEO   L'Association canadienne française de l'éducation d'Ontario

AHSBO   Associated High School Boards of Ontario

AR   Annual Report of the minister of education, Province of Ontario

CEA   Canadian Education Association

DEA   Dominion Educational Association

FWTAO   Federation of Women Teachers' Associations of Ontario

NCWC   National Council of Women of Canada

OEA   Ontario Educational Association

OPSMTF   Ontario Public School Men Teachers' Federation

OSSTF   Ontario Secondary School Teachers' Federation

OTA   Ontario Teachers' Association

OTF   Ontario Teachers' Federation

PAC   Public Archives of Canada

PAO   Provincial Archives of Ontario

RG2   Record Group 2, education department records, Provincial Archives of Ontario

RG3   Record Group 3, prime minister's office papers, Provincial Archives of Ontario

RG18   Record Group 18, provincial secretary's papers, Provincial Archives of Ontario

TBE   Toronto Board of Education, historical collection

UTA   University of Toronto Archives

The Schools of Ontario, 1876–1976

1 The Illusion and the Reality: Ontario Schools in the 1870s

I

The Philadelphia Centennial Exposition of 1876 provided an international arena for the evaluation of the Ontario school system, a system that had been carefully nurtured and consolidated during the previous three decades under the guiding hand of Egerton Ryerson. To commemorate Ryerson's retirement as chief superintendent of schools that year, the Ontario Department of Education mounted a major exhibit at Philadelphia. More than 2,000 separate articles, valued at over $10,000 and enumerated in a sixty-four page catalogue, occupied 2,750 square feet of floor space in the main display building. There were copies of educational reports and school laws, university calendars and examination papers, photographs and models of school buildings, samples of school equipment and furniture, and text books and library books. In greatest abundance were visual aids for teaching the various subjects – geometrical forms, mathematical instruments, plaster moulds of hands and feet for drawing classes, chronological charts for history classes, maps and globes, geological and biological specimens, and equipment for chemistry and physics laboratories. This 'exhibition of apparatus of every kind,' declared the Toronto *Globe*, was 'far ahead of any exhibit from any other country.' The correspondent for the rival Toronto *Mail* was 'happy to say that the Ontario Exhibit takes the shine out of them all.'[1]

International praise matched this domestic acclaim. 'The Country that exhibits the finest collection of Educational Appliances is Ontario,' declared the Philadelphia *Press*. One British commissioner asserted that the Ontario exhibit 'transcended all his expectations,' while an Australian official wrote that nothing 'so fully shows the extraordinary progress of Canada as the educational display of Ontario.'[2] From the United States Centennial Commission came a bronze medal 'for a quite complete and admirably arranged Exhibition' and 'for the efficiency of an administration which has gained for the Ontario Department a most honourable distinction among Government Educational agencies.' There was a gold medal from the British judges and a special award 'for an extensive and attractive collection, illustrative of the growth and extent of the educational system of Ontario.'[3] Deputy Minister J.G. Hodgins's presence at the International Educational Conference held in Philadelphia in mid-July reinforced Ontario's pre-eminence. No other foreign educator was in such demand as a conference speaker. Hodgins spoke at length on whatever his admiring audiences wished to hear about the Ontario school system – its courses of study, its method of teacher training and certification, and, above all, its comprehensiveness and unity.

One reason for Ontario's rich harvest of awards lay in the method of judging. Instead of competitive evaluation, the judges considered each exhibit on its own merits, leading to a liberal dispensation of gold, silver, and bronze medals. Yet the Ontario exhibit did stand out when compared with the mediocre efforts of most American states. Of the thirty-eight states in the Union, wrote John Hoyt of Wisconsin, 'perhaps half a dozen should be admitted to have done themselves credit with their educational displays.'[4] But Ontario's impact was also due to the careful planning of Hodgins and his departmental personnel. 'Other major exhibitors sent volumes and volumes of pupil work,' reported former grammar school inspector George Paxton Young, 'while Ontario ... astonished the natives by an exhibition of the material instruments of education.' The emphasis was placed on the desired process – on visual aids designed to increase the efficiency of class-room teaching – rather than on the end product. 'An intelligent enquirer at Philadelphia,' declared Hodgins, 'could understand the whole philosophy of our educational plans, take in at a glance the outlines of the entire structure of our Educational system, and could understand its practical working.'[5] Such 'intelligent enquirers' might have suspended judgment until they had had time to evaluate the product; but there was so much to see at Philadelphia that both judges and casual visitors were more likely to be impressed by Ontario's glittering array of paraphernalia.

Ontario educators had not been without doubts about accepting the invitation to exhibit at Philadelphia. 'Some hesitation was felt,' admitted Hodgins, 'when the question was considered as to how we ought ... to enter into a competition with other and more advanced countries.'[6] But this initial hesitation vanished with the realization that 'we could turn the Exhibition to good account for the Department.' First, Ontario could learn from others. 'An examination of the educational features of the Exhibition ... would place the Department in possession of valuable information.'[7] Second, the World's Fair would provide an ideal opportunity to boast of Ontario's own accomplishments during the Ryerson years. Grasping this public relations potential, Ontario officials planned 'the best method of making the educational exhibits most popular ... to the educationalists visiting the Exhibition.'[8] These seemingly incompatible purposes co-existed uneasily and vied for supremacy, not only during the Philadelphia summer of 1876, but also for the next century in Ontario education.

In the fields of science and technology, Ontario did learn from Philadelphia and from other nineteenth-century world's fairs. Impressed by Russian displays of manual training apparatus, Hodgins returned home convinced that his province was falling behind in industrial and technical education. He admitted that Ontario was represented 'by many ingenious evidences of industrial skill,' but lamented that most 'were rather striking adaptations of what already existed, rather than bold and original inventions.' Although he was 'among the last to admit it,' Hodgins concluded that Canada 'is doing very little to ensure progress or practical excellence in the future.' Even in the best Ontario schools, 'the teaching of drawing is the rare exception, not to speak of higher Industrial Training.'[9] But there were compelling reasons why it would take so long to translate this early stimulus for science and technical education into practical application. Like other Ontarians, Hodgins returned from Philadelphia with a certain feeling of self-satisfaction that proved a deterrent to educational innovation. Politicians and educators would prove reluctant to depart radically from a system that had earned, and would continue to earn, such international accolades. The forward thrust of reform, propelled by the steady urbanization and industrialization of the province, became submerged in the conservatism resulting in some measure from domestic and foreign praise. Ontario's presence at Philadelphia retarded rather than advanced educational innovation.[10]

II

Egerton Ryerson's retirement in 1876 provided the Liberal government of Premier Oliver Mowat with an opportunity to replace an appointed superintendent with a minister of education directly responsible to the legislature. 'The Chief Superintendent had hitherto been virtually a minister without a minister's responsibility,' argued Mowat. 'If responsibility was essential to all other departments of the Government, surely it was to the Education Department.'[11] Future Education Minister George Ross maintained that the powers exercised by the minister 'on a matter of such paramount importance as the education of the youth of the province for future citizenship, are too great to be entrusted to any bureau.'[12] Ryerson himself had suggested the change as the only solution to the persistent criticism he had received; a minister could answer his critics directly on the floor of the house and would at least have the support of the majority in the legislature. Conservative opposition leader W.R. Meredith seized on this latter point in arguing against the change. 'The temptation of the party in power is to back up the Minister, no matter whether he does right or wrong.'[13] While Mowat's strong Liberal majority guaranteed the passage of the education department bill, Meredith was correct in his assertion that schooling and partisan politics in Ontario would be closely connected in future years.

Adam Crooks was the logical successor to Ryerson as Ontario's first minister of education. As attorney-general in the earlier Edward Blake cabinet and provincial treasurer under Mowat, Crooks had the cabinet seniority that would bring prestige to the new ministry. As a former vice-chancellor of the University of Toronto, he had the confidence of the province's university leaders. To cap matters, Crooks was virtually hand-picked for the job by Ryerson himself. As the transition took place in the early months of 1876, Ryerson was delighted with the approach of the new minister. 'Mr. Crooks and myself understand each other,' he wrote his daughter. 'He is most cordial & seems to be thoroughly one with me on all educational matters.' Ryerson was also pleased that his long-time deputy superintendent, John George Hodgins, remained as the new deputy minister. Ryerson observed that Crooks 'takes upon himself only what requires the action or policy of the government, & places the whole management of the Department & its officers, & the Normal Schools, under Dr. Hodgins, who is virtually installed in my place.'[14]

Crooks and Hodgins nominally presided over a vast educational enterprise. Statistics for 1876 showed some 465,000 pupils enrolled in over 5,000 schools, operated at the local level by 4,900 public, separate, and high school boards. With provincial control over the determination of curriculum, authorization of textbooks, setting of examinations, and training and certification of teachers, it might also appear that Hodgins supervised the work of a large administrative bureaucracy. Yet it was a small staff that worked out of the provincial department of education offices in the Toronto Normal School building. Hodgins and a few clerks handled the routine correspondence that served to remind local trustees and parents of what was permissible under provincial law and departmental regulations. Hodgins also supervised the work of three high school inspectors and the instructors at the Toronto and Ottawa normal schools. Yet strong local appointees served as a counterweight to the power of the central departmental staff. Some 270 local public school inspectors were employees of county councils or municipal school-boards. While required to submit annual reports to the department, their tenure depended primarily on the pleasure of their local employers.

Hodgins's power was curtailed as well by Crooks's desire to set his own impress on Ontario education. The new minister ended the publication of the *Journal of Education* in 1877, and abolished the central book depository in 1879, two important functions of the department which Hodgins had supervised during the Ryerson years. Towards the end of 1879 Hodgins's position was further undermined with the transfer of legislative and legal responsibilities to Alexander Marling, a former clerk under Hodgins now installed as the minister's secretary.[15] Also functioning independently of Hodgins was the Central Committee of Examiners, an appointed group of university professors and public and high school inspectors that had replaced the old Council of Public Instruction in 1871. Originally formed to assist in the examination and classification of elementary school teachers, the Central Committee assumed greater importance after 1876 as Crooks used it as an advisory council on a wide range of policy matters. Its chairman from 1871 to 1889 was George Paxton Young, professor of philosophy at the University of Toronto and a former grammar school inspector under Ryerson. Young was such a powerful figure that one critic labelled him the '*de facto* minister of education.'[16]

Adam Crooks inherited a curriculum for the public and separate schools that had been prescribed by the department of education under the authority of the 1871 school act, Ryerson's last major piece of educational legislation. 'The great object of this Programme' was 'to secure such an education of youth as to fit them for the ordinary employments and duties of life.' The subjects listed as 'the first essentials of education for every youth' were the traditional ones of reading, writing, arithmetic, and 'the use of the English language.' A second category included the natural and physical sciences, with particular emphasis on 'our own Bodies and Minds, and the laws of their healthy development and preservation.' Next came geography, history, civics, and 'the first principles of Christian morals, so essential to every honest man and good citizen.' Curriculum revisions of 1871 had added such practical subjects as agriculture, bookkeeping, and the mechanical arts.[17] Such a comprehensive curriculum appeared a formidable challenge for Ontario youngsters and their teachers in the 1870s. But in everyday practice, most schools – especially those in the rural areas – concentrated on a limited offering of reading, spelling, writing, composition, arithmetic, and geography.

Between 5 and 6 per cent of Ontario pupils in the 1870s worked their way through the four classes or 'books' of the elementary school in seven or eight years, sat for the 'entrance' examination, and proceeded on to high school. Ryerson's 1871 legislation had brought the old grammar schools under the full authority of the provincial department of education, even though tuition fees at the secondary school level would continue in many centres for another half century. Two programs of study were now offered in the high schools. The English and commercial course was designed to educate pupils 'not only for Commercial, Manufacturing and Agricultural pursuits, but for fulfilling with efficiency, honour, and usefulness the duties of Municipal Councillors, Legislators, and various Public Offices in the service of the Country.' The more prestigious classical course emphasized 'the languages of Greece and Rome, of Germany and France, the Mathematics, etcetera, so far as to prepare youth for certain Professions, and especially for the Universities.'[18] The intention was to limit most high schools to the English and commercial course, and to authorize the classical course in a few superior schools, which would be designated as collegiate institutes. But Crooks and his department officials found this distinction difficult to enforce, as even the smallest village high schools offered Latin to their pupils. Although the terms collegiate institute and high school would persist for many decades, by 1883 the distinction came to be based on staff qualifications and physical facilities rather than on courses offered.

In 1876 there were 104 high schools and collegiate institutes in Ontario, staffed by 266 teachers and attended by 8,451 pupils. These institutions varied considerably in staff competency, facilities, and purpose from the larger cities to the smaller towns. High School Inspector J.A. McLellan singled out Brantford Collegiate 'as one of the very best schools ... [with] no better work done, in my opinion, in any school in Ontario.' In 1876 it sent five of its graduates to university, including the candidate who stood first in general proficiency at the University of Toronto matriculation examination. McLellan attributed Brantford's success largely to its principal, a man he described as 'a good scholar, inspiring teacher, and full of enthusiasm.'[19] At the other end of the continuum was Fonthill High School, a one-room, one-teacher institution, crammed with pupils who 'have never passed any Entrance Examination, and are as yet quite incapable of passing any such Examination.' Inspector S.A. Marling concluded that to call 'the school in its present state a "High School" would be but a perversion of the words.'[20] Yet such disparities existed, and would continue to exist, as long as local communities insisted on providing high school opportunities, however limited, for their youngsters, and as long as these local communities shouldered the major financial burden of schooling.

The provincial department of education hoped to weed out unqualified high school students through the introduction of the entrance examination in 1873 and the intermediate examination in 1876. The dreaded 'intermediate' was to serve as the standard for promotion from lower school (forms I and II) to upper school (forms III and IV); it also determined the bulk of the school's provincial grant on a 'payment by results' basis. So rigorous was the first intermediate examination in June of 1876 that more than half the province's high schools failed to pass a single candidate, while seven schools captured nearly half the total fixed grant distributed on the basis of results. One inspector justified the intermediate for its role in 'bringing up the poor schools and making still better the good ones.' Yet a colleague feared it would promote 'the idea of education being merely the passing of an examination.'[21] Criticism of the intermediate from both teachers and trustees led to its abolition in 1882. But the tone had been set, and the examination emphasis would continue through the end-of-school matriculation examinations. These were effectively under the control of the universities, particularly the University of Toronto, since they served the dual function of school-leaving and university-entrance. As a result, the universities played a dominant role in shaping the high school curriculum, and naturally shaped it to their own needs and interests.

Despite this university influence, statistics for 1876 showed only 25 per cent of high school leavers entering the universities and learned professions. Many students attended high school to complete the minimum academic requirements for a third-class teaching certificate. Others merely stayed a year or two before leaving for jobs in agricultural, commercial, or industrial life. And increasingly through the 1870s, girls began to make their presence felt in the once-male preserve of the Ontario high school. At Hamilton Collegiate in 1876, girls outnumbered boys for the first time in the school's history – 245 to 241. Kingston might refuse to admit girls to its collegiate, other boards might grudgingly tolerate girls in separate class-rooms, but in most centres the battle for female admission had been won. As girls proved themselves the academic equals of the boys, the old argument that the female mind could not grasp the rigours of the classical and mathematical curriculum was replaced by a new concern: were these subjects of equal value to the two sexes for their future roles in life? Crooks suggested music, drawing, and needlework to relieve girls from studies of 'less ... application to the duties of their sex.'[22] But girls were attending high school for the same variety of reasons as their brothers; many had their sights set on university entrance. Regardless of the views of Adam Crooks, they proceeded to compete on equal terms for the prizes and scholarships available in classics and mathematics.

III

Society's leaders spoke with virtual unanimity when they discussed the underlying purposes of schooling in the last quarter of the nineteenth century. Much of the academic, social, and practical justification for the various subjects of the curriculum was bound up in the theory of mental discipline, a theory that supported general education in the early grades and the dominance of a small group of subjects, especially the classics, in the high schools. The intellectual value of mental discipline was ably presented by Sir William Peterson, principal of McGill University. 'All education should be a training of faculty,' he told the Ontario Education Association. Its purposes were to 'develop and train the natural powers of the mind; to make it quick, apprehensive, accurate, logical; able to understand argument; able to search out facts for itself, to draw from them the proper conclusions; to reason, and to understand reasoning; in one word, to think.' Thus the 'real test of efficiency in education is not the accumulation of data or the acquisition of knowledge, but the development of intellectual power.'[23] Other educators stressed the moral value of mental discipline. 'The child acquires in this painstaking application the moral qualities of perseverance, patience and self-denial,' declared high school principal James Hume. 'He learns the lesson of self-control.'[24] Believing implicitly in both the intellectual and moral power of mental discipline, educators argued that a limited curriculum based on the traditional subjects was practical for all pupils. 'Farmers need, just as much as others, training in the habits of accuracy,' concluded Peterson. 'Much of what is valuable in the traditional curriculum will be quite as valuable to them as for others.'[25]

Educational leaders presented the moral aims as explicitly as any academic goals. 'Children are there to exercise self-restraint,' declared the editor of the

Canadian Educational Monthly. 'Truthfulness and honesty in word and deed are expected to be inculcated by both precept and example.'[26] Quoting from an American educator, education minister Crooks stressed that 'in the well-disciplined school, the pupil is first taught to be regular and punctual, to be cleanly in person, polite to his fellows, obedient to his teachers.'[27] His successor, George Ross, concurred. The educator's first priority, asserted Ross, was not to impart knowledge but to mould the character of his students through the suppression of 'evil tendencies' and through the search for 'what is good and true for their own sakes.'[28] The immediate goal was the inculcation of Christian values; the underlying aim was the prevention of deviant behaviour and crime. It was to the schools that 'we must look for a potent means of the prevention of crime in our midst,' stressed deputy minister Hodgins. Through the establishment of schools, hundreds of children who 'would be left to the demoralizing education of the Street ... are brought continuously under a wholesome discipline, and a humanizing and elevating influence.'[29] Indeed, one county inspector looked upon the public school system as 'the hope of the age' if it 'educates not merely in letters and figures, but in right habits ... and in correct principles, moral, social and civil.'[30]

Between 1871 and 1875 Christian morals appeared on the curriculum as a separate subject for Fourth and Fifth Class pupils. The authorized textbook was Ryerson's *First Lessons in Christian Morals* which encouraged each child to govern his 'temper, appetites, passions and propensities.' He was taught that 'the lawless indulgence of the passions and appetites involves sensuality, and sensuality ruins both body and mind.' Happiness consisted not in riches, or in the pleasures of exalted rank or station, but in 'moderation in expectations ... the exercise of the social and benevolent affections ... the formation and maintenance of good habits ... and the consciousness of His Favour.'[31] It was a change in tactics rather than in objectives that led to the dropping of Christian morals as a separate subject in 1875. Concerned about the ineffectiveness of direct instruction, critics argued that textbook teaching of morals was similar to placing 'a plant on the soilless floor of a library, watering it with textbooks on agricultural chemistry, and expecting it to grow, instead of giving it grass and light.'[32] The following year the department of education substituted optional religious exercises and prayers in 'the earnest hope that Trustees and Masters may thus be better enabled to impress upon their pupils the principles and duties of our common Christianity.'[33] Departmental officials were pleased with the results of this new approach; within a year 4,173 of the province's schools began the day with religious exercises and closed with prayers, while 3,025 went further and taught the Ten Commandments.

Other agents were also expected to contribute to the inculcation of appropriate moral values – the individual subjects of the curriculum, the authorized textbooks, and the discipline imposed within the classroom. English literature was a subject of prime importance. It would bring the pupil into 'intimate contact with ... the greatest moral power on earth,' and curb the 'inclination to read those trashy novels that are undoubtedly poisoning the intellect and moral life-blood of the readers.'[34] Mathematics and foreign languages stressed the importance of obeying rules and working within an established and ordered pattern. History, if rightly studied, was also 'a great teacher of morals.' It 'teaches us to admire and esteem the brave, the honest and the self-denying; and to despise and condemn the cowardly, the base, and the selfish. We are led to see that virtue preserves and strengthens a nation, while vice inevitably causes decay and weakness.'[35] Comparisons between the rise of the British Empire and the decline of the Roman Empire were strongly implied.

The authorized textbook was the principal vehicle for presenting this curriculum to the Ontario schoolchild of the 1870s and 1880s. The scarcity of well-trained teachers and the almost total absence of supplementary reading material created a situation in which most textbooks were memorized word for word. And among textbooks, the school reader had a central place, introducing the youngster not only to his maternal language, but also to history, geography, nature study, and science. By this time the Irish Readers, in use for over a generation in Ontario schools, were on their way out, replaced by three new domestic series – the Canadian Readers, the Royal Readers, and the long-lasting Ontario Readers. Multiple authorization did not produce a diversity of content. Readers for the early grades contained the same familiar nursery rhymes and Aesop's fables, stories about nature and young children, and descriptive passages on the origins of common household foods and fabrics. Readers for the upper elementary classes presented heroic stories from English, European, and (occasionally) Canadian history, and introduced the pupil to the poetry and prose works of the great authors of British literature – Addison, Browning, Dickens, Emerson, Hawthorne, Longfellow, Shakespeare, Tennyson, and Wordsworth.

The content of the readers was designed to shape the child's view of the past, the present, and the desired future. An omnipotent and omniscient God permeated every page, the creator of the universe and of human life, meting out both earthly and heavenly rewards and punishments. Children were told they were 'little lambs' made by God; the little girl slaving in the factory 'knows this is the way God trains my soul for heaven.' Youngsters were taught to accept misfortune and to be thankful for God's blessings. 'Make the best of the means at your disposal, as well as the talents you possess'; even the little crippled boy 'has many blessings for which he can be thankful.'[36] Well-being in the next life depended on exemplary behaviour in this life. Children were admonished to 'treat the poor kindly, and help them when we can'; they were taught the virtues of persistence, obedience, and truthfulness; they were urged to be brave, gentle, generous, and wise. Idleness and laziness were particularly sinful. 'You must not be idle. You must keep your eyes on your lessons.'[37] Economic and social concepts buttressed the status quo, and the child was not encouraged to notice that his society was less than unanimous on sensitive issues of the day. Economics stressed the sacredness of private property, the wisdom of prudent investments, and the virtues of industry and frugality – but neglected to mention the trade union movement and labour-management conflicts. There was a glorification of motherhood and an acknowledgment of the vast influence of women in shaping the life of the home – but no thought of the woman pursuing her own career outside the home.

If the nature of the curriculum and the contents of the readers failed to impress proper attitudes on young pupils, teachers could always fall back on authoritarian disciplinary procedures within the class-room and the school. Although departmental authorities were beginning to argue the superiority of positive motivation over corporal punishment as a means of reducing discipline problems, class-room control in the 1870s and 1880s continued to be maintained through the frequent and widespread application of the strap. Ottawa's Central School East reported thirty-one strappings for November 1885, while the city's monthly average throughout the decade was about sixty. Toronto's Jesse Ketchum Public School, a twelve-room school enrolling some 600 pupils, used the strap twenty-eight times between 25 October and 9 November 1888, an average of two per school day. Between four and twelve strokes on the open palm constituted the punishment at Jesse Ketchum for such offences as fighting, misbehaving in line, lying, talking back to a teacher, eating in school, neglecting to correct wrong work, shooting peas in the class-room, going home when told to remain, long-continued carelessness, and 'general bad conduct.'[38]

Assessing the moral influence of the school is more difficult than cataloguing the explicit and implicit purposes of the educational enterprise. In the first place, the school was but one of many agencies inculcating habits and attitudes. 'It is only to a very limited extent that the school can be expected to contend against the general bent and bias of society,' Goldwin Smith reminded the province's teachers in 1873.[39] One rural inspector readily admitted that the effects of the school might be negligible. After all, 'surroundings and associations influence a child's mind to a large extent.' It was therefore 'evident that home and other influences had more effect upon a child's mind than school influences.'[40] Inspector J.B. Boyle of London was especially pessimistic about the effects of the school on the rougher boys of that city. 'Our boys are in many instances, coarse in manners, in tongue, destitute of a pleasing deportment, certainly uncivil, while many do not exhibit a decent deference to their parents, masters, or those whose age or position should entitle them to respect,' he complained in 1876.[41] Archbishop Cleary of Kingston feared the schools might be doing more harm than good – at least for young girls. 'Modesty is not one of the things taught in our public schools,' he charged. 'Girls at these schools learn to be boisterous, immodest, screaming, kicking creatures, such as was never seen among pagans.' The public schools, he concluded, were 'destroyers of modesty, an abomination, and a disgrace.'[42]

External influences also compromised the achievement of academic goals. The Hastings County inspector believed that the work of the Third Class was crucial, for few students of the 1870s and 1880s continued further. Hence Third Class pupils, 'in addition to an intelligent familiarity with the branches of study always taught in that class,' should 'be trained to write, with fair facility and accuracy, ordinary letters of business and friendship ... and be able to keep an ordinary cash book, such as every farmer and mechanic should keep.'[43] E.C. Drury, later to become premier of Ontario, believed these aims had been accomplished during his school days near Crown Hill in the 1880s. 'By the time we reached the Fourth Class,' Drury recalled, 'we could read ... fluently and with expression. We could spell correctly and had a fairly broad vocabulary ... We knew enough arithmetic to serve ordinary needs.' Drury argued that despite 'all their shortcomings, I am inclined to think that the country schools did very good work.'[44] Yet what was taught or not taught varied from one school district to the next. In one school section not far from Drury's Crown Hill the idea prevailed in 1879 'that children should not learn Geography or Grammar.'[45] Writing about a part of Bruce County in the 1870s, Watson Kirkconnell related that with the exception of his father, none of the other country pupils went on to high school 'or forsook the tillage of the land.' Instead, 'the sons became farmers, the daughters farmers' wives, maintaining with toil and fidelity the ancestral traditions of their name.'[46]

And what of the few pupils who remained for the Fourth Class, passed the entrance examination, and continued on for a year or two of high school work? The average fifteen-year-old high school leaver, according to the provincial inspectors in 1876, 'should be able to read with intelligence and taste, and to express his ideas in writing with clearness and precision, should have a taste for books and some knowledge of our literature, possess accurate and available attainments in elementary mathematics ... and have a fair knowledge of general and physical geography, and of the history, government and constitution of the British Empire and the Dominion.' In addition to these explicit curricular aims, the ideal pupil should possess 'just views of his duties as a member of the Christian community.'[47] Whether these goals were realized depended on many factors: the background of the pupil, the atmosphere of the school, and the skill of the teachers. The accomplishments of J.H. Putman, a graduate of Smithville High School, were probably representative of many rural youths in the late 1870s and early 1880s. 'My knowledge of science and technical English grammar was hazy,' he recalled, 'but I had a flair for composition, was confident of my ability to spell, to solve any ordinary problem in arithmetic or geometry, knew a little algebra, had read much history as a boy, knew a little Latin, no Greek or French, and had a smattering of chemistry, physics and botany.'[48]

IV

The success of the school in accomplishing its explicit and implicit aims depended as much on the class-room teacher as on the provincial curriculum, authorized textbooks, and idealistic pronouncements from society's leaders. 'The Teacher makes the School, and the Teacher alone,' declared one county inspector in 1877. 'Programmes, Exams and Text-Books may be valuable auxiliaries, but these are mere cyphers in comparison with the live Teacher.'[49] Statistics for 1876 indicated some 6,195 teachers at work in the province's schools, 2,780 of whom were male and 3,405 female. Less than one-third of the teaching force held first- or second-class provincial or county certification; the majority were teaching on interim or third-class certificates liberally dispensed by county councils with little regard for the candidate's academic or professional training. Although the *Globe* boasted in 1883 that Toronto teachers possessed 'a degree of excellence that gives promise of a brilliant future for the city schools,'[50] rural inspectors were less charitable in their evaluation of class-room work. A frequent complaint was that too much attention was paid to 'cramming the memory rather than developing the powers of the mind.'[51] In 1876 the Simcoe County inspector paid particular attention to the question: While one class recites, how are the other classes employed? At SS no. 3, Nottawasaga, he observed 'mostly idling, laughing and playing'; at SS no. 2, Nottawasaga, 'some studying, most of them sleeping.' In the latter case the 'teacher is going to leave and does not care.'[52]

While irregular attendance undoubtedly retarded pupil progress, rural inspectors were prepared to place much of the blame on the transiency of the teaching force. The Ontario County inspector reported in 1878 that 'many considerations enable me to state ... that the wave of progress flows onward to maturity of perfection.' Yet he regretted that 'the strength of this wave is greatly diminished, and its velocity retarded, as it strikes against the rock of frequent change of teachers.'[53] The following year a colleague described teachers as 'the Arabs of Ontario.' They 'have no fixed abode,' and are 'here this year, there the next, and nowhere the third.'[54] The turnover of teachers was particularly rapid in rural areas. The fifteen schools in Oro Township of Simcoe County averaged eleven teachers each in the 1874–1900 period; one school section in Durham County went through twenty-nine teachers in the same period.[55] 'Were the same teacher retained for several successive terms, less harm would result, but this is rarely the case,' lamented one inspector. 'A new teacher, and as a rule a poor one every year, is the unfailing concomitant of the system.'[56] Each year saw a high percentage of female teachers leave for the wedding altar; there were also ambitious young men and women going back to normal school to raise their qualifications. But inspectors worried most about the large number of 'young men of ability and ambition' who annually deserted the profession because 'emoluments are small and the prizes few.' 'They aspire to something higher,' declared M.J. Kelly of Brant, 'to be lawyers, doctors, divines, and so drift into the universities, and thence into the wider fields of intellectual activity, where they hope to reap a richer harvest.'[57]

Several promising changes in teacher certification and training appeared in new regulations issued in 1877. County school-boards were henceforth restricted to the issuing of third-class certificates, valid for only three years, while the central authority assumed all responsibility for first- and second-class certification. Professional training was made mandatory for even third-class certification, not through expensive additions to the province's normal-school system, but through the inexpensive creation of county model schools. Here the teacher candidate was to receive a highly practical training in class-room management and teaching methods. The model schools proved extremely popular, requiring only a fourteen-week course, close to home, with minimum fees. They were also politically attractive; during the course of the next thirty years, they graduated over 36,000 elementary teachers at an annual cost to the provincial treasury of around $7,000. Although the model schools performed their limited task reasonably well, they attracted a host of critics. One professional journal described them in 1880 as 'fifty-two mills or teacher manufactories that bid fair to swamp, by their overproduction of an article which is now a drag on the market, the profession of teaching in this province.'[58] Rural inspectors deplored the quality of their graduates – 'too much raw material being thrust into the profession each year.'[59] Entrance requirements were low, the course was hurried, and very little time was available for practice teaching. The result was that the model schools overstocked the market with poorly trained teachers.

The system might have worked if the model-school graduates had later enrolled at either the Toronto or Ottawa normal schools to upgrade their certification and receive advanced professional training. Yet only one-quarter of Ontario's teachers did so. Many found that a third-class certificate was sufficient before marriage or a move to another career provided an escape from teaching. Others discovered that higher certification priced them out of the rural market. Still others were deterred by the barren intellectual atmosphere and rigid social rules that prevailed at the normal schools. J.H. Putman recalled his term at the Toronto Normal School in 1887 as 'flat, uninteresting and a waste of time. There was no real challenge to test intellectual power.'[60] Students were compelled to stay in approved boarding houses if they lived away from home, and could be expelled if caught speaking with members of the opposite sex. It did Ottawa Normal School students little good to protest this latter rule in 1886, demanding regulations 'in keeping with the spirit and tendencies of this enlightened age.'[61] The department of education was simply unwilling to trust the maturity and personal judgment of normal-school students, the majority of whom were from farm families, away from home for the first time. 'Here in the Normal School,' wrote Hodgins, 'there are young men and women ever ready to take advantage of any relaxation of discipline.'[62] While such restrictions may have annoyed many students, they did prepare the neophyte teacher to accept strong community and professional limitations on social and academic freedom.

Young Joseph Rowan took his first teaching position with SS no. 19, York Township, in January 1879. He and the chairman of the three-member school-board signed a standard provincial contract, calling for an annual salary of $300 paid on a monthly basis, with no obligation to teach on Saturdays or other school holidays, no salary deductions in case of illness, and thirty days' notice in writing if either party wished to terminate the contract.[63] Whether Rowan's subsequent relations with his board were calm or stormy is not known, but they could hardly have been worse than the situation in SS no. 1, Hope Township, during 1876. Here, personal animosity between the teacher and one trustee eventually led to the latter being fined six dollars for horse-whipping the unfortunate 'master' of the school.[64] All teachers had to keep a watchful eye on trustee and parent reactions if they wished to safeguard their positions. They were warned against the 'too hasty introduction of new methods' because 'our people are not prepared for such radical changes.' They were frequently pushed into 'promoting scholars before they are fit' in order to 'deceive parents and secure a re-engagement for the next year.'[65] They also had to be wary of their older pupils. 'In wintertime nearly all the back seats were occupied by young fellows ranging from 15 to 23,' recalled one teacher of his village school experience in the 1870s. 'One of the oldest pupils wore a mustache and was a local Samson. He was so strong he was able to throw a small stone with such force as to knock off a picket from the school fence.'[66]

Teachers also had to contend with limitations on academic freedom imposed by the provincial department of education. Dreams of departing from the fixed curriculum were abrupty dashed by the realization that the teacher's reputation depended on the pupils' success on the dreaded high school entrance examination. As one inspector candidly admitted, 'they naturally give most attention to those features which they think are most likely to come up on the promotion examination.'[67] The inspectors themselves contributed their share to this mechanical approach to teaching. 'An inspector came along when I was teaching a subject the pupils were not supposed to get till the following year,' recalled John Martin, a future minister of agriculture. 'But I thought it a good idea to give them a little start ... He said, "Don't you do any more thinking; the Education Department is supposed to do the thinking." '[68] In a period of inadequately trained and highly transient teachers, inspectors did guarantee that required courses and textbooks were in use and that schools were preparing their pupils for uniform provincial examinations. But J.G. Bourinot was afraid that this made the teacher 'far too much of an automaton – a mere machine, wound up to proceed so far and no farther. He is not allowed sufficient of that free volition which would enable him to develop the best qualities of his pupils, and to elevate their general tone.'[69]

Problems of student discipline, community pressures, and departmental restrictions were not sweetened by attractive salaries. 'Labourers and domestic servants are paid higher wages than many of our teachers,' complained one inspector in 1882.[70] The last two decades of the century saw teachers lose ground to other vocational groups. The average salary for county male teachers reached a high point of $404 in 1884, then dropped steadily to a low of $344 in 1899; average female salaries went from $270 to $250 during the same period. Urban teachers also saw their pay cheques dwindle; average salaries in Ottawa, for example, declined at the end of the 1870s, suffered another sinking spell at the end of the 1880s, and were actually lower in 1891 than in 1877.[71] The economic recession that lasted intermittently from the mid-1870s to the mid-1890s was a contributing factor to the teachers' financial plight. Yet teachers themselves contributed to the problem of low wages as boards encountered little opposition when they asked applicants to 'state salary required' or 'send in tenders.' There were occasional demands for a minimum-wage law to apply to teachers, but the provincial government was not prepared to take such a drastic step. 'It would be impossible in a free country like Canada to fix a minimum salary' explained education minister George Ross at the end of the century. 'All that can be done by legislation is to lay down the highest feasible standard of qualification, and to hope that public opinion will, ere long, recognize that the best policy ... is to secure good teachers even at a higher cost.'[72]

The steady feminization of the teaching profession accelerated the trend towards transiency and held salaries down. Between 1850 and 1900, the proportion of female elementary teachers jumped from 25 to 75 per cent as young girls steadily took up new positions created by the expansion of the school system. Part of the explanation for this rapid feminization rests in the scarcity of male applicants for teaching jobs. But many boards actively sought women teachers who could be paid lower salaries. Society accepted a wide disparity in male-female salaries because, as one editor argued, 'the lady teacher's connection with the profession is but temporary, and liable to be closed at any moment by her own act' of marriage. Therefore, she 'can scarcely give herself to the mastery of the profession in all its branches.' Besides, there were 'differences in the nervous constitutions or ... physical strength of the sexes.'[73] The attraction of teaching over domestic work and factory jobs, which were becoming increasingly available to women, was cemented by an aura of genteel respectability cultivated by educators and the public alike. Girls were repeatedly told that their qualities of moral virtue, patience, and kindness made them natural teachers for young children – but rarely for the higher grades or for administrative positions. In addition, a few years' experience with young children was ideal preparation for woman's 'natural destiny' as wife and mother. So society could conveniently exploit the female instincts women brought to teaching, at a minimum of expense.[74]

Women teachers in Toronto registered some modest gains during the late 1870s and early 1880s. Toronto appointed its first female public school principal in 1876 and, as a result of steady pressure from the city's Women Teachers' Association, grudgingly agreed ten years later to base salaries on years of experience rather than on grade taught. But elsewhere in the province, professional organization among both male and female teachers was virtually nonexistent. Teacher training and certification requirements, low wages, poor working conditions, and transiency all contributed to a weakness of professional spirit. County teachers' institutes were tightly controlled by the local inspectors, useful for in-service education, but hardly conducive to the development of a sense of professional independence. At the provincial level, the Ontario Teachers' Association provided a good forum for the public debate of policy questions, but it was weakened by an internal public school-high school split, by the prominent role played by university people and laymen, and by department of education control over curriculum, textbooks, and examinations. 'The Teacher's calling will remain as it is,' lamented one discouraged class-room veteran, 'so long as the ranks of teachers are recruited to the extent of twelve hundred and upwards annually, at the low age of eighteen years ... from those who by law are called infants and who are put in the same irresponsible class with lunatics, jail-birds and inebriates.'[75]

V

A European visitor who had observed both the illusion of Ontario education presented at Philadelphia and the reality of the province's schools during a two-month visit in the fall of 1879 concluded that the exhibit at the Centennial Exposition was 'nothing but a show extracted from a museum.' His quaint remarks were most uncomplimentary. At Philadelphia he had been 'very much astonished' to find so magnificent a display of school apparatus. 'Now I am here, and many schools have visited, and I find nothing as I did intend.' He discovered thirty-nine schools with no map of Canada, forty-four without a globe, and only two schools with charts of the body. As for 'philosophical appartus,' most of the teachers 'do explain they have never heard with.' He questioned whether it was 'British fair play' to mount such a display at Philadelphia when the schools of many European countries were better furnished than those of Ontario.[76] At the Exposition itself, a few inquisitive visitors had asked if the materials on display were in general use in the schools. Department officials gave a standard reply: inexpensive visual aids were 'in pretty general use,' more expensive apparatus were rarely used, but as 'teachers become better trained and the schools more efficient,' all classrooms would soon be equipped to the standards presented at Philadelphia. 'It is not the fault of the Department, but of the schools, that [the apparatus] are not so generally used as they ought to be.'[77]

The leadership and financial resources of Ontario's 4,900 local school-boards proved at least as important as the class-room teacher in shaping the educational environment of the Ontario child in the 1870s and 1880s. In the first place, the physical environment of the schoolhouse and the class-room showed enormous variation from one community to the next. Of the 5,042 schools in operation in 1876, approximately 40 per cent were of fairly recent brick or stone construction, 45 per cent were frame structures of varying durability, while 15 per cent were log buildings surviving from the earlier pioneer era of the province. The Brant County inspector found much to admire in SS no. 27, South Dumfries; he reported the 'furniture being good, as is also the heating apparatus, good clock, window curtains, six chairs for visitors, nice arm chair, small globe on iron stand, good library.'[78] At the other extreme stood SS no. 21, Wellesley, in Waterloo County, 'decidedly the most miserable school house in the county.' Standing on a low, wet corner of land, it was 'so surrounded with water in spring and fall that it is with difficulty the children get to the doorsteps.' There was no playground, no woodshed, no outhouse, no well, 'in short nothing but a wretched, bleak, desolate looking hovel.'[79] Conditions could vary even within a township. SS no. 4, Orillia, was described as an 'exceedingly good and ornamental building ... splendidly lighted and well ventilated.' But neighbouring SS no. 5 was 'a shameful old log building ... utterly inadequate to the wants of the section.'[80]

Discrepancies in school facilities were compounded by the problem of overcrowding in the cities and towns, as rising enrolments taxed the capacity of urban trustees. Peterborough was forced to house one junior class in a poorly lit and ill-ventilated basement room. 'It is unfit even to stow away unruly children as punishment,' complained the county inspector. 'It is calculated to produce melancholy, bad temper, ill-health, weak eyes and other serious evils.'[81] Barrie Public School in December 1876 lacked such basic equipment as slates, a map of the world, and cloak rooms. Pupils were promoted, 'not because they were able to pass the Examination in the class from which they were being removed, but because one room was overcrowded and it was necessary to draft a certain number on.' But in Orillia, with its five-room central school and a one-room ward school, the 'system of moves from one class to another is very thorough,' determined not by a shortage of seats, but by 'well supervised oral and written examinations.'[82]

Urban school problems were described graphically by the Toronto *Globe* in a seven-part series on the city's public schools in 1883. 'A very considerable outlay would be necessary to meet the immediate necessities of the educational interests of the city,' declared the *Globe* reporter. 'Increased school accommodation is badly needed in the various parts of the city ... Nearly every school is quite as full as it ought to be, while many of them are much fuller than they should be.' There followed a catalogue of deficiencies. At Wellesley School there were no less than fifty children awaiting admission who were excluded because of the over-crowded conditions. At Victoria Street School 'it is impossible for a teacher to do justice to a lot of little ones who are packed together as tightly as herrings in a bow or figs in a drum.' In Miss McGregor's beginners' class at Borden Street School, 'the little things are packed so closely upon the benches that they often have to sit with their shoulders fitting in toward the back of the seat sideways.' In a similar class at Church Street School, 'every time one alters his position in the smallest degree, he disturbs six or seven more who happen to occupy the same bench.' An angry *Globe* editor concluded that the chief lesson to be derived from the inquiry 'is that there is at least as much need of reform as respects children who do attend school as respects those who do not.'[83]

In a period of rapid urbanization, crowded city class-rooms were a result of both rising enrolments and more regular attendance patterns. Legislation in 1871 required at least four months' annual school attendance for all seven-to-twelve-year-olds. But 85 per cent of this age group in cities and towns were enrolled prior to the legislation; in addition, Hamilton enrolled 52 per cent of the five- and six-year-olds and 46 per cent of the thirteen-to-sixteen age group.[84] Trends first observed in the 1860s continued through the following decades as more and more parents saw economic advantages in a few years of schooling for their sons and daughters with employment opportunities declining for unskilled youngsters. Campaigns by local superintendents, such as James Hughes of Toronto, also boosted enrolments and attendance. Between 1870 and 1880, Toronto's population increased by 43 per cent, whereas public school enrolment climbed by 59 per cent, average daily attendance rose from 80 to 90 per cent of pupils enrolled, and twice as many children attended for more than 100 days during the school year. In 1875 alone, the Toronto Public School Board con-structed two new schools, doubled the size of two others, and added nine more rooms in eight additional schools. Great as this increase in accommodation was, however, Hughes admitted that it had not kept pace with demand.[85]

With urban growth becoming even more rapid in the 1880s, resulting in broader tax bases and increased revenues, city school-boards often led the provincial department in educational innovation. This was especially true when an urban system was directed by a dynamic superintendent, such as James Hughes, appointed chief inspector of public schools in Toronto in 1874. 'Some-thing like a vitalizing whirlwind had struck the schools,' declared the Toronto board's official history. 'The new Inspector had some plan ... to meet every problem.'[86] Before the end of the decade Hughes was promoting such curricular changes as the kindergarten and manual training, putting increased emphasis on music and drawing, and attacking the problems of attendance and truancy, and ungraded and overcrowded class-rooms. Crooks, Hodgins, and other provincial officials might occasionally be jealous of the leadership and promotional abilities of Hughes and his fellow superintendents in Ottawa and Hamilton. But at least provincial and city authorities agreed that improvements in teacher training, a broader curriculum, and stricter enforcement of attendance regulations were essential if Ontario schools were to keep pace with the economic and social changes brought about by the emerging urban and industrial nature of the province.

In 1876, however, just 22 per cent of the province's youngsters went to school in urban centres; the remaining 78 per cent attended one-room country schools in the 4,500 rural school sections of the province. Here in the Ontario countryside, there persisted many obstacles to educational modernization. A model rural school section would be about three concessions wide and nine lots deep with the school located in the centre. In this section the furthest farm would be about two-and-a-half miles from the schoolhouse. It would contain fifty-four farms or 5,400 acres, and would yield an assessment of $50,000 to $60,000. It would likely have a school tax of about five mills which would cost each farmer about $5 to $7 a year. This local levy would finance over 70 per cent of the capital and operating costs for the school, with the remaining funds coming in the form of provincial grants.

Unfortunately, the ideal was rarely achieved. If the assessed value of the land was low, either the section had to be huge or the tax rate very high. Small sections formed to hive off ethnic minorities, or sections split through the creation of a Roman Catholic separate school-board, severely compromised local fund-raising efforts. Even in contiguous sections composed of comparable people on similar land, badly drawn boundaries could cause widely divergent assessments. In the twenty-eight sections comprising the township of York, for example, school rates varied from 1.2 to 11.7 mills. Moreover, school taxes could differ widely within the same section since they varied with the values of the assessed property. The inequalities of the property tax were particularly noticeable in those rural sections containing small, unincorporated hamlets or villages. The villages produced the children and the farmers supplied the money.

Yet each school section's three-man board of trustees, elected annually by the local ratepayers, effectively controlled major aspects of Ontario education. Working from minimal provincial guidelines, they had the say in areas such as building and equipping the schoolhouse, hiring and firing the teacher, and deciding what was appropriate for the teacher to do both inside and outside the class-room. Originally a work of the people, the local board had its beginnings in the comparative isolation of a pioneer community, largely self-sufficient, and prone to view outsiders with a kindly condescension and a touch of suspicion. As a result, educational change advanced through rural Ontario on a broken front, depending on the wealth and inclination of local trustees and taxpayers. 'When trustees are as determined to have as good a school as the section can afford, they usually get it,' declared one county inspector. "When the determination is to have a cheap school, an inefficient school is almost invariably the result.'[87]

The one-room country school was a central feature of the rural landscape, and was often the centre of activities for the community it served. Here residents met to discuss the issues of the day, heard addresses by political office seekers, held community dances, and often worshipped on Sunday. Nor were the activities of the pupil divorced from the life of the community. The most cherished and most memorable event each year was likely to be the Christmas concert. The air was filled with the jingle of sleigh bells, the creaking of runners on the frosty snow, and the happy voices of excited children and proud parents, as the schoolhouse filled to overflowing. A good concert was often a guarantee that the teacher's contract would be renewed for another year; a poor performance could lead to dismissal. Another opportunity for close school-community interaction was the end-of-June public examination of pupils, still lingering in some parts of the province. 'Nothing could exceed the eagerness of the young aspirants to scholastic fame,' reported Hodgins of an 1876 examination in Grimsby Township. He believed that 'the spirit displayed by the Pupils, and the interest taken by the respectable gathering of visitors,' would lead to a 'general awakening of interest by Parents and Trustees, in the condition and progress of their Schools.'[88]

Yet such a close relationship between school and community often led to an unwillingness on the part of rural trustees to enforce unpopular provincial regulations. Evidence of this can be found in rural resistance to the attendance and curriculum campaigns inspired by Ryerson's 1871 legislation. Attendance certainly improved in the cities, where schools were more accessible, where fewer youngsters were absorbed into the work force, and where superintendents like James Hughes could mobilize public and newspaper support. But in the countryside, parental indifference, bad weather, and poor roads, plus the seasonal tasks of seed-time and harvest, combined to thwart the advocates of regular attendance. In 1872 the Renfrew County Inspector predicted accurately that 'the friends of education must be prepared ... to expect a great deal of disappointment' over the working of the compulsory attendance law. By 1875 the vast majority of inspectors agreed that 'of all the obstacles to the advancement of schools, the greatest is irregular attendance.' In 1876, some 60 per cent of children enrolled attended less than 100 days. Irregularity of attendance, concluded one inspector, 'is the bane and curse of the public schools; it is a log and chain upon the progress of instruction for it blasts and withers the noblest purposes of the best of teachers.'[89]

The maintenance of strong local control over the schools of Ontario is evident in 1882 revisions to the elementary and secondary school programs of study. On the surface, these revisions appeared minor, simply transferring a number of subjects from the obligatory to the optional category. But they reflected two important realities of late nineteenth-century Ontario education: first, that local conditions determined the extent to which provincial goals might be realized; and, second, that local authorities decided whether conditions in their area warranted program change. Public and separate school-boards, presented in 1882 with a revised elementary school course of study, were required to adhere to it only as far as the circumstances of the particular school would allow of its being followed; where circumstances required, 'such modifications are permitted as thereupon become necessary.' High school boards were reassured that they were not required to provide instruction in all of the optional subjects, 'but only in such as in the judgment of each Board the occasion or circumstances of their school render expedient.'[90] Changes in the course of study, 'formerly permissible with the Inspector approving,' were now left to the judgment of the trustees. The new regulations, concluded a department of education circular, 'now recognize the Trustees chosen by the ratepayers as the local officials who are entrusted with full powers of management of the Schools.'[91]

Education Minister Adam Crooks had approached his new portfolio in 1876 with considerable energy and enthusiasm. During his first year in office he visited teachers' meetings and trustee conferences throughout the province, in order to gain 'practical knowledge of the condition and working of the educational system under my charge.'[92] Thus armed, he had introduced a number of changes in 1877 – stricter certification requirements for teachers, a province-wide network of county model schools for teacher training, and a reduction in the number of required subjects on the elementary school curriculum. But with the exception of certification, these changes were practical concessions to the reality of local control, rather than bold advances of provincial power. Crooks and his successors would be confronted repeatedly by the gap between far-reaching plans for change at the provincial level and the practical operation of schools at the local level. With his own background in the Upper Canadian Grit tradition, Crooks realized that local taxation, local management, and local control were of paramount importance in Ontario education in the 1870s. 'The principal functions of the Education Department are those of supervision,' he told the legislature in 1879, 'in order to secure the satisfactory discharge, by the various local bodies and officials, of their respective duties.' The department must 'strictly refrain from taking upon itself, or interfering with powers and duties entrusted to local management, and which local experience can more intelligently deal with than any central authority at a distance.'[93]

VI

Provincial initiative was further compromised by a pitiful decline in Crooks's mental and physical health. Deputy minister Hodgins observed the deterioration as early as 1878[94] and by the early 1880s it had become evident to his close colleagues that the minister was succumbing to the ravages of cerebral paresis. Finally in January 1883, Premier Mowat had no choice but to relieve him of his cabinet responsibilities. After appointing A.S. Hardy as acting minister of education, Mowat began a lengthy search for a strong successor. Initially, speculation focused on two other members of the Liberal caucus. The Toronto *Mail* suggested Richard Harcourt, a Welland County inspector; while President Daniel Wilson of the University of Toronto feared the portfolio would go to J.M. Gibson of Hamilton, who was 'committed to co-education ... and other extreme views; and belongs moreover to the "National" or "Know-nothing" party of Canada, which means to make an end of us *Foreigners*.'[95] But Mowat was looking further afield than the provincial legislature. His first choice was George Grant, the distinguished principal of Queen's University, a man of scholarship and proven leadership ability. Grant, however, was unwilling to give up his current post; 'to abandon Queen's would be to injure it,' he wrote. Besides, he disapproved of partisan political control of the education department; 'a non-political superintendent would be best.'[96]

During November a number of factors led Mowat to offer the post to George W. Ross. Although lacking the university connections of his predecessor, and branded by the *Mail* as 'practically an illiterate man with no profession of the liberal culture of our time,'[97] Ross was said to have the support and confidence of the province's teachers. He had begun his adult life as a country school teacher, advancing quickly to such prominent positions as public-school and model-school inspector, editor of *The Ontario Teacher* (an independent educational journal of the mid-1870s), and member of the Central Committee of Examiners. More important to Mowat was Ross's prospect of preventing the riding of West Middlesex from falling into Conservative hands in an impending provincial by-election. Mowat believed that Ross might be 'the only man through whom that riding could be held ... The *coup* might be accomplished, it is thought, by making him Minister of Education; and no doubt he would make a good one.'[98] Ross was available, for the courts had unseated him recently as the West Middlesex member of the federal House of Commons. He accepted the nomination, was named minister, and held the constituency for the provincial Liberals.

'I'm so much in my element that I'm frightened,' Ross remarked to an old friend shortly after stepping into the job in the closing weeks of 1883.[99] His initial public declarations were quite conservative, spiced with laudatory references to 'an admirable system of which the country as a whole feels so justly proud,' and underlain with self-doubts about assuming the Ryerson heritage. 'What a calamity it would be if a mistake should mar in any way the excellent working of that system,' he confessed to his Strathroy constituents. He thought that 'the plan laid down by Dr. Ryerson and his predecessor made his course plain for him.'[100] Yet his task was not to be easy. Criticism of educational policies, somewhat muted as opposition spokesmen had waited first for Crooks to get his feet wet, and then for Mowat to choose a successor, was ready to surface by the end of 1883. Besides, Ross was naïve if he believed the Crooks years had not bequeathed problems of their own. 'You will now have made a slight examination of the nooks and crannies of Dr. Ryerson's den,' wrote an astute cabinet colleague at the end of December. 'Some of them poor Crooks never saw into, and some he did see he had to wink at.'[101] By the beginning of the new year, religious nooks and crannies had blown wide open, and Ross was well into his baptism of fire.

2 'The Nooks and Crannies of Dr. Ryerson's Den'

I

In 1883 some 30,000 pupils attended Roman Catholic separate schools in the cities and towns of Ontario. The Scott Act of 1863, reinforced by Section 93 of the British North America Act, had guaranteed local Catholic boards the right to maintain and, through taxation, support such schools at the elementary level. Like their public school counterparts, separate schools varied in construction, facilities, teacher competence, and pupil progress from the very best to the very worst. As far as the provincial inspectors were concerned, the best examples of pupil discipline and progress were frequently found in those separate schools staffed by members of religious orders, where boys and girls were taught separately, and where the facilities were often attached to a church or convent house. The provincial curriculum and authorized textbooks seem to have been followed for most subjects, but the religious influence often permeated instruction in reading. In December 1883, for example, Inspector James White had to remind the Kingston Boys' School that the text *Christian Duty*, 'though a very good book is not a suitable one for teaching Reading.' At Merritton Separate School he found the teacher using the *Catechism of Sacred History*, which 'is of no service for teaching either reading or religion.'[1]

Although subject to the same central authority as the public schools, the separate schools of Ontario were influenced strongly by the province's Roman Catholic hierarchy and local clergy. As Archbishop of Toronto, John Joseph Lynch was the titular leader of the Ontario Catholic population through the 1870s and 1880s. On his shoulders fell the responsibility to defend the constitutional rights of separate schools, to campaign for additional rights and privileges, to answer criticism directed at the scholastic record of these schools, and to justify clerical control in the face of a campaign by a group of reform-minded Toronto trustees for greater lay participation. Through the 1870s Lynch had impressed Ontario politicians with his moderation and his seeming intent to work quietly for Catholic school improvement, in contrast to the bitter controversy that had characterized the period of his predecessor, Bishop Armand de Charbonnel. The result was a number of small but significant separate school gains during the years of the Crooks administration: Roman Catholic model schools, easier transfer of Quebec teaching certificates to Ontario, less complicated machinery for Catholic ratepayers to place their names on the separate school tax roll, and the appointment of a Roman Catholic as separate school inspector. While Adam Crooks held to the principle that it was 'in the public interest that the children of all denominations of Christians should be educated together,' he was prepared to defend the existence of Catholic schools as a constitutional necessity and on grounds of liberty of conscience.[2]

Crooks, Ross, and the Liberal government of Oliver Mowat staked out a middle position between Catholic spokesmen who argued for full control of Catholic schools on the model of Quebec's dual confessional system, and their equally militant Protestant opponents who sought the abolition of separate schools. The latter group was the more difficult to pacify, given their numbers, their influence within the provincial Conservative party, and their vocal support from newspapers such as the Ottawa *Journal* and the Toronto *Mail*. The Mowat administration began by accepting the constitutional reality of separate schools, and sought to improve rather than abolish them. George Ross reminded his largely Protestant West Middlesex constituents that as minister of education it was his responsibility 'to promote the efficiency' of separate schools in order to parallel public school improvements. 'Our duty is to see whether the changes proposed are wise, prudent and effectual; and, if so, to make them.' As far as Ross was concerned, the province was to 'protect the liberty of the subject, not to hamper it; to extend where practicable, not to curtail.'[3] At the same time there were some 50,000 Catholic pupils attending the public schools; they must be made welcome and not forced into the separate schools by militant Protestant evangelism. While Ross was fully prepared 'to stamp our Public Schools as Christian,' he had no intention of 'destroying their undenominational character.'[4] On this point he had the support of Sir Daniel Wilson, president of the University of Toronto and a leading Protestant spokesman. 'The R.C. element is a most difficult one to deal with in educational matters,' Wilson confided to his diary, 'but it is worth a larger sacrifice to get their children into the public schools.'[5]

But if Catholic children were encouraged to attend public schools, this meant that the government had to be as open to suggestions from Catholic leaders as it was to Protestants on sensitive curriculum matters. One of Adam Crooks's last acts as education minister in late 1882 was the withdrawal of Walter Scott's poem 'Marmion' from the high school English curriculum, on the grounds that it was objectionable to Roman Catholic tastes. Archbishop Lynch had publicly criticized the poem as an ill-disguised condemnation of mediaeval religion. But what pleased one branch of the Christian church proved anathema to the other. Championing the Protestant cause, the Toronto *Mail* vehemently opposed what it considered undue Catholic influence on the Mowat government and the education department. 'It is not Mr. Crooks who presides in the Education office,' thundered the *Mail*, 'it is Archbishop Lynch.' The *Mail* also suspected that Catholic influence had been behind the 1875 decision to drop the formal study of Christian morals from the elementary school course of study. Not satisfied with optional religious exercises, the *Mail* through 1882 and 1883 championed a move to make opening exercises and scripture reading obligatory in all schools. If the Bible was already in seven-eighths of the public schools on an optional basis, asked the *Mail*, why should it be 'arbitrarily excluded from the other eighth?'[6]

Protestant pressure for compulsory Bible reading increased during the autumn of 1883 as George Ross, himself an active Presbyterian layman and Sunday School teacher, took over the education portfolio. Early in 1884 Ross concurred, on the grounds that 'religious instruction is an essential factor of our system of education.'[7] Henceforth, schools must begin each day with Christian prayers and readings, 'without comment or explanation,' exemptions being granted where parents objected. But it proved easier to authorize scripture passages than to prepare a series of readings acceptable to all segments of the population. The selections were first prepared by Brantford lawyer W.H.C. Kerr, and then referred by Ross to representatives of the province's leading churches. There was no public outcry against minor revisions suggested by several of the Protestant clergy, but a storm of protest greeted Ross's acceptance of Archbishop Lynch's recommendation that 'who' be substituted for 'which' in the opening line of the Lord's Prayer. The Toronto *Mail* denounced the new 'Ross' Bible, charging that the Protestant Bible had been 'mutilated,' and once again raised the issue of an unhealthy relationship between the Catholic hierarchy and the Mowat government.[8] At first Ross stood firm behind his decision. 'Was there anything more reasonable,' he asked, 'than that [Catholic] representatives should be consulted when the representatives of other denominations were consulted?'[9] But further compromise was necessary to meet the criticism of the province's militant Protestants. This came in 1887 when the 'full' Bible (including the word 'which') was authorized as an alternative to the 'Ross' Bible.

Obviously, George Ross was not to be blessed with the same calmness in church-state relations in education that had characterized most of the Crooks years. The fires of controversy had been slowly refueled through the Marmion and Ross Bible episodes, lingering concerns over the presence of 'unqualified' religious teachers in Catholic schools, and the absence of the secret ballot in separate school elections. The year 1885 brought the Northwest Rebellion, the execution of Louis Riel, and an intensification of the debate over the desired cultural character of the new Dominion. As the Toronto *Mail* and the Loyal Orange Order became more anti-Catholic, Catholics themselves became more determined to defend and extend their separate school rights. Lynch grew increasingly outspoken through the 1880s, declaring that Catholic children attending public schools were 'tinctured with Protestant ideas,' and he defended clerical influence in Catholic schooling on the grounds that the bishops had 'to answer for the souls of those confided to their care.'[10] Thus any hopes that earlier constitutional provisions had solved the church-state question in Ontario education were dashed by the renewed animosities of the 1880s.

The provincial election of 1886 brought forth the full power of the *Mail*'s campaign against the position of the Roman Catholic Church in Ontario political life and education. The Ross Bible was still a controversial issue, as were a number of recent school law amendments that made it easier for tenants and business corporations to direct their taxes to separate school boards. While Ross stressed the themes of undenominational public schools, and parallel improvements in efficiency in both public and separate schools, Premier Mowat tackled the larger question of the future of Catholicism in the province. In a published letter, entitled 'Protestantism Not in Danger,' and addressed to Rev. G.M. Milligan, a leading Toronto Protestant, Mowat attempted to show by rational argument that amendments which improved one school system did not encroach upon the other. In a second published pamphlet, 'The No Popery Cry,' the premier made a much more emotional appeal. There was no Catholic threat because Protestants outnumbered their brethren five to one. As a public servant, Mowat did not believe that the badge of a true Protestant was to be earned by 'hating or ostracising Roman Catholics.'[11] Ultimately, the December election results seemed to indicate acceptance of the Mowat-Ross policy of improving rather than curtailing separate schools. The Liberals increased their majority, capturing fifty-nine seats against thirty-one for W.R. Meredith and the Conservatives.

II

Roman Catholics and their separate schools were harmful enough in the eyes of the Toronto *Mail* and its Anglo-Protestant readers, but French-speaking Ontarians and their bilingual schools were viewed as an even greater threat to the cultural solidarity of the province and the nation. A generation earlier, Ryerson had had no reservations about schools using languages of instruction other than English, sanctioning both French and German in school regulations of 1851. In subsequent years, German-language schools in Waterloo County slowly declined in number, but French-language instruction in eastern, northern, and southwestern Ontario expanded as the province's French-speaking population rose. By 1883 there were twenty-seven schools, largely concentrated in Prescott and Russell counties, which were exclusively French, plus uncounted others scattered across the province which were predominantly French. Educators were concerned that too many children left such schools with an inadequate grasp of English. 'The English subjects are the weakest and require special drill,' reported Inspector James White of a bilingual school in Amherstburg in 1883. 'Since last year little if any improvement is noticeable, in fact the school seems to have gone back.'[12] Not only had these schools become 'nurseries ... of an alien tongue,' charged the *Mail*, but also 'of alien customs, of alien sentiments, and ... of a wholly alien people.'[13] Principal Austin of Alma College in St Thomas called for a total elimination of all French-language instruction, because in his mind, 'it is a barrier to the progress of the Anglo-Saxon civilization in the Province of Ontario.'[14]

Rebuffed on the separate school question in the 1886 election, Meredith and the Conservatives quickly added the bilingual school issue to their arsenal. Once they had discovered the problem, the solution seemed simple: eliminate French as a language of instruction and insist upon the use of English in all schools. But education minister George Ross found neither the problem nor the solution quite so simple. On at least one occasion he referred to it as 'that most disturbing of all questions.'[15] While the Conservatives and the Toronto *Mail* tended to advocate a cultural solution, Ross and Mowat insisted on an educational one: improve the quality of English-language instruction rather than eliminate the use of French. Departmental regulations of 1885 made the teaching of English compulsory in these schools, while still permitting the teaching of other subjects in French. In his annual report of 1887, Ross was pleased to note that the Franco-Ontarians were 'complying so cordially with the Department's recommendations.'[16] But this did not satisfy the *Mail*, which had sent its own reporters through Prescott and Russell counties, and concluded that English-language instruction was the exception rather than the rule. Nor did it satisfy Meredith, who accused the department of education of failing to maintain the 'integrity of the English language.'[17]

Anxious to defuse such political dynamite, Premier Mowat in May 1889 named Professor A.H. Reynar of Victoria University to head a three-man commission to investigate the enforcement of English-language regulations in both French and German bilingual schools. The commissioners had nothing but praise for the German-English schools of Waterloo County, but they discovered that more than half of the French-English schools in Prescott and Russell failed to devote the prescribed amount of time to English. Confirming the reports the *Mail* had been publishing for several months, the commissioners found that of sixty-nine teachers employed, only three had ever attended high school, and only two had attended model schools and thus qualified for provincial certification. They also discovered the widespread use of unauthorized, French-language textbooks from Quebec, and a heavy Roman Catholic clerical influence in these supposedly public schools. But their recommendations were closer to Ross's commitment to school improvement than to the Conservative campaign for the elimination of French as a language of instruction. Reporting in August, the Reynar commission called for effective bilingual training schools, more rigid certification requirements, and authorized bilingual texts. Admittedly, they concluded, education was to be imparted in English, and any departure from this practice was to be 'partial' and so that 'the end sought may thereby be more fully attained.' Yet, to raise the educational standards of these schools, 'time must be allowed and patience must be exercised.'[18]

Such moderate recommendations proved totally unacceptable to the newly formed Equal Rights Association, a volatile organization that quickly provided a focus for Ontario's Anglo-Protestant spokesmen to attack both bilingual and separate schools. At its founding convention in Toronto in June 1889, the ERA proclaimed that, since 'the use of the French language as the language of instruction tends to perpetuate evils,' English should be the only language used in Ontario schools, that every teacher should be able to 'use the English language efficiently in imparting instruction,' and that schools should use only textbooks authorized by the department. Concerning separate schools, the convention charged that recent school law amendments made it too easy for those schools to claim the support of Catholic ratepayers, and urged that steps be taken to strengthen the public schools, 'our national system.'[19] The Equal Rights Association stepped up its attack throughout the summer and autumn months. 'Let us see that our Protestant money is not, against our will, diverted to separate schools,' thundered spokesman D'Alton McCarthy. 'We want no treason taught in our public schools.'[20] At a mass meeting of the association in October, McCarthy led the delegates in demanding that unless Premier Mowat removed the twin 'evils' in the schools, he would be turned out of office in the coming election.

Pressure from ERA and Orange Lodge members within his own party drove Meredith towards an increasingly aggressive stance. The Conservative leader fired the opening salvoes of the coming election campaign in a fiery speech in London on 16 December 1889. He demanded repeal of recent separate school amendments and a return to the limited Catholic rights of the 1863 Scott Act. Switching to bilingual schools, he denied the 'extraordinary view' that 'in this English province of Ontario the French language ought to be taught side by side with the English language.' French should be tolerated only for giving rudimentary instruction to pupils who knew no English. Premier Mowat, he charged, was too much allied with the Catholic hierarchy and with French-Canadian nationalists who had a dream of achieving the 'establishment of a nation in our midst.'[21] While Mowat defended his government's record against Meredith's attack, George Ross had to face a more personal challenge on educational issues from Toronto school inspector James Hughes. For many years an active Conservative and Orangeman, Hughes contested the 1890 election as an Equal Rights candidate in Peel. There was no love lost between these two political rivals and educational spokesmen. In the 1886 campaign they had fought to a saw-off in a seven-hour marathon debate in Strathroy; in 1890 they confronted each other again on a public platform in Brampton, amid reports that Hughes would become minister of education should Mowat and the Liberals be defeated. But Hughes lost the Peel campaign, while Meredith once again failed to carry the province. Mowat and the Liberals won fifty-nine seats against thirty-two for the opposition.

The anti-separate-school and anti-bilingual-school campaigns of 1886 and 1890 were repeated by the Conservatives in the 1894 provincial election. Each attack proved to be a failure, however, because the majority of Ontario voters were prepared to accept the middle course steered by Mowat and Ross. Throughout the 1880s and early 1890s, Mowat repeatedly declared that separate schools were 'a fact in our Constitution, and we have to accept them whether we now like it or not.'[22] He argued that it was his duty, not to curtail their rights and privileges granted in 1863 and 1867, but to guarantee that they functioned as efficiently as the public schools – thus the various amendments and regulations of the 1870s and 1880s. These changes no doubt helped the separate school system grow in size. During the twenty-year period following Ross's appointment in 1883, the number of separate schools increased from 194 to 419, while average attendance jumped from 13,705 to 29,920. Yet by refusing to sanction separate textbooks, separate high schools, separate normal schools, and a deputy minister for Catholic schools, Mowat and Ross ensured that these schools functioned as an integral part of a unified provincial educational system. When attacked for permitting the use of French in the bilingual schools, Mowat and Ross refused to crush the language by immediate anglicization; but they did act upon the recommendations of the 1889 commission that called for closer adherence to departmental regulations. When the same commissioners once again toured Prescott and Russell counties in 1893, they found that their recommendations were slowly being put into practice – the time given to instruction in English had increased in the majority of schools.

III

Thwarted on the issue of bilingual schools as they had been on separate schools, Conservative editors and politicians focused their educational criticism during the 1890s on yet another aspect of cultural nationalism: were Ontario schools deficient in inculcating appropriate patriotic sentiments in their pupils? A number of Conservative speakers took advantage of an 1892 legislative debate on textbook pricing and authorization policies to address the ideological content of school-books. One member found the revised *Ontario Readers* 'singularly deficient' in inspiring patriotism as compared with former editions. The *Third Reader* failed to mention the battle of Queenston Heights or the taking of Detroit in the War of 1812; the *Fourth Reader* omitted that 'we ever had a fight with the inhabitants of the country across the line, or that we were victorious.' Fine binding, typography, and illustrations were all very well, but what was wanted was 'sentiment inculcated into the scholars which would lead them to become good, patriotic Canadians.' Another member called on the government to follow the American example 'and teach young Canadians loyalty to the Union Jack, the beaver and the maple leaf.' A third member objected to the exclusion of a passage describing an 1812 naval battle 'where the English ship licked the Yankee ship'; such passages should be retained 'to teach the children of the country to shed blood and hate their neighbours.'[23]

Conservative critics had little cause to complain. All the graded readers used in Ontario schools during the 1880s and 1890s introduced the young child, not only to language and literature, but also to his historical heritage and contemporary political society. As the pupil reached the higher grades, formal courses and textbooks in history and geography were added to strengthen the attachment to Canada and the British Empire. George Ross felt strongly that all Ontario school-books should reflect a Canadian sentiment. In geography, this approach meant an emphasis on Canadian place-names ahead of foreign rivers, capes, straits, and bays; the fact that many of these geographical places were equally unheard-of to the average Ontario pupil was incidental to the fact they were Canadian. In history there was a similar emphasis on the Canadian experience. Ross believed that national history 'shows the young the springs of public honour and dishonour; sets before them the national feelings, weaknesses and sins; warns them against future dangers by exhibiting the losses and sufferings of the past; enshrines in their hearts the national heroes; and strengthens in them the precious love of country.'[24] He urged teachers to cultivate 'a Canadian sentiment' in their pupils as the first step in developing 'the great forces which make for national life.' If Canadian achievements were properly impressed on schoolchildren, then 'an impetus will be given to Canadian patriotism, and an intelligent interest will be taken in Canadian affairs, which will place the future of the country beyond all doubt.'[25]

The formation of the Dominion Educational Association in 1892 gave Ross an opportunity to obtain a new Canadian history textbook under non-partisan auspices. He used the prestige of his presidential chair to persuade the new association to sponsor a national competition for a history text suitable for all provinces. 'Can't we agree upon certain broad features common to the whole of this Dominion with which we can indoctrinate our pupils, so that when a child takes up the history of Canada, he feels ... that he is taking up the history of a great country?'[26] Five years later the winning manuscript was published: *The History of the Dominion of Canada* by Toronto lawyer W.H.P. Clement. Although approved for use in Ontario schools, the book never completely replaced other texts, and was generally unpopular with teachers. Nevertheless, it reflected a move towards the fusion of national and imperial loyalty in the province's class-rooms. Introduced during Queen Victoria's Diamond Jubilee year, it was intended to 'convey a fair and inspiring impression of the grandeur and importance of the heritage committed to us as Canadians and as citizens of the British Empire.' Riding the crest of the imperial wave, Clement ended his 341-page account by exhorting pupils 'to look forward to the still wider federation of all the lands which fly the Union Jack.'[27]

But what was the proper balance between Canadian patriotism and broader imperial sentiments? The latter had a particularly strong appeal during the 1890s, with the Diamond Jubilee and the renewed interest in imperial solidarity among public groups in Britain. And to many Anglo-Ontarians of the day, imperialism was a growing and urgent expression of national sentiment. This is shown most clearly in the reaction to an 1893 education department proposal to substitute Canadian for British history on the high school entrance examination, a proposal that appeared to have the 'almost unanimous' support of the most experienced teachers and inspectors.[28] But such a move was anathema to the Toronto *Empire*, a new Conservative journal whose name indicated its sympathies. 'Is British history to be driven out of our public schools?' asked the *Empire*, interpreting the move as a 'blow at the Mother-land.' While Ross admitted that 'it is impossible to teach Canadian history without touching Great Britain,' he clearly indicated his own preference. 'I say with all due respect to the powers that be, Canada first and the rest afterwards.'[29] But with the approach of a provincial election, and the fear that Meredith and the Conservatives would add the 'loyalty' question to their attacks on separate and bilingual schools, the Mowat government found it prudent to backtrack. Early in 1894 Ross announced that British history would remain on the high school entrance examination.

By the end of the decade Ross answered his critics by blending the imperial and national visions into one homogeneous outpouring of patriotic sentiment known as Empire Day. Capitalizing on an idea first proposed by Clementine Fessenden of Dundas, whose 'national patriotic scheme of education' would focus around an annual Flag Day, Ross persuaded his government and the education ministers of other provinces to adopt the concept of Empire Day, where love of country would be encompassed within the larger imperial embrace. According to Ross, the name Empire Day 'suggests that larger British sentiment which I think now prevails.' The date selected for the annual school celebrations was the school day immediately prior to the May 24 holiday for Queen Victoria's birthday, an ideal day for 'bringing before [the schoolchildren] the relations of Canada to the Empire.'[30] Henceforth the highest type of citizenship would imply a love for and loyalty to both the Canadian nation and the British Empire – the two became inseparable in Ross's statements. 'There is no antagonism between Canadianism and Imperialism,' he suggested. 'The one is but an expansion of the other.'[31] Later Ross was to remark that one of the most pleasant features of his tenure in the education office was 'to instil into the half million school children of the Province a greater love of Ontario, for Canada, and for the Empire than was previously entertained.'[32]

The 24 May 1899 issue of the Toronto *Globe* devoted much of its front page to a description of the first Empire Day festivities in the cities and towns of the province. In Petrolia, the children marched to the opera house, led by the high school cadets; in Galt the officers, bugle band, and a colour party of the 29th Battalion led 1,500 youngsters to Dickson Park; in Guelph another 1,500 pupils assembled on the collegiate grounds for a drill display, speeches, and a sports program; in Mount Forest, Empire Day was celebrated 'right royally at the public school here.' The centre of Ontario's public celebrations was the Toronto Normal School and its adjoining Model School. Girls from the normal school, dressed in white, presented a tableau portraying the poems of Rudyard Kipling, then went through 'some graceful evolutions' to the tune of 'The British Grenadiers.' There was a rifle drill by the model-school boys and the lusty singing of such patriotic songs as 'Rule Britannia' and 'Soldiers of the Queen.' One county inspector concluded that 'Empire Day is come to stay'; the following year he called it 'the most popular day in the school year.'[33]

Empire Day succeeded because of its compatibility with concepts of loyalty and patriotism prevalent in turn-of-the-century Ontario. Those years witnessed an increase in national and imperial zeal throughout English-speaking Canada, as schoolchildren received a daily dose of flag-saluting, allegiance-pledging, patriotic singing, and poetry reading. To a certain extent this was a manifestation of Canadian nationalism. With the racial and religious tensions of the 1880s behind them, the opening of the West before them, and the prospect of continued prosperity ahead in the new century, Canadians developed a greater pride in their country. Yet in many respects Canadian nationalism lost its solid mooring as it became caught up in the greater emotional appeal of British imperialism. Britian's renewed interest in her empire, her military exploits overseas, the formation of the Imperial Federation League – all promised a larger adventure than any narrow nationalism could hope to offer. And English-Canadians responded as never before with support for imperial preference, inter-colonial steamship and cable connections, the celebration of Queen Victoria's Diamond Jubilee, and, above, all, Canadian participation in the South African War. According to one historian, by the turn of the century 'there was no single topic which moved Canadians as powerfully and as emotionally as "The Empire".' In English Canada, 'the empire was an article of faith like God.'[34]

IV

There was more to late nineteenth-century Ontario education than religion, language, and patriotism; indeed, educators of the 1880s and 1890s faced economic and social pressures that were as significant as the cultural challenges. In 1883 George Ross inherited a school system that had been formed in the earlier years of the nineteenth century when Ontario's economy and society were much closer to the pioneer stage. The simple curriculum of the elementary school, with its emphasis on the three Rs and the values of honest labour, had been considered sufficient for the vast majority of country boys and girls who would step into their parents' shoes as farmers or farmers' wives. The practical skills of farming and home-making could be acquired naturally in the process of growing up. For town and village youngsters who entered small shops, business establishments, or domestic service, there had always been possibilities for learning necessary skills on the job. The tiny minority of pupils who continued on to high school were for the most part destined for careers in teaching or the learned professions; here, a limited academic curriculum was deemed in the best interests of all. But by the 1880s Ontario was shifting with growing momentum from an overwhelmingly agricultural to an emerging industrial economy, and from a rural to an urban society. This industrial and urban development raised new questions about the relationship between the school and the wider world of adult life.

There remained general agreement that the basic function of the primary grades was to lead the child to mastery of the three Rs. Critics did not question Adam Crooks's assessment of the role of the upper elementary grades in providing instruction 'sufficient for any career in life' as well as meeting 'the wants of all the classes.'[35] The debate of the 1880s and 1890s centred around whether the traditional academic curriculum or a more practical course of study provided the more appropriate preparation for any career. The transfer of the mechanical arts, bookkeeping, and agriculture from the required to the optional list of subjects in 1877 had pleased those who criticized the overloaded curriculum, yet disturbed those who advocated a closer relationship between schooling and practical life. Traditionalists clung to the mental discipline argument to support the limited, academic curriculum, arguing that 'practical skill in every department of life requires intelligence and general mental activity ... promoted by training in habits of observation and reflection.' This could best be secured by providing the best instruction in reading, writing, arithmetic, literature, and the ordinary subjects of the elementary school course. But to other educators, these 'ordinary subjects' seemed more oriented to high school entrance than to preparation for life. Inspector W.R. Bigg charged in 1881 that the elementary schools were 'mere feeders' to the high schools, 'to which all pupils rush, as soon as they have been sufficiently crammed to pass the Entrance examination.' Bigg urged a broader role for the elementary school in the 'great work of general education.'[36]

David Boyle was one teacher who believed that pupils were 'over-educated along mathematical and literary lines of a narrow type,' whereas scientific, technical, and agricultural teaching were of more general value. 'Children are

rushing to the cities, frightened away from their schools by impractical instruction.'[37] One county inspector argued that many of the older pupils 'remain at
home in idleness, owing to a supposed want of practicality in the school
programme.'[38] Mayor W.H. Howland of Toronto presented a lengthy case for
practical elementary education to the Royal Commission on the Relations of
Labour and Capital in the 1880s. Schoolboys, he argued, 'are educated to a point
which just makes them unfit to go into the manual occupations and they go into
callings where they have almost to starve for the rest of their lives.'[39] Any move
towards a more practical elementary education, argued one inspector, would
win increased public support. 'Everything that makes clear to parents the
relation between the school education of their children and their honourable
success in life is good, and binds together school and home in support and
helpful accord.'[40] By 1888 the Toronto *Globe* could report on 'the cry coming up
from the people that the education given to children was not of the practical
character it ought to be.'[41]

The problems involved in providing 'practical' schooling can be illustrated by
the fate of agriculture as a subject on the elementary curriculum. Agriculture
had the support of the province's leading educators; it was consistent with the
general pressure for more practical instruction; and it bore a close relationship
to the life and work of the majority of the population. Even after the curriculum
reforms of 1877 moved it from the required to the optional list, agriculture might
have been expected to be a popular school subject. But such was not the case. It
has been estimated that by the end of the century, fewer than 1,500 students, less
than one-half of one per cent of the rural school population, were studying the
subject. At no time during the 1880s and 1890s did the agricultural enrolment
reach 5 per cent of the total for rural schools.[42] Agriculture failed as a school
subject for a number of reasons – the difficulty in finding qualified teachers
among seventeen-year-old female model-school graduates, the lack of suitable
textbooks, and its omission from the high school entrance examination. A more
fundamental reason for its failure, concluded one teacher in 1888, was that 'it has
not been sought by those who use it most – the farmers.'[43] Farm parents decried
any 'textbook' teaching of agriculture, while farm youngsters tended to view the
school as a release from, rather than an extension of, their routine daily chores.

While educators hoped that a more relevant curriculum would keep rural
children in school, they put their hopes on compulsory attendance laws to keep
urban youngsters in the class-room. By the mid-1880s, it was obvious that the
attendance legislation of 1871 was not securing the desired results. The percentage attendance of school-age children had inched up from 42 per cent in 1872 to
just 50 per cent in 1887. Various explanations were offered: in Carleton Place
irregular attendance was attributed to job opportunities for youngsters in a
milling and manufacturing town; in Essex County it was the unwillingness of
elected trustees to enforce legislation against their neighbours; in Kingston the

culprits were identified as poverty and the 'absence of proper family control.'[44] Although urban attendance was consistently higher than rural (62 per cent to 47 per cent in 1890), it was the city environment that had made truancy visible and created the pressure for governmental action. 'Truancy is not an evil in rural schools,' observed George Ross. 'It creates some trouble, however, in urban schools.'[45] By the mid-1880s, Ross had come to believe that the taxpayer 'has a right to expect that those for whose education he is compelled to provide should be obliged to attend school.'[46]

Undeniably, early attendance laws lacked teeth. More important, many non-attending children in the 1880s had compelling economic motives for absenting themselves from school. They and their parents saw the short-term gains of employment outweighing the delayed advantages of higher earning power through extended schooling. Ross pinpointed farmers' sons, 'whose labours are required on the farm, and who consequently attend [only] during the winter months.'[47] But child labour was also a prominent feature of the urban work world, providing an estimated 11 per cent of the Toronto work force in the early 1880s. The introduction of machinery made physical strength no longer essential in many routine factory jobs. Persistence and drudgery were needed, and children, who could be paid depressed wages, filled the bill admirably. A federal commission investigating mills and factories in 1882 found that the children invariably worked as many hours as the adults and that 'the appearance and condition of the children in the after part of the day ... was anything but inviting or desirable.' As for Ontario's compulsory school attendance law, 'we were unable to find any place in which this act is enforced.'[48] Similar observations were recorded by the federal Royal Commission on the Relations of Labour and Capital in 1889 and the Ontario Royal Commission on the Prison and Reformatory System in 1891.

The publicity surrounding these reports persuaded the Mowat government that public support would tolerate stiffer attendance laws, despite fears of interfering in a traditional sphere of family authority. The resulting 1891 legislation empowered police commissions or municipal councils to appoint truant officers, who were given authority to enter factories and shops where children were employed, and initiate court proceedings against erring parents. Thus was created the notorious truant officer, who became for many youngsters the most powerful symbol of the school system's encroachment on their private freedom. Although enforcement continued to be somewhat lax in rural areas, attendance statistics gradually improved, reaching a provincial average of 57 per cent by 1900. In the long run, however, compulsory attendance legislation had to reflect as much as lead public opinion. Children attended school more regularly in the late 1890s for a variety of reasons: better class-room accommodation, more enlightened teaching methods and disciplinary procedures, and growing parental awareness of the economic value of schooling. Perhaps most important were the declining employment opportunities for children. As early as 1892 the Ontario factory inspector reported very few children at work. 'Even fruit and vegetable factories, which four years ago employed so many without regard to age ... by the adoption of machinery, can to a large extent do without them.'[49]

The campaign for stricter enforcement of attendance laws was paralleled by that of the Women's Christian Temperance Union for the inclusion of 'temperance education' on the elementary school course of study. Like the attendance movement, the WCTU campaign appealed to those citizens concerned about the social and moral challenges of the emerging urban environment. Temperance advocates believed it was possible to obtain a dry generation through the instruction of children in the physiological dangers of drink. As one inspector put it, 'when King Alcohol is dead, the universal verdict will be that education killed him.'[50] The Toronto *Globe* gave its support by pointing out that 'if the cause of temperance is ever to make the progress it ought to make, the subject must be taught in the schools of our country.'[51] As a leader in the temperance cause himself, George Ross had no difficulty in interpreting WCTU pressure as a broadly-based public demand. The new subject was introduced into Ontario schools on an optional basis in 1885 and became compulsory eight years later. As with so many successful school crusades, temperance education had support from both humanitarian reformers interested in saving the individual and from conservatives desirous of preserving the social order.

Yet Ross was not so naïve as to believe that stricter attendance laws and 'textbook' teaching of temperance were sufficient in themselves to produce a younger generation equipped to meet the moral challenges of an uncertain future. The inculcation of any kind of higher morality, if possible at all, was dependent on educational factors that went beyond the subjects of the curriculum. Ross tended to put his faith in the provisions regarding religious instruction, in the obligation of teachers to enforce moral precepts, and in particular, in the personal character of the teaching force. By 1894 he could report that the scriptures were read in 90 per cent of the rural schools, and in all but two urban schools, while devotional exercises were used in 93 per cent of rural schools and all urban schools. Legislation in 1896 made it a statutory obligation for every teacher 'to inculcate by precept and example, respect for religion and the principles of Christian morality, and the highest regard for truth, justice, love of country, humanity, benevolence, sobriety, industry, frugality, purity, temperance and all other virtues.' But all these regulations, continued Ross, were 'of little consequence compared with the moral power qualities of the teacher.' He hoped that higher salaries and higher qualifications would strengthen the teacher's influence in the formation of the character of the pupils.[52] With such a teaching force, Ross believed that 'the training of the school-room is a great moral therapeutic, that it subdues, restrains and refines those who come under its influence, and that it contributes to law and order in the state.'[53]

The real issues at stake for Ross, in both curricular reform and moral training, were the limits of the elementary school and its potential usurpation of the traditional rights of the family, the church, and the community in the child-rearing process. The addition of temperance to the curriculum was the exception that proved the rule. Ross fervently believed that school efficiency rather than extension of the curriculum was the best possible preparation for an industrializing and urbanizing society. 'As to the limitations of a public school course, I am somewhat conservative,' Ross told the inaugural meeting of the Dominion Educational Association in 1892. 'I believe it is the worst ... and the most dangerous thing in the world for a minister of education to extend the public school course beyond its proper and safe limits.' '[Call me] Tory or Conservative if you like,' Ross challenged his fellow educators, but 'the three Rs seem to fix the limits fairly well.'[54] Ross saw himself as the inheritor of the Ryersonian tradition, boasting that 'to the present time there has been no radical change ... so far as the elementary schools are concerned.' Minor changes from time to time were prompted, not to extend or alter the role, but simply 'by a desire ... to make the free schools more efficient.'[55]

V

During the last two decades of the nineteenth century, the Ontario high school felt the pressure of economic and social change more strongly than the elementary school. Between 1883 and 1904, for example, high school enrolments more than doubled from 11,483 to 27,759. In 1871, some 5 per cent of elementary school graduates continued on to high school; thirty years later the figure was near 10 per cent. In the small town of Arnprior, this meant that the average size of the First Form class increased from sixteen in the early 1880s to thirty-five in the late 1890s. In Toronto it resulted in an eight-fold increase in the high school population between 1870 and 1900, and the construction of two new collegiates. The explanation for this increase in attendance is complex. One-third of the schools continued to charge tuition fees (from $2 to $27 per year in 1886) yet their enrolment increases were not significantly lower than in schools which had abolished fees. Certainly urban population concentrations made high schools geographically accessible to more children; rising affluence made extended schooling less of an upper-class luxury; and the demand for advanced training in business and industry encouraged teenagers to remain longer in school. While the high schools did little in the way of specific vocational training, they did provide a year or two of general education that employers increasingly sought from job applicants.

The incorporation in 1871 of the old grammar schools into the full embrace of the provincial system had produced considerable standardization in Ontario secondary education. One casualty was William Tassie, the famous headmaster who had attracted pupils from across the province and from abroad to the Galt Grammar School. In 1872 Galt had headed the list of the first six schools to be awarded collegiate institute status. The emphasis on external examinations and the demand for co-education proved anathema to Tassie, leading to his resignation nine years later. But there were other schoolmen who adjusted to the demands for uniformity and built academic institutions that attracted scholars from throughout the province. One such individual was John Seath, principal of St Catharines Collegiate from 1874 to 1884. 'I was one of Mr. Seath's pupils,' recalled a native of York County, 'because it was a common saying among teachers, "if you want a first-class certificate or university scholarship, go to St. Catharines."'[56] Seath's potential career as a sharp-tongued critic of the system – and a Conservative supporter – was ended when Ross appointed him as a high school inspector. The spotlight shifted in the late 1880s and 1890s to tiny Strathroy Collegiate under principal James Wetherell. 'The school has now a provincial reputation,' boasted the town newspaper in 1891. 'Its pupils come from every section of the province and the tuition imparted has made its graduates names in almost all ranks of life.'[57] Scholars even folowed the great headmasters when they changed schools. Thus when Thomas Kirkconnell left Port Hope High School, 'the parents and pupils in half of Durham county transferred their allegiance ... to his new school at Lindsay.'[58]

The private schools that survived the institution and consolidation of the public high school system constituted a conscious and often expensive rejection of the state system. The 1880-1 report of the provincial department of education listed seven such boys' schools and seven ladies' colleges. The founders of these schools have been described as being 'stimulated by a variety of motives, not all of which were concerned with the academic needs of the province's youth.' Religious idealism, sentimental attachment to old English institutions, patriotic and imperialistic notions, the desire to create a leadership class imbued with the ideals of Christian service – all were factors which contributed to the evolution of Ontario's boarding schools.[59] These private schools were patronized by parents who sought for their children either denominational education, superior or more specialized teaching, or social advantages – in short, 'advantages that the emerging state schools did not or could not offer.'[60] With its endowment lands and provincial grants, Upper Canada College in Toronto was the wealthiest and most prestigious of the late nineteenth-century private schools. High school inspector J.A. McLellan (a UCC old boy) was particularly complimentary in his evaluation of the school in 1881. If sufficient funding were forthcoming to permit the employment of first-rate masters, declared McLellan, 'higher results in national education will be won, with profounder influences upon the moral, intellectual and industrial life of our community.'[61] Education minister Ross, in laying the cornerstone for Upper Canada's new campus in 1891, praised the institution lavishly and virtually dedicated himself to its preservation. 'Anything wrong that should happen to such a college, with such a career,' declared Ross, 'would be nothing short of calamity.'[62]

Yet Upper Canada and its fellow institutions faced an increasing barrage of criticism during the latter years of the century. 'Now that our numerous Collegiate Institutes afford every facility for a first-class secondary education,' observed Charles Mulvaney in 1884, 'it is thought by many that Upper Canada College has survived its usefulness.' Financially pinched high schools looked with envy at the College's generous state endowment and demanded a more equitable division of the available money. Reform politicians and labour groups regarded it – with good reason – as a privileged institution, designed for and patronized by the wealthier families of the province. 'In these democratic times, little is venerated,' complained G. Mercer Adam in his 1893 official history of Upper Canada.[63] Adam was articulating what seemed plainly evident to all private schools by the end of the century – a very minor role in the provincial scheme of education. With the steady improvement of public high schools and the democratic tendencies of North America, Ontario's private schools could never fill the role that Eton, Rugby, and Harrow had filled in England. These British transplants, declared Richard Harcourt, Ross's successor as education minister in 1899, were 'of doubtful relevance for Ontario,' where social values called for free secondary education for all.[64]

Increasing enrolments in the public high schools brought to the fore the questions of purpose and curriculum. How could the secondary school, traditionally influenced by and subservient to the needs of the university, appeal to the increasing number of non-academically-oriented pupils coming from the elementary schools? Reformers believed that the needs of all elementary graduates could only be served by broadening the purpose and curriculum of the high school. The *Canada School Journal* argued in 1878 that 'it would be a great mistake to suppose that the only, or even the principal, function of these schools is to prepare students for a university course.' Its rival, the *Canada Educational Monthly*, demanded that the high school curriculum should be largely influenced by the fact that the majority of school leavers entered agricultural and commercial pursuits.[65] This trend became more pronounced with each passing year. By 1894, for example, while some 951 students left Ontario high schools for university, teacher training, and the learned professions, more than twice that number moved directly from high school into agricultural or mercantile life.[66] Whereas Adam Crooks had earlier maintained that high schools were 'intended to furnish higher education to a very limited number of our population,' George Ross argued in the 1890s that 'as by far the largest number are those who enter a High School for a superior [i.e., general] education, it is but fair that the curriculum should be framed with a special view to their benefit.'[67]

A limited number of new subjects did make inroads into the secondary school course of study in the 1880s and 1890s, although they were usually justified as advantageous for all pupils. Physical education won support for its perceived benefit in relieving an examination-ridden curriculum, providing recreation in crowded urban environments, and building character through organized games and gymnastics. In 1885, collegiate institute status was made dependent on the provision of a suitably-equipped gymnasium. The scientific subjects also gained converts at this time. Some spokesmen argued their practical and utilitarian value in an age of industrial progress; others stressed their equality with classics and mathematics in training the mind. 'The main reason for the introduction of science into our schools,' declared Ross, 'is the mental discipline to be obtained.'[68] By the end of the century, physics, chemistry, and botany had found a place in the Ontario high school curriculum. Business and commercial education had also established a beachhead, although for different reasons and for a narrower clientele. 'As the subjects of a commercial course are practical,' admitted the department of education, 'many parents believe that if their children take them at school, they will be in a better position to earn a livelihood.'[69] As early as 1882, nearly half the pupils in the lower high school grades studied bookkeeping; fourteen years later a two-year commercial course was introduced, leading to a terminal diploma rather than to university matriculation.

Like commercial education, the emerging demand for high school technical education was grounded in late-nineteenth-century economic change. The 1881 census had demonstrated modest industrial development in the province. In the ten-year period since the previous census, the number of industrial employees rose from 87,000 to 118,000; by 1891 the total reached 167,000. Industrial growth raised questions about the relationship between practical training and public schooling throughout North America and Western Europe. As production shifted from small shop to large factory, and from handicraft to power-driven machinery, an Ontario labour publication observed that there was no longer a 'place for an apprentice to go to find assistance or get instruction when learning his trade.'[70] As vocational training ceased to be the responsibility of the employer, it became increasingly fashionable to look to the school to take this subject into its curriculum. In its 1889 report, the federal Royal Commission on the Relations of Labour and Capital concluded that 'instruction in technical schools is calculated to replace the old system.' The commission saw national economic benefits as well. 'If we are to become a great manufacturing country,' it reported, 'more attention must be given to training our people to become artistic and skilled workmen.'[71] Education minister George Ross agreed. The 'commercial prosperity of a country,' he argued in his 1884 annual report, 'may be advanced and promoted by thoroughly trained mechanics.'[72]

In the long campaign to introduce a more practical-vocational dimension to Ontario secondary schools, advocates stressed these twin benefits of upward mobility for the working man and increased prosperity for the nation. But even more than the promoters of science, physical education, or even commercial education, the supporters of technical education had to battle against the well-entrenched academic tradition of the Ontario high school. 'What is demanded is not true education at all,' complained one principal, 'but merely instruction, especially instruction that will speedily equip for work in the factory.'[73] Initial efforts by the provincial department of education came outside the formal school system, through support for evening classes in the Mechanics' Institutes and financial grants for schools of engineering at Queen's and the University of Toronto. High-school-level technical education was initially offered in the new Toronto Technical School in 1891, an institution initiated and managed, not by the city's high school board, but by a business-labour group. The local labour council argued for an extension of technical education to other high schools because 'the community at large would be better for it.'[74] Yet firm resistance to vocational education continued within the teaching ranks. Being products of mid-nineteenth-century grammar schools and liberal arts courses at university, most principals and teachers were loath to compromise the academic environment of the collegiate institute by adding technical courses. So the Toronto Technical School remained an exception to the rule, an appendage to the local and provincial school systems, rather than a 'rung' on the educational 'ladder' leading from elementary through high school to university.[75]

The more divese nature of the high school population challenged traditional approaches to teacher preparation as well as curriculum. Professional training of secondary school teachers became easier to justify as the high school was forced to place less emphasis on learning for learning's sake and concentrate on making the curriculum relevant to heterogeneous classes. The older model of teacher as scholar would no longer suffice. 'While the very best teachers are so by a gift of nature, and cannot by any process be manufactured,' argued one inspector, 'yet as these are seen only now and then in a generation, training must be provided for the great majority.'[76] The idea was by no means a popular one. Universities regarded professional training as an insult to their arts and science graduates, and as an implied criticism of their own teaching methods. This view persisted for many years at Queen's, where according to C.F. Lavell, anyone found advocating high school teacher training was 'a scarcely endurable heretic.'[77] But in 1885 the department of education took an initial step, by designating five of the province's better collegiates as teacher-training institutes. Successful completion of a four-month course was henceforth required for certification as a high school teacher. In 1890, high school teacher training was centralized in a School of Pedagogy within the Toronto Normal School. Seven years later the school was transferred, as the Ontario Normal College, to Hamilton, where it was closely associated with the Hamilton Collegiate Institute. But the continuing hostility of many university professors prevented the locating of high school teacher training in a university environment.

Despite the lip-service paid to the needs of a more diverse student population, the introduction of a few new subjects, and the requirements for teacher certification, the Ontario high school of the 1880s and 1890s departed little from its traditional academic orientation. In fact the classical subjects won even greater prestige (and more students) when in 1894 Latin was added to the list of subjects required for model- and normal-school entrance with the amalgamation of the teacher-training and university matriculation programs. 'The University,' admitted George Ross, 'practically determines the course of study in all our High Schools.' Its influence upon the educational forces of the country could not be overestimated.[78] For all his statements about the importance of general education, Ross continued to measure the high schools in traditional terms. He argued against free tuition, since 'nearly one-half of the whole work of our High Schools is devoted to qualify young men and women for the professions, by which they may become self-supporting.'[79] Ross boasted of the 'abundant supply of students always available for the universities' as one of the 'obvious tests' of high school excellence. He unabashedly proclaimed that Ontario high schools 'may not unfairly be regarded as the most perfect system of secondary schools in any English-speaking country.'[80] As with the elementary schools, increased efficiency rather than drastic change was the operative phrase of Ross and the provincial department of education.

VI

Critics of Ontario education had difficulty making their voices heard during the 1890s. The praise that began at Philadelphia in 1876 was repeated and reinforced at subsequent world's fairs. At the Paris Exhibition of 1878 the Ontario department of education exhibited in six classes and won awards in each – more awards than Britain and other parts of the Empire won altogether. The climax in international acclaim came at the World's Columbian Exposition in Chicago in 1893. Twenty-one prizes went to Ontario: for kindergarten and primary work, secondary and superior instruction, normal schools and model schools, art schools and mechanics' institutes, and schools for the deaf and blind. Capping them all was a special award for 'a system of public instruction almost ideal in the perfection of its details and the unity which binds together in one great whole all the schools, from kindergarten to the University.' One British judge at Chicago called it 'the finest practical system of public education ... that the world affords today.'[81]

International acclaim was matched by domestic regard. A publication aimed at potential British immigrants boasted that 'the educational institutions of Ontario are such to place it in the very front rank among the nations of the earth.' J.G. Bourinot agreed that 'it is to Ontario we must look for illustrations of the most perfect educational system.' The *Educational Weekly* magazine was not the least surprised that 'the efficiency and worth' of the Ontario system won praise throughout the Western world. 'Whatever defects may be detected by those who scan it in details only, as a whole it challenges the admiration and wins the approval of all who know it.'[82] Even Conservative leader W.R. Meredith, while critical of separate schools, bilingual schools, and textbook policies, admitted that 'it is a system the superior of which does not exist in any part of the world.'[83] In recognition of Ross's leadership as minister of education, five Canadian universities awarded him honorary degrees. When the Dominion Educational Association was founded in 1892, Ross was the natural choice as its first president. 'I was quite content to be a follower and took for granted that we had in Ontario the best system of schools in the world,' recalled J.H. Putman of the 1880s. 'Ross had said so on many occasions.' Young pupils were given the same message, as a geography textbook told them that 'the educational system of Ontario is very perfect.'[84]

No doubt the accomplishments in education during the long years of Premier Mowat's administration were considerable. Any quantitative comparison with other Canadian provinces or American states reflected credit on Ontario. Annual provincial expenditures for education more than doubled in the quarter-century between 1871 and 1896; when the growth of population is taken into account, this increase amounted to about 50 per cent per capita. Indeed, this was to be expected; it would have been strange if Mowat, who had brought so many social issues within the closer purview of the government, had not given importance to education. Ross maintained that the state's duty was not discharged when elementary education was provided, and that the young should be encouraged to continue on into high school and university. While unwilling to legislate the complete abolition of high school fees, he was quite prepared to defend the higher per-pupil cost to the government of secondary schools. 'There is no good reason why the state should not encourage its citizens to acquire the highest culture which their means will afford.'[85] Each year saw an increase in the total number of schools, teachers, and pupils; each year also saw improved attendance and retention rates. And Ross worked continually for improvements in textbooks, for higher standards in the training and certification of teachers, and for adult education for artisans and mechanics. By 1893 illiteracy among Ontario's adult population had been reduced to less than 10 per cent, while among persons between the ages of ten and twenty it stood at less than 6 per cent. Little wonder that the Ontario exhibit at Chicago that year was displayed under a banner reading 'Education – Our Glory.'

Naturally the system did have its critics. 'Is it not time,' asked the *Canadian Educational Monthly* as early as 1880, 'that we stop patting each other complacently on the back in the belief that no country has a superior or more complete school organization than we have in Ontario?'[86] Despite the improvements initiated by the Mowat government, had the schools kept up with changing times? 'Our educational system has always been an anachronism, and has by no means kept up pace with the social development or the intellectual development of the race,' charged one high school principal. 'Our system in respect to its curriculum has never been superior to what ought to have existed in the last century.'[87] Critics also felt that the legacy of the Philadelphia and Chicago triumphs made the province unwilling to look outside its own borders for new ideas. Inspector John Dearness urged teachers in 1897 to look to Sweden for leadership in physical and manual training, to Germany for deportment and compulsory attendance, to France for agricultural and technical education, and to Nova Scotia for elementary science. 'If we studied the school systems of other nations with impartiality,' concluded Dearness, 'we should find some feature in every one of them that we might copy with advantage.'[88]

Considerable criticism was directed at two of George Ross's key concepts – uniformity and the ladder system. Uniformity of curriculum, textbooks, and teaching methods was seen to lead to rigidity, which was 'destructive of liberty, of the best personal effort, of the highest results.' Rigidity subordinated the teacher 'to the autocratic fiat of an almost irresponsible inspectorate,' charged one journalist. Teachers became 'simply slave-drivers, exacting the tale of bricks without straw, at the autocratic bidding of some Pharaoh of the hour.'[89] The public and high school inspectors were once described as the 'official tentacula' by which the minister of education 'grasps and apprehends ... the especial agents through and by whom he perceives and acts.'[90] Individually inclined principals and teachers chafed under the authority of these external agents. 'If we as Principals explain why we have adopted a certain course, we are met immediately with the reply, "This is not in the Regulations," and a man had better break all the commands of the decalogue than to depart one jot or tittle from "The Regulations".'[91] Behind the inspectors stood the centralizing legacy of Ryerson and the continuing commitment of Ross to uniformity. 'Ontarians take the ideas of a Ryerson or a Ross, and crystallize them with a machine through which every Ontarian must go,' wrote one party supporter to Conservative leader James Whitney in 1899.[92]

Rigidity through uniformity was compounded by rigidity through continued adherence to the ladder concept, which tied the elementary school to high school domination, and the high school to the university. 'Our system is pre-eminently an educational ladder,' declared Ross, 'and so every advance a boy makes in his ascent should be so definite that there should be no necessity for retracing his steps in order to reach the top.'[93] High school principal W.N. Bell criticized this educational ladder on the grounds that it was 'framed in the interests only of the man who is bent on reaching the top rung – the university.' Bell was one who had succumbed to the 'persuasive eloquence of the advocate' of this approach. 'How beautiful seemed the road commencing in the Kindergarten and proceeding through the grades up to the fair gate called Entrance. The child with his "shining morning face" was depicted as always looking up. And when he passed this gate there opened before him another pleasant and inviting ascent to another fairer and grander gate called Matriculation. Through this he went ever upward to the splendid summit of graduation.' But, concluded Bell, 'the orator failed to tell us that only one in a hundred reached his goal.'[94]

University spokesmen joined in the attack on the schools during the 1890s. In his many addresses to the OEA, Principal George Grant of Queen's stressed two themes. First, was the 'uniformity fetish' or the concern for centralization. 'Military precision might be all right in its place, but its place is not in education.' Second, Grant charged that there was no adequate measure of Ontario's educational quality because of the lack of data on which to make comparisons. He called for open and independent criticism rather than the useless statistics of the annual reports. 'But first we need information.'[95] President James Loudon of the University of Toronto questioned the supposed efficiency of the school system, when the average Ontario university arts graduate was three or four years older than his German counterpart. Loudon's own conclusion was that too much time was wasted in the elementary grades, and that language study was deferred while other subjects were unduly fostered.[96] But George Ross could live with criticism from the province's teachers and universities; some of it was ill-founded, much of it was contradictory, and most of it could be blunted or refuted by Ross's comprehensive grasp of the educational scene and his eloquence as a public orator. But more hard-hitting and politically damaging criticism of Ross's educational policies was soon to come from the Conservative opposition in the provincial legislature.

During William Meredith's long term as Conservative leader, the opposition attack had been largely focused on cultural questions such as separate schools and bilingual schools. Ross had ridden out the storm, owing in part to the moderate position of the government on both questions, and in part to the political strength of the Mowat administration. But the political situation changed dramatically after 1896. Mowat left Queen's Park for the federal cabinet, and the strength of the Liberal administration soon declined under his successor, Arthur Hardy. Meredith in turn gave up the Conservative leadership, first to George Marter, and then to James Whitney. Whitney soon proved himself a suitable match for the government in general, and Ross in particular. Whitney de-emphasized the separate and bilingual schools questions, and concentrated his educational attack on the area where Ross had been least successful. This was the call for a new relationship between schooling and the socio-economic demands of a growing urban-industrial society, particularly the role of the schools in the vocational preparation of tradesmen, office clerks, factory workers, and farmers. In the 1897 session of the legislature Whitney pleaded for more money for the elementary schools so that instruction might be widened to make them more useful to the agricultural and industrial community. He regarded the elementary school as of prime importance in the education of the children of the 'poorer classes' who had to be given 'an opportunity for attaining sufficient education to fit them for their future lot in life.'[97] During an extensive speaking tour of the province in the summer and autumn months of 1897, Whitney placed a major emphasis on education. His favourite theme remained that of government neglect of the elementary school, which he cleverly termed 'the poor man's college.'[98]

Ross's reply to Whitney's criticisms in the 1897 session was a wide-ranging defence of all aspects of Ontario education; it constituted his most eloquent report on his long years of stewardship. He began by denying that 'the so-called centralizing policy' was his doing; it was begun by Ryerson and fully completed before Ross himself took office. Besides, nearly every other Canadian province had adopted the Ontario pattern of centralized examinations; was that not testimony to their value? He denied that elementary schools were being neglected for the benefit of the high schools and universities; the very fact that high school attendance had increased so dramatically was proof of elementary school efficiency. But the greater part of Ross's speech was a defence of his high school policy. 'High schools are not maintained for purposes of higher education alone,' he argued, pointing to new subjects on the curriculum and the increasing numbers of students preparing for elementary school teaching or jobs in business and industry. Why shouldn't the government respond to local initiatives to provide for high school education? 'Are we to say to the people of Ontario,' that 'if you wish to secure for your children a higher education, then this Legislature will grant you no further assistance?' Such a policy might do 'for Abyssinia or Patagonia, but not for the Province of Ontario.' Some critics charged that Ontario was over-educating the bulk of its citizens, encouraging them to aspire beyond their station in life. 'Who has the right to fix any man's station in life?' demanded Ross. 'Who has the right to say to the humblest citizen of Ontario that he has not a right to aspire to any position to which manhood and character are the qualifications?'[99]

It was a strong defence that Ross offered. Yet he did not stop there. During the next two years he became more defensive and less willing to listen to criticism. Ross reached a pinnacle of self-satisfaction in an 1899 political address. 'In education I am unable to propound a new policy,' he grandly announced. 'My contention is that the school laws of Ontario are equal if not superior to the school laws of any Province.' Reflecting on the tribute from Chicago in 1893, Ross reminded his audience that 'we have proven that our school system is in competition with the school systems of the world.' What of the future? 'In the line of general education I think we have gone about as far as we need to go. All we need to do is maintain the efficiency of the teaching profession.'[100] At the time of this address, Ross had just left the education department to replace Arthur Hardy in the premier's chair. Throughout his sixteen years as minister of education, Ross clung to the nineteenth-century liberal outlook that stressed a fixed and limited academic curriculum, with emphasis on mental and moral training, as the best possible school preparation for any life career or vocation. But James Whitney sensed that urbanization and industrialization were placing new pressures on the relationship between schooling and life which traditional educational approaches could not meet. More radical than Whitney were a growing number of educational, social, and industrial reformers who advocated a complete revision of educational philosophy and practice to fit Ontario children for the more complex urban-industrial environment of the new century. Their efforts would come together in the New Education and Industrial Education movements of the 1890s and early 1900s.

3 The New Education Movement – Those 'Yankee Frills'

Ontario teachers were formally introduced to an alternative educational approach in 1886, when J.E. Wetherell, principal of Strathroy Collegiate, addressed the Ontario Teachers' Association on 'Conservatism and Reform in Education Methods.' Wetherell went to great lengths to distinguish between what he called the 'Old Education' and the 'New Education.' The former 'stored the mind with knowledge, useful and useless, and only incidentally trained the mind,' while the latter 'puts training in the first place and makes the acquisition of knowledge incidental.' The Old Education was devoted to the study of books while the New Education 'is devoted more to things than books.' The old approach 'was eminently subjective, dealing largely in abstractions' while the new 'employs objective methods, preferring the presentation of truth in the concrete.' Rather than beginning with 'the unseen and the unfamiliar,' the New Education 'begins with the seen and the common and gradually develops the reflective faculties by reference to knowledge already obtained ... by the child.' Finally, while the Old Education was too one-sided, the New Education promised to develop 'the whole being, the mental, the moral, the physical.'[1]

The end-of-the-century reform movement that took the name 'New Education' could trace its roots to earlier nineteenth-century European education reformers like Johann Pestalozzi and Friedrich Froebel. Inspector James Hughes of Toronto once proclaimed that 'if all the work of all the great educators of the past were destroyed, all that is vital in modern education' would be found in the writings of these two men.[2] Teaching and writing in early nineteenth-century Switzerland, Pestalozzi had advocated a complete change in the purpose of the school: it should develop the child's own powers and faculties rather than impart facts, show not so much what to learn as how to learn. In mid-century Germany, Froebel had extended Pestalozzian ideas with his pioneer work in kindergarten education. Froebel placed even greater emphasis on the activity of the child, on 'learning by doing,' and on the overriding importance of play and physical activity in the education of the young child. By the end of the nineteenth century the ideas of both these men were well known to North American educators, through a proliferation of books and an endless number of convention addresses. One book that attracted more than its share of attention was Hughes's *Froebel's Educational Laws for All Teachers*; an American kindergarten leader claimed it did the most to emphasize 'the universal character of Froebel's principles.'[3]

But the United States, not Europe, provided the immediate source of inspiration for Ontario school reformers. J.H. Putman identified psychologist G. Stanley Hall and educational philosopher John Dewey as the two greatest influences on him at the time of his appointment to the Ottawa Model School staff in 1894. Hall's 1880 article, 'The Contents of Children's Minds upon Entering School,' moved child study away from the speculative inquiry of pioneers like Froebel and helped give it a scientific base. Hall's central thesis was that young children have special characteristics which must be studied and appreciated before effective teaching and learning can take place. In 1894 he delivered a series of lectures on child study in Toronto, and the following year a child study section was formed within the Ontario Educational Association. Although Ontario teachers had to wait till 1917 for a personal visit from John Dewey, they were as familiar with his ideas as with those of Hall. As early as 1889 high school inspector James McLellan had co-authored with Dewey a major textbook, *Applied Psychology*, which introduced Ontario normal school students to scientific psychology and child-centred teaching methods. F.W. Merchant journeyed to Chicago 'to sit at Dewey's feet' just prior to assuming his new duties as principal of London Normal School in 1900.[4] Ontario disciples were familiar, not only with Dewey's principles, but also with his picturesque turn of phrase. 'The child is the centre of the educational system, as the sun is the centre of the planetary system,' parrotted Frederick Tracy,[5] a University of Toronto philosophy professor.

Putman, McLellan, Merchant, and Tracy were representative of a growing number of Ontarians reacting against traditional nineteenth-century curriculum and teaching methods and willing to embrace the more child-centred pedagogy offered by the New Education movement. They were joined by Adelaide Hoodless, the promoter of domestic science education; James Robertson, the federal agricultural commissioner who campaigned for rural school improvement; and J.J. Kelso, the Toronto humanitarian crusader who provided the link with the related child-saving and urban-reform movements. Within the Ontario cabinet, pedagogical reform found support from J.M. Gibson, provincial secretary in the 1890s; Richard Harcourt, Ross's successor as education minister in 1899; and W.J. Hanna, provincial secretary in the later Whitney administration. But the foremost Canadian advocates of the New Education were the husband-and-wife team of James and Ada Hughes. As inspector of Toronto schools since 1874 and promoter of the kindergarten, James was the earliest champion and acknowledged philosopher of the movement. The New Education was 'more of a revolution than an evolution,' he declared, arguing that new aims, new methods, and new principles must be substituted for old.[6] As Toronto's first public kindergarten teacher, his wife Ada came to see social as well as pedagogic dimensions to the reform movement. 'The traditional methods of the old education are not equal to the demands of the new conditions and modern needs,' she declared. The New Education was crucial for wider social reform. 'The possibilities for the uplift of society,' could only come 'through the better understanding and more intelligent training of child life.'[7]

Under the leadership of people such as J.J. Kelso and James Hughes, there developed in Toronto and other Ontario centres by the end of the century a loosely knit 'child saving' movement which focused its attention on a variety of interconnected school and school-related reforms. To improve the quality of childhood and the nature of family life, reformers stressed infant care and child-rearing practices, child psychology, improved housing, day nurseries for working mothers, supervised playgrounds, and sex- and family-life education in home and school. In the area of child and family welfare, they worked for factory legislation for women and children, proper care and placement of neglected children, detention homes, industrial schools and juvenile courts for delinquent children, and changes in legislation affecting desertion, divorce, support, and child custody. Out of their concern for child and family health they campaigned for the reduction of infant and child mortality, for maternity and children's hospitals, pure water and pure milk supplies, compulsory vaccination and immunization, medical and dental inspection in the schools, fresh-air camps for slum children, and special care and education for mentally and physically handicapped children. The child savers viewed themselves as altruists and humanitarians, dedicated to rescuing those who were less fortunately placed in the social order. But like most moral crusades, the child-saving movement reaffirmed faith in traditional values and stressed the positive capacities of traditional institutions. Thus two of their earliest successes in protecting the youth from social ills – the temperance curriculum of 1887 and the compulsory attendance legislation of 1891 – established the pattern of using the institutional school to regulate youthful behaviour.

The transformation of the school via the New Education movement was central to the child-saving crusade. New methods of instruction stressed learning by activity rather than memorization; correlation of the subject matter around the child's own widening experience; enrichment of class-room study with material drawn from the school's immediate neighbourhood; and the substitution of love for fear, and of interest for authority, in class-room discipline. The purpose of these child-centred methods was not to preach permissiveness, but rather to lead the child to his own acceptance of traditional moral values that had once been externally imposed by adult society. The end had not changed – despite James Hughes's talk of revolution – only the means to that end. Likewise the curriculum was broadened, not to introduce the principle of free choice, but to encompass the occupational, civic, and moral training which the family in the new urban environment seemed no longer able to provide. The new subjects were the mechanical, agricultural, and household arts; social studies, especially civics; hygiene and physical instruction; and moral education, grounded in religious faith but executed in practice in ethical decision making. The New Education reformers also sought to improve rural schools, partially under the guise of equality of educational opportunity, but also to strengthen rural life and stop the drift of country children to the wicked and materialistic cities.

II

The kindergarten was an early example of the link between the curricular reforms of the New Education and the social and moral crusades of the child-saving and urban-reform movements. Shortly after his 1874 appointment as Toronto's public school inspector, James Hughes spent what he later described as an 'epoch-making morning' visiting a private kindergarten in Boston. 'I saw an educational process that was intended to develop vital centres of power and skill and character, instead of merely storing the memory and giving an abstract training in reasoning.' Fired with enthusiasm, Hughes at once set about learning all he could of the Froebelian kindergarten movement that was exciting American urban school reformers. 'I shall be the first man in Canada to establish a kindergarten,' he boasted.[8] Every year he concluded his annual report to his trustees with the same words: 'It must ultimately become part of our system, and I trust it may soon.' With the backing of Toronto's two leading morning newspapers, and the support of education minister Adam Crooks, Hughes began convincing a sceptical public. Finally, in September 1883 Canada's first public kindergarten began in Toronto's Niagara Street School with seventy children under the direction of Ada Marean – the future Mrs James Hughes. London, Hamilton, and Ottawa followed suit, and by the end of the 1880s, the province offered financial grants and teacher-training classes, and at least one commercial firm in Toronto specialized in the sale of kindergarten materials.

The kindergarten meant different things to different people. To some humanitarians, it suggested the emancipation of the child from traditional and insensitive restrictions, the enhancement of spontaneity and creativity. When carried too far, this view led some critics to consider the kindergarten 'in the light of a new kind of play, for the conduct of which little or no training is required – or of a nursery where babies are taken in charge – in order that their mothers may have more leisure for running about.' Such was the complaint of a London kindergarten teacher in 1894. 'The very last thing to be appreciated is the educational value.'[9] But schoolmen did note the educational value of the kindergarten. It engaged in what later came to be called reading readiness, or as a contemporary inspector put it, 'preparing the pupils for the prosecution of their studies in more advanced classes.'[10] It was a new bottom rung on the educational ladder! But its advocates hoped that the methods of the kindergarten would have some effect on improving primary-grade teaching methods. One inspector did note such an improvement in 1889, and attributed the change 'to the diffusion of a knowledge of the principles and methods peculiar to the Kindergarten system.'[11] George Ross agreed that kindergarten methods lay at the foundation of all successful primary work. He argued that 'anything done to improve primary education would be of great advantage to our Public Schools.'[12]

Yet if kindergarten instruction suggested freedom and creativity to some critics, and improved primary teaching methods to some supporters, it also suggested uniformity and control. Kindergarten teachers evolved a complex and highly structured methodology of play activities which channelled childhood spontaneity into a desired social behaviour. All play activities, however, were not equally valid. Music, games, and marching were most important; while calling for great activity, they kept children within a highly structured program and prevented 'disagreeable romping.' Proponents of this social function of schooling claimed for the kindergarten almost the entire gamut of social improvement – from the prevention of pauperism to the salvation of man. Rev. Alexander Jackson catalogued the benefits in an 1896 address to the OEA. Kindergarten training, he argued, 'would supply our country with intelligent, tactful and capable mothers ... improve the quality of the citizens which it would turn out of the public schools ... [and] materially lessen the number of criminals and the cost of their care.' Finally, as national economic growth became a topic of public concern, "the kindergarten system would save children for their usefulness to the nation.'[13]

While not denying the benefits of this structured pre-school experience for middle- and upper-class children, reformers above all emphasized the necessity of the kindergarten for the children of the poor. J.J. Kelso promoted the 'mission kindergarten' as second only to a 'mother's own good teaching' among preventive social-service agencies. Here, the 'little ones are gathered from the streets and alleys' and 'they are saved from acquiring evil and untidy habits.'[14] Advocates of charity and public kindergartens insisted that the child continually learned things before he entered the formal school. He could learn vice, crime, intemperance, and despair in the slum; however, he could learn desired social relationships and moral values in the kindergarten. Although the ideal was never fully attained in Ontario, the kindergarten movement also proposed to reach out beyond the class-room and influence the lower-class child in his poverty-stricken home environment. In some centres, kindergarten teachers were at first placed on half-day teaching schedules, leaving time for both mothers' meetings and home visitations. Through these meetings the teacher tried to bring the mothers into closer contact with the school program and discuss general domestic questions of mutual interest. Home visitations personalized this contact, with the teacher tactfully discussing issues of nutrition, hygiene, and child development.

Hughes's enthusiastic campaign for the kindergarten, similar to his later crusades for other aspects of the New Education movement, was a manifestation of his developing philosophy of education and his concern for social cohesion in an urban environment. He argued that the kindergarten provided a 'bridge from the nursery to the school,' between the play activities of childhood and the work activities of the class-room. 'Play is the work of childhood,' wrote Hughes in recalling his own boyhood in Durham County. 'It develops a tendency to work, and cultivates in the energetic player the physical force and the characteristic aggressive spirit that enjoys work and accomplishes mighty deeds.'[15] Hughes envisaged the kindergarten as a miniature community within which the child learned the skills and moral values of responsibility and co-operation, so necessary for social living. The process of moral growth involved the 'transference of the child's interest from evil to good in so natural a way that the child is not conscious of the external, guiding influence in making the change.[16] He saw the kindergarten as especially valuable for Toronto urban schools. More and more children were attending from slum dwellings and lower-class backgrounds, where school readiness and acceptable middle-class social and moral attitudes were not stressed. As with so many educational innovations, the kindergarten was proposed, not solely to open wider horizons for under-privileged children, but also to channel these youngsters into socially desirable patterns of behaviour.

By 1902, almost twenty years after introducing the first public-school kindergarten, James Hughes could feel justifiably proud of his creation. That year there were some 120 kindergarten class-rooms in the province, where 247 trained teachers taught more than 11,000 five-year-olds. Hughes could take satisfaction in the fact that his educational rival and arch political enemy, George Ross, admitted that 'there is no department of our school work more useful than the course of instruction in our Kindergarten schools.'[17] In April 1902 Hughes was at his poetic and prophetic best in an article on 'The Future Evolution of the Kindergarten.' To Hughes, the kindergarten was not just 'a system adapted to any special stage of human development ... not a philosophy designed for an epoch in human progress ... not a process through which the race must pass, and which will cease to be of value, when the race has grown beyond it.' No, the kindergarten was a 'universal ideal,' 'broad enough to make it the true basis of growth to higher stages of consciousness for every existing condition of humanity' and 'deep enough to be the vital principle that must guide mankind in its advances through clearer insights and grander achievements to higher and higher conditions in its definite and conscious growth toward the infinite.'[18]

III

Hughes was not prepared to admit that Froebelian principles ended at the kindergarten level. 'Froebel wrote a philosophy for the university as well as the kindergarten,' he maintained. 'The application of principles should change as the child ascends through the advancing periods of its growth, but the laws of true educational development apply universally.'[19] Hughes believed that the subject of manual training or industrial arts provided the natural extension for Froebelian ideas to influence the entire school curriculum. He saw it as a logical development from the controlled play activities of the kindergarten, as both the starting point and the perpetual means of all other educational development. 'You cannot kindle all children by literature,' Hughes argued. 'A very large proportion were not meant to be deep lovers of book learning.' Other subjects had their place, but more could be kindled with art and manual training 'than by all the others put together.' Why? 'Because God meant men and women to be productive.'[20]

Hughes envisaged an integrated and comprehensive manual training program that would permeate the entire elementary school curriculum. It would begin in the kindergarten, since 'all kindergarten occupations and clay modelling exercises are perfect types of manual training for young children.' Youngsters in First and Second Book classes would take up pencil drawing and cardboard construction. In Third Book classes, sewing would be available to the girls while the boys moved on to knife work with soft wood. Up to this point the manual training activities could be handled by the regular class-room teacher and, it was hoped, be integrated with the other subjects of the curriculum. But special rooms and specially trained teachers would be needed for Fourth and Fifth Book classes. Here, the girls would concentrate on sewing and cooking, while the boys followed a standard curriculum, based on English and Swedish models, that combined drafting, the introduction of hand tools, and the making of such 'useful' wooden articles as sock darners, corner shelves, and towel rollers.[21]

As with other elements of the New Education, manual training was in part an attempt to preserve the traditional values of a society threatened by urban-industrial growth. Hughes looked back on his early years in Durham County with fond memories. 'The boy whose childhood is spent in the country has better opportunities for the natural development of mind and body than the boy who is brought up in city or town.' Problems encountered in doing chores or investigating the natural environment of the farm 'gave me the best possible training for the recognition and solution of the problems of life.'[22] Unfortunately, this ideal rural environment was not possible for the many thousands of young children growing up in crowded cities. But manual training – an institutional re-creation of the challenges of earlier days – offered possibilities for both mental training and character development.

Beginning in 1886, Hughes's yearly reports to the Toronto Public School Board included a strong plea for the new subject. The aim of the movement, he wrote, 'is not to make mechanics or expert manufacturers, but to train a race of skilful and intelligent men.' He was careful to preserve a balance among educational, social, and practical benefits. Manual training would develop the observant powers, provide for the application of knowledge, allow opportunities for the child to observe his success and progress, create a higher respect for labour, increase the earning potential of the individual, and benefit the nation industrially.[23] By 1897, Hughes was emphasizing the social and moral potential of manual training. It made pupils constructive rather than destructive, contributed to the nation's moral development, preserved the taste for work, increased respect for honest labour, led to more originality in the products of labour, and provided a great moral force for combatting the vices of drunkenness and lack of thrift.[24]

There were vigorous objections to manual training at the time. Many middle-class parents regarded it as something menial and decidedly inferior to book learning, associating it with the training schools for poor and delinquent children. Teachers complained that the elementary school curriculum was already overloaded. 'In the present crowded state of the programme of studies,' resolved the staff of Toronto's Wellesley Street School in 1895, 'it would be impossible to give one half day each week to the subject.'[25] Strenuous opposition came also from trade union leaders. In part, the unions objected on economic grounds; they feared manual training would undercut the apprenticeship system, take work away from properly qualified tradesmen, and produce second-rate workers – 'botch carpenters' was the term used. Labour spokesmen also feared that manual training would trap working-class children by denying them the type of education that would increase their chances of upward social mobility. 'Manual training would be prejudicial to the interest and welfare of mechanics generally,' Robert Glocking told the 1888 meeting of the Trades and Labour Congress.[26] Yet manual training gradually won additional converts. At their annual meetings, Ontario teachers listened regularly to spokesmen such as W.H. Huston proclaim that 'shopwork disciplined the mind and trained the student in order and method,' or J.H. Putman argue that young people should have something useful to do, otherwise they would 'become somewhat listless, and pass through a period when they are in a kind of comatose, stand-still, won't-be-interested-in-anything condition.'[27] Regular manual-training classes were established in 1889 at Woodstock College, a private boys' school, and in 1896 in Kingston's public elementary schools.

The Macdonald Education Movement provided the much-needed funds for urban school-boards to initiate the new subject. Federal agricultural commissioner James Robertson persuaded tobacco millionaire William Macdonald to donate large sums of money to a number of innovative projects associated with the New Education – manual training, domestic science, school gardens, and rural school consolidation. Although the improvement of rural schools was the ultimate aim of Macdonald and Robertson, their first project was the establishment in 1899 of the Macdonald Manual Training Fund. Robertson later claimed this was a necessary first step in helping rural education; since country people were accustomed to following an urban lead, successful practical work in city schools would create a demand for comparable improvements in rural schools.[28] Despite this political ploy, Robertson was as convinced as Hughes of the cultural and moral values of the subject; he saw it 'as an educational means for developing intellectual and moral qualities of high value in all children.'[29] Under Robertson's direction, Macdonald Manual Training Centres were guaranteed staff and maintenance for three years, at no cost to local school-boards. At the end of this three-year demonstration period, it was hoped that local and provincial authorities would be so convinced of the subject's value that they would take over the centres and extend the work. The first centre in Ontario opened in Brockville in April 1900; during the next school year additional centres were opened in Ottawa and, to Hughes's satisfaction, Toronto. Within three years the Macdonald fund was maintaining centres in twenty-one Canadian cities, paying the salaries of forty-five teachers at a monthly cost of $3,600 and offering manual training to some 7,000 boys.

While Hughes and his colleagues sought to adjust male schooling to the demands of the new urban-industrial order, a growing number of women in late nineteenth-century Canada attempted similar reforms in the education of girls. Foremost among these was Adelaide Hoodless, the country's leading promoter of domestic science or home economics. Hoodless saw the growing independence of women as a mixed blessing – the advantages of the new freedom had to be weighed against potential personal and societal disaster. Young women working in factories, shops, and offices had too little time to devote to domestic concerns, were exposed to 'too much of the seamy side of life,' and were deprived 'of the refining and protecting influences of home life at a time when the character was being formed.'[30] The home, in contrast, constituted 'a second heredity, a moral shaping by suggestion, example and influence.'[31] The management of the home, she believed, 'has more to do in the moulding of character than any other influence, owing to the large place it fills in the early life of the individual during the most plastic stage of development.'[32] But the new urban-industrial world created opportunities for women to neglect their role in the home. 'Instead of finding the chief pleasures and duties of life in the Home circle, our young women seek a career. Inventions and changed conditions have altered the whole structure.'[33] The result, she concluded, was contrary to natural law and a threat to domestic life. 'The subversion of natural law,' she told the National Council of Women in 1902, 'which makes man the bread-winner and woman the home-maker, cannot fail to have an injurious effect on social conditions, both morally and physically.'[34]

Hoodless believed that the school system of the day compounded the problem, through its failure to adjust to the demands of the new society. When the home was the manufacturing centre 'from which the necessities of life were produced,' little was demanded of the elementary school except the three Rs. But 'changes in industrial conditions demand a readjustment of educational methods and courses of study.'[35] Yet theoretical questions still took precedence over practical problems in the school curriculum, with unfortunate results for home-making. 'If practical knowledge formed part of the education of every girl we would not see so many domestic shipwrecks.'[36] The answer seemed to lie in the New Education which 'aims to affiliate school with life, to correlate all subjects into a unity of physical, mental, moral and spiritual action.'[37] In particular, the answer was domestic science in the elementary school. Hoodless saw the new subject as fulfilling the twin aims of integrating school life with desired home life, and preparing women for their all-important role at the centre of that home life. 'Girls should be educated to fit them for the sphere of life for which they were destined – that of the homemaker.'[38]

Like Hughes, Adelaide Hoodless pictured a comprehensive elementary school curriculum in domestic science that began in the kindergarten. 'Small tables are set with all the necessary dishes, cutlery, napkins, etc., and real dinners are eaten by the little ones.' The youngsters would also engage in bed-making, laundry-folding, knitting, and stocking-darning. Graduated exercises in sewing and cooking would continue through First Book to Fifth Book classes. The teaching of 'cookery' would include far more than 'simply imparting a knowledge of the preparation of certain dishes.' It would also entail 'instruction on the nature of food and the art of choosing suitable, nourishing and at the same time economical articles of diet in order that the smallest incomes may be made to serve the needs of even large families.'[39] Hoodless's 1898 textbook, *Public School Domestic Science*, included calorie charts and chemical analyses of different types of foods, and chapters dealing with the parts of the body, the relation of food to the body, infants' diets, and household management.

In 1897 Stratford became the first city in the province to make domestic science an integral part of its public school curriculum. Again, it was the Macdonald Manual Training Fund, rather than support from the provincial department of education, that helped the new subject gain a foothold in urban centres. Although the Macdonald Fund provided no direct money for domestic science, it challenged local boards to provide some activity for the girls while the boys were in manual training classes. Ultimately, domestic science was accepted, not solely for its limited educational purposes, but for its more sweeping social and moral promises. 'There are tremendous possibilities involved in this new movement,' wrote Hoodless, 'not only as an educational factor, but as a social power.' In the city, domestic science would help alleviate the social problems of slum housing by instilling into girls the desire and the 'executive ability' to turn 'hovels into homes.'[40] In the country it would attack a main source of social dislocation – rural depopulation – by imparting to country girls a fitting appreciation for rural life, by training 'proper farm wives' to create and maintain an agreeable home life.[41] Above all were the ethical considerations. 'Character is formed in the home, and largely under the influence of the mother,' Hoodless argued, 'and unless women are educated so as to realize and faithfully perform the duties and responsibilities of homemakers, we cannot expect a higher type of citizen.' There was no branch of education so conducive to ethical instruction as domestic science, 'dealing as it does directly with the home and the occupations carried on there.'[42] Finally, the new subject might stem the tide of women leaving the home. 'Girls should have special opportunities for acquiring a knowledge which not only develops character but fits them for their God-given place in life.'[43]

IV

While James Hughes and Adelaide Hoodless sought to make city schools more relevant to the social needs of the turn-of-the-century urban environment, other reformers concentrated their attention on the rural schools. 'The rural school problem is the most important question before the people of Ontario today,' journalist W.R. Parkinson told the 1903 OEA meeting. Lamenting the 'growing tendency towards urban life,' Parkinson concluded that the rural school and the provincial education system were not doing enough 'to keep the boy on the farm.' Rather, 'the whole trend of his training' was 'calculated to fix his attention on the High School, then on the University, and finally to induce him to enter professional life.' Even the unsuccessful young man was likely to 'come back filled with the idea that his father and mother are slow, and that he is too clever to earn his living by soiling his hands at the plough.'[44] Parkinson took for granted a basic assumption that found wide support at the time: a reformed rural school would halt the decline in rural population and restore the idyllic virtues of country life.

Reformers could point with pride to a few rural schools in the province that seemed to relate to their immediate communities and serve the larger needs of agrarian society. One such institution was the Rittenhouse School, located near the village of Jordan Station in the heart of the Niagara Peninsula fruitlands. Moses Franklin Rittenhouse was the personal benefactor of this school; his was a classic Horatio Alger story, as he rose from Lincoln County farm boy to prosperous Chicago lumber baron. Local trustees in 1890 accepted Rittenhouse's offer to bear half the costs of a new schoolhouse on the site where young Moses had been educated back in the 1850s. The result was a handsome two-room, brick structure, well endowed with the latest in teaching aids and library books, electricity, and indoor plumbing. But that was not the end of Rittenhouse's beneficence; in due course he provided money for domestic-science and manual-training rooms in the basement, and for an adjacent music and lecture theatre which made the school the centre for community activities. He also employed a landscape gardener to beautify the grounds with a variety of shrubs, trees, and hedges, 'making it not only a paradise for the children but also a beauty spot from which other sections might receive inspiration.'[45] But other school districts lacked a philanthropist of comparable wealth and generosity. The Rittenhouse School remained the exception to the rule; local effort was not sufficient to provide the ideal rural schooling demanded by the agrarian visionaries.

At the secondary level, turn-of-the-century agrarian reformers initially put their hopes on the continuation schools. Beginning in 1896, these were formed around Fifth Book or First Form classes that had sprung up in many village and rural elementary schools. Within three years, many of these schools added the Second Form, and by 1906 some offered the entire high school program. Continuation schools were especially successful in Carleton, where Inspector R.H. Cowley soon had the county blanketed. They provided a preferred alternative to the cost of erecting a central county high school or to the high non-resident fees charged by Ottawa Collegiate. As a local member of the legislature remarked, 'these classes relieve us from the necessity of sending our children from the good, innocent farm life to the cities and towns for high school education.'[46] Farsighted educators cherished the hope that the continuation schools would provide a type of secondary education particularly suited to rural, agricultural needs. But the majority of country dwellers cherished no such desire. They wanted the new schools to be miniature reproductions of traditional town high schools. Cowley himself observed with amazement that the farmers were intensely interested in their sons learning Latin. 'There appeared to be a glamour about it that pleased them. They would speak with pride to their neighbours, while their eyes brightened up.'[47] As early as 1899, the department of education admitted that the objectives of the continuation schools were identical to those of the town high schools. 'A different course of study ... could not be thought of.'[48]

While the continuation school provided a partial answer to the problem of rural secondary education, it was educator James Robertson and philanthropist William Macdonald, working together in the Macdonald Education Movement, who provided the most concerted attack on the problems of rural elementary education. 'In our educational progress not much has been done for the girls and boys in rural schools compared with what has been given to and made possible for the children in towns and cities,' Robertson wrote to Premier Ross in 1902.[49] But once manual training had gained a foothold in urban schools, Robertson and Macdonald could turn their attention to their original concern – the rural school. Their reform thrust was essentially conservative. Robertson claimed that its aim was not to destroy anything that existed in rural districts – 'except weeds' – but rather to 'build up something better than is now known and done, and thereby replace what is poor.' Its vocational aim was to provide more competent leaders for the horticultural and agricultural population while its social aim was to 'help the rural population to understand better what education is and what it aims at for them and their children.'[50] Rural discontent and unrest could be defused through greater support for and confidence in the country school.

The first Macdonald-Robertson venture in country education was the Macdonald Rural Schools Fund, which saw school gardens established at five rural schools in each of the five eastern provinces in 1904. The designated Ontario schools were all in Carleton County, largely due to the efforts of Inspector Cowley. As with the manual training fund, Macdonald bore the costs of establishing the gardens and maintaining supervisory personnel for three years. The pupils were shown the value of seed selection, crop rotation, and protection against weeds, insects, and disease. Supporters claimed both practical and social values for the school gardens. Robertson maintained they could be used 'for the training of children to habits of close observation, of thoughtfulness,' with the result that the child 'becomes a better pupil and the promise of a better citizen in every sense.'[51] The department of education saw them as bringing school life closer to social life and giving children 'brighter impressions of the work of the farmer.'[52] Cowley was the most starry-eyed supporter. He claimed the gardens would 'cultivate the sense of ownership and a social spirit of co-operation and mutual respect for one another's rights' and 'provide an avenue of communication between school and home, thereby strengthening public interest in the school as a national institution.'[53] As school gardens spread from Carleton County to other parts of the province, their success led to the very popular school agricultural fairs, which began in North Dumfries Township (Waterloo County) in 1909. Like the gardens, the rural school fairs were seen as conservative social forces. They would 'prepare the boys and girls for the farm, create in them a greater love for farm life, make them more efficient workers, more practical thinkers, and more intelligent citizens.'[54]

Initial enthusiasm for school gardens led to an even bolder scheme for the regeneration of rural education and rural life – the Macdonald Consolidated School Project. This plan sought to extend the benefits of the gardens and add those of manual training and domestic science by amalgamating several small rural school districts and building one large, consolidated school. 'It has not been difficult in Canada to arrange routes for the collecting of milk or cream to one central place,' argued Robertson. 'It would not be more difficult to arrange for the collection of children on various roads to one central school.'[55] Macdonald money again provided for the construction of a new building and part of the extra operating costs over a three-year period. Interest was keen throughout the province, as correspondents from several counties wrote education minister Richard Harcourt begging that the one Macdonald demonstration school allotted to Ontario be established in their locality. Finally, a site near Guelph was chosen, to give the school close proximity to the Ontario Agricultural College. Robertson saw several immediate practical advantages of consolidation: better buildings and equipment, higher qualified staff, better classification of pupils, improved attendance, an enriched program, and the opportunity of obtaining a high school education close to home.[56] But again there were important social aims. Journalist W.R. Parkinson believed consolidation the best possible solution to the problem of rural de-population. It would 'keep boys and girls at home, save them from the bedizening influences of city life, and turn them into an intelligent rural constituency.'[57] Education minister Richard Harcourt confided to Macdonald that he knew of 'nothing which would tend to make our farmers' sons and daughters more contented with rural life.'[58]

Harcourt's enthusiasm for consolidation was consistent with the support he gave to all facets of the New Education movement during his years as education minister from 1899 to 1905. A new tone is evident in the department's annual reports during the Harcourt years – the challenge of scientific and industrial development. 'The progress of science, in this latter part of the nineteenth century, has revolutionized all our industries,' Harcourt prefaced his 1899 report. 'The curriculum of fifty years ago will not do today.'[59] His annual remarks to the OEA were less defensive and more conducive to change than those of Ross had been. 'We have reached the time when our course of study should be remodelled,' he told the teachers in 1903. 'The needs, the conditions, the circumstances of today must dominate the situation.'[60] Those circumstances demanded that the schools address themselves to practical preparation for the industrial world. 'The training given in our High and Public Schools should be as practical as possible,' he declared, 'and the subjects taken up should have in view the pursuits that will necessarily be followed by the great majority of our citizens.' Practical training had the potential for making the pupil intelligent, industrious, and law-abiding. And the subjects promoted by the New Education reformers seemed to fill the bill. To Harcourt, manual training was essential 'if we are to have well-trained mechanics, farmers, and merchants'; it would furnish effective relief from an altogether too bookish curriculum; help co-ordinate 'the training of hand and eye' so vital for young children; and give 'a due regard to the dignity of labour.'[61]

Harcourt at once began corresponding with local school-board chairmen, principals, and other educators, urging them to introduce the new subjects. 'The change will come, must come. Why delay it?' he asked a Lindsay school principal. 'You would popularize your schools immensely by making the change.' He implored James Mills, president of Ontario Agricultural College, to preach the virtues of domestic science in the Guelph area. He offered a substantial yearly grant to the Welland Public School Board because he wanted 'to have a commencement made in some of our best schools.' He expressed annoyance when a Brantford supporter raised the question of cost. 'You must not ask me to decide now about the extent of the grant since you know that I am desirous of giving aid to the full extent. If I make a mistake I want it to be on the side of generosity.' Pelham Township was promised a special grant if trustees would 'seriously take up a good consolidation scheme.'[62] It may have seemed strange for a former provincial treasurer to be so lavish with public funds, but Harcourt knew that legislative approval for a formal system of provincial grants would be forthcoming only if local communities led the way. 'We will follow the principle which governs our entire system,' he told the OEA in 1902, 'that of aiding and supplementing local effort. We will commence by offering a small grant to any section which will supplement it by a sum twice as large.' Such stimulation was necessary, Harcourt believed, because people usually were slow to demand reforms which involve increased taxation.[63]

During 1903 and 1904 Harcourt moved vigorously to guarantee a future for manual training and domestic science in the province's elementary schools. When initial Macdonald Fund money expired, the new subjects became eligible for fixed annual provincial grants in addition to percentage grants based on teachers' salaries and equipment costs. And in the face of strong teacher opposition, Harcourt mobilized his departmental personnel to champion their retention as optional subjects during a sweeping revision of the elementary school curriculum. Through most of 1903 and into 1904 the province's teachers had an opportunity to discuss the most thorough proposals for curricular reform since Ryerson's retirement. Not surprisingly, the more traditionally oriented university and high school spokesmen within the OEA mounted a strong campaign against the new subjects. They met their match in Harcourt and high school inspector John Seath. 'These new subjects have come to stay,' warned Seath, 'and it would be well for all of you to realize the fact and to use the movement as it may be used, for the proper ends of education.'[64] In the end, the advocates of the new subjects carried the day at the 1904 OEA meeting; the revised curriculum regulations announced later in the year retained manual training and domestic science as optional subjects, and added art, nature study, and agriculture. By the end of 1904, Harcourt could take justifiable pride in the progress of school reform; manual training and domestic science classes were spreading throughout urban Ontario, school gardens and school libraries dotted the rural countryside, and the new consolidated school at Guelph seemed a welcome omen of things to come.

V

Innovations in health care, recreation, child morality, and auxiliary classes – areas where the New Education merged with the broader child-saving movement – had at least as much influence on early twentieth-century Ontario pupils as the various curricular changes. Proposals to link the public school with the growing public health movement fell on receptive ears; the school was an institution that provided a captive audience, since one entire age group was compelled to attend. As early as 1881, education minister Adam Crooks, who usually championed a limited role for the school, saw merit both for the child and the state in 'giving familiar information to each child of the rules of health, and in protecting him against bad ventilation, lighting and heating, and other defects of the school-house.'[65] Soon the newly formed Ontario Board of Health and its supporters within both the medical and teaching professions embarked on a four-fold crusade: school sanitation, control of infectious and contagious diseases, the inclusion of hygiene in the curriculum, and, finally, medical inspection of schoolchildren.

The provincial board of health launched the campaign by charging in its 1883 report that many Ontario schoolrooms were 'in a very unsanitary condition' and that 'neglect of precautions to prevent the spread of contagious and infectious diseases' was all too common.[66] It was one thing, however, for a board of health and a department of education to set minimum sanitary standards for schools, but quite another thing to persuade local trustees to apply them. Rural ratepayers in Middlesex County defeated an 1891 motion to ventilate their schoolhouse by a whopping twenty-eight to one vote. Local trustees were reluctant to follow 1886 board of health requirements that called for the exclusion from the school of any children in direct contact with smallpox, cholera, scarlet fever, diphtheria, whooping cough, measles, or mumps; the line of least resistance was to close the schools entirely when faced with a major outbreak. It was even harder to enforce compulsory vaccination laws for all schoolchildren in the face of public hostility to what one Toronto mayor called 'a dirty, filthy practice.'[67] Meanwhile, public health officials sought to make subjects like physiology and hygiene compulsory for all students, because the 'susceptible minds of the young' were 'particularly adapted to receive and retain such information.'[68] Physical education was also important because, as James Hughes argued, it would 'make men healthful and less liable to disease' and 'remove hereditary diseases and counteract hereditary tendencies.'[69]

By the turn of the century it was evident that neither poorly-enforced sanitary regulations, poorly-trained teachers, nor hastily prepared hygiene curricula could by themselves win the battle against childhood disease. What was needed, declared the Ontario Board of Health in its 1899 and 1901 reports, was to have 'physicians visit the schools to examine for suspects ... and to follow up the absentees to their homes.'[70] Toronto's chief medical officer at first dismissed school medical inspection as 'a pure fad, instituted principally by women' who were 'apt to give way to sentiment' and listen 'to the talk of agitators' who wanted 'easy billets for their friends, with good pay and little work.'[71] But under pressure from the local Council of Women and *Telegram* publisher John Ross Robertson, the Toronto public school-board in 1910 agreed to conduct an initial medical survey of pupils and appoint their first school nurse. Brantford began medical inspection that same year, and by the First World War twelve other Ontario school-boards had followed suit. The Women's Institute led the campaign in rural Ontario, and in 1914 its Parkhill branch secured in the North Middlesex school inspectorate the first medical inspection of country pupils. By this time the school nurse had become the front-line worker in the school health movement. She did the routine inspections, examinations, and readmissions, kept medical records on all pupils, and taught health to teachers and pupils through lectures and demonstrations. In Toronto schools there were the celebrated Little Mothers' Leagues, where senior elementary girls learned infant care at first hand as they brought their baby sisters to school to be bathed, dressed, fed, and put to bed.

Led by Toronto dentist Dr J.G. Adams, the campaign for dental inspection was much more flamboyant and emotional than that for medical inspection. Adams gained as many opponents as supporters with his unsubstantiated claims that 'there are not less than one million permanent teeth going to destruction in the mouths of the school children of Ontario.'[72] The Niagara Falls town council flatly opposed inspection of pupils' mouths, 'energetically protest[ing] against this kind of paternal legislation.'[73] Other groups could not agree that dental inspection was a matter of special priority; they argued that the state of pupils' eyes and ears was more crucial for school learning. By about 1910, however, with the initial acceptance of medical inspection and statistical information on the poor state of children's teeth before them, school trustees in urban centres were prepared to begin dental inspection. Again, it was the school nurse who undertook most of the preventive dentistry in the class-rooms. She examined teeth, persuaded parents to have cavities treated, demonstrated the proper use of the tooth-brush by conducting 'tooth-brushing drills,' and provided needy children with free brushes.

Toronto's widely acclaimed 'open air' schools illustrate the extension of the school health movement beyond purely medical concerns into the broader area of moral rehabilitation. Beginning in 1910 with an open-air class-room on the grounds of the Hospital for Sick Children, the public school-board opened two summer 'Forest Schools' in 1913-14, and in 1916 converted the two upper-storey rooms of Orde Street School into year-round, open-air class-rooms. The Forest Schools were designed for underprivileged tubercular children, and combined education, nutrition, health care, and morality in May-to-October outdoor sessions. Medical workers were heartened when children during the first summer of the program gained an average of five pounds in weight.[74] Yet the 'highest aim' was moral rather than physical. Dr W.E. Struthers, the board's chief medical officer, hoped the experience in the open air and the comradeship of morally upstanding teachers would 'give these children a new ambition, a desire to make good in life, a desire to be useful.' These were the children 'who will otherwise be physical weaklings, who will fill the class of the shiftless, fill the reformatories ... the prisons, penitentiaries, and asylums, who make the loafers and criminals of adult life, who never had the asset of a healthy, vigorous, clean body, or knew the inspiration of a clean mind.'[75]

Toronto reformers also championed the supervised playground as a corrective for the debilitating physical and moral environment of underprivileged urban children. Most citizens agreed that people in urban areas needed plenty of fresh air and exercise, but the major concern and dominant motive of the playground leaders was a belief that there was little for the child to do in the city during the summer vacation, and that idleness led to delinquency and crime. Again, the loose coalition of child-savers like J.J. Kelso and schoolmen like James Hughes went to work. During the winter of 1907-8 they organized the Toronto Playgrounds Association to 'save many spirited youngsters from the police court and the prison cell.'[76] Within three years they could boast two community and seven school playgrounds, all effectively supervised by a teacher who 'takes the place of a wise mother.' Not only did she minister to her pupils' physical and recreational needs; she also protected them 'from all kinds of evils by seeing that their language and character are at all times proper' and told them 'appropriate stories to kindle their imagination and store their minds with pure and high ideals.'[77] There were also 'vacation classes' at Toronto's Hester How School where the one requirement for pupils wishing to attend was that they come with 'clean hands and face.' Here some 600 children were provided with 'useful occupation during the midsummer holidays.'[78]

From health and recreation it was a small step into the area of children's morality. Not resting on its laurels after seeing temperance introduced into the school curriculum, the Women's Christian Temperance Union found new villains to pursue – cigarette smoking, immoral literature, pornographic picture cards, and the motion-picture industry. A storm of protest was created in

London during 1911 when the local WCTU president charged that 'the vicious tendencies of today start in the Public Schools and Collegiates.' London may be no worse than the rest of the province, added May Thornley, 'but the conditions are terrible to consider.' Thornley demanded a joint clean-up campaign from city council and the school-board. But the mayor refused to be stampeded into a city-wide morality drive. 'Let the parents of the boys and girls be taught the responsibility they have for their children,' he responded. 'They should be taught morality in the home.'[79] The WCTU and other provincial reform groups disagreed; in the years before the First World War they were active in scrutinizing textbooks and library books for the slightest hint of impropriety and in agitating for anti-cigarette lectures at school assemblies. The WCTU in 1905 also introduced sex education into Ontario schools through the 'advanced purity' lectures of Arthur W. Beall, the WCTU's 'Purity Agent.' Six years later the department of education took over the work and appointed Beall as a special lecturer. Invited into schools by local officials, Beall continued to lecture Ontario pupils – largely on the dangers of masturbation – through the 1920s and into the 1930s. The department took no official notice of his work in its annual reports, and at least one inspector was 'never convinced that public lectures on this subject to young boys will do more good than harm.' Yet thousands of Ontario pupils would remember Beall delivering what he came to call his 'eugenics' lectures.[80]

Early twentieth-century reform groups also interested themselves in special schooling for mentally deficient pupils, as stricter enforcement of compulsory attendance laws brought more handicapped children into the schools. According to Dr Helen McMurchy, provincial inspector of the feeble-minded, 'in the ordinary school class there is little that the best and kindest teacher can do for the mentally defective child, who is simply a drag on the rest of the class, and cannot learn by ordinary methods.'[81] Reformers were encouraged by the work done in small, special classes at the hospital school of the Orillia Asylum. If handicapped children in the public and separate schools could also be taught in segregated classes, perhaps they might be prepared for responsible, productive adulthood, and rescued from the feared perils of poverty, delinquency, and crime. Provincial legislation in 1911 and 1914 permitted local boards to establish classes for the physically handicapped, 'promotion classes' for slow children, and 'training classes' for mental defectives. By the time of the First World War, five Ontario school-boards were operating these various kinds of 'auxiliary classes.' And Toronto's inspector of public schools was referring to the 'education of the feeble-minded' as one of his board's 'chief pressing problems.'[82]

VI

Thirty-nine years after his initial appointment as inspector of Toronto public schools, and thirty years after his introduction of the kindergarten, James

Hughes approached retirement in 1913. The finale for the Grand Old Man of the New Education Movement was his presidential address that year to the Ontario Educational Association. 'Modern Tendencies in Education' was the carefully chosen title for his remarks. Still as vigorous as ever, still something of a rebel, Hughes delivered a message that praised the many reforms he had championed and initiated during his long career. Unfortunately, his wish to be 'Minister of Education for 30 years' never came true.[83] But his dreams and hopes survived in a younger generation of Ontario schoolmen, many of whom heard his valedictory address. One of these was J.H. Putman, appointed inspector of Ottawa public schools in 1910. Putman quickly reorganized the city's kindergartens, extended manual training into the lower grades, abolished external examinations, reoriented physical training away from military drill towards gymnastics, and introduced nature study, school gardens, pottery classes, and field trips. 'I may modestly claim,' Putman wrote later, 'to have had some share in giving this city a system of elementary education the least academic and the most practical of any in Canada.'[84] More than anyone else, Putman provided the link between the New Education reforms of the early 1900s and the Progressive Education movement of the 1930s.

The year 1904 had marked the high-water mark for the curricular reforms of the New Education movement. The new Conservative government which took office in 1905 by no means sabotaged the program; indeed the Whitney administration tried to sustain the reform thrust through increased provincial grants and the appointment of supervisory personnel. But the movement gradually fell prey to the twin perils of teacher indifference and public criticism. The New Education made fresh demands on the province's teachers – a better understanding of the nature of the child and a greater familiarity with the life of the community. 'We can improve our schools only as we improve our teachers,' stated Putman in 1913. 'Compared with the teacher every other factor pales into insignificance.'[85] Yet the majority of teachers of the day were immature, poorly trained, and inexperienced. Rather than accept the new challenges, most retreated into the security of traditional concerns. Staff meetings in Toronto public schools in 1913 dealt with routine questions of marking registers, width of margins in work books, playground and lunch-room supervision, and end-of-day dismissal procedures.[86] With Hughes's retirement there was no one in the Toronto system to inspire those teachers with the promise of the New Education. Instead, they were admonished 'to give the major portion of our time and energies to the essential subjects.'[87]

Nor was the public convinced of the social value of the new subjects. The editor of *Saturday Night* complained that the products of Toronto schools could 'dress dolls and fry beef steaks,' but were unable to 'write decent hands [or] add up a column of figures.'[88] 'We see education sugar-coated to a degree that must make it nauseous to a sensitive palate,' wrote young Vincent Massey in 1910.

'Froebel's belief in the divinity of the child – whatever that means – results in child worship. This, in turn, often gives rise to adolescent impudence, which is anything but divine.'[89] A Galt principal saw the new subjects as 'interfering with the teaching of the branches essential to the foundation of an English education' and thus 'detrimental to our highest educational interests.' Therefore, urged William Linton, 'feathers, frills and fads should find no place in our system.'[90] Frills were bad enough; worse still they were 'Yankee frills' promoted by Hughes and his high-powered American friends. And American ideas were highly suspect during the decade of the Alaska boundary dispute and Ontario's decisive rejection of the proposed Canadian-American reciprocity agreement. Principal John Henderson of St Catharines Collegiate received nods of approval when he charged at the 1911 OEA meeting that most of the fads in Ontario education could be traced to American sources. His comment that 'what may be good for the United States may be very bad for Ontario' needed no further elucidation.[91]

Kindergarten developments are representative of the slowdown in reform in the years prior to the First World War. Statistics for 1911 were superficially impressive – close to 200 kindergarten classes, with over 350 teachers and some 20,000 youngsters. Yet nearly half of these classes were in Hughes's own Toronto system. Throughout the province the movement had faltered since the early enthusiasm of the 1880s. 'At first there was quite a rush of the infantile community to the classes,' wrote Brantford's inspector as early as 1889, 'but the novelty seems to have passed, and there is less enthusiasm manifested now.'[92] Poor management and poor public relations left the province's teachers and the general public unconvinced of the value of kindergartens. One kindergartner placed the blame on the failure of the department to appoint a provincial inspector; this left supervision to principals and trustees 'not understanding the work.'[93] A professor charged that the poorly-run kindergarten subverted the true aim of education. 'It does not inculcate punctuality; it permits the little ones to come and go as they please,' said E.U. Birchard. 'It does not teach obedience to authority, but permits them to follow the inclination of their own wills.'[94] One Toronto inspector questioned if even the best run kindergarten was 'living up to its promises of years ago' since so many youngsters still remained too long in the First Book classes.[95]

Similar problems befell the manual training movement. By 1911 the subject had been introduced in just 26 of 279 urban municipalities and in only one rural school district. 'Even in those places where the subject has been introduced, it is a difficult matter to bring it to a point where it is looked upon as an integral part of the course of study,' complained provincial supervisor Albert Leake. 'The grade teacher has held aloof and the manual training teacher has refused to have any connection with other school subjects.'[96] Hughes and other advocates were criticized for 'attempting to make intellectual studies or some wonderful science out of what is valuable only as it is made practical.'[97] But was it even practical?

Vincent Massey believed it 'doubtful if the manufacture of hat-racks and towel-rollers has much more bearing on the average man's life than a course in history.'[98] The solution seemed to be to stress the industrial and vocational purposes of manual training, rather than the cultural. Led by Albert Leake, this trend was evident even before Hughes's retirement. 'The foundation of all technical education is the Manual Training course of the elementary school,' wrote Leake in 1903.[99] At first manual training, like the kindergarten, was aimed at the inculcation of community values, not the occupational preparation of the child. But by the time of the First World War manual training had shifted from the principles of work to the introductory teaching of trades.

On all sides the curricular and administrative reforms of the New Education were at a standstill or in hasty retreat. Domestic science was opposed in rural areas because it seemed to threaten rather than bolster the home. 'Let them take up the work of the home there,' wrote one village trustee. 'It will help make the home what it should be – the best place on earth.'[100] A teacher dismissed domestic science as 'too much fuss and feathers.' It was 'too great an attempt to exalt into some wonderful science what needs mostly practical experience, coupled with common sense.' The girls should be put to work at home, and judged by practical results. Even nature study in rural schools 'seems to have bidden us a sad farewell' becuase 'no one seems to have known exactly what she was.'[101] The consolidated school movement had also faltered. Three of the five rural sections withdrew from the Guelph consolidation when Macdonald money expired in 1910. By that date only one other consolidation had been formed in the province – in Hudson Township near New Liskeard. Although consolidation was judged a pedagogical success, increased transportation, salary, and maintenance costs drew local opposition. 'If we could *guarantee* no increase in taxation, we *might* carry each section,' wrote one inspector, 'but even then we should have a stubborn fight.'[102] Most important for the failure of consolidated schools was the lack of any perceived need for school reform in the countryside. The one-teacher, ungraded rural school was still giving a satisfactory account of itself.

What, then, was the significance of the New Education movement that ruffled the water of Ontario schools in the twenty years preceding the First World War? Certainly the New Education and the larger child-saving crusades were permeated by a high degree of compassion for the child. The reformers suffered for the child labourer, for the mentally and physically disabled child, the undernourished and underprivileged child, the unhappy and the unadjusted child. They turned to the schools as strategic centres for humanitarian reform. Here they made the first great strides since the mid-nineteenth-century common-school movement in reforming pedagogical practice. They urged greater understanding of the nature of the child, attempted to take into account each child's personality and background, and encouraged natural growth geared to the child's experience. Of course these pedagogical changes were often geared to conservative purposes, as the reformers grappled with the question of what forms of instruction would be most conducive to desired social ends. It has been argued persuasively that much of the motivation for reform grew from 'a desire to order, contain, and mitigate the destructive aspects of urban-industrial growth.' Reformers regarded the school as the best instrument for the preservation of social order and traditional moral values.[103] Through subjects like manual training and domestic science, through carefully regulated playgrounds and forest schools, it was hoped to produce in children a character suited to the needs of the times: industrious, clean, thrifty, law-abiding, God-fearing, sound in body and pure in mind. Whitney's provincial secretary, W.J. Hanna, after reciting the specific advantages to the boy of the various aspects of the New Education, perhaps best summed up the hope of the school reformers. 'If you launch him with this equipment, he is not likely to prove a serious civic problem,' he told the Civic Improvement League in 1916. 'Launch a generation of him and your civic problems are largely solved.'[104]

That social control and social improvement were central to department of education thinking is evident in a 1915 teachers' manual that was required reading for all normal-school students. In a key chapter entitled 'Education for Social Control,' the anonymous author catalogued the main purposes of education. First came the role of the school in teaching youngsters the means of individual 'social control.' Second, the school must disseminate knowledge, for upon knowledge depended 'intelligence, social progress and happiness.' Third, 'by free education for all in our public schools,' society met the demand for social improvement. Taxpayers cared 'little for the advantage of individual pupils'; they were preoccupied mainly with the welfare of society. Finally, through practical subjects, the school met the demand for 'industrial efficiency' and thereby responded to the need 'to make each individual a productive social unit.'[105] If the realities of both school and the larger society had forced the reformers to scale down their hopes of improving society through the school, those same realities continued to support the goal of fitting the schoolchild for his place in that society. In many ways, the difference between the 'old' and the 'new' education was a difference in means, not in ends.

4 Industry, Efficiency, and Imperialism

I

Taking office in February 1905, at the mid-point of a decade of agricultural and industrial prosperity, the Conservative government of James Whitney faced a new set of educational concerns. Although the problems of urbanization, first identified and debated in the 1880s and 1890s, were far from solved, politicians and social critics in the new century began to focus their attention on the related phenomenon of industrialization. If urbanization had called into question the social role of the elementary schools, then industrialization forecast new vocational roles for high schools. Out of urbanization had come the New Education movement, a loose coalition of social and humanitarian reformers; by 1904 their reform thrust had reached a plateau, at least in the area of curriculum reform. Many of these New Education leaders were already making the transition to the Industrial Education movement, a more powerful and better organized pressure group that lobbied for agricultural, commercial, and technical training in the high school, not for esoteric moral or cultural ends, but for the specific purpose of assisting Canada's economic growth.

Whitney developed his party's educational policies during the nine years prior to 1905 when he served as leader of the opposition. His insistence that more attention must be paid to the '95 per cent of our children who cannot go further than the public school' implied that the schools must do more to train future workers for agriculture, industry, and commerce. Such practical training would be beneficial both to the child and to the state. It would 'fit them for their future lot in life' and 'make them more useful to the agricultural and industrial community.'[1] Whitney claimed that industrial training 'is the most striking single fact in present industrial progress' and that 'the most noteworthy improvement in educational work in the near future is likely to be based on this fact.'[2] By 1905 he believed that discontent with the schools had become general. Too many parents and professional educators had come to believe that 'a kind of lethargy had crept over the whole system' and that 'the schools were not giving the kind of instruction best designed to fit the child for later life.'[3] Whitney made much of this charge during the 1905 election campaign. 'I told the people upwards of two hundred times on the platform,' he later wrote, 'that the reform and improvement of the educational system would be the first question to which we would turn our attention.'[4]

The new premier could count on support from a number of new faces in the higher echelons of the provincial education department. The new minister was Robert Pyne, a doctor who had sat on both the Toronto public and high school boards, and whose close personal friendship with the premier guaranteed cabinet solidarity in educational matters. A.H.U. Colquhoun, another close friend of Whitney's, came in as deputy minister after John Millar's sudden death in 1905. Colquhoun was to handle administrative matters; policy formation and development were vested in the re-created position of superintendent of education. That post was filled by John Seath, a veteran high school inspector who served as the chief architect for Whitney's educational reforms. 'Viewed in large, the history of education in Ontario from 1906 until a few months ago is the history of Dr. Seath,' declared the OEA's obituary tribute in 1919.[5] His domineering and authoritarian personality won both respect and hatred from teachers and principals; 'Olympian Zeus' and 'the autocrat of the education department' were two nicknames he acquired. 'There is a feeling growing that the Minister of Education is too much under the influence of the Superintendent,' grumbled one Conservative supporter in 1906. 'He might be under a worse influence,' replied Whitney.[6]

Whitney later admitted that an initial inquiry into rural schools in 1905 revealed conditions 'more serious than had been anticipated.' Because of insufficient financial support, the displacement of population, poorly paid and minimally qualified teachers, 'heroic measures were needed to improve matters.'[7] The government placed its major hope for strengthening rural education in improving the calibre of the teaching force. 'There is a much more pressing question than that of consolidation,' education minister R.A. Pyne told the 1906 OEA meeting. 'If we are going to have better schools we must have better teachers.'[8] Good teachers were not likely to be attracted by the salaries then offered by local boards. Even the city of Toronto could not offer beginning women teachers more than an annual salary of $324; this compared with $321 paid to charwomen at the post office, $421 for street sweepers, $528 for city-hall stenographers, and $546 for stockyard labourers.[9] Salaries were even lower in rural areas. 'Today we must pay the man who splits our wood at least $1.50 a day,' Pyne observed. 'We can get a teacher – a poor one, indeed – at less than a dollar a day.'[10] Low salaries and poor working conditions caused both a steady stream of better teachers to the higher-paying western provinces and their replacement by poorer, minimally qualified young recruits, fresh from the model schools. Many of these newcomers retained the peripatetic tendencies of their earlier colleagues, staying only a short time in the rural schools before they too moved on to city schools, to marriage, or to other careers. The fifteen one-room schools in Oro Township of Simcoe County were typical of rural Ontario; they averaged ten teachers each in the 1900-14 period.[11]

Legislative action was soon forthcoming as a new school act in 1906 put the main features of the Conservative rural education policy into practice. Provincial annual grants to local school-boards were more than tripled, from $120 to $380 million. These grants were no longer to be paid solely on the basis of average attendance, which was consistently lower in rural areas. Some were incentive grants, allocated in a manner designed to assist the purchase of more class-room equipment, provide better school accommodation, and encourage higher salaries for better qualified teachers. To underline this latter point, minimum salary scales of $300 to $500 were set for rural teachers, and special grants were made available so that even the poorest school sections in the province could afford such expense. These changes were part of a comprehensive attack on the rural school 'problem' which also included increased grants for Fifth Book classes and continuation schools. But there would be no special grants for consolidated schools; their unpopularity in rural areas persuaded Whitney to abandon this earlier dream for country school improvement so vigorously promoted by James Robertson and Richard Harcourt.

The incentive grants were frankly designed to help 'those that help themselves.'[12] Given the strong tradition of local school control, each inspector was cautioned to use his judgment in securing improvements in accommodation and equipment, 'having due regard to ... the capabilities of the present premises, and the financial competency of the boards.' The key to the situation, the department advised its inspectorial corps, is 'reasonable persistence.'[13] Inspector D.D. Moshier of Lambton West was prepared for especially strong rural opposition to minimum teacher salaries. The new scheme, he informed provincial secretary W.J. Hanna, 'provides a salary for individual teachers without regard to his or her worth – a labour union principle strongly opposed by people of the rural sections.' He feared the government had moved too quickly 'to awaken an educational Rip Van Winkle.' Yet by the fall of 1906, thanks to 'reasonable persistence,' Moshier was 'really surprised at the gains I am making,' reporting that '75 per cent of the men I reach in the school houses view the act favourably when they understand it.' As a result of his efforts, teachers' salaries in each of the five townships of his inspectorate exceeded provincial minima for 1907.[14]

Moshier had also stressed to Hanna a point that was not lost on the Whitney administration: higher minimum salaries implied a pool of more highly qualified teacher candidates. The key to this puzzle lay in finding a solution to the model school problem. For nearly thirty years these local training institutes had been over-supplying the province with third-class certificates, and deterring teachers from enrolling in the supposedly superior normal schools. Harcourt had sought unsuccessfully for some way of resolving the model school dilemma. 'I wish we had fewer of them,' he confided to a political supporter in 1901. 'There are too many weak schools ... It would help if the weaker ones were closed.'[15] But neither partial closure nor a lengthening of the term was acceptable to the Ross government as it scrambled to retain the rural vote. The new Whitney government, however, felt no emotional commitment to the model schools; both the premier and the minister of education were convinced they had to go. Pyne closed forty of them in 1906, permitting only those in remote areas of the province to continue. For the majority of prospective teachers, the normal school would now constitute the only path to certification. The move provoked surprisingly little opposition, as communities faced with the loss of a small model school became excited at the prospect of gaining a more prestigious normal school.

New normal schools were 'in active demand' throughout the winter and spring of 1906. Renfrew lauded its advanced kindergarten and manual-training facilities, while Paris boasted of its suitability for nature study because of the rich and varied flora along the 'rugged banks of the Grand and the Nith' rivers.[16] Under John Seath the department made a careful study of several locations, based on population densities, rail connections, vigour of local school systems, and proximity to existing normal schools in Toronto, Ottawa, and London. When the new locations were announced on July 13 – Peterborough, Hamilton, Stratford, and North Bay – the Toronto *Globe* commented dryly that all were in constituencies 'represented in the legislature by Conservative members.'[17] Stratford was a surprise choice over Berlin, but the latter 'has never been a good Model School centre for the Germans do not encourage their children to become teachers.'[18] A disappointed Liberal from Bruce County complained bitterly that Owen Sound had lost out to North Bay. 'Of all the God-forsaken places to put a normal school – at North Bay!'[19] But this was part of the Whitney government's active program to stimulate the social and economic development of northern Ontario. The six districts of 'New Ontario' more than doubled their population in the first decade of the new century, from 100,000 to 218,000. There was a fear, however, that 'existence in pioneer settlements easily tends to neglect of education.' Therefore, argued Pyne, 'it is of vital concern that the training of children in rough and sparsely settled districts should be carefully looked after.'[20] Thus the rationale for the North Bay Normal School which, with its low enrolment, remained an economic liability for many years.

With normal-school graduation now the accepted entry point into the teaching profession, each year showed more first- and second-class teachers in the province and fewer third-class and permit holders. Salaries inched upwards, reaching a record high in 1909, when they averaged $484 for rural males and $399 for rural females. Teacher affluence seemed to be reflected in the number who forsook summer jobs in favour of 'study at education centres in Canada or the United States' or 'vacation trips by land and sea.'[21] And with the co-operation of the Toronto newspapers, the OEA secured some success in its campaign to end teacher-wanted advertisements that forced underbidding through demands to 'state salary required.' Yet problems remained; teacher turn-over remained alarmingly high, and the percentage of male teachers continued to drop, falling to 14 per cent in 1915. Even the small gains recorded seemed to benefit urban schools more than their rural counterparts. In 1909, for example, while only one-quarter of all first-class teachers taught in rural areas, over 90 per cent of third-class and permit holders were found in the country schoolhouses.[22] And the normal schools, while increasing the professional component of training, may have been more remote from the rural scene than were the model schools. 'From a Normal School to one of the country schools is a precipitate tumble,' wrote one veteran teacher in 1914. 'It is like learning the rules for swimming from a guide-book and then being suddenly upset into deep water.' So the teacher 'experiences a rude awakening when she confronts the problems of the building, its discomfort and meagre equipment, the parents, the pupils, and herself.'[23]

Curriculum changes were also seen as urgently required to improve country schools, thereby strengthening country life. Despite the continued drift of farm youngsters towards the city, Pyne hoped that 'the great mass of the rural population' would remain 'associated with country life.'[24] In this latest attack on the rural school problem, agriculture was once again encouraged in the elementary schools. Its purpose was 'to interest boys and girls in country life and to impart a kind of instruction useful to them in the work of the farm.'[25] Its subject matter was drawn from nature study, with some emphasis on field husbandry, botany, and horticulture. In the class-room and outside in the school garden, the child's interest in his environment and future vocation were to be emphasized by learning through observation, activity, and experience. Improved textbooks, increased provincial grants, and summer courses for teachers at the Ontario Agricultural College did lead to an impressive rise in the number of elementary schools offering agriculture – from 6 in 1905 to 264 in 1914. Yet this latter figure still represented less than 5 per cent of all rural schools. As in the 1880s, there was little consumer demand for a subject that did not lead to high school entrance. Besides, charged one critic, 'it has simply been added to the general course of study,' and remained 'unco-ordinated with the situations in which it is supposed to function.' As a result, many teachers regarded agriculture as an extra burden, while many inspectors considered it unnecessary.[26]

In a 1914 report on rural schools commissioned by the department of education, Harold Foght of the United States Bureau of Education found much to admire in Ontario's country schools. He praised the provincial grant schedule, the professional nature of school inspection, improvements in teacher-training, well-constructed school buildings, and curricular developments in nature study, school gardens, and agriculture. 'Yet the fact remains,' lamented Foght, 'that the average rural school in the Province is unable to offer enough of what is vitally interesting to the larger boys and girls to keep them in school.' Its curriculum should be of as high a cultural level as that of the town school, but 'a culture intimately related to present and future problems instead of to traditional things ... rooted to the agricultural community.' But this could not be accomplished through the one-teacher school and the small rural administrative unit. 'The best the small schools can do is prepare the children for the lower grade of some town high school,' while the small administrative section frequently left the schools 'in the hands of honest, well-meaning men, but ignorant of school needs.' Only through school consolidation and township-sized boards, argued Foght, could the country school offer country youth a rural-oriented curriculum and solve 'the problems of country life.'[27] Everyone except rural trustees seemed to agree, but the Whitney government was not about to alienate that important segment of the voting population. Thus in 1914, as in 1885 or 1900, the rural school problem was 'the biggest school problem of Canada.'[28]

II

Pyne's plans for teacher improvement also included changes in the professional training of high school teachers. The Ontario Normal College in Hamilton, isolated from the academic mainstream and lacking in prestige, was abolished, replaced by faculties of education at Queen's and the University of Toronto. 'Thus at last teaching may become a real profession,' argued one university supporter. 'The aloofness of the university may disappear, something approaching to educational solidarity and brotherhood be established, and every schoolhouse even in the remotest settlements reap the advantage.'[29] Such hopes that upgraded training would entice significantly more arts and science graduates into high school teaching were not realized. In August 1909 Smiths Falls High School advertised for a specialist to teach classics and English. Between 7 and 21 August the promised initial salary rose from $1,200 to $1,250 to $1,300 as candidates failed to appear. Just twelve years previously a 'crowd of applicants' underbid one another for the same position in this school, with the successful appointee settling for $700. One teacher attributed the shortage to the 'exodus to the Northwest' and the 'gratification of larger ambitions' in the other professions and the business world.[30] To fill the ranks, local high school trustees followed the lead of their elementary counterparts and hired more women staff members. During that same ten-year period the proportion of female high school teachers rose from 25 to 45 per cent of the provincial total.[31]

The shortage of high school teachers was also due to the rapid expansion of secondary-school enrolments in the years preceding the First World War, as ever larger proportions of elementary school graduates continued their education.

Toronto, for example, saw a 79 per cent increase in population and a 165 per cent increase in high school students between 1900 and 1910, with a consequent increase in the number of collegiates from three to eight. Faced with such pupil growth, the chairman of the London Board of Education argued that while that city's collegiate 'will continue to prepare students for University or professional life, it will not subordinate to these the claims of those students who come demanding solely a good general education.'[32] Increasingly during the early years of the century, more schoolmen were beginning to define a 'good general education' not in terms of a limited curriculum of traditional academic subjects, but of a much broader curriculum with optional courses drawn from both the academic and practical sides. 'The day for arguing the relative importance of Mathematics, Classics, English, Moderns, and Science has long ago vanished,' principal John Henderson of St Catharines Collegiate told the 1901 OEA meeting. 'We are confronted with a number of new subjects knocking at the door.' Agricultural and commercial subjects and industrial training were 'seeking to be admitted to a full recognition as part of the course.'[33]

What came to be termed 'the high school debate' was formally launched in 1901 at a curriculum conference sponsored by Queen's University and the Kingston Board of Education. Queen's registrar John Watson argued against electives to the applause of most of his academic colleagues. The reformist position was taken by Kingston Collegiate principal W.S. Ellis, who called for the high schools to stand on their own, cease being feeders to the university, and offer a combination of core subjects plus freely chosen electives, including programs in vocational education.[34] Watson continued the debate in the columns of the *Queen's Quarterly*. Ellis's plan, he charged, would lead to an unfortunate division of students between 'those who are from the first intended to enter a profession, those who are to be engaged in industry and commerce, and those who are intended to be artisans.' Both the future scholar and the future tradesman stood to benefit from a common high school program.[35] But the problem with Watson's proposal, argued Dean N.F. Dupuis of the new faculty of applied science at Queen's, was that it emphasized the literary subjects at the expense of the scientific and technical. 'An educational scheme which makes no provision for science, or which places it upon a lower level, is covertly discouraging its pursuit.' Clearly, this would not suffice in the face of twentieth-century commercial and industrial development.[36]

Under Superintendent John Seath's direction, the department of education was now prepared to move away from the principle of high school uniformity. Revised regulations in 1904 recognized no less than seven different high school programs: general, commercial, manual training, household science, agriculture, university matriculation, and normal-school entrance. The greatest controversy arose over the separation of the university and normal-school routes, and the provision that Latin and a modern language would no longer be compulsory for the latter. Queen's professor James Cappon identified Seath as the major villain and charged him with leading 'a general movement against literary or humanistic education as a whole.'[37] Seath replied that the languages had no monopoly on education for cultural purposes and that the high schools must be freed from 'men whose interests are universitywards and whose greatest glory comes from the University success of these students.'[38] This so-called Latin debate of the early years of the century had considerable implications for subsequent high school development: the traditional literary subjects were clearly on the defensive; John Seath was emerging as the major champion of change within the department of education; and the new regulations forecast a multi-purpose role for the Ontario high school, a role that could include direct vocational training.

As part of its concerted effort to improve rural education, the Whitney government in 1907 launched two-year agricultural programs in six Ontario high schools – Essex, Lindsay, Perth, Morrisburg, Collingwood, and Galt. The objective was primarily vocational, that the rising generation 'might be trained for farm work.'[39] Eight years later, a national survey concluded that Ontario was the only province making 'any effort to offer in connection with the general provisions for secondary education, an organized course for those remaining in rural life.'[40] Yet progress was indeed disappointing; by 1918 only twenty-five secondary schools offered agriculture. And only four of those were continuation schools, the institution supposedly designed to offer courses rooted in the needs of rural life. Neither the agricultural courses nor the agricultural teachers (OAC graduates without formal teacher certification) were accepted as equal by academic staffs. Nor did the high school students themselves seem enamoured with the agricultural course. It began in the middle of September when most farmers' sons had plenty of harvest work to do; when they did attend school they sought release from farm work. Rural high schools continued to find the majority of their pupils preparing for university or normal-school entrance, and had difficulty finding enough students to justify the offering of agriculture. One student of agricultural education has maintained that 'it was not considered essential by the majority of the people.' It did not teach the three Rs, nor was it part of the educational ladder which led from the school to an urban profession or career, the inevitable destiny of many rural youth. Agricultural education failed because it conflicted with one of the school's most important functions, that of providing an avenue of socio-economic mobility for its pupils.[41]

While progress in agricultural education was disappointing, the early twentieth-century campaign for high school technical education was a resounding success. Local developments reflected the growing industrialization of Ontario's cities and larger towns. The Toronto Technical School flourished under the leadership of William Pakenham, appointed principal in 1902. The school and its 1,800 pupils moved into permanent quarters, came under the jurisdiction of the newly formed Toronto Board of Education, and edged closer to the educational mainstream by changing its name to the Toronto Technical High School.

Beginnings had been made in Kingston and Brantford, where collegiate principals like W.S. Ellis and A.W. Burt added small technical departments to otherwise academic schools. Sault Ste Marie wanted to begin, because 'the failure of the boys of the Town and District to get the necessary training along technical lines' meant that 'all positions of importance ... are filled by Americans, many of whom have no interest in or desire to build up the country.'[42] Hamilton was ready with architect's plans for Ontario's first specially designed vocational high school. What deterred these centres was the government's failure to devise a provincial policy and grant system.

But the Whitney government could not ignore growing public demand for a comprehensive provincial policy in technical education. Educators and manufacturers were well aware of Germany's highly developed system of technical high schools whose graduates were contributing to the development of German technology. In Ontario the campaign was led by the Canadian Manufacturers' Association, which used its annual meetings and its monthly journal, *Industrial Canada*, to promote the importance of technical education in economic development. 'If our manufacturers had in their factories a class of labour more intelligent and skilled than can be procured in other industrial centres of the world,' declared the CMA, 'the manufacturing establishments in Canada will be able to more than hold their own in the race for commercial supremacy.'[43] The CMA campaign was soon joined by the Trades and Labour Congress of Canada. Labour spokesmen could support any move that 'opens to the mechanic an opportunity to rise above the routine of ordinary drudgery, instructs him in conception and technique, and remedies deficiencies caused by his daily environment.'[44] Soon the TLC and the CMA were co-operating in briefs and deputations calling for provincial action.

The Ontario legislature finally passed the Industrial Education Act in 1911. For the potential early school leaver, provision was made for two-year general industrial schools, follwed by special industrial schools with more theoretical instruction. For the elementary school graduate aiming for 'minor directive positions in industrial establishments,' boards could establish technical high schools or technical departments within existing secondary schools. Most important, there would now be generous provincial grants for all forms of vocational education – whether technical, commercial, or agricultural. The significance of the act was not lost on its principal advocates. *Industrial Canada* believed that Canadian manufacturers and 'practically all mechanics' would benefit. The Toronto *Mail and Empire* saw the act as representative of Whitney's attempts to come to grips with industrial and urban development. It would 'complete the solution of the main problem of education, namely, to bring the school instruction into correspondence with the affairs of life.'[45] With minor changes over the years, the Industrial Education Act of 1911 provided the basis for a provincial policy on vocational education until superseded by the federal-provincial arrangements of the Technical and Vocational Training Assistance Act of 1960.

The 1911 act provided the stimulus for an immediate expansion of vocational education facilities in the large and medium-size cities of the province. By 1914 general industrial schools were established in Brantford, Hamilton, London, and Toronto, special industrial schools in Haileybury, Sudbury, and Toronto, technical high schools or departments in seven centres, and evening industrial schools in no fewer than twenty-seven. Toronto had been somewhat upstaged by Hamilton in 1909 when the latter city opened the first building specially designed as a technical school. But 'with all due respect to Hamilton,' stated the chairman of Toronto's industrial advisory committee, 'we want to make this the centre for Technical Education in Ontario.'[46] The resulting Central Technical School opened in 1915; at a cost of $2,000,000 it was the most expensive high school built in the province to that time. The following year the Toronto board moved its commercial classes out of rented quarters into the all-new Central High School of Commerce. By 1919 there were sixteen technical and commercial high schools in the province with a full-time enrolment of nearly 7,000 students. Though the Ontario high school would still be criticized for its bookish atmosphere, its rigidity, and its university and teacher-training orientations, even its severest critics saw the introduction of vocational education as a hopeful sign for the future.[47]

The greater success of technical education compared with agricultural education can be explained both by the increasingly industrial orientation of the province and by the declared priorities of the Whitney government. The question of agricultural or industrial education was part of a larger debate over what kind of social ethos and economic future should prevail for the province and the nation. Would the future be based on land, agrarianism, rural values, and the independent farmer and craftsman, or would it be based on factory production, urban values, the industrial capitalist, and the hourly-paid worker? Both rural populists and urban progressives hoped to use the school to shape the future. The agrarian movement, however, was primarily a rural and small-town phenomenon, antagonistic to the new urbanism, and striving to preserve the old order. The progressives, on the other hand, with their sights set firmly on future commercial and industrial prosperity, were prepared to accept the new urban life as an inescapable reality. Whitney was conscious of the tension between these conflicting futures, and sought to bolster both through reforms in rural as well as technical education. In the end, however, the government put its weight behind an educational future more closely related to industrial than agricultural growth. Whitney clearly recognized that Ontario was passing through a transitional phase in its economic history in the early 1900s. As his biographer aptly concluded, 'the Conservatives observed the change and acted.'[48]

The differentiated high school programs that accompanied agricultural, commercial, and technical education meant a redefinition of the concept of equality of educational opportunity. Under George Ross in the 1880s and 1890s, the school system had functioned as a unifying force, providing similar learning experiences for all children. But in 1913 James Robertson asserted that 'equality of opportunity to enter a school designed to prepare leaders, is not what is needed.' Instead, 'equality of opportunity, to mean anything real, must have regard to the varying needs, tastes, abilities and after lives of the pupils.' Schools must now 'serve them all alike in preparing them for occupations they are to follow.'[49] Now the school was to function less as the great equalizer and more as the great selector, selecting the most talented for the higher level jobs, and selecting from the rest those destined for office and factory employment. In the past, much of this sorting process had taken place after young people left school; now the school would predetermine those choices. Albert Leake, former provincial director of technical education, wrote in 1913 of 'at least two castes' in the school population, 'those who are the elect and those who are not, i.e., those who can absorb the printed page and pass the prescribed examinations and those who for both mental and financial reasons are not able to do so.'[50] The academic high school would provide the captains and generals for twentieth-century society, while the vocational courses would prepare the infantry troops for the industrial army.

III

While the campaign for technical education and the Industrial Education Act had attracted the interest of the province's manufacturing and labour groups, the Ontario press through 1910 and early 1911 focused its attention on a more explosive educational issue – French-language schooling. In January 1910 the city of Ottawa was host to more than 1,000 delegates attending the Education Congress of French Canadians of Ontario, a meeting organized to discuss the interests of French-language bilingual schools. Premier Whitney declined an invitation to attend, and expressed his fears that the Franco-Ontarians 'propose to ask for changes in the law and practice for our educational system which cannot be considered for a moment.'[51] For years, Whitney had managed to keep both the separate school and the bilingual school questions out of provincial politics, in the belief that the policies of his predecessors in the 1880s and early 1890s had harmed the Conservative party. During his early years as premier, Whitney was moving towards a position of guaranteeing Catholic separate school-boards a more equitable share of local corporation and utility taxes. But in March 1910 he wrote that demands put forward by the French-Canadian Congress in Ottawa had so complicated matters that he found it 'quite out of the question to deal with the subject thoroughly during the stress of the session.'[52] And so the bilingual school issue, as it had done in the late 1880s, once again pushed aside the separate school question.

For three days in January, the Franco-Ontarians assembled in Ottawa debated their difficulties, their needs, their hopes; they heard reports from various investigative committees; they listened to speeches on social issues. But they did not stop with rhetoric. The congress proved more aggressive than any Franco-Ontarian gathering of the past as it sought to extend as well as defend the educational rights of the minority group. Resolutions were passed calling for French-language instruction in all schools where the majority of pupils spoke that tongue; for an authorized series of French readers and textbooks; for the study of French reading, spelling, grammar, composition, and literature in schools where 25 per cent of the pupils were French; for supervision of all such schools by bilingual inspectors; and for French subjects on the high school entrance examinations. The congress ended by giving birth to l'Association canadienne française d'éducation d'Ontario, under the presidency of Senator N.A. Belcourt, and vowed to carry the fight into the political arena.

To the Franco-Ontarian leaders, the grievances seemed genuine, the requests legitimate. But if the Ottawa congress inspired the cultural minority, it chilled the blood of many leaders of the province's Anglo-Saxon mainstream. It was bad enough, complained some, that the French-speaking minority was approaching 10 per cent of the provincial population; worse that it was behaving like an aggressive minority. Approval of these requests by the provincial government would place French on a virtually equal footing with English in the elementary schools, and fundamentally re-order the Anglo-Protestant tradition in Ontario education. As in the 1890s, the bedrock opposition of old Ontario loomed to confront the perceived threat posed by the francophone minority.

Like the campaign for technical education, the movement to strengthen (or curtail) French-language bilingual schools was set against a background of educational and technological change. The 'cult of efficiency' argument was making considerable inroads into American educational administration in the years preceding the First World War. This involved the application of the views of Frederick Taylor – an industrial theorist and efficiency expert – to public education systems in order to develop improved models of management and production. There was a growing concern with educational 'products' and 'results' that could be measured. Studies were made of the percentage of children of each age enrolled, the average length of time required for children to complete a definite unit of work, the percentage of children continuing into high school, and the 'quality' of education dispensed. 'Efficiency must be made the criterion of education, of educational systems, and of public aid dispensed,' thundered the Ottawa *Citizen* in attacking French-language schools.[53] That Ontario's bilingual schools were not measuring up to arbitrary standards of efficiency seemed confirmed by F.W. Merchant's confidential report to the government following his 1908 study of English-French schools in the Ottawa Valley. Pupils were leaving these schools proficient in neither language; too few were continuing on to high school. Merchant's major recommendation was to increase efficiency by improving teacher-training facilities.[54] The Franco-Ontarians, it was argued, must be brought within the rapidly changing mainstream of educational development.

Ottawa public school inspector J.H. Putman was one Ontario educator who viewed the bilingual school issue as essentially a problem in educational efficiency. He agreed with Merchant that poorly prepared teachers were at the root of the problem; but rather than adopt Merchant's idea of improved model-school training, Putman called for an expansion of French-language instruction at the high school level. In a series of newspaper articles in July 1907, Putman was highly critical of the lack of secondary school opportunities for French-language pupils, especially in a mixed-language city like Ottawa. 'No one can say that the French of our city do enjoy equal rights if they are taxed to support secondary schools, and yet denied one which they can use.' Build a French-language collegiate, he argued, and the problems of equality of opportunity for city young people and poorly prepared teachers for eastern Ontario bilingual schools would vanish. Indeed, such a step would lead to greater harmony among the country's two linguistic groups. High standards in the French-language collegiate would attract English pupils; in turn, many French-speaking students would ultimately transfer to English high schools to perfect their second language. By such a 'constant interchange of pupils,' French and English would 'come together without either sacrificing their self-respect.'[55]

If the efficiency argument had an appeal, particularly to bureaucrats and businessmen, it was the cultural rationale behind French-language schools that aroused the emotions of far more Anglo-Ontarians. They could agree with Putman that French and English should come together, but it was anglicization, not a mutual development of cultures, that was desired. Early in January the *Sentinel*, the official publication of the Orange Order in Ontario, charged that the 'avowed aim' of the Ottawa congress was 'the Gallicizing of the public and separate schools in Eastern Ontario,' and steadfastly opposed any moves to entrench French-language instruction. When the deliberations of the congress confirmed the *Sentinel*'s worst fears, the threat posed to the schools became a threat to the entire nation. 'It is part of the great ambition of the French that French be equal with English. All that would mean to the destiny of Canada cannot readily be imagined. It would almost inevitably mean French domination and papal supremacy.'[56] One Orangeman warned Whitney that any government move to legalize bilingual schools would be 'an un-British act, as well as an act of folly' and promised that 'future generations would anathematize the name of Whitney as the destroyer of the Public School system of Ontario.'[57] As the French fact was beginning to make itself evident in many segments of Ontario life, francophobes saw the schools as the first line of defence. 'We cannot force people to use English in their homes, or to read English books,' declared the Toronto *Star*. 'We can touch the question only through the schools, which are public institutions.'[58]

What pressed the Whitney government to act was not the expected opposition from the ultra-Protestant Orange Order, but rather the unanticipated reaction from Ontario's English-speaking Catholic bishops. Here the leader was Michael Francis Fallon, recently appointed Bishop of London, whose diocese included a number of bilingual schools in Essex and Kent counties. Fallon seemed to echo the concerns of the efficiency advocates as he viewed with alarm the poor calibre of instruction in these schools which, he charged, 'encourages incompetency, gives a prize to hypocrisy and breeds ignorance.'[59] Yet the type rather than the standard of education seemed to be his major concern; his solution was rigid control rather than any qualitative improvement. No friend to French-Catholic educational interests after his earlier, unhappy days at the University of Ottawa, Fallon was prepared to use the bilingual school issue to restore Irish supremacy among the Ontario hierarchy. He also saw potential gains for Catholic separate schools if those schools could be viewed as the equal of the public schools in promoting Anglo-imperial ideals. 'We are playing our part in the making of a great English-Canadian nation and so far as I am concerned I intend ... to take my side on the manifest destiny of Canada.'[60] One friend of the bishop later wrote that Fallon never accepted the 'lose your tongue, lose your faith' argument of French-speaking Catholics, and 'was of the firm opinion ... that the future welfare of Canada would be best served by the predomination of the English-speaking portion of the population.'[61]

Fallon made his views known to the government in a private meeting with provincial secretary W.J. Hanna in Sarnia in the spring of 1910. Bilingual teaching should be 'discouraged and prohibited,' he argued, because he was 'assured that in certain sections of the County of Essex there were children today going to the public school who could not speak English.' He asserted that 'we are in an English-speaking Province on an English-speaking continent where the boys and girls going out to fight the battle of life must be equipped, first with English.' Hanna was frankly afraid that voter support or opposition throughout the diocese would depend directly on the government's reaction.[62] Indeed, by August Fallon appeared to have the support of most of the province's English-speaking bishops, who declared that a bilingual school system would 'injuriously affect the education of our children' and 'give an inferiorly-educated body of Catholic citizens to the province and to the country.'[63] Not satisfied with the continuing silence of the Whitney government, Fallon made his views public in October. The bilingual school system, he charged, 'is absolutely futile as concerning the teaching of either English or French, and utterly hostile to the best interests of the children, both English and French.' The fault lay neither with the children nor the teachers. 'It is with the system, and it is against the system, and the threatened extension of it, that I protest.'[64] The Toronto *Star* described the bishop's charges as a 'scathing indictment of the Education Department' and forecast that 'his charges of inefficiency in bilingual schools are so serious that they cannot be ignored by the government.'[65]

Whitney's initial response to the demands of l'Association canadienne française d'éducation d'Ontario had been to maintain the status quo by refusing to allow 'the creation of a new, additional statutory class of schools organized upon a racial basis.'[66] Fully aware of the pedagogical deficiencies of the bilingual schools through Merchant's 1909 report and a subsequent review by John Seath in the spring of 1910, he had hoped to follow the course laid down by Ross and Mowat in the 1880s. This involved trusting to time, having faith in the French-speaking communities to observe the regulations, and providing additional teacher-training facilities. But the press campaign following Fallon's public statement showed no signs of abating. Soon there were rumblings of discontent within his own party. Early in 1911 backbencher G. Howard Ferguson, a future premier and education minister, introduced into the legislature a motion asserting that 'no language other than English should be used as a medium of instruction' in any Ontario school.[67] Although later modified by Ferguson, the intent of the original motion was crystal clear. For the rest of 1911 Ferguson continued his crusade; in the words of his biographer, 'he seemed imbued with the demands of a great mission.'[68] That mission was to use Ontario schools to promote Anglo-Saxon culture for the benefit of the entire nation. 'We want British traditions and British ideals to be instilled into the minds of the rising generation,' he thundered, 'so that as our young men and women seek new homes in the great western country and mingle with the foreigners there, the Ontario men and women will put the impress of their character and personality on the community in which they live.'[69]

In an attempt to gain time, Whitney in November 1910 had commissioned F.W. Merchant once again to conduct a thorough investigation of the province's English-French schools. In the course of the next fifteen months, Merchant personally visited 538 of the 642 teachers in schools where French was a teaching language. Presented in February 1912, Merchant's thorough and judicious report tended to confirm Fallon's pronouncements. His study showed that bilingual schools were indeed 'lacking in efficiency' and demonstrated that 'a large proportion of the children in the communities concerned leave school to meet the demands of life with an inadequate equipment in education.' He advised that French remain the language of instruction in the primary grades, and that English be introduced gradually so as to become the main teaching language by the third form, 'depending on the ability of the student and the language conditions of the locality in which the school is located.'[70] The system must be flexible, with inspectors possessing wide discretionary powers. Above all, as Merchant had indicated in his earlier reports, there must be improvements in the academic and pedagogical training of teachers for bilingual schools. The Merchant report was a sympathetic document, stressing improvement rather than restriction; it did not forecast the harsher measures which the Whitney government subsequently adopted.

IV

Whitney announced his new bilingual schools policy a short half-hour before the end of the spring session of the legislature in April 1912. 'Regulation 17,' as it became known, went far beyond Merchant's recommendations for the gradual replacement of French by English as the teaching language. The vital paragraph read: 'That instruction in English shall commence at once upon a child entering school, the use of French as the language of instruction and communication to vary according to local conditions upon the report of the supervising inspector, but in no case to continue beyond the end of the first form.' Government funds would be contingent on the employment of teachers able to instruct in English; only authorized textbooks could be used; and additional inspection of bilingual schools would ensure enforcement of the new regulations. Whitney justified this policy on two grounds: first, it was in the interest of the Franco-Ontarians themselves, who needed an adequate knowledge of English in order to thrive in Ontario; second, it was merely a formalization of existing practices first laid down by Mowat and Ross in 1890.

Department of education officials and the province's teachers played little role in determining the new policy. 'The opinion of the expert is quite overlooked,' complained *The School* magazine. Regulation 17 'overlooks the Merchant report, wrests the problem out of the domain of education, and seeks solutions in the opinions of every man but the schoolmaster.'[71] Merchant himself was out of the country at the time, visiting industrial schools in Europe and the United States, before taking up his new position as director of technical education. John Seath opposed the plan on grounds that it would 'prove injurious to the interests of pupils in many such schools,' in addition to being virtually unenforceable.[72] Rather than relying on his educational officials, Whitney was guided more by political and religious counsellors. Howard Ferguson seemed to have the premier's ear, and years later contended that 'I, personally, was largely responsible for the establishment of Regulation 17.'[73] Certainly Bishop Fallon's views were influential. In January 1912 Fallon had written education minister Robert Pyne spelling out the conditions he considered absolutely necessary for an efficient government policy. The parallels between this letter and Regulation 17 are extremely close.[74]

Resistance to Regulation 17 was most dramatic within the Ottawa Separate School Board, now controlled by a French-speaking majority. Under the leadership of trustee Sam Genest, the board in December 1912 voted to resist the government's policy, claiming that the aim of the regulation was Anglicization rather than education. Genest had declared that he 'would sooner see the separate schools go by the board than have the French language taken out.'[75] This led in turn to the government cutting off provincial grants, the board encouraging teacher and pupil walkouts, and finally in 1915 to the government placing the board under trusteeship. By early 1916 one Conservative supporter in Ottawa was warning Ferguson of 'a great national crisis undoubtedly developing here.' J.S. Crate's prophesies were indeed foreboding: 'The French will decide not to pay taxes and resist efforts at collection. As French children march the streets some parents talk of fighting and dying for their religion. They are becoming fanatical on this question and the situation is full of dangerous possibilities.'[76]

The situation was equally bleak throughout much of eastern and northern Ontario. Inspector W.J. Summerby reported during the fall of 1913 that Franco-Ontarian trustees refused to meet with him, teachers refused to answer his questions, pupils left their class-rooms as soon as he entered, and English-speaking Catholics were being coerced into submitting to unilingual French instruction. SS no. 2, Bonfield, 'want no Inspector if grants not paid. Will follow Priest.' Summerby was most discouraged. 'All my talk to these people seems to have little effect upon them,' he complained to his superior in Toronto. 'They have given their case into the hands of their leaders and they rest there. One cannot move them.'[77] While Summerby rode out the storm, his counterpart in Nipissing, Henri St Jacques, found the situation impossible. The ratepayers of Sturgeon Falls, he reported in September 1913, 'looked upon my inspection as useless and [will] disregard any recommendations from my part.' St Jacques, unwilling 'to simply draw my salary and reduce my work to that of a statistic collector,' submitted his resignation.[78]

While the years of the First World War intensified English-French animosity and saw the bilingual schools question spill over into federal politics, they also saw the beginning of a temporary resolution of the conflict. In September 1916, Pope Benedict XV addressed a letter to the Canadian hierarchy, counselling moderation. The Ontario bishops were themselves anxious to end the dispute because of the dangers it posed for all Catholic schools. 'If the Catholic Bishops of Ontario were to join in the agitation against Regulation XVII,' declared their memorandum, 'our whole Catholic school system would be abolished.'[79] Then in November the Judicial Committee of the Privy Council ruled that Regulation 17 was within the jurisdiction of the Ontario government, thus ending any formal legal basis of French opposition. When the same court ruled against the suspension of the Ottawa Separate School Board, Genest was sufficiently pacified to assert that 'it is not the intention ... to create any unnecessary trouble.'[80] But temporary resolution of the crisis was also due to a moderation in government policies, a move towards improving rather than curtailing the bilingual schools. As early as 1913, revised regulations had permitted French-language instruction beyond the first form 'in the case of pupils ... who are unable to speak and understand the English language.'[81] Three years later acting minister of education Howard Ferguson announced that the regulations would be enforced 'without injury to the feelings, prejudices, or preferences of any element within the Province.'[82]

Ferguson was now prepared to accept the advice of Seath, Merchant, and other senior officials within the department of education. 'The most serious need of the English-French schools,' declared a departmental memorandum in 1916, 'is a competent supply of teachers with a teaching knowledge of English.'[83] Emphasis must be on continuing to develop 'the efficiency of the Model Schools.' By September 1917 chief inspector John Waugh could report that among the province's bilingual schools, 'the present condition is greatly improved as compared with conditions of a year or two ago.' Although bilingual schools in eastern Ontario left much to be desired, schools in the North and in Essex and Kent counties were complying with the regulations. Most encouraging of all was that 'the inspectors have been admitted without question to all the schools.'[84] Eighteen months later Waugh reported that of 243 English-French schools in the province, 108 were 'fully complying' with departmental regulations, while another twenty-seven 'have agreed to comply.'[85] Although any ultimate resolution was still many years in the future, the bilingual schools issue was far less volatile by the end of the First World War than it had been during the 1910-12 period.

The more moderate policy towards French-language instruction during the later years of the First World War resulted in part from the fact that anglophone Ontario had identified a new villain – German-language instruction. German had become an increasingly popular subject of study at the high school level, not only among Waterloo County Germans, but also among Anglo-Saxon students preparing for university programs in modern languages. As late as 1915 one high school inspector noted that 'the bias that justly prevails against the German rulers and the German people does not appear at all in the attitude of the schools toward the German language.'[86] Yet soon the wartime hatred of things German was extended to the language. The result was that by 1918, enrolment in German classes had fallen from 15 to 5 per cent of the total high school registration. The decline continued steadily through the 1920s, as anti-German prejudice remained, and the department of education dropped German as a requirement for prospective modern-language specialist teachers.

More important in the easing of the French-language school problem was the government's gradual abandonment of coercion and its return to the policy of patience, encouragement, and assistance laid down by Mowat and Ross in the 1880s and 1890s. During the height of the Regulation 17 controversy, George Ross, then an aging member of the Senate, reminded his successors at Queen's Park that education 'should be adapted to the needs of the whole people.' Where two languages were of 'more than local utility,' Ross continued, 'every sound principle of pedagogy' confirmed bilingual schooling.[87] Howard Ferguson, the militant Anglophone backbencher of 1911, and at various times acting minister of education during the First World War, eventually realized the failure of coercion. He later wrote that the 'thou shalt not' wording of Regulation 17 was 'the kind of declaration [that] always breeds trouble.' If it had stressed only that 'English shall be taught for a certain length of time,' then Ferguson believed that there would never have been the resulting agitation.[88] By 1916 the Conservative government, now led by Premier William Hearst following Whitney's death two years earlier, had tentatively substituted the carrot for the stick. Eleven years later the premier of the day, Howard Ferguson, would confirm the legitimacy of the Mowat-Ross policy of accommodation towards French-language instruction.

V

The bilingual school controversy was set against a background of racial consciousness and imperialism that excited the minds and stirred the passions of English-speaking Ontarians in the first two decades of the century. In the years following the South African War and the introduction of Empire Day, Ontario school-books extolled the glories of the British Empire and Canada's place in that imperial sun. A 1904 history text, *The Story of the Canadian People*, contrasted 'French failure through the folly of absolutism, monopoly and feudalism' with 'British success through the wisdom of self-government, freedom and equality.' Second only to the expansion and consolidation of the dominion, the 'most important fact of recent Canadian history has been the strengthening of ties binding Canada to the British Empire.' Students were told of the Colonial Conferences, transoceanic cable lines, the Diamond Jubilee, Imperial penny post, the building of the CPR ('an event of great moment to the British Empire'), and the sending of Canadian troops to South Africa. There was seldom any hint that some Canadians might be less than enthusiastic about these developments, and no mention of French-Canadian opposition to participation in the Boer War.[89] Textbooks in English history expanded the benefits of imperial membership to lands and peoples beyond the seas. In 1906, emphasis was on 'the wonderful work being done in civilizing and *enlightening* the millions of subject people'; four years later, with a slight change in wording, another text underlined 'the wonderful work being done in *controlling* and civilizing the millions of subject people.'[90] [italics added]

What was implied in the history texts was made more explicit in the geography books. The *Ontario School Geography* of 1910 was probably the most racist textbook ever authorized for use in the province's schools. Pupils were told that the Caucasians were 'the most active, enterprising and intelligent race in the world.' In contrast, the Yellow race included 'some of the most backward tribes of the world'; the Red race were 'but little civilized,' and the Black race while 'somewhat indolent ... often impulsive in their actions,' were partially redeemed because they were 'faithful and affectionate to anyone for whom they care.' But not all Caucasians were equally progressive. France was characterized by urbanites who were 'fond of excitement' and backward rural dwellers. On the other hand, the 'people of the United Kingdom are noted for their energy, intelligence and high ideals,' unless, of course, they were Irish! The Scots were 'an intensely patriotic people, industrious, thrifty, and noted for their zeal in education and religion.' The English were 'noted for their respect for the law, their ability to adapt themselves to new conditions in new countries, and their enterprise in developing commerce and manufactures.' Here, history and geography marched together in the cause of imperial glory as pupils were again reminded that the British 'have won where others failed.'[91]

A 1910 edition of the *Ontario Fourth Reader* surpassed all others in its imperial message. This was the reader for children in the two senior elementary years, the last contact with formal schooling for many youngsters. As a parting message in the years before the First World War, the reader served well the interests of the British Empire. The first picture in the volume was a portrait of the late King Edward VII; he looked out approvingly on 400 pages of words to which he could not possibly have taken exception. On the flyleaf, beneath a beautifully coloured Union Jack, appeared the motto, 'One Flag/One Fleet/One Throne.' The first page was Kipling: 'Oh Motherland, we pledge to thee / Head, heart and hand through years to be.' There were verses from Henley: 'Mother of Ships whose might / England, my England.' There was a hymn of empire by Scott: 'Strong are we? Make us stronger yet; / Great? Make us greater far.' There was Thomson's 'Rule Britannia,' Campbell's 'Ye Mariners of England,' Macaulay's 'The Armada,' Byron's 'The Eve of Waterloo,' and Tennyson's 'Funeral of Wellington.' The praise of militarism and imperialism was not limited to poetry. There were short prose essays by Russell on Balaclava, Southey on the death of Nelson, and Goldwin Smith on the glories of London. Five full pages were devoted to an unsigned article from the *Atlantic Monthly* stating that, thanks to her colonial and naval power, Britain could win any conceivable war against any conceivable enemy, including the United States.

Older boys in the senior elementary and high school grades were also subjected to the cadet movement. As early as the 1890s, the military-imperial lobby had championed cadet training, rifle drill, and physical exercise as panaceas for a host of problems: to counteract the prevailing 'soft' influence of female teachers; to check the debilitating influence of urban slum living; to teach the virtues of obedience, punctuality, and precision; and, above all, to provide military training for defence of country and empire. Provincial legislation in 1896 permitted any high school board to establish classes in military instruction, and offered encouragement through a fifty-dollar annual grant. By 1900 there were cadet corps in thirty-three Ontario schools. Rapid expansion came after 1909 when Lord Strathcona established a half-million-dollar trust fund to provide Canadian schools with $20,000 a year for physical and military training. Strathcona's objectives seem to have been all-inclusive. While desiring 'to bring up the boys to patriotism and to a realization that the first duty of a free citizen is to be prepared to defend his country,' he also hoped the program would be 'of the highest value in developing the moral, physical and intellectual qualities of the children.'[92] But control of the Strathcona Trust by the federal militia department meant that the military and patriotic emphases took precedence over physical culture. What the minister of militia wanted in 1909 'was not only the bodily development of children of all classes and both sexes,' but also that all boys acquire an elementary knowledge of military drill and rifle practice so that they could if necessary 'take part in the defence of their homes and country.'[93]

The military orientation of the cadet movement intensified after the 1911 appointment of Sam Hughes, James Hughes's younger brother, as minister of militia in the federal cabinet. A lifelong supporter of school drill, the younger Hughes had entered a plea for an 'Empire Militia' six years earlier, stating that if he were in control, he would divide the Empire according to school divisions, beginning with boys at the age of twelve, and when the boys were older 'I would have them drafted into regiments and brigades.'[94] In 1911 Sam Hughes went before the OEA and left no doubt as to where he thought teachers should stand. Dismissing criticism as 'maudlin, sloppy sentimentality,' he lauded the cadet movement as a necessary first step in Canada's being 'ever ready at a moment's notice to repel any invasion upon her shores.' If only every school in the country had a cadet corps, 'the guarantee of perpetual peace would surely result.'[95] He promptly announced that 40,000 boys would go into training that summer. 'In five years from now,' he asserted in 1912, 'I want to have some hundreds and thousands of our youth trained to shoot and march.'[96]

The fusion of the cadet movement with Empire Day observances underlined the military-imperial atmosphere of early twentieth-century Ontario. Responding to the Boer War in the spring of 1900, the Toronto Board of Education built its Empire Day celebration around a cadet parade from the University Avenue Armouries north to the parliament buildings in Queen's Park. One thousand schoolboy cadets took part, Governor-General Lord Minto took the salute, and the streets were lined with admiring citizens. As the cadet movement grew, so did the annual parade. Soon the boys were joined by their white-bloused sisters, carrying baskets of freshly-cut flowers to decorate the monuments in Queen's park. And each year the youthful marchers heard inspirational messages from prominent citizens, quite frequently from the Governor-General himself. In 1909, for example, Earl Grey implored the Toronto school cadets 'to remember what Empire Day means.' For Grey it was 'the festival on which every British subject should reverently remember that the British Empire stands out before the whole world as the fearless champion of freedom, fair play and equal rights; that its watchwords are responsibility, duty, sympathy and self-sacrifice.' Grey concluded by laying on Toronto's young manhood 'a special responsibility ... to be true to the traditions and to the mission of your race.'[97] Thus Empire Day came to evoke more than past glories; it was meant to help build an even greater imperial future.

Empire Day celebrations were also used to indoctrinate central and eastern European immigrant children in appropriate national and imperial outlooks. The 'Canadianization' of the foreign-born child was becoming a concern in urban areas and in northern Ontario schools in the early years of the century.

Fort William trustee J.R. Lumby viewed the school as 'the only agency that can be called upon in the whole machinery of civilization to perform the duty of moulding the second generation of foreign-born into Canadian citizens.' The process began in the kindergarten where, through games and exercises and 'without consciously learning,' the little child 'absorbs the rudiments of English.' It continued through the primary and upper grades, through the *Ontario Readers* and the history and geography courses. Finally, there was the annual Empire Day pageant. Every year in Fort William, 'the entire school population, over two thousand strong, musters and marches through the streets of the city.' The parades brought together 'children of twenty-seven races, uniting to carry Canadian flags and sing Canadian songs and to hear addresses from prominent men on patriotic subjects.'[98]

Having consciously promoted nationalism and imperialism for more than two decades, it was not difficult for the provincial department of education to increase the propaganda campaign with the outbreak of the First World War in August 1914. That fall, all elementary and secondary schools were directed to add to their history courses units on 'the war, its causes, and the interests at stake.' This was not to be an objective, dispassionate study, but one designed to stir emotions and show that Canada 'owes loyalty and filial service to the Mother of Nations.' The study was buttressed by a series of pamphlets entitled 'The Children's Story of the War,' by questions relating to the war on departmental examinations, and by appeals to 'generously disposed citizens' to offer prizes for student essays on 'one or more of the phases of the present struggle.'[99] Boys in the high school graduating class were granted diplomas without having to write departmental examinations if they enlisted for overseas service or volunteered for farm work. Children in all grades were involved in a steady round of raising funds, collecting scrap metal, knitting socks, and sending letters to the boys at the front. Male teachers were encouraged to enlist through guarantees that their positions would be held open for them after the end of hostilities. Those who did not enlist were often placed under suspicion by the local community. The Hamilton Board of Education, for example, required every teacher to declare that 'he or she is pro-British in his or her sympathies, and a Loyal British Subject, or else face dismissal.'[100]

After cautioning its readers to 'keep their heads' about the war, the leading teachers' magazine, *The School*, devoted three issues in the spring of 1915 to a very British version of the war's causes, and made suggestions for incorporating the events of the war into history lessons. Always there were patriotic watchdogs to monitor the actions of the educators. When the Toronto Board of Education, for example, proposed as an economy measure to stop flying the Union Jack over its schools, the IODE expressed outrage. 'If there was no British flag, and no sentiment connected with it,' declared the provincial executive, 'there would be no general enlistment, nor would the millions of soldiers of Great

Britain be available.'[101] The patriotic response of the province's pupils, teachers, and schools was a product of the national-imperial orientation that had permeated Ontario society and education for two decades. After describing this 'schooling in imperialism' at the turn of the century, Arther Lower concluded that it was 'not surprising that fourteen years later, those boys rushed off across the seas to fight for a country they had never seen – to fight as perhaps men had never fought before.'[102]

5 Post-war Change and the Education of the Adolescent

I

'Everyone is hoping that the end of the war marks the opening of a new age,' reflected the editor of *The School* magazine in January 1919, 'an age in which the ideals of all the people of the world will be raised to higher and nobler levels; and education will be called upon to do great service in bringing this about.' Such statements were common in the months following the end of the First World War, as public spokesmen forecast a crucial role for the school in moulding the post-war generation. Most began by re-affirming their faith in the past greatness of the province's school system. 'That Canada was able in the recent war to make an important contribution to the defence of herself and the Empire is perhaps the most striking proof of the efficiency of public education in Ontario,' declared the Toronto *Mail and Empire*, adding that education 'will play the greatest part in the rebirth of the world.'[1] Principal W.L. Grant of Upper Canada College employed much more flowery language to make the same point. 'Spread over the welter of incoherent ideas the broad sunlight of education,' declared Grant, 'and the miasmas will disappear.'[2] Realizing the challenge before provincial educational authorities, the Ontario minister of education conceded in 1919 that 'the world today looks to the schools more than any other agency to heal and guard the past and to direct and stabilize progress in the future.'[3]

Society's leaders generally agreed on those aspects of the past which the schools should guard and how they might 'direct and stabilize progress' in the years ahead. Judge J.H. Scott of Perth saw the schools 'as an agency for the development and propagation of some of the lessons in which we were drilled during the war and which should not be allowed to be forgotten.' To Scott, these lessons included the veneration of the British Empire and monarchy, the importance of history and the flag, love of country, and 'the habit of saving and the practice of thrift.'[4] President Robert Falconer of the University of Toronto offered an even deeper anchor in the sea of post-war uncertainty. 'Definite ideals have to be taught to the children in the schools,' wrote Falconer. These included 'the ascertained body of moral truth and the spiritual traditions of our people.'[5] Canadian industrialists added economic imperatives to this list of education's goals. The managing director of the Mond Nickel Company called on the schools to develop in their students a 'knowledge and breadth of mind in economic matters,' and a 'saneness of view regarding industrial and all other social relationships.' In short, education must train each youth 'to understand his economic and social place and responsibilities in our present, highly organized, industrial society.' This must happen 'if industry is not to drift more and more towards deadlock, the signpost that marks the down-hill slope to revolution.'[6]

There was nothing new in this view of the relationship between schooling and society. Since its origins in the middle decades of the nineteenth century, public education had been expected to buttress the accepted political, religious, and economic norms. What gave these directives a greater sense of urgency in the immediate post-war years was the uneasy feeling that many traditional social norms were threatened. Instead of swinging back to normal in 1919, Canadian life swung sharply away from the past, away from the ordered society of the Victorian and Edwardian eras. As the last year of war drifted untidily into the first year of peace, unrest was growing across the country. Industrial tensions led to greater union militancy and a rash of strikes, culminating in the Winnipeg General Strike of 1919. Equally disturbing to traditionalists were outbreaks of agrarian discontent, which shook governments across Canada and spawned reformist political parties at both the provincial and national levels. But the revolution in attitudes and moral values posed an even greater challenge to the defenders of the pre-war social ethic. This revolution expressed itself through new dress styles and new codes of social behaviour, the flouting of prohibition and the decline in church attendance, and in a general questioning of established authority. In response, a number of citizens' groups appeared on the Ontario educational scene, ready to save the pupils – and, by implication, the entire society – from the social and moral dangers of the post-war era.

The Ontario Federation of Home and School Associations was the largest of the post-war citizens' movements in education. Its guiding spirit was Alice Courtice, former proprietress of a private girls' school and a member of the Toronto Board of Education. In 1916 Courtice had founded the Toronto Home and School Council with representatives from nine city schools; three years later the provincial federation was organized. By 1920 the movement received official recognition, with a $2,000 grant from the provincial department of education and status as a section within the Ontario Educational Association. That year the annual convention heard reports from fifty-three local associations. There had been new victrolas purchased for Kingston schools, a supervised playground financed in Welland, first-aid equipment for Peterborough schools, efforts to censor vaudeville shows in London, and the 'encouragement of bird clubs' in New Toronto.[7] The movement grew quickly over the next two decades, claiming more than 400 local associations with a total provincial membership of 25,000 by 1941. The pattern was similar across the country; by mid-century the Home and School had become Canada's largest voluntary association.

Yet despite its size, the Home and School was never an effective force for radical change. True, it helped bridge the gap between parents and teachers as schools took on responsibilities once considered the prerogative of the home. And it lobbied continuously for improvements in school medical services and the health curriculum, better school libraries and student counselling, and the extension of manual training and domestic science. But these efforts coincided with education department priorities, and in no sense re-oriented the schools towards different social purposes; in a way the Home and Schoolers were co-opted by the educational bureaucracy to serve the latter's own ends. The movement's major weakness was its inability to translate its concern for the vanishing social and moral norms of the pre-war world into a positive program for the new era. Members could talk nobly about the 'social uplift' received through attendance at Home and School meetings, and hope that 'this social uplift will ... give the community a broader outlook.'[8] But such talk had little impact on the Ontario class-room of the 1920s.

The Junior Red Cross movement shared many of the idealistic goals of the Home and School, but it had the advantage of reaching directly into the elementary school class-room. By 1925 the Junior Red Cross had organized 921 class-room clubs involving over 30,000 Ontario pupils. For the pupils themselves, weekly Junior Red Cross meetings – often held after recess on a Friday afternoon – provided a change of pace from regular school routines. But the movement's organizers viewed it as more than a pleasant diversion. Junior Red Cross leaders promoted habits of cleanliness, proper diet and regular exercise, care of teeth, deep breathing and 'sleeping with open window.' In the area of citizenship, they encouraged the development of restraint and self-control, the inculcation of accepted manners and moral standards, and better behaviour in the schoolyard and on the streets, all under the guise of 'character building.' The Junior Red Cross put its emphasis on the development of desirable habits and attitudes, rather than on textbook mastery and success on examinations. 'It brings the school into a wholesome and practical relationship with society and the affairs of life,' declared provincial president S.B. McCready in 1923. 'It is a socializing agency and it fits young citizens in our classrooms for their maturer citizenship in the school of life.'[9]

The thrift campaign in the schools was another attempt to promote character education through self-directed practice. It began in 1906 when the Dominion Penny Bank Act provided for the incorporation of school banks. Participating class-rooms devoted a portion of every Monday morning to receiving deposits, counting cash, and tabulating balance sheets. Its success in Hamilton was typical; by 1914 some 6,152 Hamilton pupils had over $28,000 on deposit. For the next four years the campaign was integrated into the war effort, as children across the country were encouraged to purchase war savings stamps. The return of peace in 1919 saw the goal of peacetime 'thrift' substituted for that of wartime victory. When Toronto trustees considered excluding the Penny Bank in 1923 – on grounds that it interfered with regular class-room work – they were successfully opposed by the city's businessmen and industrialists. Bank inspector J.R. Littleproud saw the chief value as 'the development of thrift habits among girls and boys.' But thrift was not an end in itself, merely a vehicle for character building. 'In sacrifice and self-denial, in resisting the allurements of unnecessary pleasures, in saving rather than spending, comes the true development of character – the stalwart, rugged, honest character which overcomes all obstacles.'[10] Thrift and frugality, then, would produce a generation of industrious young people.

The National Council of Education was the most ambitious private attempt to channel schooling along conservative pathways in these volatile years. The original impetus for the NCE came from the Canadian Industrial Reconstruction Association, a group of Ontario manufacturers formed during the latter years of the war. Its immediate aim was to 'maintain industrial stability and to secure wise consideration and prudent treatment of problems of reconstruction.'[11] Concern over the leftward drift of the country increased with the outbreak of the Winnipeg General Strike in the spring of 1919. Quickly the CIRA broadened its support base and its areas of concern. With support from Rotary clubs, several Protestant churches, and leaders in the highest echelons of the social register, the newly formed NCE held a massive conference on character education in Winnipeg in October. Speaker after speaker urged national goals for Canadian schools, reorientation of education towards preparation for life rather than as a means to livelihood, recruitment of teachers of good moral character, strengthening of patriotic education, and an emphasis on teaching young people to appreciate the values of Christian society. The National Council remained alive through the 1920s, but its grandiose plans for the moral regeneration of Canadian youth and Canadian schools soon expired. Although its goals were not at variance with those of provincial departments, its promotion of a national bureau of education ran into opposition from the provinces, jealously protecting their constitutional rights. The NCE's failure has been attributed also to its 'attempt to superimpose aristocratic leadership in order to exert a controlling influence for esoteric purposes over the schools of the people and the democratically constituted school authorities.'[12]

II

If the post-war world expected much from the school, it demanded miracles from the teacher. 'The teacher after all holds the key to the educational citadel,' wrote education minister Henry Cody in his 1918 annual report. 'On the teachers is being thrown to-day a burden which should be borne also by the other educational factors of the community – the home, the church, and the press.' Cody recognized the heavy demands on teachers – 'their task makes special drains on the nerves and on the soul' – and realized that higher salaries and higher occupational status were essential to bolster their 'low spirits.'[13]

There had been a number of earlier attempts to found professional teachers' organizations – the College of Preceptors and the Teachers' Protective Association in the 1880s, the Ontario Teachers' Alliance in 1908 – but all had run into stubborn opposition from the department of education and massive indifference on the part of most practising teachers. They year 1913 was especially bleak for outspoken teachers. The Toronto Board of Education attempted 'to stifle in the teachers all active interest in politics'; a small-town principal was advised to 'keep out of such things' when he campaigned for public control of hydro power; and a rural principal was threatened with dismissal 'because he would not vote against local option.'[14] But it was not until the closing years of the First World War that teacher anger at their low status and low salaries combined to produce successful attempts at organization.

Salary increases during the war had not matched the rise in the cost of living. The equivalent real purchasing power of a public school teacher's salary in 1920 was about 88 per cent of what it had been ten years earlier, for separate school teachers 79 per cent, and for high school teachers 80 per cent. And the differential between male and female salaries continued to increase; the average female public school teacher earned 55 per cent of her male counterpart's salary in 1910, but by 1920 this had fallen to 49 per cent.[15] In 1919 the Ontario girl with high school graduation plus one year at normal school earned less in a teaching job than an inexperienced stenographer who had never been to high school and who had taken only a six months' business course.

Teachers' salaries were the responsibility, not of the provincial government, but of the thousands of local school-boards that dotted the Ontario countryside. 'I respect all honest, faithful teachers as the pluckiest beings on earth,' wrote one discouraged woman teacher to the minister of education, 'but I can have no respect for people who say they want their children educated, but who do not want to pay for it.'[16] Another teacher was more specific. Jennie Stead of Walkerton estimated that $416 of her $577 annual salary was eaten up by room and board. 'Judge for yourself,' she challenged the minister, 'how far the balance will go in meeting the present cost of living.' Stead warned Cody that 'proposals for joining certain organizations are being made to us' whereby salary demands would be presented in a more militant fashion. 'Is there no other way by which we may receive just remuneration without having to resort to these *union* methods?'[17]

First to organize at the provincial level were the female public school teachers – perennial recipients of low salaries and sexist slurs on their dedication to the profession. Members of the Women Teachers' Guild of London contacted their sister organization, the Women Teachers' Association of Toronto, in May 1917, suggesting a joint meeting. The torch was picked up by Helen Arbuthnot of the Toronto WTA, leader of a skilful though unsuccessful campaign to affiliate the WTA with the Toronto Labour Council in 1912, and a moving force behind the 1917 provincial superannuation legislation. The Federation of Women Teachers' Associations of Ontario was born the following year at the Easter OEA meeting, responding to the challenge of Berta Adkins that only such an organization would 'reduce sexism and raise the status of women teachers.'[18] As the first secretary of the FWTAO, Adkins proved to be an organizational wizard. In her own area of St Thomas, amidst cries of trade unionism, communism, and selfishness from local school-board members and respected citizens, she attained 100 per cent membership. By 1920 she had enrolled more than 5,000 of the province's 12,500 female elementary teachers.

The initiative taken by the women left their male counterparts behind, and contributed to the division of Ontario teachers' organizations along male-female, elementary-secondary, and religious and linguistic lines. The male public school teachers, conscious of their minority position, yet determined to protect their favoured economic status, established their own organization, the Ontario Public School Men Teachers' Federation at the 1920 OEA convention. Meanwhile high school teachers from Toronto, Hamilton, and Western Ontario met in secret during the 1919 Christmas holidays and founded the Ontario Secondary School Teachers' Federation. Their initial idea was to organize a federation of only male teachers from the high schools and collegiates, but low numbers soon persuaded the leaders to include both men and women, and to invite teachers in the continuation and vocational schools. Within a year, some 90 per cent of the province's secondary school teachers had joined the OSSTF.

Such united action on the part of teachers was opposed by conservative elements within Ontario society. President J.H. Scott of the Ontario School Trustees' and Ratepayers' Association argued in 1922 that 'the so-called Federations are unnecessary.' The only legitimate reason for teachers' organizations was to 'confer and co-operate for their mutual advantage and the elevation of their standards.' Scott believed that local teachers' institutes and the provincial OEA were sufficient for this purpose. His chief complaint was the use of force and 'unionism' to compel 'acquiescence of their demands.' The Educational Committee of the Council of the United Counties of Stormont, Dundas, and Glengarry added to the charges of unionism and coercion, asserting that the federations were virtually dictating hiring and termination policies.[19] Even more alarming was the fear that teachers' federations were the first step along the road to radicalism, socialism, and communism; such at least was the view of the editor of the Chesley *Enterprise* who advised FWTAO organizer Jennie Stead to 'pack her kit and head for Russia.'[20] Conservative citizens' groups such as the

Home and School, the Red Cross, and the Penny Bank saw their own campaigns as providing pupils with defence mechanisms to ward off radical preaching from militant teachers. The National Council of Education saw its mission in part as preventing educational decision-making powers from passing into the hands of these new teachers' federations.

Salary increases gained in Toronto in 1920 demonstrated the importance of united action on the part of teachers. City teachers had refrained from pressing salary claims during the war, but united now in the Toronto Teachers' Council they campaigned for an across-the-board increase. To achieve its goal the council held at least forty strategy meetings, produced a sixteen-page booklet explaining why teachers deserved better pay, convened a mass rally on the University of Toronto campus, lobbied individual trustees, and spent thousands of dollars on an elaborate press campaign. The result was a 25 per cent increase for male teachers, and a 15 per cent increase for female teachers. The council had refused not only to endorse equal pay for equal work, but even equal increases, thus strengthening the conviction of the FWTAO to continue with its own organization.

Rather than a first step to greater economic and political triumphs, the year 1920 marked the high point of early organized teacher efforts in Ontario. True salaries did rise somewhat faster than the cost of living during the remainder of the decade, and collective bargaining and greater security of tenure became unofficial norms. Yet the exhilarating economic victories seemed to take the starch out of all three associations. The very existence of three groups rather than one meant that the individual bodies went their separate ways; even the joint Toronto Teachers' Council withered after the successful 1920 salary campaign. There was also the long-established Ontario Educational Association, whose continuing presence denied the new federations a role in the important area of professional development. The conservative philosophies of most of the early presidents also proved a restraining factor on radical action; the selection of a reserve army colonel, William Michell of Toronto, as the first president of OSSTF, set a pattern of respectability and restraint. Finally, the movements failed to generate support in the rural parts of the province; continuation-school teachers were conspicuously absent from the ranks of OSSTF, as were the one-room country school teachers from the FWTAO. The high-minded idealism of the urban founders simply did not penetrate the village class-room and the small school on the back concession.

Most disappointing of all was the decline of the women teachers' association as membership dropped from 4,300 in 1921 to 3,400 in 1922. FWTAO organizers had the worst of male suspicions confirmed, as they encountered thousands of young girls in the country schoolhouses who were not prepared to commit themselves to a professional career and the long, hard battle for better salaries, pension plans, and fringe benefits. 'Most girls expected to marry and forget the

harrowing experiences of the classroom and the country school,' stated the federation's historian.[21] As members drifted away, the FWTAO itself diluted its economic and professional goals and moved towards a more idealistic platform
stressing the teacher's role in reconstruction and the value of education to
society. The executive joined the purity campaign and petitioned the government to censor motion pictures, vaudeville performances, and comic books, and
opposed sex education in the schools. Even the once-militant Women Teachers'
Association of Toronto became, in the words of one student of the period,
'another Junior League or a kind of Big Sister Association.'[22]

By the early 1920s it was evident that neither the voluntary citizens' movements nor the organized teachers' federations would succeed in altering the basic
thrust of Ontario education. The Home and School, Junior Red Cross, and
Penny Bank were accepted because they supported the goals of the educational
administrators. The National Council of Education was rejected because it challenged the control of that bureaucracy. Teachers' federations found their field of
action tightly circumscribed by bureaucratic control of the provincial educational system. Departmental officials could give tacit, although not public, support to salary campaigns in the belief that higher wages would attract better
candidates to the teaching profession. But any hopes that the federations had of
exercising greater professional control were dashed by the fact that decisions on
curriculum, text books, and examinations were the prerogative of the provincial
department of education. If Ontario schools were to be changed in the 1920s, the
thrust would have to come from within the provincial education establishment.

III

Several months before the end of the First World War, prior to the mushrooming of the various citizens' groups and teachers' federations, Conservative premier William Hearst had brought into the provincial cabinet the man designated
to rescue Ontario education from within. Henry J. Cody, rector of St Paul's
Anglican Church in Toronto, became minister of education in May 1918.
Although an outsider to the department, Cody was no stranger either to education or to the inner ranks of the Conservative party. A brilliant scholar and outstanding Christian leader, Cody had served on the 1905 University of Toronto
royal commission and later on the university's board of governors; he had
shared speaking engagements with Hearst and other cabinet ministers, had been
the most vocal clerical supporter of Union Government during the 1917 federal
elections, and a determined champion of the war effort and the imperial connection. Hearst saw Cody as boosting the education department's sagging morale,
restoring public confidence in a somewhat tired government that would soon
face a general election, and 'moulding the character and the citizenship and
determining the future destiny of this province.' Rarely has a government placed

so much faith in one person. 'You will be the instrument,' Hearst told him, 'not only of raising and improving educational standards in this Province, but the moral standards of our people in setting up new and better ideals of life and conduct.'[23]

No radical social or political reformer, Cody was determined to build a post-war society on the traditional foundations of Protestant Christianity, political conservatism, and Anglo-Saxon racial superiority. Schooling could play a crucial role in checking rampant libertarianism by instilling habits of respect and discipline in young minds. 'The weakening of religious faith, the loosening of the bonds of parental control, the absence of real discipline from school life,' he told the province's teachers, 'are all causes that have led to the undermining of the foundations of respect and reverence.'[24] There must be respect and reverence for British as well as for Christian contributions to mankind. 'Who stands if Freedom falls? Who dies if England lives?' Such was the slogan adopted by Cody during the early years of the war. He preached that the genius of the British people had been granted by God, and that it was to the credit of the Britons that they had set out to share their genius with backward people.[25] Cody had visions of a new Canada 'united in common sentiment, tradition and readiness to serve King and country.'[26]

The new minister moved quickly to strengthen patriotic teaching in the schools of Ontario. History – 'the great vehicle of patriotic instruction' – was given a renewed emphasis when British and Canadian history were reinstated as high school entrance examination subjects. 'The value of the subject in promoting patriotism, in providing material for a clear grasp of Canadian civics, and in expounding Canada's Imperial relations and her place in the Empire,' Cody declared as an article of faith, 'is generally recognized.'[27] The *Ontario Readers*, revised in 1909-10, remained in use through the 1920s and 1930s, thus guaranteeing that yet another generation of Ontario youngsters would be exposed to an over-riding emphasis on traditional moral and political values, Britain's past military glories, and Canada's place in the Empire. Not content to rely solely on the authorized readers, Cody published in 1919 a booklet entitled *The Great War in Verse and Prose*, which was placed in quantity in each school library with instructions that excerpts be read by the class-room teachers as often as possible. Cody's introduction enumerated the issues that had been decided, the lessons learned, and the revelations of the war, not the least of which was 'a truer conception of the meaning of Empire.'

Cody's promotion of imperialism and moral rectitude went far beyond the formal school curriculum. He sought to attract returned soldiers into the teaching profession, whose 'moral force and influence' would more than compensate for their lack of academic qualifications.[28] He promoted the League of Empire, which fostered imperial unity through teacher exchanges and student pen pals. He supported the work of the Boy Scout and Girl Guide movements, and heartily endorsed a compaign undertaken by the IODE and the Navy League to interest pupils in the achievements of the navy and merchant marine. A long-time supporter of the school cadet movement, Cody did nothing to deny the rumour that he planned to make such military training compulsory. Whether he had a coherent policy of extending the movement is uncertain, but the number of cadet corps soared from 168 in 1918 to 248 in 1919. It was on this issue that the first rumblings of opposition to Cody were heard. The province's agrarian leaders, through the columns of the *Farmers' Sun*, kept sniping at Cody throughout most of 1919. Insinuating that the minister of education believed Canada to be 'but an outpost of London, England,' the *Sun* charged that Cody's purpose, 'more or less openly avowed, was to make the public schools of Ontario a means of Imperialistic propaganda.'[29]

If there was scattered opposition to the cadet movement, there was still unanimous public support for Empire Day during the immediate post-war years. Cody was astute enough to harness Empire Day enthusiasm to the twin causes of immigrant assimilation and the checking of subversive political ideas. 'We want those in our land who, when it comes to the crisis,' declared Cody, 'will bear their share in the defence of the liberties we enjoy.'[30] The potential threat could be overcome if political, educational, and religious efforts were united in the common cause 'of unification, of assimilation, of Canadianization, of Christianization.'[31] Cody heartily applauded the motives of the Robert Simpson Company in making annual Empire Day presentations of Union Jacks to Toronto schools with large foreign enrolments. 'The idea behind the gift,' declared a company executive, 'is to inculcate in the minds of the rising generation a definite feeling of loyalty and respect for both the flag and the Empire.'[32] Although the language was considerably more explicit than he would use personally, Cody could also support the statement of the mayor of Toronto on the occasion of the 1919 Empire Day parade. 'It would do the people of Winnipeg good to see such an inspiring sight,' proclaimed Mayor Tommy Church. 'There is no room for Bolshevism or European socialism in Canada and we are going to have none in Toronto.'[33]

Yet Cody never placed all his hopes for educational reconstruction on patriotic pronouncements concerning imperial unity. The lack of leadership in Ontario education throughout the war years resulted in a host of problems for the new minister. Former minister Robert Pyne had neglected the portfolio in favour of military hospital work; acting minister Howard Ferguson had been burdened with the Regulation 17 albatross. Leadership within the department – apart from F.W. Merchant's work in technical education – had suffered because of the aging John Seath's unwillingness to surrender the post of superintendent before his death in early 1919. On 8 April of that year, Cody made his Queen's Park debut as a spokesman for both the education department and the Hearst government's reconstruction platform. Speaking on second reading of a consolidated school bill, Cody ranged over the entire educational system, outlining his proposals to extend equality of educational opportunity. There would be improved medical and dental inspection of school pupils, extended and more rigidly enforced compulsory attendance regulations, encouragement of consolidated schools in rural areas, help for vocational schools and for instruction in agriculture and manual training, and more money for rural teachers' salaries and for the teachers' pension fund.

Cody's major contributions to Ontario education were his 1919 compulsory attendance requirements. The School Attendance Act (effective 1 Jan. 1920) required local school jurisdictions to appoint attendance officers, while the more controversial Adolescent School Attendance Act (effective 1 Jan. 1921) extended the age of compulsory schooling from fourteen to sixteen. The latter act reflected the growing view that fourteen-year-old school leavers were no longer prepared for the vocational and social challenges of the post-war urban-industrial world. Industry now demanded more highly trained workers; inadequately prepared school drop-outs, competing for jobs with recently demobilized soldiers, could not hope to find employment during a period of industrial slowdown. But these early teen-age years were equally important in the formation of moral character. Cody believed that 'it is impossible to teach under the age of fourteen all that a boy or girl ought to learn for effective citizenship.'[34]

The implementation of compulsory schooling for fourteen-to-sixteen-year-olds proceeded smoothly in most urban areas of the province. Some labour spokesmen complained initially of the difficulty it would pose for poorer parents denied the earning potential of their children for two additional years. Some trustees feared their schools would not be able to accommodate the hordes of teen-agers now forced to remain in the class-room. But the government had prepared the ground with earlier permissive legislation, with amendments to the Factories Act prohibiting the employment of youngsters under sixteen and to the Mothers' Allowances Act providing support for children up to age sixteen, and by permitting attendance exemptions for youngsters whose employment was essential to the family's economic welfare. By the end of 1921 newly appointed provincial attendance officer J.P. Cowles reported that 'the increase in urban centres is considerable.' St Catharines showed the highest gains – 145 per cent for fourteen-year-olds and 41 per cent for fifteen-year-olds – while Fort William, Windsor, London, Guelph, Woodstock, Hamilton, and Peterborough were 'all doing well.'[35] Throughout the decade the government continually boasted of the success of the act and equated increased attendance with social progress. 'Many juveniles who formerly spent the years of their early adolescence in unnecessary employments, often intermittent and unprofitable, or in actual idleness,' declared the 1923 department of education report, 'are now under systematic training and discipline.'[36]

More radical in conception – and ultimately less successful in execution – were the provisions of the Adolescent School Attendance Act calling for part-time classes. These were to begin in September 1922 for fourteen-to-sixteen-year-olds who had been granted work permits, and the following year for all sixteen-to-eighteen-year-olds who had not completed a recognized high school program. These classes were to be partially vocational in scope – 'interlocking, to a certain extent, the activities of the school with those of industry' – but their main intent was social. They were to furnish 'means of training in the duties of citizenship and in the right use of leisure.'[37] Unfortunately, local school-boards were not enthusiastic about this new responsibility, and business and industry showed some reluctance to co-operate. 'Does one imagine for a moment,' wrote an eastern Ontario critic, 'that the employer is going to upset his whole office or factory routine, in order that this young man or woman may take 400 working hours off in the course of a year, in order to attend classes?'[38] Toronto was the centre of the most determined opposition, as the board of education dragged its feet for three years. Part-time classes for sixteen-to-eighteen-year-olds were never implemented, while those for fourteen-to-sixteen-year-olds became unnecessary by the end of the decade as full-time attendance became the norm for town and city youngsters.

And from the rural areas of the province came opposition to both the part-time and the full-time attendance provisions of Cody's legislation – provisions that ironically had to be enforced by the United Farmers' government following the 1919 election. Continuation school inspector G.K. Mills saw no point in keeping rural youth at school till sixteen 'when all that is offered them is a little more grammar, geography, history, etc., taught by a young girl.'[39] W.H. Casselman, UFO member for Dundas, charged in the 1923 session of the legislature that school attendance for fourteen-to-sixteen-year-olds was 'an economic evil, because it tended to educate the boys and girls off the farms.' No 'hot-house academic education' could instil the qualities necessary for success in life's battles.[40] Repeated pressure from Casselman and other UFO backbenchers forced the government of E.C. Drury to back down. In the final days of the 1923 session, education minister R.H. Grant announced greater freedom to exempt fourteen-to-sixteen-year-olds in rural areas and the indefinite delay of provisions for part-time attendance for sixteen-to-eighteen-year-olds. The impact of greater exemptions was immediately apparent, as adolescent attendance dropped 20 per cent in rural inspectorates the following year.

But public opposition to the attendance acts was not immediately apparent in the summer and fall months of 1919. Henry Cody and his cabinet colleagues entered the November election campaign with a solid record of progressive educational and social legislation behind them. Premier Hearst made the most of Cody's achievements on the campaign trail. 'He has planned and is rapidly carrying out the most complete and comprehensive educational program ever presented to this or to any other country,' declared the premier. Cody had stimulated

'a greater interest in Education ... and a new enthusiasm has been created in educational affairs.'[41] Yet these achievements were to no avail; although Cody
retained his own seat by acclamation, the Conservative government fell before
the combined onslaught of the United Farmers of Ontario and the Independent
Labour Party. The Hearst government appealed neither to traditional groups
clinging to the status quo nor to the militant post-war agrarian and labour
groups seeking a new social order. Cody's reforms, like those of the government
in general, had provoked resentment among traditional rural Tories without
winning working-class support. The farmers, he confided, 'believe that I have
been exclusively devoted to university matters and that my desire is to train up a
group of Imperialistic jingoes in the schools.' On the other hand, 'the Labour
people feel that my policy of wide-open technical and industrial education will
trench upon the labour union monopoly of skilled labour.'[42]

IV

The focus of public attention on the high school that began with the Adolescent
School Attendance Act continued throughout the decade of the 1920s. The publicity was not always favourable, as a situation in Ottawa in the autumn of 1927
revealed. During the month of October, Rev. E.B. Wyllie of Erskine Presbyterian Church filled the columns of the city's two English-language newspapers
with a steady stream of allegations about student behaviour at Ottawa Collegiate. The school was a veritable cesspool of sin – marked by unsupervised dances, disrespect for teachers, moral impropriety, the acquisition of undesirable
habits, hip-flask drinking at student parties, and wild escapades in automobiles.
Wyllie demanded a crack-down by school authorities.[43] Pressed by editorials in
both the *Journal* and the *Citizen*, the Ottawa Collegiate Institute Board called on
the provincial government to establish a commission of inquiry. Premier G.
Howard Ferguson responded by naming Mr Justice R.A. Orde of the provincial
supreme court as a one-man commission.

Wyllie provided Orde with additional allegations at a public hearing on 9
November. Lavatory walls were covered with grafitti and 'obscene pictures.'
There were dances where 'conditions would make even the most worldly hesitate
to have their children go, especially young girls.' There had been a sleigh-ride
party across the river to Hull where 'a good deal of roughness and drinking took
place.'[44] But Wyllie would provide no specific evidence and refused to reveal his
sources. Other witnesses were unable to corroborate his charges. Justice Orde
concluded that Wyllie's charges were unfounded, and he rapped the clergyman's
knuckles severely. 'Any one with experience of school life,' Orde reported,
'knows that there have always been instances of insubordination, and of
immoral or improper conduct' when teenagers gather. But 'as long as human
nature is as it is, these things will continue.' These habits, he concluded, 'are quite
independent of any system of schooling' and were no more prevalent in the
Ottawa Collegiate Institute than in any other school.[45]

The significance of this 1927 controversy lay neither in Wyllie's charges nor in Orde's dismissal of them. What the incident revealed was the growing public interest following the First World War in the high school years. For the first time the majority of Ontario teenagers were attending high school, and were staying longer than pre-war students. At Ottawa Collegiate, Principal A.H. McDougall was ultimately responsible for the academic performance and out-of-class behaviour of more than 2,000 students. Four years earlier the school had been split into two campuses; by 1927 there were 881 pupils in the old building (soon to be re-named Lisgar Collegiate) and 1,187 students in a new location several blocks away (the future Glebe Collegiate). The same expansion was occurring in Toronto. Riverdale Collegiate in the city's east end jumped from 448 students in 1918 to 1,180 ten years later, despite the channelling of hundreds more students into the newly-opened Danforth Technical School and the Eastern High School of Commerce. Such enrolment increases were not confined to Ontario's larger urban centres. One-room country schools added Fifth Book classes for those students continuing on to grades 9 and 10. Villages sprouted continuation schools; towns up-graded their continuation schools to high school status. September 1921 saw a province-wide increase of 23 per cent in high school enrolments. While Ontario's population rose by 17 per cent during the decade of the 1920s, secondary school enrolment quadrupled. When Toronto high school inspector William Michell was asked in 1928 how to halt the trend, his only suggestion was to 'kill the stork.'[46]

Principal McDougall cited four factors that he believed accounted for the rapid rise in high school attendance: enactment of compulsory-attendance legislation, abolition of fees, vanishing employment opportunities for early school leavers, and the intangible 'desire on the part of more parents for secondary education for their children.'[47] Yet McDougall's first two points were more symptoms of change than causal factors in themselves. Ontario's Adolescent School Attendance Act, which raised the school-leaving age to sixteen years, took effect in September 1921. But 'the movement had started before the war,' concluded one principal. 'The real effect of the war was to check the rising tendency to attend secondary schools. When the damming back was removed by the termination of the war, we had the sudden great rise in attendance.'[48] Nor could the explanation be found solely in the question of tuition fees. The final abolition of fees might have had some effect for the 50 per cent of Ontario high schools still charging them in 1920, but enrolment jumps in these schools the following year were not significantly greater than in schools which had voluntarily abolished tuition fees years earlier.

More satisfactory explanations for the growth in attendance are to be found in the economic and social climates of the post-war period. Technological advances in business and industry were rapidly reducing the need for unskilled labour; unlike previous decades, early school leaving was now more likely to lead to unemployment rather than a job. 'Each day in High School adds $25.00 to his life's earning,' was the trumpet call of popular magazines of the day. 'Modern business, with its intensity and complexity, calls for the highest degree of training for those who seek success in it,' declared a department store executive.[49] Toronto businessman John Wanless painted a glowing picture of 'modern merchant princes' as he told the province's teachers that 'matriculation is valuable to a business man who is called upon to fill the commanding position of business administrator and head executive.'[50] The partial social and political emancipation of women produced similar economic challenges for the teen-age girl, who was now expected to 'do something' after she left high school. She must 'take a thorough training in her chosen line of work' for 'the untrained worker, however clever, will be left behind in the race for efficiency.' Stay in school, ran the litany, and eventually the young girl would be prepared to join 'the mighty stream of business women pouring, day in and day out, into office, bank or store.'[51]

Increased high school attendance promised more than economic benefits. Many parents were concerned about the social and moral temptations confronting their offspring during the 1920s, and thus tacitly supported the strictly supervised atmosphere and the socialization role promised by the high school. Schoolmen throughout the province spoke frequently of this 'character building' and 'citizenship training' mission. In broader terms, the Ontario high school assumed many of the attributes of the nineteenth-century elementary school and became an institution of child custodianship. With its diverse curriculum, physical facilities, extra-curricular activities, and opportunities for peer-group contact, the high school also offered an exciting interlude between the carefree days of childhood and the responsibilities of adulthood. 'It often means an entrance into a new world, cultural and social,' wrote one principal in 1923, 'in fact a complete revolution in the life of the student, transferring him from one plane of life to another vastly different.'[52]

These pupils, who streamed out of the elementary schools and into the high schools in ever-increasing numbers during the 1920s, came from a wider socioeconomic background than ever before. 'The High School is now a common meeting ground for the children of all the classes,' wrote inspector I.M. Levan in 1920. 'Here the sons and daughters of the tradesman, the mechanic, the labouring man, the professional man, the Protestant and the Roman Catholic, mingle together and work together in the spirit of amity and equality, regardless of distinctions of class and creed.'[53] Though egalitarians still complained of the underrepresentation of children from unskilled labouring backgrounds, the character of the student population had shifted from the more élitist orientation of the pre-war years. 'Many of the pupils no longer belong to those social levels in the community for whose children a complete high school education and subsequent entrance upon the university is regarded as a social and professional necessity,' concluded a national study in 1929. Such a phenomenon had definite implications for the curriculum. 'Such pupils may enter high school and then drop out again if their education does not appear to be satisfying any strong and rather immediate need.'[54]

Many of these young people were part of the new youth culture of the 1920s. Increases in productivity, affluence, and leisure time all contributed to creating what came to be called the flapper age or the jazz age. Large numbers of youths who were brought up in comparative affluence, free of concerns about involvement in production, began to develop a different style of life around the new technology of the twentieth century. More rapidly than their parents, they embraced the automobile, the movie theatre, the radio, and new styles of dress and dance. 'For the girls, there was the freedom of daringly short skirts, bobbed and marcelled hair, cosmetics openly applied, and the boyish silhouette,' recalled a former student of Ottawa's Glebe Collegiate. 'For the men, escape from the tyranny of hard collars, the ever-present coat and stovepipe pants to the ease of soft collars, rainbow-hued sweaters and bell-bottom trousers.' These daring dress styles were enough of a threat to the older generation; worse still were the behavioural traits that seemed to accompany such changes. 'To complete the picture, add the Charleston, the college boy's coon coat, loud-checked plus-fours, and a tin lizzy bedizened with a smart remark for every rattle.'[55] To many veteran school personnel and other upholders of traditional moral values, all this seemed to be leading youth straight down the path to hell.

'We who taught in high schools played ostrich then,' recalled Ontario's Chief Director of Education, J.G. Althouse, two decades later. 'We didn't admit even to ourselves that we had a task with any but the able and the industrious.'[56] But school principals could not help but notice that the spirit of the age and the enrolment of a larger proportion of the adolescent population had combined to produce a new challenge for the Ontario high school. Principals found themselves forced to devote precious planning time to such concerns as smoking around the school-yard, drinking at dances, what to do about fraternities and sororities, and how to prevent students from leaving classes for temporary employment just prior to the Christmas holidays.[57] A.M. Overholt of Brantford Collegiate saw the principal as 'responsible for the manners, morals, mental habits and to a large extent the characters of those placed in his charge.'[58] Ontario educators realized that the challenge of the 1920s could be met only by expanding the social role of the high school. The underlying debate of the period was whether this role should be realized through expanded curricular offerings or through extra-curricular activities.

V

The increased attendance triggered a construction boom that was not matched until the 1960s. While the new high schools and the additions to older buildings were partially funded through provincial grants, over 90 per cent of continuing costs fell on the shoulders of the local authorities. This burden was assumed out of necessity, in order to keep pace with enrolment, but civic pride was also involved. 'One can scarcely pick up a newspaper published in any part of the Province without reading an account of the opening of some new educational institution,' declared the *Canadian School Board Journal* in 1923. The new Sarnia Collegiate Institute and Technical School was touted as the most completely developed composite school in Canada. Delta Collegiate in Hamilton was a veritable palace, 'a beautiful building of Tudor-Gothic architecture.' Interior facilities matched exterior grandeur as Toronto's new Jarvis Collegiate boasted a conservatory with fountain and pool to serve as an aquarium, an auditorium seating 1,000, a large modern cafeteria, a gymnasium with swimming pool and showers, armouries, and rifle range, plus 'metal lockers built into the corridor walls to serve more than 1000 pupils.' These institutions were sold to cost-conscious taxpayers in a variety of ways. The new Kingston Collegiate and Vocational School was advertised as 'another new factory, unique in that it will have no competitor and its products are always marketable.' Meanwhile, Belleville Collegiate acquired virtual cathedral status at its cornerstone laying ceremony, with the Anglican Bishop of Ontario invoking the divine blessing and the assembled throng lustily singing 'Praise God from Whom All Blessings Flow.'[59]

Vocational education programs in the trades and business subjects were viewed as an important curricular response to the changing economic needs of the 1920s. Non-university-bound students, instead of being early drop-outs from an academic program, could now be channelled into specialized technical or commercial programs, equipped with social and vocational life-skills, and funnelled into the market-place. By 1928, some 21,000 pupils – more than one-quarter of all Ontario high school students – were enrolled in full-time vocational programs in forty-two schools. While this expansion was aided by federal money, it was also due to the pressures of industrial development within the province, to the foundation laid by Ontario's own Industrial Education Act of 1911, and to the direction given the movement by provincial director F.W. Merchant during the second decade of the century. Before the First World War, vocational education had been confined to the larger urban centres; during the 1920s it spread to the medium- and smaller-sized cities from one end of the province to the other.

Peterborough's assessment of vocational education needs was typical. A massive survey in 1920 discovered more than 1,500 fourteen-to-eighteen-year-olds not attending school. Although most were employed, their employers demanded better general and specific training – 'a more satisfactory preparation for citizenship and for their future vocations.'[60] So the Peterborough Board of Education added a vocational wing to its collegiate. The new vocational facilities provided a great diversity of curriculum offerings. Sarnia Collegiate

Institute and Technical School offered drawing, commercial design, blue-print reading, electricity, machine shop, tool and die making, welding, auto mechanics, carpentry and cabinet making, clay modelling, millinery and dressmaking, cooking, bookkeeping, shorthand, typing, and navigation. By the end of the decade the new Ontario Training College for Technical Teachers at Hamilton was preparing instructors for these new programs, and the University of Toronto was accepting technical-school graduates into its faculties of applied science, household science, and commerce. 'Ontario's programme of vocational education is the most diversified and highly organized in Canada,' reported the federal director of technical education.[61]

Consistent with the motivation behind Ontario's initial move in 1911, vocational education in the 1920s was designed to serve economic ends. Henry Cody sounded more like an apologist for the National Policy than a minister of education when he declared in 1918 that 'Canada has been thrown into the mid-stream of world life and the manufacturers of Canada will compete against the manufacturers of the world. You cannot do everything by tariff, which will never take the place of the good article. To get the good article we must have skilled workmen, and to get good workmen, we must get the education.'[62] Merchant's annual report for that year echoed the call for 'the organization of education to provide better trained workers for these industries and trades.'[63] Whether the results lived up to the initial hopes is difficult to document. Merchant's successor as director of technical education admitted in 1927 that 'some schools are unable as yet to furnish concrete evidence that the purpose is being attained.' The only example that D.A. Campbell could cite was the Ford Motor Company's policy of accepting into its tool-making department only graduates of Windsor-Walkerville Technical School.[64] Tom Moore, president of the Trades and Labor Congress of Canada, questioned how far vocational education really assisted boys and girls to find the occupation for which they were best suited. He also feared that 'a slight knowledge of a trade might be disappointing and frustrating when its real or more advanced practice was entered upon.' But like most supporters of the movement, Moore was convinced of one thing – that 'technical education as a whole filled the void left by the passing of the old apprenticeship.'[65]

Vocational schooling was also justified in terms of 'making useful citizens.' Occasionally this was argued on the specific grounds of industrial harmony as business and government sought ways of riding out the period of post-war labour unrest. 'Instructors may do much for students in giving them the proper attitude towards work, towards their job, towards their employer,' asserted the principal of London Technical High School. 'Instructors may do a service of national importance by becoming ambassadors of a better understanding between labour and capital.'[66] More often, educators employed a much broader definition of 'good citizenship' as they argued their case for vocational education. Merchant linked 'specialized training in the subjects and operations which are fundamental to trades and industries' with 'the essentials of a general education as a basis for citizenship.' Cody believed 'that such institutions should teach good citizenship as well as good workmanship.'[67] With the onset of the depression in the early 1930s and the failure to establish any empirical proof of the economic success of the vocational schools, Ontario educators began to put this citizenship mission ahead of the job-training role. Departmental officials in 1931 repeated the twin aims – 'to develop our students as responsible and cultured citizens, and second, as partially trained and ready to enter some field of employment' – but concluded by suggesting that 'the first of these is the most important.'[68]

But the separate technical or commercial high school – so strongly championed by John Seath in the years before the war – was not always seen as the best model for attracting students into vocational courses nor for 'moulding citizens' once they were enrolled. Although the larger cities kept the specialized vocational schools they had already established, new school construction in the smaller centres during the 1920s tended towards the composite school model. These were not like American high schools, where university- and work-bound students took common core subjects and then split away for electives. The Ontario composite high school retained a curricular and administrative split between academic and vocational classes. But students from the two divisions were expected to rub shoulders in the hallways and in extracurricular activities, thus in theory at least fostering the link between general and vocational education. The composite high school also offered a greater possibility for attracting more pupils into vocational courses than did the lower-status technical school. In cities with segregated facilities, all too many elementary school graduates were seen as 'simply drifting – going in crowds to the collegiate because their chums are going.' But with the composite school, argued a Sarnia administrator, 'the principal meets all the students' and 'he has that one advantage – he will actually come in contact with them, and give them advice about courses.'[69]

Principals had always advised students about courses and post-school opportunities. But what had generally been done in an informal way prior to the war now became formalized during the 1920s. The larger proportion of adolescents in attendance, the impersonal atmosphere of the large schools, the troublesome social and moral trends of the decade – all combined to launch the guidance movement. 'High school courses are hampered by a lack of opportunity for the teacher to take personal interest and have personal contact with the student and his individual problems,' charged C.L. Burton of the Robert Simpson Company. 'Our high school boys should find themselves in a way that is not characteristic of them to-day.'[70] But by the end of the decade, general or personal guidance had lost out to the more specific form of vocational guidance. The vocational schools needed to justify their existence and keep the support of the manufacturers and labour groups. Thus vocational guidance and job placement became priority concerns. London had one of the most comprehensive programs, beginning with a survey to determine the job aspirations of elementary school graduates, followed by school pressure 'if the student is contemplating an occupation for which he is manifestly not suited.' This was followed by pre-registration in either an academic or vocational secondary school program, individual and group guidance during the first two years of high school, and job placement and follow-up by school guidance officials.[71] The provincial department of education institutionalized the process at the end of the decade by providing a certificate in vocational guidance through summer courses at the Ontario Training College for Technical Teachers.

Like the composite high school and the vocational-guidance movement, extra-curricular activities were seen as answering many of the social needs of the 1920s. Progressive principals saw extra-curricular activities as important in the process of socialization, in the growth towards adult responsibilities, and in the fostering of social efficiency. Thus they came to be regarded as more than mere adjuncts to the academic program; they could furnish boys and girls with actual laboratory training in many of the important experiences they would have in later life. The student newspaper could 'cultivate alertness, accuracy and co-operative work habits.'[72] Student governments, with carefully controlled powers, could engage in group planning activities. At Toronto's Northern Vocational School the student council planned and managed social and athletic events, conducted opening exercises in the auditorium, and looked after 'such disciplinary problems as smoking, bad language, and unbecoming conduct in halls and washrooms.'[73] High school assemblies could do much to foster 'a healthy school spirit, to train the pupils in public speaking, in self-control, in orderly habits, in consideration for others and in respect for authority.'[74] School athletics promised 'the cultivation of the virtues of courage, endurance, persistency, self-control, of patience and good humour in adversity, and of temperance and modesty in triumph.'[75] Like other extra-curricular activities of the 1920s, school sports – if kept in proper perspective – provided a 'wholesome' outlet for adolescent energies, kept teenagers in school, and provided the social dimensions of education missing from the formal curriculum.

With parties and dances arranged by the school, with a dazzling variety of school clubs to engage his interests, with the inspiration offered by assemblies, with weekly football or basketball games, the high school student of the 1920s might be thought of as fortunate indeed. Yet student populations lived under tight control. There were regulations on attendance and lateness, student dress and hair styles, completion of homework assignments and obedience to school rules – all in the name of character development. In some cases the rules and regulations were more strict than in previous decades, for the high schools of the 1920s were dealing with a much less selective student group than that of the past, and were also reacting to a stereotype of 'flaming youth' engaged in flouting pre-war norms and conventions. Almost without exception, the provincial inspectors drew a close connection between discipline and control on the one hand, and the ability of the high school to measure up to its academic and moral purposes. Although they praised the contributions of a school's extra-curricular program in character training and citizenship development, the inspectors left no doubt that such activities were subordinate to the academic role of the high school. R.B. Anglin, for example, saw much value in the morning assemblies at Ontario's Shelburne High School in fostering 'the good spirit that is evident in the school.' But the essence of his report was contained in one short sentence. 'The main attention of the school,' he concluded, 'is rightly focused on the regular studies of each day.'[76]

VI

Despite promising beginnings, the 'regular studies of each day' changed little for the vast majority of Ontario teenagers enrolled in academic programs during the 1920s. Amidst considerable fanfare in the fall of 1920, the provincial department of education established a Committee on High School Education, with a broad mandate to consider the implications of larger student numbers on the purposes and curriculum of the secondary school. Its 1921 report did lead to the elimination of tuition fees and the reduction of the high school course from six to five years. But its recommendations for the academic program were minor: a somewhat lighter course load, more options suited to local needs, and a slight easing of examination pressures. The committee of principals, inspectors, and university representatives was not prepared to follow the lead of its American counterpart, a committee of the National Education Association which recommended a social-service orientation in its 1918 report, *The Cardinal Principles of Secondary Education*. It did not translate the ideas of F.W. Merchant into recommendations for new courses bearing on education for leisure, for home-life, and for citizenship. Rather, the Ontario committee continued to put its faith in the traditional academic subjects as the best preparation for adult life.

As a result, the 1920s proved no different than earlier periods; despite alarming drop-out rates, most pupils – backed up by their parents – pinned their hopes on university matriculation. The result was an academic program mainly determined in the interests of the approximately 15 per cent of students who did proceed to some form of higher education – either university or normal school. This situation could have been justified if the matriculation courses were also those which served as 'preparation for life.' The academicians argued that they were; the critics charged that 'the predominantly formal trend of high school studies as they at present exist would seem to make this position untenable.'[77]

This formal trend manifested itself through the subjects of study, the methodology employed in the class-room, the prescribed textbooks, and the domination of final examinations. Students endured daily doses of English and history, ancient and modern languages, mathematics and science. There was no place for the new social-science disciplines, little opportunity to study the contemporary worlds of business or labour, or to examine the changing role of women in society. A few gifted teachers might use the traditional subjects to focus on these contemporary concerns. But most used a deductive rather than an inductive approach, starting with a prescribed body of knowledge that must be mastered rather than with the immediate interests of the students. The rationale continued to be based in part on the mental discipline argument of the 1880s; mathematics, for example, was justified on the basis of its 'training in quick, logical thinking.' There was also the strongly held belief that a fairly well-defined body of literary knowledge comprised the essential content of a liberal or general education. English and other languages, for instance, promised the student a 'broadening, cultural value ... [which was] a real asset to him in whatever business he may become engaged.'[78] Inspector A.J. Husband spoke for the majority of schoolmen when he argued that the subjects were designed 'not only to develop in the boys and girls the trained mind which is becoming more of an asset every day in the industrial and commercial world, but also to bring to them the refinement and culture that will be a constant source of satisfaction to them in life.'[79]

In the final analysis it was the examination system – particularly the externally set and externally graded examinations at the end of the upper-school year – that controlled the academic curriculum of the Ontario high school. These 'departmental' examinations were administered by the Joint Committee, consisting of university appointees and department of education personnel; all courses of study and textbooks were drawn up to meet these examination requirements. Academicians defended the formal examinations as the best test of a student's intellectual mastery and the best predictor of future success at university. Critics charged that they tested only one's ability to memorize factual information and were not an indicator of future success 'in life.' OSSTF president W.H. Tuke singled out the departmental examinations as 'foremost of the handicapping influences' in high school development, 'deadening initiative on the teacher's part ... and encouraging wrong ideals of work among the pupils.'[80] Yet when the provincial department suggested substituting teacher-set examinations at the end of the decade, the response was unfavourable. The universities refused to surrender their voice on the joint examining committee and were reluctant to trust their own graduates in the upper-school class-rooms to assume this responsibility. Local school-boards also relied on uniform external examinations; favourable results in comparison with other cities were always publicized as 'bearing testimony to the excellent organization and efficient teaching in our schools.'[81] But just as strong a resistance to change came from the high school teachers themselves. Although they spoke in terms of preserving standards, the basic problem was a lack of an individual and collective self-confidence in directing education affairs.

Most Ontario high school teachers felt more comfortable serving the demands of traditional scholarship than responding to the new social challenges of the 1920s. It was not that their middle-class backgrounds conflicted with community expectations of exemplary behaviour and lofty dedication to the cause; indeed this very background often made the teacher uncomfortable in the new social climate of the decade. He was expected to supervise a host of new extra-curricular activities, offer vocational guidance to his pupils, keep in touch with the burgeoning commercial and business orientation of the period – all in the name of social efficiency and citizen-making. 'Teachers as a class,' related principal A.M. Overholt of Brantford Collegiate in 1921, 'are men who pay their debts, keep out of the police court, out of the bankruptcy courts, lead quiet lives, read a great deal.'[82] But that was not good enough for Overholt. 'Too few of us know anything of the industrial life of the towns and cities in which we live ... Let us lift ourselves out of cold isolation and come into closer and more vital contact with our citizens, and let our pupils see that we have interests that extend beyond the confines of our classrooms.'[83]

The breadth of vision of new high school teachers was compromised in 1920 when the provincial government closed the faculties of education at Queen's and the University of Toronto and centralized all high school teacher training in the new Ontario College of Education. Department of education personnel – especially Superintendent John Seath – had never been happy with the two faculties of education created in 1907. Seath felt uneasy about this delegation of authority, preferring 'a provincial college of education to be controlled wholly by the Government.'[84] Particularly troublesome to Seath was the situation at Queen's, caused in part by personality clashes, high operating costs for a limited student enrolment, and conflicting views of the balance between theoretical and practical courses in the training of teachers. University of Toronto president Robert Falconer was convinced that his faculty 'would not have been attacked at all if it had not been that the Department of Education had designs on closing the Faculty at Queen's for several years.'[85] Nothing was done during Seath's lifetime, but the new United Farmers government, prompted by critical comment in the legislature on the relevancy of the training offered, closed the two faculties in the spring of 1920 and established the Ontario College of Education. While OCE was nominally a part of the University of Toronto, the department of education exercised real control, even over funds to be spent on class-room supplies. Dean William Pakenham held that the minister had 'as much control over the College of Education as the Normal School at Stratford.'[86] Principal R.B. Taylor of Queen's regretted the move, not only for his own university, but for the teaching profession in general. 'Even at its best, teaching is a narrowing profession, and the teachers will have still less outlook if they do not have the advantage of the give and take of university life.'[87]

But the closing of the two faculties of education was consistent with the inward-looking tendency that had historically characterized the Ontario department of education. There was to be no external professional challenge to departmental expertise during the decade of the 1920s. The educational aims of the post-war citizens' movements were quickly co-opted by the provincial department of education, while their political aims were successfully resisted. The Ontario Educational Association grew more fragmented than ever, as its teacher and trustee sections split over rural school reform proposals. Many teachers transferred their professional allegiance to their new federations; but like the OEA, the teachers' movement was so fragmented that any united front against the provincial bureaucracy was impossible. Nor could *The School*, the leading teachers' magazine, offer any consistent opposition. Edited by the OCE staff, *The School* was dependent on department of education financing. Typically, it cheered the department's move to abolish the position of superintendent of education in 1919 and applauded its re-creation four years later.

The new superintendent, F.W. Merchant, was a respected and even brilliant educationalist and administrator. There were few, however, in the provincial bureaucracy who could match Merchant's vision. Most were promoted from within the Ontario system, and were dedicated to preserving those virtues of centralization that had won international acclaim for the previous half-century. Fresh perspectives might have been provided through appointments from outside the ranks and the re-employment of persons who had gone beyond the province for graduate study in education. But the great mecca for such study in the 1920s was Teachers' College, Columbia University, the hotbed of progressive education. Not even Merchant could consider hiring Columbia graduates. 'Canadian teachers who are to be leaders in educational thought and practice should be trained in institutions permeated with British and Canadian sentiment.'[88] Thus the system would continue to be developed along traditional lines by those whom it had itself developed.

By the end of the 1920s public zeal for educational reform had dissipated. American educators had responded to the social challenges of the decade by altering both the curricular and extra-curricular components of the high school program – through courses in social studies and life-adjustment as well as through student councils, athletics, and the assembly hall. While Ontario schoolmen accommodated growing pressures for vocational guidance and a rich smorgasbord of extra-curricular activities, they held the line at the door of the academic class-room. 'With us the objectives of our high school course might be termed scholarship and character; in the American school their great objective might be stated as citizenship,' a Toronto principal told the OEA in 1922. 'Our objective seems to be largely individual, while theirs seems to be a social objective.'[89] The survival of this difference seemed evident at the end of the decade to Fred Clarke, a British educator with experience in both Canada and South Africa. Clarke believed that the Ontario high school had 'avoided the two main dangers that were set for it ... the English one of class privilege ... also the other one of too easy diversion from the high road of tradition in pursuit of the gaudy attractions of the up-to-date, or the values of the immediately vocational.'[90] Clarke was gratified that Canadian high schools had generally avoided 'the excesses of countless electives, of freak units, and of sentimental pandering to immature impulse and sheer whims among pupils, such as have marred high school work in the United States.'[91] There was, however, a price to be paid. The basic conservatism of the Ontario educational experience was a mixed blessing for students and society alike.

6 *Equality of Educational Opportunity*

I

While the urban high school of the 1920s forecast future developments in Ontario education, the rural elementary school confirmed the ever-present conservative tradition – a remembrance of things past. Every morning from early September till the end of June, some 200,000 country children arrived at the schoolhouse door – to learn their lessons, play with friends, and receive their social and moral preparation for responsible adult life. The school buildings had changed little in the half-century since Ryerson's retirement. Most were plain, rectangular structures of brick or stone, consisting of one class-room together with a small entry hall or cloak room where the children hung their coats and stowed their lunch boxes. The familiar wood stove dominated the back of the class-room, with teacher's desk and blackboard at the front. Depending on the annual harvest and the inclination of the trustees, a few dollars might be spent each year on interior or exterior painting, new library books or maps. A major change for many rural schools in the 1920s was the switch from double to single desks. But comforts such as central heating and indoor toilets were usually dismissed as too expensive or apt to spoil the children. The surrounding school-yard was usually a half-acre in size, containing two outdor privies, a well and an iron pump, often a woodshed, but no play apparatus.

Rural trustees frequently complained of how they were bound by the myriad of school laws, rules, and regulations built up over the previous half-century by provincial politicians and department of education officials. There seemed to be a regulation to cover everything – from the size and drainage of school sites, to the construction and fireproofing of buildings, to class-room space (16 square feet and 250 cubic feet per pupil), to the sanitary condition of the water closets and the water supply. All these were subject to an annual evaluation by the school inspector who had the power, if the grading were too low, to withhold provincial grants. Yet Queen's park officials were astute enough to realize that desired improvements could not outpace local perceptions of need. The inspector was cautioned to use his judgment in securing the necessary or desirable changes or additions having due regard to 'the interests of education, the capabilities of the present premises, and the financial abilities of the Boards.'[1] And local trustees and ratepayers continued to hold the power of the purse during the 1920s. They raised approximately 70 per cent of the money for operating costs and bore the full burden of capital expenses unless the price of a new school building exceeded 10 per cent of the assessment of the section.

Local trustees also had full control over the appointment of the teacher. Higher salaries, the lessened drain to the western provinces, and the greater number of high school graduates contributed to an abundant supply of elementary school teachers during the 1920s. 'If a school loses its teacher,' wrote Inspector E.W. Jennings of Victoria County, 'another is generally secured before I am aware of the vacancy and this without advertising.' Yet there was no greater premanency in the profession than there had been before the First World War. 'I do not think that more than three per cent of teachers who enter ever intend to make the work their profession,' complained Inspector W.J. Dallas of Kent County. 'With few exceptions those who teach do so only temporarily; the men until able to enter the university and the women until marriage.'[2] The average rural teacher had 4.3 years of experience at the beginning of the decade, and those years were frequently spread over more than one school. Sometimes the teacher moved on at the wishes of the trustees; perhaps her Christmas concert had not been satisfactory, or she had been judged too lenient with the majority of the pupils, or too strict with the trustees' own children. Sometimes she moved of her own volition, to better her financial position or her matrimonial prospects. 'A minimally attractive girl could hope to find a solvent husband in a matter of two or three years,' recalled John Galbraith of his boyhood days in Elgin County. 'If she didn't she moved on.'[3]

New teachers coming from the provincial normal schools were not totally unprepared for the demands of rural teaching. 'I live on a farm and attended a rural school myself so that the problems of a rural school will be familiar,' wrote one applicant for a position in Algoma District.[4] Throughout the 1920s, almost one-half of the normal-school students were farmers' daughters, products of country elementary and high schools. No fees were charged, and the $250 to $300 expense for room and board was within reach of most farm families with ambitions for their daughters. The strict normal-school rules no doubt pleased anxious parents. Students were told which normal school to attend, were forbidden to stay in non-authorized boarding houses, and were not allowed to dance at any official school functions. In the same way the uniformity of the normal-school curriculum and teaching styles prepared the new teacher to function within a uniform provincial program. The local inspector was expected to provide leadership and inspiration for the neophyte teacher. Although still an employee of the county, the inspector of the 1920s had to meet academic, professional, and experience requirements laid down by the provincial department of education and was a far cry from the amateur dilettante of the 1870s. Yet with more than 100 teachers to supervise, with trustee and ratepayer disputes to arbitrate, he rarely saw the teacher in the class-room more than twice a year.

As the decade of the 1920s continued, more and more country teachers found themselves taking on the advanced work necessitated by the growth of Fifth Book classes and continuation schools. The imprecise boundary between elementary and secondary schools encouraged this growth. Although elementary schools, both public and separate, normally ended with the Fourth Book – what later would be termed grade 8 – provision existed for them to offer the Fifth Book – the equivalent of the later grades 9 and 10. In fact, the local board was obliged to offer Fifth Book work if pupils who had passed the high school examination desired it, provided the school section was outside an established high school district. As prolonged school attendance became more prevalent, Fifth Book classes mushroomed throughout rural Ontario, from 431 schools at the beginning of the decade to 1,316 schools enrolling 6,618 pupils by 1930. Quality instruction was usually lacking, with immature and inexperienced teachers attempting to cover the first two years of high school work, dividing their already limited time over ten rather than eight grades. But these classes were inexpensive. One 1929 estimate claimed savings of $600,000 a year by conducting Fifth Book classes rather than sending pupils to regular high schools or collegiate institutes.[5]

While the back concessions spawned new Fifth Book classes, the small villages of Ontario turned their advanced classes into continuation schools. First established in 1896, continuation schools numbered 189 by 1923 – more than the total of high schools and collegiates – and grew to reach a peak of 220 in 1930. Most villages found continuation schools more attractive than regular high schools; they could easily be established by existing public school boards, could be partially staffed with lower-salaried elementary teachers, and did not require such a large outlay of funds for accommodation and equipment. The typical continuation school of the period was a two-teacher institution offering the four years of lower- and middle-school work to about fifty pupils. The school might have its own building, or else share accommodation with the village elementary school track meets, Hallowe'en parties, and Christmas concerts. These limited tory were usually missing, as teachers taught a limited curriculum on a shoe-string budget. Low enrolments naturally precluded many of the extra-curricular activities found in the large urban high schools, but the pupils had their inter-school track meets, Halloween parties, and Christmas concerts. These limited opportunities had to be balanced against the obstacles of sending the pupil into a city or town high school. The latter course of action was often financially prohibitive. It was also fraught with dangers of another kind, for the young person sent away to school, 'subject to other surroundings, customs and associates, and without parental control, care and influence, is being weaned away from home.'[6]

During his 1926 exchange visit in Ontario, British inspector E.G. Savage expressed surprise at finding such a large number of continuation school pupils taking French and Latin while so few took the 'practical' subjects. Savage had anticipated that 'these schools, serving rural areas, would have developed along lines more definitely related to the needs of the population rather than along the academic lines as set by the universities.'[7] But their development was no surprise to Ontario's own continuation school inspectors. 'The parents who send children to our Continuation Schools seem to desire education along the old established lines,' reported J.P. Hoag in 1921.[8] That year only 3 of 160 continuation schools offered agriculture – a proportion even lower than in the high schools and collegiate institutes. What Savage failed to grasp was that the curriculum was determined as much by local ambitions and perceptions as by the universities. Although agrarian leaders talked nobly of the need for the continuation schools to prepare more scientifically-oriented farmers, most parents and pupils viewed them as a means of escape from the limited employment opportunities of rural Ontario. Fifty per cent of their pupils in 1921 came from farms; only 17 per cent returned.[9] The rest went on to careers as teachers and nurses, office workers and salespersons, doctors and lawyers, and they soon scattered across the entire North American continent.

II

A 1922 pamphlet issued by the department of education laid two charges against the country schools: they were expensive and they were inefficient. Statistics showed a 'somewhat alarming' increase in the number of very small schools; some 482 out of 5,200 rural schools reported an enrolment of fewer than ten pupils. The financial loss in maintaining these schools was 'startling' – an average cost of $151.31 per pupil against $80.26 for the total province, with the bulk of the difference picked up by the local ratepayers. There were perceived social as well as financial losses. Inspector R.S. Miles of Lanark County concluded that 81 of his 120 schools had insufficient pupils to 'choose sides for a good game of baseball.'[10] Small size and high per-pupil costs made it difficult for rural schools to provide the more varied curriculum offered in the towns and cities; there was little physical education, manual training, or domestic science, and not much agriculture was taught. Support services were also lacking; there were few auxiliary classes and little evidence of medical and dental inspection in rural schools. 'This is unfair to the country boys and girls,' concluded the department. 'We should provide them not with what was good enough for their grandfathers many years ago, but what is the best obtainable educationally to-day.'[11]

While there was no empirical evidence on the ideal school size, Chief Inspector V.K. Greer suggested later in the decade that with less than fifteen 'there are not sufficient pupils to give that healthy stimulation which is needed, and that healthy spirit of rivalry which is essential for real success; and the teacher herself is not inspired to do her best work.' Greer suggested a 'desirable' enrolment of twenty to forty, a figure that was 'well above the norm so long as the seven square mile school section remained the standard pattern in rural Ontario.'[12] The problem was not a new one in the immediate post-war years, nor was the proposed solution. As part of his 1919 legislative package Education Minister Henry Cody had returned to the idea of school consolidation, first proposed by his predecessor Richard Harcourt fifteen years earlier. The Consolidated Schools Act of 1919 was permissive in nature, providing the mechanism whereby two or more school sections might unite for the purpose of constructing a larger consolidated school. Such a school was viewed by reformers as a panacea for most of the problems of rural education. A larger student enrolment would permit graded class-rooms and a broader curriculum, encourage the better teachers to remain in the countryside, and improve the quality of instruction. It would also address itself to the social concerns of rural areas by providing a community focus and enabling youngsters to complete their schooling close to home.

The new Wellington Consolidated School in Prince Edward County was reported in the fall of 1922 to be 'the finest consolidated school yet built.'[13] Each morning five school buses brought the rural children into the village to a building that boasted eight regular class-rooms, plus manual-training and domestic-science rooms, gymnasium and auditorium, library, and teachers' room. It offered instruction to the end of high school and provided the village with a luxurious community centre. The Wellington consolidation was prompted by necessity – the village and seven surrounding school sections all needed new buildings – and nurtured by the dogged efforts of the county school inspector, F.P. Smith. Yet Wellington was the exception rather than the rule. By 1925 only twenty-seven consolidations had been effected; these represented seventy-one school sections or slightly more than one per cent of the provincial total. Just one year after Cody's Consolidated Schools Act of 1919, departmental officials advised his successor, Education Minister R.H. Grant, that under current rural conditions consolidation would be 'impossible to secure either through the operation of voluntary effort or the enactment of Departmental regulations.'[14]

Fear of higher costs, dislike of transporting children long distances each day, and a natural resistance to change all helped kill consolidation. W.J. Goodfellow used his 1923 presidential address to the Rural Trustees' Section of the Ontario Educational Association to attack the supposed advantages of graded schools. 'Things are made too easy for the child. They come out like hot-house plants exposed to the winter weather.'[15] The following year the consolidated school was blamed for a host of real and imagined ills; the large attendance, for example, would 'make it more difficult to control epidemics, as the whole countryside is affected instead of one small section.' Meanwhile the one-room school acquired a lengthy list of virtues. 'Give them fair play,' concluded one trustee, 'and in the future as in the past the pupils from these little rural schools will make the province of Ontario the best place under heaven in which to dwell.'[16] As early as 1920, R.H. Grant realized that consolidation was not the answer to Ontario's rural school problem. 'The school section is the unit of administration which is closest to the people,' he wrote in his annual report, 'and those who compose it desire to know exactly what the substitute is before they abandon the present system.'[17]

Despite the physical limitations of the buildings and the intellectual short-comings of the teachers, most of rural Ontario in the 1920s put great faith in the country school. Many farmers considered that its limited offerings were all that was necessary in an agricultural environment – a minimal supplement to strong backs for the young boys and domestic talents for the girls. Other spokesmen simply listed the perceived social and moral advantages of the multi-graded rural class-room. 'The pupil is thrown more on his own resources and yet can have at intervals a personal supervision, direction and encouragement that the teacher in an urban school can hardly hope to give.' As for academic advantages, candidates from ungraded country schools passed the high school entrance examination at an average age of six months younger than town children, and then went on to hold their own in the high schools. 'The briefest survey of the college class lists and the younger professional groups in any town,' declared *The School*, 'would convince any unprejudiced inquirer that the Ontario rural school more than holds its own.'[18] More starry-eyed defenders saw its very simplicity and purity in terms of the agrarian myth. S.B. McCready, the former director of elementary agricultural education for Ontario, dedicated his 1920 textbook, *The School and Country Life*, 'to the girls and boys in the country schools who will in the great days that are to come make country life the sure foundation for sound democracy.'

Within the rural section, the school continued to be an object of sentimental attachment. It had always been there. There was an undeniable stability about it. 'What had once been an ingenious improvisation,' recalled John Galbraith, 'was by way of being considered part of the natural order of things.'[19] The names of section pioneers, long dead, remained carved on desk tops. In its log-book were recorded the names of the few boys and girls who had reached positions of distinction. A half-dozen thus recorded from the years were cherished as evidence that the school which had produced these prodigies must necessarily be an excellent one. The decade following the First World War saw the one-room country schoolhouse at the peak of its long career. It had accommodated the reforms of the Whitney government and survived the dislocations of the war. Now it would make its last triumphant stand, prior to the onslaught of economic depression, rural depopulation, and the centralizing tendencies of Queen's Park.

From 1919 to 1923, rural school reform was sustained at the political level by the United Farmers' government. No political party had enunciated its educational policy so precisely: 'To provide equal educational opportunities for all the children ... by greatly extending and improving educational facilities in rural districts.' Agriculture Minister Manning Doherty hoped that an improved rural school would not 'point the young folk to the cities, but enable them to get a fairly complete education in the country.'[20] Agricultural schools were established at Ridgetown and Kemptville, grants for rural teachers' salaries rose from 40 to 70 per cent, a director of rural school organization was named, and consolidated schools and continuation schools were encouraged. Yet the thrust for change was short-lived. 'It is a significant fact that Mr. Drury in his earliest speeches as Prime Minister had much to say of an educational awakening,' declared the *Canadian Forum* in 1922. 'It is equally significant that during the past two years he has been almost silent on the subject.'[21] Perhaps the turning point came as early as February 1920, when the government declined an offer from Vincent Massey to finance a comprehensive survey of the Ontario school system. Massey was suspect to a farmer government because of his family's involvement in the agricultural implement business. Besides, the idea of any external commission was anathema to departmental officials and to the cautious UFO minister of education – R.H. Grant. The year 1923, however, saw a new political leader emerge with yet another proposal to solve the rural school 'problem.'

III

Premier Howard Ferguson kept the education portfolio for himself following the victory of his Conservative party in the 1923 provincial election. Political observers both then and later have attributed this move largely to Ferguson's desire to watch over and solve the contentious bilingual school question.[22] Yet the new premier saw a very practical reason for hanging on to education. 'There is an army of people in the province who occupy a position more or less unique – teachers, supervisors and inspectors are closely in touch with community life.' It was politically advantageous for a busy premier to keep in touch with such people.[23] It was also politically beneficial for Ferguson to associate his name directly with the major thrust of the provincial department of education during the 1920s – extending equality of educational opportunity. Ferguson told the 1924 Easter meeting of the OEA that he was 'intensely interested in the development of further educational opportunities out in the country. We have to take more education to the doors of the people.' Ferguson's support for extending educational opportunity brought different things to different sections of the province. For the urban centres, it meant more money for auxiliary classes and vocational schools. For the rural communities – 'I have always been more closely in touch with rural education, I confess, than I have been with urban education' – it meant larger grants for Fifth Book classes and continuation schools.[24] For Northern Ontario it meant a series of imaginative responses to the challenge of geographic distance. It would even lead to a better deal for the bilingual English-French schools.

While few Ontarians questioned the principle of extended educational opportunity, many took issue with particular applications of it. Indeed, by 1925, the battle lines had been firmly drawn on two of Ferguson's more controversial reform proposals – the township school-board and the transfer of the first year of university work to selected high schools. Neither idea originated with Ferguson. Township school-boards, for example, had been permitted under Ryerson's 1871 school act. Although five had been formed at that time, only one in Morrison Township of Muskoka District survived till the 1920s. Yet the proposal had been revived periodically as a means of ending the inequalities and limited opportunities provided by the three-member, one-school section boards in rural Ontario. Ferguson raised the issue in his first annual report of 1923, then prepared the ground for action the following year. 'The present situation is too serious to be permanent and ... some measure of dealing with it must be found,' he wrote at the end of 1924. He promised 'a central board without destroying the representation of school sections' and added that 'no desire exists to force upon the Province a change in its educational structure which has not popular support.'[25]

April 1925 was the crucial month, as the township school-board plan was formally introduced and effectively killed within a two-week period. Introducing the bill in the legislature on 1 April, Premier Ferguson made his case on grounds of extending educational opportunity. 'The country pupil is not getting as good a chance educationally as the city pupil,' he argued. 'It is my earnest desire to have such conditions provided in the schools that the youth of rural communities may have equal opportunity with those of the towns and cities.'[26] The bill provided for permissive, as opposed to mandatory, township organization, with the ultimate decision put to a vote of the ratepayers. If approved, township boards of from three to ten members would replace the small school sections. Although opposition was not pronounced in the legislature, Ferguson withdrew the bill after second reading to give interested parties a chance to study it and offer constructive criticisms. The most interested parties were the rural trustees themselves, prepared to gather for the annual OEA convention in Toronto. They came, not to study or offer constructive assistance, but to defeat the proposal.

Once the weak sister of the OEA, the trustees' section was by the early 1920s the largest and often the noisiest group within the association. Trustees felt threatened both by the rise of the teachers' federations and by the moves of the department towards consolidation and larger units of local administration. In response they opened their section membership to ratepayers so as to enlist taxpayer support, launched a province-wide journal, and began holding annual county conventions to encourage grassroots participation. On the evening of 14 April most of the 1,009 registered delegates among the rural trustees crowded into Convocation Hall of the University of Toronto to hear the premier address the general membership. Ferguson spoke again of equal educational opportunity, suggesting that both teachers and trustees 'talk up the bill over the next year and when you come back here next year you will be able to give us some sound advice on the subject.'[27] But the trustees were not prepared to wait that long, many believing that Ferguson 'would ram it through at the next session regardless.'[28] The following morning the rural trustees set aside their regular agenda for an emergency discussion of the bill. Close to noon a motion was put from the floor opposing the bill. The vote was immediately taken, the motion carried, and the session hastily adjourned. The trustees had won the first round of the battle.

Department officials were stunned but not completely taken by surprise. Deputy Minister A.H.U. Colquhoun jokingly advocated modifications to the criminal code, especially 'the clause respecting murder so that I could dispose of the whole Trustee Association after due notice to their families.'[29] Chief Director F.W. Merchant never expected to convert local trustees 'because you can scarcely expect them to commit suicide.' He was more interested in the position of the rural parents and taxpayers. 'What about the ratepayers who are behind those boards? They are the people whose opinions we wish to get.'[30] So in June, Ferguson circulated a copy of the bill with an explanation of the government's position to 'those interested in rural education' in order to 'clear up misconceptions.' The premier argued vigorously that township boards would not 'take away from the people control of their schools'; they would not 'be the thin edge of the wedge for the establishment of consolidated schools' since that decision would still be a local one. Furthermore the plan would not increase costs – 'one of my main reasons for proposing the scheme is to *reduce* the cost.' Again, he asked for constructive criticism and not 'merely an expression of your disapproval,' and urged his readers to keep uppermost in their minds the welfare of their children.[31]

Events of 1925 established the pattern that would continue for the next four years. Each year until 1929, Ferguson introduced the township school-board bill into the legislature, only to withdraw it 'for further consideration' before a vote was taken on second reading. Each year he praised its virtues in his address of welcome to the OEA, only to have the rural trustees' section overwhelmingly condemn it. As one thoughtful trustee analysed the situation, the head-on clash resulted largely from the fact that both the statement of and the solution to the rural school 'problem' had been imposed from without. 'The people are in fact fairly well satisfied with the present system and while they are not unconscious of its minor defects, they have never felt the need of any radical change,' wrote Sydney Williams. Because the suggestion came from 'sources entirely apart from the rank and file of the people,' Williams was not surprised that 'it should meet with opposition before ever it was judged on the strength of its merits or demerits.' People opposed the bill because they did not 'realize the need of a change ... The serious problems the Bill aims to solve are not real to the body of the people.'[32] Ottawa public school inspector J.H. Putman could readily identify with the thinking of his Lincoln County boyhood that continued to dominate rural residents. 'All sensible people do like to manage their own affairs and especially the affairs that touch them intimately,' he wrote during the height of the controversy. 'They have sprung from the race proud of its freedom. They are a people who would rather that half the things they do were wrongly done than that they should do the right thing through compulsion.'[33]

Ferguson was an astute politician. He realized the danger of forcing provincial change on an unwilling rural electorate. 'I am not going to arbitrarily impose this scheme upon the ratepayers unless it is acceptable,' he replied to one opponent who criticized his apparent dictatorial urge.[34] Instead, he turned to another aspect of school re-organization – the transfer of first-year university work to selected high schools. After praising the work of the Fifth Book classes and continuation schools in an address to the OEA, Ferguson casually remarked that he did 'not know why almost every public school should not have an extended course.' When that remark drew the applause of the delegates, Ferguson went on to a more controversial point. 'I do not know why the first year's work in the University should not be done in certain first-class schools out in the country.'[35] This was the first public exposure of what the University of Toronto would vilify as 'the premier's proposal.' Ferguson, Merchant, and other departmental officials gave this plan a high priority during the remainder of the decade. 'We will take the first year university work and place it in the high school,' the premier stubbornly proclaimed five years after the first pronouncement.[36] Unlike the township school-board controversy, Ferguson made no deference to local autonomy and university freedom. But the university professors were not unlike rural school trustees; when cornered in their own backyard they were prepared to fight.

Ferguson argued the scheme on the bases of costs, convenience, and equality of opportunity. The financing of a year's university work for a promising young person 'can be substantially reduced to the individual parent by extending the courses of study in certain local centres that are properly equipped for that purpose.'[37] The proposal would also counteract the growing impersonality of higher education. Ferguson believed that universities had become so large that 'it was utterly impossible to give much personal attention to the individual student.' Courses were laid down and the undergraduates pursuing them were 'turned out much as a big industry carries on mass production.'[38] This impersonality, claimed the premier, led to a high attrition rate at the end of the first year, and a reluctance on the part of the drop-outs to return to their home communities once they had had a taste of city life. All the accompanying social and vocational problems, however, would be substantially reduced if higher training were available close to home. Underlying the entire argument was the thrust for equal educational opportunity. Ferguson claimed that at least 50 per cent of the University of Toronto's students came from that city. Western's dean of arts produced similar figures for London students, and speculated that more students from Kingston attended Queen's than went from Hamilton to all universities combined.[39]

University of Toronto President Robert Falconer was not completely adverse to the proposal. He had always believed that 'the Arts degree ... should be kept within the reach of as many as possible.'[40] Falconer also saw Ferguson's plan as preventing 'the waste and the disabilities that attend to so much of the education of this Continent.'[41] But among members of the Faculty of Arts, the subject was judged to be 'the most important and critical question since the new university act of 1906.' According to the faculty council, the proposal would destroy the integral relationship of the four years of the honours course. University work was best done in a university atmosphere, where there was 'more opportunity for originality and initiative in teaching,' a greater variety of subjects available, and where out-of-town students could benefit from the advantages of residence life.[42] Professor W.J. Alexander charged that the scheme would be too costly for local school-boards, would only 'postpone the sifting to the close of the Second Year – a disastrously late period,' and would mean that the curriculum would be shaped by the bulk of the high school teacher's work, 'and this work must be done with school-boys and school-girls.'[43]

Ferguson pushed harder with his university proposal than he did with the township school-board bill. At the end of December 1926, he wrote Falconer wanting information on what steps the University had taken to meet this 'suggestion' since the government had decided on this proposal as a matter of policy and 'I am exceedingly anxious that this scheme should be put into effect at the beginning of the term of 1927.' Falconer replied that he was unable to overcome faculty opposition because 'the matter is so encompassed with difficulties.'[44] From that point on, both sides dug in their heels and gave no sign of any willingness to seek a compromise. Ferguson kept the idea alive through the 1929 election campaign, but – as with the township school-board issue – met defeat at the hands of a vested interest which argued its case very persuasively. A compromise solution of sorts was finally reached after Ferguson left the premier's office, when in 1931 the University of Toronto put into effect the requirement of honour matriculation or upper-school graduation for entrance into the Arts program. The change reduced the pass course in Arts to three years, ended admission at the end of middle school, and effectively transferred a year of study to the high schools and collegiate institutes. Although accomplished on the university's own terms so as to solve 'the problem of increasing numbers and consequent overcrowding,' it was consistent with Howard Ferguson's original proposal.

IV

Rebuffed on the issue of the township school-board and the transfer of university work, Ferguson finally tasted victory on the French-language school question. He was the first to admit that the infamous Regulation 17 of 1912 – the measure he had supported so vigorously as a back-bencher in the Whitney administration – simply was not working and was never likely to work. Throughout the 1910s and early 1920s a large number of supposedly bilingual schools – particularly in the rural parts of Prescott and Russell counties – openly defied Regulation 17 and functioned primarily as French-instruction schools. Inspector J.C. Walsh reported in the fall of 1922 that he had been denied entrance to twenty-nine of forty-five schools. As for another twenty-eight schools on his list, 'I fear I shall be refused in most of them.'[45] The department of education could have withheld provincial grants in such a situation, but Ferguson was quick to point out that in a small country school the grants did not amount to a great deal and the church authorities usually made up the difference and carried on the school.[46] The result was that, instead of introducing youngsters to the English language, Regulation 17 had led to a stubborn defence of the mother tongue and a continued inferior level of schooling for many Franco-Ontarians. Once a strong supporter of restrictive measures, Ferguson by the mid-1920s was anxious to find a way of improving rather than eliminating the bilingual schools.

A negative defiance of Regulation 17 was only one part of the campaign conducted by L'Association canadienne française de l'éducation d'Ontario during the early 1920s. At least as effective was ACFEO's support of a positive alternative to the restrictive measure of 1912. The alternative was simply that a second language could best be introduced to elementary school pupils by using, not suppressing, the mother tongue. So ACFEO supported 'free schools' in Pembroke, Green Valley, and Windsor. And with the co-operation of the University of Ottawa it instituted its own bilingual high school entrance examinations and its own normal school. This independent teachers' college was crucial to the ACFEO campaign, since the four existing English-French model schools were viewed as agents of anglicization, designed to prepare teachers to implement the detested Regulation 17. Meanwhile Senator N.A. Belcourt had resumed the presidency of ACFEO and begun a diplomatic campaign to win support from influential groups of English-speaking Canadians. One group very willing to co-operate was the Unity League of Ontario – a group of progressive academics and young professionals. In 1922 the Unity League commissioned the aging James Hughes to report on the progress of bilingual schools in Ottawa. Although a prominent Orangeman, Hughes was sympathetic to the French language, and his report stressed positive accomplishments rather than weaknesses.

A key figure in the Unity League was Professor C.B. Sissons of Victoria University. A cousin and close friend of UFO Premier E.C. Drury, Sissons helped pave the way for a series of discussions between ACFEO officials and the government. Despite Drury's assertion that 'he regarded it as one of the two or three most important tasks before him,'[47] the solution of the bilingual school problem remained beyond his grasp. There was the usual opposition of the Orange Lodge to contend with, the caution of a new and inexperienced government, plus the fear that the leader of the Conservative opposition, Howard Ferguson, would exploit any settlement for political advantage. But the main stumbling-block appears to have been the UFO minister of education, R.H. Grant. 'Right at the outset the minister warned his chief not to expect anything from him,' related Sissons, 'since he represented a county with 87 Orange Lodges.'[48] Sissons noted later that 'Grant was averse to grappling with the question, and told Drury once in my presence that some one else would have to be minister if Regulation 17 was rescinded.'[49] This threat of resignation was enough to tie the premier's hands, since Grant's departure might have precipitated a political crisis among the UFO.

There was little indication in the summer of 1923 that Howard Ferguson's electoral victory was the first step towards a resolution of the issue. This was the man who had introduced the notorious 'English only' resolution into the provincial legislature in 1911 and who had led the government defence of Regulation 17 during the war. 'There is no man in public life in Canada who can more fully be trusted,' declared the *Orange Sentinel.*[50] ACFEO officials were equally certain of no amelioration; 'I hope this is only a bad dream,' lamented Belcourt.[51] Ferguson's retention of the education portfolio was dictated in part by his own awareness of the explosive potential of the bilingual schools issue. Already convinced of the futility of Regulation 17, he nevertheless kept his thoughts to himself throughout 1923 and early 1924, 'so long as smouldering fires are periodically stirred up and break into fresh flame.'[52] Yet the conciliatory efforts of ACFEO and the Unity League were beginning to pay dividends, and towards the end of 1924 Ferguson was carefully making preparations to move. An exchange of correspondence between two members of the League in November suggested that Ferguson 'was going to go very much further than we could possibly imagine.'[53]

Ferguson was moving towards a position of bilingual school improvement rather than bilingual school abolition. This position was as educationally sound as always, but hardly politically opportune in the mid-1920s. The public announcement of the policy change came in April 1925, during a debate in the legislature on bilingual instruction. After reiterating that his major aim was to see the English language adequately taught to every pupil in the schools of Ontario, Ferguson suggested that how this could be done had to be determined. Then came the bombshell. 'I am not wedded to Regulation 17 and I do not think the Department is ... If our methods can be improved upon I am perfectly frank in saying that it is the duty of the Government to take that into consideration and accept suggestions.' There would be a comprehensive survey of the whole situation, whose purpose would be to suggest better methods for Franco-Ontarians to secure their education in English.[54] Ferguson gave the province six months to digest this and, when opposition failed to develop, announced the make-up of the survey commission in early October. The chairman would be F.W. Merchant, the much-respected senior department of education official, now making his third survey of English-French schools in the province. To assist Merchant, Ferguson wisely chose Judge J.H. Scott of Perth, an Orangeman who had previously defended Regulation 17, and Louis Coté, an Ottawa lawyer who had never been close to ACFEO.

For two years the Merchant Commission busied itself gathering statistics on the English-French schools of the province, visiting some 843 class-rooms in 330 schools. Its September 1927 report was a condemnation of the level of achievement in schools where French was used as a teaching language. Conditions in the bilingual separate schools of Cochrane and Hearst were typical of what the commissioners found: every staff member was a teaching sister on a temporary certificate, unauthorized French-language history and geography textbooks were used, and French continued as the major language of instruction through to the Senior Fourth class. Such a situation produced depressing results: lack of proficiency in reading and writing in both languages; poor achievement in arithmetic because of an undue amount of time spent on languages; and few pupils surviving through to the high school entrance examination.[55] Statistically, the Merchant report confirmed that the Cochrane-Hearst pattern was repeated throughout the province: only 13.5 per cent of the teachers held first- or second-class certificates (the bulk of them in the Ottawa and Windsor urban schools), English reading was unsatisfactory in 70 per cent of the schools, and arithmetic unsatisfactory in 65 per cent.[56]

These findings were not new, merely duplicating the results of Merchant's earlier report in 1911. Nor were the recommendations; again Merchant called for better training and closer personal supervision of the teachers. What was new was the government's acceptance of improvement of bilingual teaching rather than its restriction. 'We must rely more upon the personal influence brought to bear upon our schools by means of sympathetic and helpful advice and supervision and efficient teaching,' Ferguson announced to the press the day after Merchant's report was released, 'rather than upon ... general rules which do not and cannot possibly provide for the great variety of conditions that exist.'[57] The new policy involved a legitimization and upgrading of the University of Ottawa's Normal School, and the creation of a special departmental committee, consisting of the chief inspector and new directors of English and French instruction, to consider each bilingual school case in consultation with the local inspector. Regulation 17 remained on the books till 1944, but from 1927 on it was a dead letter. No longer was any attempt made to dictate the stage at which French could be used for instruction or studied as a subject; the end would be emphasized rather than the means.

The reaction of English-speaking Ontarians to the new policy of 1927 was favourable. Although Ferguson was giving the French language a new position in the province's schools, there were few who bothered to object and still fewer who seemed determined to make an issue of the decision. The conciliatory efforts of the Unity League and ACFEO itself helped pave the way for public acceptance of the settlement; there was also relief that an issue so damaging to national unity had finally been resolved. Even more important was Ferguson's own argument that the policy itself had not been changed – every child was to leave school with some measure of fluency in English – but that a more satisfactory means of implementing that policy had been determined. Ferguson was undoubtedly motivated by a combination of political and educational factors. The solution of such a long-standing problem in national unity did guarantee him the Franco-Ontarian vote, improve Conservative party fortunes in Quebec, and advance his candidacy as a potential national party leader. Yet despite these political overtones, Ferguson saw the problem as an educational issue: how to advance educational opportunity for the province's tens of thousands of French-speaking pupils. Regulation 17 had driven them out of the schools ill-prepared to face the challenges of twentieth-century society. The new procedures were designed to encourage attendance and raise the educational skills and vocational opportunities of an important provincial minority. In any case, Ferguson confided to a friend in 1929 that he hoped 'there will be no further French question in our schools.'[58]

The new policy survived the resignation of Howard Ferguson in 1930 and continued under the administration of his successor, George Henry, premier and minister of education for the next four years. Henry told ACFEO secretary Edmond Cloutier that he was determined to give a fair trial to the recommendations in the hope that 'this policy can be maintained in all its essentials without hindrance.'[59] To oversee the operation, Henry kept veteran investigator Frederick Merchant on the departmental payroll as chief adviser, four years after his official retirement as chief director of education. By the time of his final departure in 1934, Merchant could report considerable progress. Sixty per cent of the teachers now held first- or second-class certificates, while teachers without valid certificates had vanished from the scene. Better teachers meant improved pupil learning in both languages, higher retention rates, more French-speaking pupils proceeding through the high schools and, to come full circle, a pool of improved candidates for the University of Ottawa Normal School. 'From the very nature of the problem, progress must necessarily be slow,' Merchant confided to Henry, 'but it has been much more rapid than I expected, especially in supplying the fundamental need for a larger body of qualified teachers.'[60] This statement was a fitting conclusion to the lengthy career of this veteran Ontario educator, whose French-speaking father had changed the family name from Marchand to Merchant when young Frederick was a boy.[61]

V

Bilingual schools, township school-boards, and the university proposal all provided exciting copy for the province's newspapers, but Ferguson had a number of other projects underway within the department of education. Each addressed itself to the central concern of educational opportunity and each possessed a popular appeal that the politically astute premier was quick to exploit. Nowhere was this more evident than with the 'schools on wheels' – the railway-car schools that began serving the isolated bush settlements of northern Ontario. The idea for these peripatetic schools originated with J.B. MacDougall, a veteran northern educator who in 1919 became assistant chief inspector of schools with particular responsibility for the North. After documenting the many conventional attempts to educate 'hundreds of children unhappily placed' in the northern wilderness, MacDougall concluded his 1922 annual report with a call for 'added devices and a special policy ... such as the travelling school or itinerant teacher.'[62] He found a receptive listener in Ferguson, who saw immediately that railway-car schools could be incorporated into his own master plan for extending educational opportunity. Ferguson had a special affinity for the North, dating back to his 1914 appointment as minister of lands, forests, and mines in the Hearst cabinet. Here was an opportunity to fulfill his oft-repeated assertion that he was 'exceedingly anxious to do everything possible to promote educational facilities in Northern Ontario.'[63]

The twentieth of September 1926 was a red-letter day in Nandair, a tiny hamlet on the Canadian National transcontinental railway line, five miles north of Capreol. That day the first railway-car school opened for business with Fred Sloman as teacher, and nine previously un-schooled youngsters as pupils. Six days later a CNR engine picked up the car and moved it north to Anstice, the next stop along the line. Thus began a pattern that lasted almost forty years and at one period included seven such schools on wheels. There is little doubt that the school cars fulfilled their primary function of providing basic schooling for isolated youngsters in the North. It was quite common for children to travel up to twenty miles to attend classes – often by boat in the good weather and by snowshoes, dog team, or skis in winter. There were oft-repeated stories of an Indian boy who came thirty-two miles by canoe with a week's supply of food, and of two young brothers, ages nine and eleven, who came forty miles, set up a tent in mid-winter, thatched it with balsam boughs, and camped out in below-freezing weather. Denied schooling for so long, the children often made rapid progress once the opportunity was available. No records exist of the total number of youngsters who went on from the travelling class-rooms to complete their high school education in the larger towns and cities, but Sloman alone is said to have 'graduated' more than 500 during his forty-year career.[64]

The same year as the schools on wheels made their first visits to Nandair and Anstice, department of education correspondence courses first penetrated the North. Ontario was some years behind the western provinces in this aspect of educational extension work, as traditional school inspectors argued that this approach 'would not adequately meet the needs of children who were out of reach of a school.'[65] But in 1922 a concerted campaign was begun by the Associated Boards of Trade of Northern Ontario, picked up by another vision-ary northern Ontario inspector, Neil McDougall, and ultimately given the stamp of approval by Premier Ferguson. Beginning in early 1926, correspon-dence lessons were sent out from Toronto to children on the 'frontier fringe' – those in isolated settlements of the near and far North beyond the reach of organized schools – as well as to physically-disabled, home-bound youngsters, and adults who would not feel comfortable sitting in an elementary class-room. Interest grew steadily, so that by the time of the Second World War some 2,500 pupils were enrolled up to the end of grade 10; many were completing the grades faster than pupils in regular class-rooms and more than holding their own on high school entrance and lower-school departmental examinations. Although far less spectacular than the schools on wheels, the correspondence courses were estimated to have cost one-eighth the total price for the school cars, and to have served eight times as many people during their first ten years of operation.[66]

The extension of educational opportunity in the 1920s meant more than bringing the child to the school, or taking the school to the child. Central to the campaign was the belief that if the child were to benefit academically, he must first enjoy good health. But except for some pioneering work in Peel and Lincoln counties, school medical and dental inspection had not spread beyond the urban centres of Ontario by the end of the First World War. Prompted by interest from the Women's Institute and the department of agriculture, the provincial educa-tion department in 1919 undertook a comprehensive survey of the health needs of rural schools. Results from the first county surveyed gave some indication of the extent of need: of seventy schools, only six were properly heated and only three adequately lighted; of 2,539 pupils, only seventy-three were free of medical defects.[67] The problem seemed to rest in the weakness of the rural school section and the rural municipality; the solution pointed to a transfer of public health responsibility from local to provincial control. The education department assumed full responsibility in 1922, but two years later control was vested in the department of health as the effort to improve the health of schoolchildren was subsumed by the much wider campaign of infant and child health.

The decade of the 1920s also saw thousands of mentally and physically handicapped youngsters taking advantage of auxiliary classes for the first time. The school's responsibility for training the mentally handicapped – roughly those with IQs between fifty and seventy-five, and known as the 'feeble-minded' – was no longer in question. A provincial report in 1919 called for compulsory medical examinations for all school beginners as a means of identifying the feeble-minded ones, followed by compulsory assignment of such pupils to segregated training classes. Later that year a survey of Guelph public school pupils revealed that some 3.5 per cent would benefit from such special instruction.[68] Classes began to mushroom in Ontario's larger cities and towns during the next decade, as a healthy economy and larger provincial grants saw equality of educational opportunity translated from ideal to practice. For the first time, too, the movement had effective leadership. S.B. Sinclair was brought out of retirement in 1920 to serve as provincial inspector of auxiliary classes; the former principal of Ottawa Normal School was a trained psychologist and had devoted many years to child study and the New Education movement. Eight years later, Ontario boasted some 207 auxiliary classes, of which 152 were for educable mentally-retarded pupils, although Sinclair himself was the first to publicize the unmet needs of some 2,500 retarded rural pupils.

There was less public support for special classes for children at the opposite end of the mental scale – the gifted. Provincial regulations of 1917 recognized fourteen types of auxiliary classes, including 'advancement classes for children who are far above the average both physically and mentally,' but London was the only centre to give consistent support to such classes from 1928 through to the 1950s. Here a carefully selected group of pupils in the upper elementary grades received enriched instruction in the academic subjects, plus French, typing, public speaking, drama, choral speaking, and student government. The pupils planned much of their own timetable, worked through much of the curriculum on their own, and participated in group projects. 'The man in the street was sure a race of prigs would be engendered,' wrote London's two advancement class teachers. 'Some have said that these classes are only for the rich people. But the number of homes where the income is less than average is greater than the number where the income is above average.'[69] Yet the London board was constantly charged with establishing an intellectual élite, a practice incompatible with democratic principles. Opposition increased during the depression years, when the classes were considered a costly luxury, and the London experiment survived only through the determination of the two teachers and the insistence of Inspector G.A. Wheable. Elsewhere in the province, the gifted child had to make do with early promotion, grade acceleration, and ability grouping.

VI

Greater educational opportunity for all Ontario children was a constant source of pride to Howard Ferguson during his seven years as premier and minister of education from 1923 to 1930. Although many of the specific developments owed much to local initiative and to a buoyant economy, Ferguson did not hesitate to identify his government with these advances during the provincial election campaigns of 1926 and 1929. There was the steady rise of the urban high school, with its expanding opportunities for vocational education. There was the resolution of the bilingual school controversy. The railway-car schools – and to a lesser extent the correspondence courses – attracted international press coverage and caught the fancy of city-bound residents of southern Ontario. Improved medical inspection services and auxiliary-class funding showed a concern for the physically and mentally handicapped. The new Ontario Training School for Boys at Bowmanville replaced the old, prison-like industrial schools of the 1880s, and a new apprenticeship act in 1928 helped bridge the gap between vocational schools and the world of work. What did it matter if university personnel turned down Ferguson's plan to transfer the first year of arts and science instruction to the high schools? The very proposal had demonstrated his concern for extending educational opportunity at the local level. Nor did the furor over the township school-board issue hurt him; Ferguson's reputation as a concerned educator and an astute politician was assured when he withdrew the legislation. Meanwhile rural education benefitted from a new two-year normal-school course and a steady increase in the number of Fifth Book classes and continuation schools.

Equality of educational opportunity was a catchy political slogan. But there was also a strong philosophical commitment on the part of Howard Ferguson – a mixture of liberal idealism and social conservatism. He certainly saw greater loyalty and patriotism as important by-products of extended educational opportunity. 'It is one of the problems of the Department of Education,' he wrote, 'to lay down in its schools, principles and methods that will bring about cohesion, unity of spirit and purpose amongst all our people.'[70] This could be accomplished partly through the history curriculum, where a new public school textbook 'designedly written in simple story form' and with 'a romantic tinge' would interest the children in their country's past.[71] Empire Day had a special role to play as it provided schoolchildren with an opportunity for studying 'the greatness of the British Empire' and for proving that 'you have the right stuff in you.'[72] Loyalty and unity were especially important to Ferguson in the schools of northern Ontario, an area heavily populated with continental European immigrant families and supposedly ripe for Bolshevik propaganda and agitation. Throughout 1928 and 1929 there were continual stories out of north-western Ontario that certain schools were being used as centres for the distribution of communistic literature. Ferguson had his departmental officials and local school inspectors constantly on the alert to track down such rumours. And he used the opportunity to promote the nation-building possibilities of the railway-car schools. The system was 'exercising a wholesome Canadianizing influence all along the lines' as 'communities are being wrought over into the fabric of loyal Canadian citizenship.' The next generation would fall naturally into their places as loyal citizens since 'Bolshevik propaganda finds no place or acceptance wherever the school car operates.'[73]

There were the usual criticisms of the provincial department of education during the 1920s – the bureaucratic structure, the centralized control, and the plethora of rules and regulations on minute matters. Visiting British schoolmen such as exchange inspector E.G. Savage and teacher-educator Fred Clarke were quick to single out these characteristics. Clarke considered the provincial bureaucrats as something like a 'Central Departmental Providence, dispensing standardized blessings to a docile population' and doubted whether this was 'really the last word in human reason.'[74] Many Ontario educators undoubtedly shared such views, but their natural hesitancy and worry over job security kept them quiet. One exception was William L. Grant, who as principal of the independent Upper Canada College did not depend on departmental favours. Like his father, Principal George Munro Grant of Queen's, a generation before, he called for fresh ideas and new blood within the department to overcome 'the trades union and closed shop' mentality. 'Our Ontario educational system won a medal for efficiency at the Chicago World's Fair in 1893,' he told the OEA, 'and since then it has tended to sit like Endymion, wrapt in the contemplation of its own perfection.'[75]

Yet Ferguson placed full confidence in his senior officials, referring to education as 'the best organized department in the public service.'[76] He credited the efficient operation to A.H.U. Colquhoun, who as deputy minister since 1905 provided a large measure of stability. While Colquhoun handled administrative matters, chief director F.W. Merchant developed policy positions for Ferguson's approval. Working closely with Merchant at the end of the decade were V.K. Greer as chief public and separate school inspector and George F. Rogers as senior high school inspector. University of Toronto officials dubbed this trio the 'Queen's Own,' because of an alleged favouritism shown towards their alma mater in Kingston. It would have been equally appropriate to call them the 'London Mafia,' since all cut their administrative teeth with the London Board of Education which had earned praise for its highly innovative system. Ferguson placed particular confidence in Merchant – who seemed to have inherited the power and knowledge once possessed by John Seath, without Seath's abrasive personality. Merchant 'knows more about the problems than anyone else,' Ferguson confided to his successor, George Henry. 'If you could hear what educational people over here (i.e., England) have to say about him – that he is the biggest man in education in the real sense anywhere in Canada.'[77]

This respect seems to have been mutual. When Ferguson stepped down in late 1930, Judge J.H. Scott of Perth told him he had been assured 'time and time again, by the chief officials of the department, that its business has never been so satisfactorily administered as under your direction.'[78] Despite the battles over bilingual schools, township school-boards, and the university proposal, Ferguson enjoyed his seven years as minister. And his record was generally satisfactory. Although English-French tensions continued, he had at least ended the fifteen-year-old cultural strife that dated from Regulation 17 in 1912. Although his township school-boards and university proposals had gone down in flames, Ferguson kept the ideal of educational opportunity before the population and supported local initiatives in this regard. As a successful politician, he saw distinct advantages in not bull-dozing ideas through stubborn local opposition. On one occasion he was reported as saying that the school act would be changed 'just as quickly as the people will let it'; at another time he cautioned against departmental interference in what he considered the business of the local school-boards.[79] 'If I haven't done anything else,' he declared, referring to his tenure as minister of education, 'I have attracted public attention to education and put some energy into it.'[80]

7 The Ontario Taxpayer and the Depression

Economic disaster did not hit the schools of Ontario in any sharp, dramatic way in the months immediately following the New York stock market crash of October 1929. The depression was more like a slowly advancing wave – turned back at the schoolhouse door with varying degrees of success in September 1930 and September 1931, before sweeping over the educational scene in 1932-3. The immediate effects were obvious – fewer jobs for school graduates, crowded class-rooms for drop-outs coming back to avoid unemployment, little money for school improvements and additions, few positions for newly trained teachers. Hard times led to sharp words and rancour between teachers and trustees, and between school-boards and municipal councils. Economics forced the Roman Catholic separate school question back into the political arena, with all the bitterness of the 1880s. Yet these years of financial hardship proved to be years of innovation in education, as imaginative remedies were devised for desperate situations. Before the end of the decade, Ontario education underwent substantive changes in financing, rural school administration, and curriculum reform. Ironically, seeds sown in the prosperous twenties needed the depressed thirties before bearing fruit.

As premier and minister of education from 1930 to 1934, George Henry was expected to find answers to the problems of school finance caused by the depression. Initially he struck an optimistic note. 'Whatever economies may be necessary,' he wrote in 1931, 'the Government does not propose to cut down the aid to education given by the Legislature.'[1] But the worsening economic situation forced cutbacks, and Henry was soon perceived by teachers and trustees as a dispenser of bad news. Provincial grants to local school-boards were reduced by 10 per cent in the fall of 1932, followed by further reductions of 10 to 20 per cent in the spring of 1933 and again that autumn. Between 1930 and 1934 total annual expenditures on schooling in the province dropped by one-third. A future minister of education, Duncan McArthur, wrote a future premier, Mitchell Hepburn, that 'this reduction is simply passing the burden on to the municipalities.'[2]

Most of Ontario's city boards had erected large and commodious buildings to cope with the rising enrolments of the 1920s. In nearly every case such capital expenditure had been financed through long-term debentures; interest charges still had to be paid despite the revenue shortfall in the 1930s. Vocational education was especially hard hit, as federal contributions ceased in 1929 with the expiry of the Technical Education Act, and provincial grants were reduced to a level comparable to grants for academic classes. Yet in the long run, rural school-boards were even harder hit by provincial cutbacks, since they had long depended on the province for a greater percentage of their funds than did city schools. By 1933, some rural schools in northern Ontario were approaching desperate straits. SS no. 1, Harley Township, near New Liskeard, found it 'next to impossible to collect the taxes enough to keep the school going.' Nearby Bucke Township considered it 'out of the question' to finance both schooling and local relief efforts.[3] Rural school inspectors were quickly urged to pull back on their school improvement campaigns of the 1920s. As early as the spring of 1931, chief inspector V.K. Greer cautioned that 'no undue pressure toward the erection of new school buildings be used this year.'[4]

There were almost as many suggestions for saving money as there were concerned trustees. Suburban school-boards around Hamilton and Galt simply stopped paying non-resident fees for their pupils attending the city high schools. London attracted province-wide attention to its system of 'staggered' classes at Central Collegiate; longer use of the facilities during the day was reported to have staved off the need for a ten-class-room addition at a cost of $106,000. Everyone wanted to eliminate the 'frills and fads,' except that few could agree on what the 'frills' were. In Hamilton, this concern meant cutting back on manual training, domestic science, and music. To the chairman of the Ingersoll Board of Education, it meant that many pupils enrolled in Latin and French 'would be better off learning some of the fundamental principles as applied to business, or studying elementary engineering, or useful mechanical crafts.'[5] But to George Rogers, the former high school inspector who had succeeded F.W. Merchant as chief director of education, the fads and frills were the latest office machines and power tools continually requisitioned by the commercial and technical schools.[6]

Reducing the number of children and teenagers enrolled in the schools was seen as a major cost-saving venture. Lowering the school-leaving age from sixteen to fifteen years, and raising the entry age from five to six years, were propositions advanced at a July 1932 meeting of Ontario mayors in Kingston, and picked up by Liberal leader W.E.N. Sinclair in the provincial legislature. Yet both parts of this proposal were fraught with difficulties. The York Township Collegiate Board of suburban Toronto, for example, argued that 'it was better for students to be attending school than having nothing to occupy their minds,' and actually reduced from $100 to $25 the annual fee for pupils returning for their seventh year.[7] And the government accepted the argument of Chief Director Rogers that raising the school-entry age would be a move in the wrong direction. 'As this Province becomes more completely industrialized,' argued Rogers, 'it may be found necessary to *lower* the minimum age of entrance, especially in urban centres where mothers of families have, for economic reasons, to go to work.'[8] It seemed that the depression of the 1930s called for an extended role for the school in ameliorating and preventing social problems.

The Associated High School Boards of Ontario arose in 1932 as one organization dedicated to cutting the cost of secondary education. Initiated by a number of York County boards, the AHSBO was in part an attempt to untangle the complicated and unsatisfactory financial arrangements existing between county councils and district high school boards. It also represented an effort to form a trustees' organization with a constituency parallel to that of the OSSTF, the teachers' federation most successful in maintaining salary levels during the opening years of the depression. The AHSBO immediately declared war on an unpractical high school curriculum, exorbitant teachers' salaries, the power of the OSSTF, and the alleged collusion between the department of education and the teachers' movements. Provincial officials took the new group seriously, as Deputy Minister Colquhoun advised Premier Henry to 'promise consideration to any proposals that they may care to place before [you] in definite form.'[9] The Associated High School Boards of Ontario enjoyed some success as salaries for high school teachers were reduced over the next two years. Yet politics made strange bedfellows, for before long the AHSBO and the OSSTF had joined forces to counter a challenge from municipal councils for control of school financing.

At its September 1932 annual convention, the Ontario Municipal Association requested the Ontario government to give municipal councils the power of supervising and controlling the expenditures of local school-boards. Support for such a move had developed over the previous months as cities and towns throughout the province sought ways of cutting taxes. Numerous studies showed that municipal expenditures outstripped school expenditures during the 1920s and early 1930s, despite the fact that the increase in school population was about five times that of the total municipal population. Yet, according to the legislative law clerk in 1933, 'the danger is that the taxpayer is being educated to believe that it is school expenditures and those alone which are weighing him down.'[10] 'It looks to us,' declared the secretary-treasurer of the OPSMTF, 'as though the City Council of Windsor, having gotten into a financial jam during these exceptional times, is out to squeeze the Educational system of the City, and the Teachers, in order to make ends meet.'[11] Teachers and trustees joined forces to counter the challenge from municipal bodies. OSSTF secretary S.H. Henry charged that any transfer of educational power to councils would put schools 'on the level of the municipal Street Cleaning Department.'[12] But it was the reality of Ontario's separate school system that squelched the move to municipal control, for neither public nor separate school ratepayers were willing to hand over control of their schools to city councils which in all likelihood would include both Protestant and Catholic aldermen.

The public relations efforts of Ontario teachers' groups contributed in part to the maintenance of a relatively favourable public image towards education during the depression years. Teachers contributed generously – though sometimes after some arm-twisting by boards of trustees – to local relief efforts, and in 1937 began assisting their less favoured colleagues in Saskatchewan. But the most successful public relations venture was the annual promotion of Education Week, begun by the OSSTF in 1930 and soon supported by the elementary federations and by the provincial department of education. 'The best defence of the school is accurate and widespread publicity,' declared the OSSTF *Bulletin* in 1932. 'A community which is well informed about the objectives of its schools and the actual work being done by day is not likely to be stampeded into senseless slashing of its school budget. Inform the community and its schools are safe.' Soon the pattern of Education Week was established in most urban centres, with visitors' days or visitors' nights in the schools, talks to service clubs, special church services on Sunday, and publicity items in local newspapers and on radio stations. By 1936, J.M. Paton, OSSTF publicity committee chairman, concluded that the annual week had established 'in the minds of the people a definite sympathetic interest in the cause of education' – not to mention a more positive image for the teacher.[13]

Teachers at both elementary and secondary school levels weathered the depression decade with a modicum of success. As job prospects declined in business and industry, a teaching career at least offered some security. 'With the prospect of 50 dollars a month – every month – why it sounded like pure heaven!'[14] By early 1933 the training colleges were jammed – 2,200 at the normal schools (despite the fact that 1,500 graduates from the previous year were still unemployed), plus 560 OCE students competing for an estimated 150 high school positions. The inevitable result was a lowering of salaries, as school-boards slashed their budgets and desperate teacher applicants underbid one another. The extremes were found in the one-industry smaller cities which were close to bankruptcy and whose affairs had been taken over by the province, and in depressed rural areas where cash returns from the autumn harvests had plummeted. The rural school financial crisis was at its worst in 1935, when the provincial government stepped in to ensure teachers at least a $500 minimum salary. The teachers of the day made much of their martyrdom, yet in retrospect they had one of the favoured occupations. Although salaries slipped, they decreased much more slowly than for wage earners and salaried employees in the private sector, with the result that the average Ontario teacher's income possessed more equivalent real purchasing power in 1933 than in 1929 – $1,050 to $797.[15]

Given the relative comfort of the teaching profession, the lack of teacher militancy during the depression years is not surprising. Federation magazines could welcome the birth of the CCF party, or point to the accomplishments of Russian collectives, but most members opted for the shabby respectability of the low-status professional in preference to the militant image of the trade unionist. There was some interest in union affiliation among vocational school teachers in Hamilton, but neither the OSSTF nor the elementary federations formally considered the question. Nor was the economic situation desperate enough to push the three federations towards amalgamation. Although they co-operated in salary negotiations in many localities, there was enough male sexism to keep the two elementary federations apart, and enough academic snobbery to keep the OSSTF at some distance from both elementary groups. Only when the prospect of automatic membership was held out by a new government in 1944 did the three groups come together under the Ontario Teachers' Federation. Meanwhile, as the economic climate slowly improved after 1935, each federation made its own small gains in raising salaries, securing written contracts, and earning a measure of job tenure.

II

While school trustees and municipal councillors argued over educational costs, innovative schoolmen were generating a number of far-reaching reform proposals that were both pedagogically and financially appealing. In the early 1930s, reform interest centred on what Ontario educators called the intermediate school, otherwise known as the junior high school throughout most of North America. The intermediate school was the darling of many educators and psychologists. By combining the upper elementary and lower secondary school grades (usually grades 7 to 9), it could address itself to the particular academic and emotional needs of the early adolescent population, and smooth the transition from the teacher-centred elementary school to the subject-oriented high school. Some spokesmen saw the intermediate school providing more efficient preparation for the labour market. The Toronto *Globe* viewed it as directing pupils 'while they are finding themselves, and while their future most suitable form of education is being determined.' Such a school would serve as 'the laboratory in which the mentality and taste of boys and girls would be tested and their future career be settled, with a minimum loss of time and effort to the pupil and to the community.'[16] Not the least of the intermediate school's attractions was its economic advantage. Hundreds of under-enrolled elementary schools (a result of the declining birth-rate of the 1920s) could easily be transformed into intermediate schools, thus taking the pressure off the high schools at a time when their enrolments were mushrooming yet finances dictated no new building programs.

Several Ontario school-boards had begun to experiment with various kinds of intermediate school arrangements. Led by Inspector J.H. Putman, who had long criticized the eight-year elementary/five-year secondary pattern, the Ottawa Public School Board in 1929 drew together all its Fourth Book classes (grades 7 and 8) in five centrally located schools. Students spent half the day with their home-room teacher for instruction in reading, language, and mathematics; then they rotated among specialist teachers for classes in science, history, geography, oral French, physical education, manual training, and home economics. Teachers were carefully selected on the grounds of experience, scholarship, and ambition; preference went to those 'who had an adequate knowledge of the psychology of adolescence, and whose personalities were such as would appeal to early adolescents.' Pupils were reported to prefer the variety of teachers, the change of class-rooms, and the richer curricular and extra-curricular programs. And their academic performance surpassed that of a Kingston control group in areas such as arithmetic skills, spelling, and reading comprehension.[17] Of course the Ottawa intermediate schools were not junior high schools on the American model: there were no optional subjects and there was no Grade 9. Nevertheless, Putman predicted as early as 1930 that 'the intermediate school has come to stay. It will soon be an integral part of every progressive urban school system in Ontario.'[18]

While Ottawa began with its upper elementary grades, other municipalities pushed towards an intermediate-type school by experimenting with the lower secondary school grades. These were the Fifth Book classes, the first two years of high school work offered in the elementary school building by the elementary school teacher. Between 1930 and 1934 the number of Fifth Book classes jumped from 1,316 to 1,716. Before 1930 they were largely a rural phenomenon – a means of providing a modest amount of high school work close to the family farm. But during the depression years they were promoted by urban schoolmen as a way of saving money and providing a more relevant curriculum for many adolescents. Such classes had existed earlier in Toronto, but they had been phased out in 1925 as the high school building program caught up with demand. Now in the 1930s, enrolments were again rising and there were no funds for new high schools. By September 1932 Toronto had 953 pupils in three kinds of Fifth Book classes: commercial, academic (in areas of the city where high schools were crowded), and special non-commercial (for the disinterested pupil putting in time until age sixteen).

Innovative arrangements for these 'middle years' were not confined to major urban systems like those of Ottawa and Toronto. Three country schools near Tamworth began sending all their Fourth and Fifth Book pupils to one central school, where agriculture, home economics, and manual training were provided;

this was advertised as Ontario's only rural intermediate school. Meanwhile Forest Hill Village Community School in suburban Toronto, a school that included the entire range of elementary and secondary grades under one administration, treated its grade 7 to 9 pupils as a distinctive sub-unit. Here, in what may have been the closest Ontario copy of the American junior high school, students were presented with a complete rotary system of teachers, a variety of optional subjects, guidance counselling, and extra-curricular activities. From 1930 on, the junior high school question was a feature at annual meetings of the OEA, the teachers' federations, and the Urban School Trustees' Association. Educational journals like *The School* and the *Canadian School Journal* kept the issue continually before the public.

Provincial proposals for intermediate schools first surfaced at the time of Howard Ferguson's plan to transfer the first year of university work to the high schools in the mid-1920s. Ferguson had in mind a comprehensive grade reorganization, resulting in primary, intermediate, and secondary divisions. The primary grades (for children ages seven to eleven) and the intermediate grades (for eleven- to sixteen-year-olds) would be included within the elementary school and made universally available in both urban and rural communities. Secondary schools would concentrate on the sixteen and older age group, up to and including the first year of university work. With local support developing, senior departmental officials in the early 1930s threw their influence behind the intermediate school. F.W. Merchant, now serving in a consultant's role as chief adviser to the minister of education, argued its practical, psychological, pedagogical, and financial advantages – plus the opportunity 'to fix once-and-for-all the upper limits of separate schools.'[19] Chief director George Rogers sang the praises of this 'educational clearing house or distributing station.' As a bridge between the elementary school and the high school, it would sort for occupational purposes as well as 'open up possibilities in moral and in social training.'[20]

Yet the main object of the department, according to the legislative law clerk who was close to the scene, was reducing the cost of education.[21] Hence the hope that the new intermediate schools would be staffed primarily by lower salaried elementary school teachers and operated by elementary school boards; hence the name intermediate school rather than junior high school. 'The intermediate school is essentially a senior division of the common school under the administration of the public or the separate school board,' declared the department.[22] Such boards had always been able to do this through Fifth Book classes; the intermediate school bill, introduced in the legislature in 1934 and again in 1936, was designed to encourage the movement through incentive grants. But once it reached the political arena, the intermediate school idea was in deep trouble.

The designation of the intermediate school as a branch of elementary rather than secondary education did not automatically win the support of the elementary teachers. Many feared that eight years' work would now have to be covered in six years. In addition, the removal of the two upper grades would deprive the elementary schools of 'the senior pupils who are leaders in school organizations, sports and all those things which are essential to a good working school unit.' Gone as well would be most of the male teachers, for as one Toronto trustee explained, 'our experience shows that the men will not compete for positions in the junior grades.'[23] However, the two elementary teachers' federations – the FWTAO and the OPSMTF – ultimately gave their support to the proposal, once the government made clear that an intermediate school 'will not be required to limit its staff to teachers with secondary school teachers' qualifications.'[24] But it was precisely that point that antagonized the high school teachers; indeed they feared that their lower-salaried elementary colleagues would capture all the places in the new intermediate schools as they had in the old Fifth Book classes. The OSSTF devoted much of its Easter 1934 provincial council meeting to the intermediate school question. With George Rogers of the department of education as a captive listener, speaker after speaker tore into the government's bill. Intermediate schools were attacked on pedagogical, psychological, and economic grounds. But the real issue was jurisdiction; which federation would control the intermediate school teachers? The sudden withdrawal of the bill in the spring of 1934 was therefore welcomed by the OSSTF, although the federation was astute enough to realize that other forces besides itself had been at work.

It was the century-old separate school problem that ultimately defeated the intermediate school proposal of the mid-1930s. The imprecise boundary between elementary and secondary education in Ontario had allowed Roman Catholic separate school boards to move into Fifth Book classes without violating the Scott Act of 1863 and without arousing widespread opposition from public school supporters. But with money scarce in the 1930s, any further extension of separate school work in the lower high school years would mean less tax money available for public school efforts. Judge J.H. Scott of Perth, Ferguson's confidant throughout the 1920s on religious and linguistic matters, painted a vivid scenario of separate school expansion throughout the entire high school grades – and consequent Protestant unrest. Scott warned Premier Henry that the intermediate school bill, by opening the door to both public and separate school boards, 'will precipitate a peck of trouble for the Government.'[25] With an election approaching, Henry faced the prospect of Protestant antagonism if he pushed through the intermediate school bill in its existing form, and Catholic opposition if the legislation were amended to exclude the separate schools. Henry took the easy way out and withdrew the bill in March 1934. Two years later the successor Liberal government of Mitchell Hepburn in its turn withdrew an intermediate school bill, again because of the separate school question. 'If this political obstacle cannot be removed, there will be no

Intermediate Schools,' wrote a contemporary observer.[26] Such was the price Ontario was destined to pay.

III

One hundred thousand pupils annually attended the separate schools of Ontario during the 1930s. This number had doubled since the turn of the century, and in doubling had increased the separate school proportion of the total elementary population from 10 to 17 per cent. Separate school attendance was largely urban – 76 per cent as opposed to 56 per cent in the public school system – due to the historic and continuing urban destinations of Roman Catholic immigrants. Accommodation, equipment, and teaching competency varied from excellent in many towns and cities to unsatisfactory in remote rural areas, much the same as in the public schools. Comparisons of quality between public and separate schools were not undertaken in any official way, although the high school principals of Toronto were 'unanimous in saying that these [separate school] students as a whole do poorly, and that a good student from these schools is rare.'[27] Most Protestants would have agreed, and would have blamed the deficiency on alleged inferior teaching and the supposed inordinate amount of class-room time spent on religion. Catholic clergy countered by emphasizing the importance of church influence on the schooling of the young. 'The strength and solidity of the child's life and works depend on the Catholic education received in youth,' declared Rev. M.J. Brady at the cornerstone laying of St John's Separate School in Kingston in 1932. 'Man is created for eternal life, [and] Catholic education always takes this into consideration.'[28]

Separate school board participation in the proposed intermediate schools was linked in the minds of many public school supporters with the even more explosive question of separate school board sharing of corporation and utility tax revenues. Such revenues were eagerly sought by the generally poorer separate boards during the financial crisis of the 1930s. Large Catholic families and low residential property assessments combined to generate too many pupils and not enough funds. In Ottawa at this time, it was estimated that half of the city's children were educated in the separate schools at a cost of $32 per pupil and at a tax rate of 14.8 mills, while for the other half attending the public schools, a tax rate of only 7.9 mills permitted expenditures of $84 per pupil.[29] Two possibilities existed for relieving the burden on Catholic homeowners and channelling more money into separate school coffers: either increased provincial grants or a share of local corporation and utility taxes.

Provincial grants could have been raised without reference to the legislature and without risking a heated political debate. But this was not likely to happen during a decade when across-the-board cuts in provincial school grants had quickly become an annual occurrence. Nor did this approach have the support of the recently formed Catholic Taxpayers' Association, which campaigned for a permanent, legislated settlement rather than one dependent on the whims of future governments. From its formation in 1932 under the leadership of Martin Quinn, the CTA mounted a consistent lobby for a guaranteed share of local corporation and public utility taxes. An 1886 amendment had permitted, but not obliged, company directors to pay to separate schools the portion of their school taxes which was in proportion to the number of shares in the corporation owned by Catholics. That amendment had no teeth and had proven ineffective. Now, almost half a century later the Catholic Taxpayers' Association wanted such a division of taxes made mandatory, extended to public utilities, and split on the important basis of student populations.

Howard Ferguson had survived his seven years as premier and minister of education without the separate school question entering the political arena – a factor of some significance in the 1927 resolution of the bilingual schools issue. Certainly Catholic demands for publicly supported high schools had been growing since before the First World War. Fifth Book classes and continuation schools were used as back-door approaches to secondary education; indeed by 1924 some seventeen separate schools with 475 pupils were engaged in middle-school work. But before it became politically volatile, Ferguson manoeuvred the entire issue of separate high school rights into the judicial arena. 'I have always sought to remove from the field of controversy all our educational problems,' Ferguson wrote Catholic Bishop Michael Fallon of London. 'The judicial determination is, to my mind, the one way of bringing this about.'[30] For two long years, from 1926 to 1928, the famous Tiny Township case dragged through the Ontario, Canadian, and British courts. Finally on 12 June 1928 the Judicial Committee of the Imperial Privy Council decided in favour of the government; Catholics had no legal claim to financial support for any secondary schools they might erect, or to exemption from support of public high schools. Yet Ferguson kept Catholic support by partially shifting provincial grants from an incentive to an equalization basis, thus providing more funds for poorer separate school boards. But no principles were conceded, no political gambles taken.

George Henry was not as successful as his predecessor in keeping the separate school controversy out of politics. Ferguson warned Henry in the fall of 1933 that in 'the school question you have your most delicate and difficult problem,' and urged the establishment of a commission that might recommend that the corporation tax issue be settled by the courts.[31] But Henry took no action until the last day of the spring 1934 pre-election session of the legislature, when he announced that a list of questions to clarify the Catholic tax position would be submitted to the courts. This belated move – which lacked the acute sense of timing Ferguson had displayed with regard to bilingual schools in 1925 – satisfied neither side. The Catholic Taxpayers' Association feared its economic demands would not be met, while Protestant Orangemen feared they would be.

Although the Depression was the over-riding factor in the Conservative defeat in the ensuing election, Henry firmly believed that the Orangemen had sat on their hands while Catholics voted solidly against him because he had not met their demands for more tax revenue.[32]

Led by the flamboyant Mitchell Hepburn, the Liberals were now in power for the first time since 1905. Hepburn's approach to the separate school question bore many similarities to that of the last Liberal premier, George Ross – separate schools were a fact of life and should be maintained at a level of efficiency equal to that of the public schools. Hepburn had promised the Catholics nothing beyond 'a fair hearing' during the 1934 election campaign, but there were indications early in 1935 that he was seeking a solution that ameliorated the inequities in the distribution of corporation taxes. 'There's no doubt in my mind,' he told Martin Quinn and a CTA delegation in January, 'that when the original school act was drafted they did not anticipate, at that time, that we were going into an industrial age such as we are in at the present time.'[33] Three months later he publicly acknowledged that an inequality existed. Previous governments had recognized this by making additional grants to separate schools, but now 'a practical solution should be applied, and that is the problem we must solve as soon as possible.'[34] Hepburn was defining the problem and suggesting a solution in an economic, rather than a political or religious context, with rational underpinnings rather than emotional overtones. Whether the Ontario voters would agree to such a re-definition was still to be seen.

Finally in April of 1936 – after the intermediate-school bill had been withdrawn to defuse the situation – Hepburn introduced the tax assessment bill, the most important piece of Catholic school legislation in over seventy years. Corporations, which hitherto had an option in the matter, were now obliged to divide their school taxes in proportion to the religion of their shareholders. If the corporation was so large or complex that such a religious census could not be undertaken, then the taxes would be apportioned in each municipality according to the ratio of Catholics to Protestants among the total population – not, as the Catholics requested, on the basis of school population. No provision was made for the second Catholic request, a share of public-utility taxes. It was an economic issue, argued the premier, not a religious one. He cited the phenomenal growth of twentieth-century manufacturing, using Windsor as an example. 'Such has been the growth of corporations there that today about half the taxable property is owned by corporations, which means that about half that taxable property might be shut off from the separate schools.'[35] If the province must support separate schools, he asked, 'what is more obvious than to use the taxation from those people to equip and maintain the schools.'[36] Amid heated debate, an alleged threat on Hepburn's life, and the revolt of three. Liberal members, the tax assessment bill passed on a vote of sixty-five to twenty at about five o'clock in the morning of 9 April.

Unfortunately for Hepburn and the province's separate school boards, the act proved both practically unworkable and politically unwise. It was impossible to determine for purposes of assessment who were Catholic school supporters in large complex corporations. In Hamilton, Toronto, and Windsor (where the Ford Motor case was not finally determined by the courts until 1941), the difficulties were so great and there was so much litigation that the financial position of the Catholic schools was actually worse than before the contentious legislation had been passed. 'My personal belief,' wrote a solicitor for several cases, 'is that this Act may cause even more sectarian bitterness in hundreds of municipalities as a result of forcing Separate School supporters to clog up the Courts of Revision with appeals, etc., which should be unnecessary.'[37] Whatever the outcome of individual court cases, militant Protestants jumped on the fact that any additional funds for separate schools could come only at the expense of local money for public schools. The Toronto *Telegram* charged that Hepburn's 'idea of a fair compromise is to plunge his hand deeper into Protestant pockets for the support of separate schools.'[38] Hepburn's prorogation of the legislature within hours after the bill's passage simply meant that political opposition was transferred from the confines of Queen's park to the battleground of the province.

The East Hastings by-election of December 1936 killed any hopes that Protestant voters might accept the tax assessment act as an economic rather than a sectarian measure. Here in the heartland of Orange Eastern Ontario, Conservative leaders Earl Rowe and George Drew stirred up anti-separate-school prejudice and sent the Hepburn Liberal candidate down to defeat. Ontario's Protestant majority was simply not prepared to accept what it considered unwarranted financial concessions to the Catholics. The message was not lost on Premier Hepburn, who in the 1937 spring session of the legislature, stunned both Catholic and Protestant voters by announcing his support for repeal of the controversial legislation. Thus Hepburn was able to defuse the issue for that year's general election campaign, retain Catholic support because he had tried to resolve the financial inequalities, as well as keep Protestant support because he had pulled back in time. His re-election, plus the slowly improving economic situation of the late 1930s, enabled Hepburn and his advisors to consider other ways of easing the burden on separate school supporters. That assistance would not come by way of tax changes at the local level, but in the less contentious form of provincial grants.

IV

These setbacks on intermediate schools and the tax assessment question were the exception rather than the rule for the Hepburn government in the field of education. The new administration implemented a number of significant changes in the school system – despite the financial stringencies of the decade and despite the premier's personal interest in issues far more flamboyant than education. As opposition leader in the early 1930s, Hepburn had shown little interest in school questions. But by the spring of 1933 the annual reductions in provincial grants demanded action. 'In view of the recent developments,' Hepburn wrote Duncan McArthur, his future deputy minister and later minister of education, 'I think we ought to direct considerable of our attention against the policy of that Department.' According to Hepburn, there were 'several very able men in the province working on the matter now.'[39] The framework of an educational platform was put together over the next fifteen months and emerged gradually as the June 1934 election approached. There were the usual promises to make curriculum more relevant and increase provincial grants. There were crowd-pleasing pledges to reduce the number of departmental examinations and abolish the new requirement of a second year of normal-school training. And there were hints of 'a much over-due over-hauling' of the department of education, which should be headed by 'a man outstanding as an educationalist and equally outstanding for executive ability.'[40]

Hepburn's first minister of education in the July 1934 cabinet had shown little previous evidence of either 'outstanding' educational or executive ability. The member for Simcoe Centre, Dr Leo J. Simpson was a Barrie physician whose only experience in education had come as a school-board trustee. But Simpson was a veteran party organizer and a close ally of Hepburn's in the troublesome pre-1934 years when the new leader struggled to establish his authority over an undisciplined party. Actual leadership was assumed by the new deputy minister, Duncan McArthur. This was the outstanding educator Hepburn had been seeking for over a year – a Queen's University history professor, member of the Kingston Board of Education, and a man who had the respect of the province's teachers. Hepburn had failed to lure McArthur into the political arena as a Liberal candidate in the 1934 election, but the subsequent offer of the senior civil service position in the department had its appeal. Eventually, McArthur would have a taste of both worlds, for he moved from deputy minister to minister following Simpson's death six years later.

McArthur's arrival meant the departure of what George Henry had called his 'triumvirate of specially able men' within the department.[41] A.H.U. Colquhoun retired after twenty-nine years as deputy minister, F.W. Merchant left as special adviser, and George Rogers stepped down from chief director to senior high school inspector. McArthur's assumption of all three of these responsibilities demonstrated both Hepburn's confidence in him and the vengeance with which the new premier cleaned out the Tory-dominated civil service. How much McArthur would be able to accomplish in the depths of the Depression was questionable. Certainly Leo Simpson did not wish to raise any false hopes. 'Education is not a spectacular department,' he said, 'and we do not wish it to be.'[42] Yet there was a feeling that McArthur, perhaps because of his professorial background, might make a difference. 'We fancy he will effect a distinct change in the whole atmosphere of Ontario education,' wrote the editor of *Saturday Night*, 'a change which will be definitely for the better.'[43] Teachers and trustees seemed to catch this spirit of optimism, for the 1935 OEA convention turned out to be one of the most productive and constructive in years. 'The era of drift appears to be passing,' concluded the highly partisan Toronto *Globe*.[44]

McArthur moved quickly towards solving two enduring problems in Ontario education – local school financing and rural school administrative reorganization. Not one, but two committees on school costs were established in 1935. The first was the OSSTF Committee on Educational Finance, significant in that it marked the federation's first major step into educational policy questions and launched the political career of its chairman, York Township English teacher J.W. Noseworthy. The OSSTF committee set out to show that the public was not over-spending on education and to prod the province into assuming a greater proportion of the costs. More comprehensive in scope and more representative in its membership was the government's own Committee of Enquiry into the Cost of Education, chaired by McArthur himself. This latter committee was clearly designed to defuse public criticism over still another cut in provincial grants. In addition, it appears that its hidden agenda included consideration of alternative methods of assisting separate schools should political factors force the withdrawal of the tax assessment bill.[45] Despite their different origins, the two committees reached similar conclusions and made almost identical recommendations in their 1935 and 1938 reports: equality of educational opportunity could only be achieved through larger units of rural school administration and through the province assuming a greater proportion of the total cost.

The Hepburn government quickly implemented the recommendations of the McArthur committee. Larger provincial grants were now possible as economic conditions improved throughout the province. By 1938 the total money committed to school grants surpassed pre-depression highs; by 1941 it amounted to a doubling from 10 to 20 per cent of the provincial share of total educational costs. Hepburn justified this move in stating that 'the burden of local taxation on real estate may be lightened.' In addition, the province was moving away from incentive grants – helping those districts best able to help themselves – towards equalization grants which channelled more money 'to those districts which, by reason of their small assessments, are least able to provide for the financial support of schools.'[46] Among the major beneficiaries were the separate school boards, whose local financing had always been weak and whose hopes had been dashed by the repeal of the tax assessment bill in 1937. By 1941 any statistical breakdown of provincial grant figures showed advantages for the separate schools – 7.3 cents per pupil per day for example, as against 5.6 cents for public school pupils. Minor opposition came from the Ontario Public School Trustees and Ratepayers Associations, formed to 'advance and protect the interest of the public school system of Ontario.' But legislative grants were less controversial than changes in local tax structures; the government and the department of education had found a way to pursue educational equality throughout both public and separate schools without arousing a political storm.

Politicians and educators of the late 1930s were well aware of the precedent being established as the provincial share of total school costs doubled from 10 to 20 per cent. Education Minister Simpson warned that developments along these lines must be gradual, that too sudden changes might upset the entire educational system. Consequently limits were placed on annual increases available to boards. 'When things come too easily,' he suggested, 'they are too often abused.'[47] Yet larger provincial grants were seen as the only way of equalizing school costs, guaranteeing equality of educational opportunity to all children, and assisting poorer rural areas to survive against the powerful forces of urbanization. It was ironic, too, that while school financing was being centralized, decisions on curriculum, examinations, and promotions were gradually being transferred to local levels. What was needed was a unit of local school administration strong enough to assume responsibility for academic decisions and still capable of raising the bulk of its money locally. Such a unit existed in urban areas – the municipal board of education. Perhaps the time was ripe to try once again for rural school administrative reform.

Howard Ferguson had never been as rigidly committed to the township school-board as his opponents in the 1920s believed. To him it was simply a means to an end – that of improving educational opportunity in rural areas – and if a better means could be found he would gladly support it. As early as 1925 Ferguson suggested an intermediate-sized board, larger than the old school section yet considerably smaller than an entire township. 'If you had fifteen or sixteen sections in a township I would make two school areas of it,' he told the OEA. 'I would not have the board too large and cumbersome.' The precedent existed in a 1921 provision which permitted the formation of a township school area of any part of a township lying contiguous to a city or town. This was an early recognition of the phenomenon of suburbanization in the townships surrounding Toronto. In 1928 the first township school area was established in North York. Four years later all the school sections in York Township were joined under a township public school board. Savings were estimated at $10,000 during the first year of operation, despite a reduction of nearly four mills on the average tax rate of the eleven sections.[48]

By 1932, then, the initial promise of suburban school areas plus the steadily worsening economic situation combined to provide a climate favourable to legislation permitting the formation of township school areas in rural regions. Township councils were then given the power to organize part or all of the township into a school area, thus abolishing the sections. Neither trustee nor ratepayer approval was necessary, yet the councillors were close enough to the people so that any move to create a school area would appear to be a local action. Despite the incentive of an extra $100 per year in provincial grants for every school under a township area board, only twelve such areas were formed in the next five years. But there was one official in the department of education determined to throw his weight behind the re-organization as soon as his superiors gave the green light. That individual was V.K. Greer, who since 1926 had been chief inspector of public and separate schools, and who from 1938 until his death seven years later translated the township school area from theoretical ideal to practical reality.

Greer forecast similar advantages under the township school area as others had earlier promised under the township school-boards. It would equalize assessment across a broader area, eliminate local frictions caused by 'the jealousies and prejudices of a too-restricted community,' attract 'better types for the teaching profession' through greater assurance of permanency, and secure co-operation for such 'needful school services' as Fifth Book classes, school health services, and instruction in agriculture, home economics, and manual training.[49] All these and many other advantages were demonstrated in Nassagaweya Township of Halton County, where one of the more successful school areas was established in 1939. Eight teachers were now employed for the seven schools under the area board, including specialists in manual training, home economics, agriculture, and music who rotated among the schools; Fifth Book work was concentrated in one school; pupils' supplies were provided out of board funds; teachers got higher salaries; and the buildings received regular maintenance. Yet local taxes were reduced in five of the sections and held constant in the other two. This was accomplished through reduced costs of administration and more economical purchasing of supplies.[50]

But McArthur and Greer could proceed only as fast as local opinion would permit. By 1940, due largely to Greer's persuasive efforts at local community gatherings, some 516 former school sections had been reorganized into 100 township areas. This represented close to 10 per cent of the rural schools in the province. But almost all the township areas were in the economically depressed and sparsely populated regions of the Laurentian Shield; only a handful were in the agricultural heartland of the South. Opposition persisted within the rural trustees' section of the Ontario Educational Association where in 1940 'with cheering and yells of triumph the great majority of delegates gave vent to their feelings' and carried a motion condemning the department of education's encouragement of the larger unit.[51] Like his more astute predecessors, McArthur was aware of how far the province could move in the face of opposition from local authorities. 'This is a democratic country,' he stated in the spring of 1939, 'and we do not intend to force the larger unit of school administration on you. If you want it you can have it, but there will be no Hitlers in the educational system of Ontario.'[52]

V

Improvements in the high school program were as important in McArthur's mind as rural administrative re-organization. Statistics for September 1932 had shown a 10.6 per cent jump in high school enrolments, a rate of increase sustained through the remainder of the decade. Some schoolmen claimed the increase had little or nothing to do with the depression, but was due to higher university admission requirements or was 'but a trend of the times.' Others argued that more pupils were kept out of school to supplement family earnings than were kept in school because there were no jobs for them.[53] Yet the majority of senior administrators, who had to provide the pupil places, and school trustees, responsible for raising the bulk of the money, saw a close connection between the state of the economy and adolescent school attendance. Toronto trustee John Corcoran asserted that depression-induced attendance cost his board $300,000 extra a year, yet concluded that 'there is no more effective welfare work being done anywhere.'[54]

Out of the depression came a re-statement by educators of the importance of social goals in the high school. What had seemed somewhat idealistic in the individualism of the 1920s now appeared eminently practical in the depths of the depression. 'While this period is a time of storm and stress for all youth, it is also a seed-time of ideals,' declared Leo Simpson. 'These ideals depend largely upon the influence of the environment, and the environment of the school room forms one of the most important factors of such influence.'[55] The chairman of the Toronto Board of Education concurred. 'The secondary schools,' declared Adelaide Plumptre in 1934, 'have at the present time a unique opportunity for influencing thought and characters in a very large number of students – and that during adolescence, the most plastic period of educational life.'[56]

Many educators who had viewed extra-curricular activities as 'frills' in the 1920s now came to appreciate their value in keeping high school students occupied during the depression years. Carefully managed student councils could also co-opt rebellious youth into supporting authority, and thus head off any drift towards radical political thought and action. So in 1935 East York Collegiate in suburban Toronto began a perfect system. Those senior students chosen to enter the charmed circle were expected to help discipline unruly pupils, co-operate enthusiastically in all school projects, and show complete loyalty to the principal. Kennedy Collegiate in Windsor had its Forum, a staff-student council which regulated and supervised the activities of 'one thousand adolescents assembling together every day, forming a fair-sized village.' Principal George Campbell insisted that 'education for character is of paramount interest on the collegiate program,' and boasted that Kennedy graduates were well trained to assume leadership roles in adult clubs and societies.[57] A decade earlier, the Kennedy Collegiate Forum might have been ridiculed by conservative Ontario educators as too American. But by 1933, veteran Toronto principal

E.A. Hardy could remark that 'the extra-curricular life of a modern secondary school plays almost as important a part in the education of the boys and girls as the prescribed class room work.'[58]

The principal difference in high school policy formation between the 1920s and the 1930s, however, was the attempt to address contemporary social realities through the regular academic program in addition to extra-curricular activities. The June 1938 graduating class of Gananoque High School demonstrated the disharmony between traditional programming and contemporary reality. Of the fifty-five students who left school with either junior or senior matriculation, forty-one found direct employment before the end of the year, nine were still seeking work, while only five continued their education at normal schools, business, or agricultural college.[59] Since small-town Gananoque was unable to offer technical and commercial programs, all fifty-five had been enrolled in the university-oriented matriculation program. Yet not one of the graduates proceeded directly to university. Even in composite schools in larger centres, the majority of students continued to choose the academic program at the beginning of their first year without any exposure to technical or commercial education. While some educators argued the relevance of the matriculation program for all youngsters, progressive schoolmen of the late 1930s could no longer contain their dissatisfaction. Education minister Simpson conceded that the matriculation program would remain for university preparation, but warned that it could no longer 'mould the course of the whole secondary school.'[60]

Defeated on the junior or intermediate school concept, Ontario officials quickly changed their tactics while remaining true to their declared strategy of a more flexible grade 9 year. If grade 9 had to remain in the high schools, why could it not be 'a common first year,' permitting wide choice of options, and delaying for one more year the traumatic decision on the part of each student as to the choice of a matriculation, technical, or commercial program? The curriculum for such a year, proposed by a departmental committee early in 1937, and commonly referred to as the 'McArthur Plan,' included English, social studies, health, mathematics, science or agriculture, French, home economics or general shop, music or art, and business practice. The elimination of Latin caused consternation among classicists and supporters of the classical tradition. But McArthur saw the elimination of Latin as the only way to ensure that grade 9 could be 'a year of testing ... in which the boy can try himself out along different lines under the guidance and direction of teachers, that he might reach conclusions regarding his particular capabilities and aptitudes.'[61] Shop work and home economics were not intended to train for direct employment, wrote chief director of education J.G. Althouse eight years later, 'but would provide an opportunity for practical vocational guidance, and at the same time offer an activity programme which would be attractive to youth and probably have the effect of holding their interest longer in school.'[62]

Lyndhurst Continuation School in Leeds County claimed to be the first secondary school in the province to implement the new program in its entirety. Lyndhurst was helped, in no small measure, by the fact that, coincident with the new regulations, a new building with fully equipped home-economics and general-shop rooms was constructed. Change came more slowly throughout the rest of the province. In Toronto, for example, only two of the ten collegiates had the facilities to offer the new subjects in September 1937 and $269,000 was not available for the necessary renovations to the other eight buildings. Qualified teachers were also in short supply, and the depression years discouraged attendance at the specialist summer schools in home economics and industrial arts. Public support was sometimes lacking, especially when expensive new accommodation and equipment were involved. Students of Milverton Continuation School used their column in the weekly Milverton *Sun* to argue the advantages of the new curriculum and to lobby for an addition to the school building in the face of 'considerable opposition to such a venture.'[63] The provincial department of education was prepared to exempt local boards where financial conditions were particularly acute but fully expected the introduction of the new grade 9 'in its entirety' when it did not 'place an undue burden on the ratepayers.'[64] When wartime emergencies brought a halt to school construction in late 1940, some ninety-five Ontario high schools and 20 per cent of the grade 9 pupils were fully immersed in the new program.

The new program had far-reaching implications for the smaller village high schools and continuation schools. How could a 50-pupil or even a 100-pupil school justify expensive home economics and industrial arts facilities for one grade 9 class? Iroquois Falls High School cast about for other arrangements in November of 1937. Should it share facilities with the local public schools or with neighbouring towns?[65] Tiny Lions Head Continuation School on the Bruce Peninsula found it had no facilities, no money, no qualified teachers, and no interested students. The department, fully aware of the problem, exploited the situation to push for larger rural high school districts. Legislation was passed permitting county councils to establish such districts and transportation grants were made available to bus students from small communities which could not offer the new courses to larger towns which did. Fifth Book classes were the first to suffer; between 1937 and 1940 their number dropped from 1,715 to 1,370 and their pupil population fell from 11,621 to 10,987. Most continuation schools held out till the end of the Second World War, but the writing was on the wall for these distinctive Ontario schools. The move to larger rural high school districts simply paralleled the trend towards township school areas at the elementary level.

Additional high school changes carried the philosophy of the McArthur Plan beyond the grade 9 level. Inspector Rogers spoke of the reforms as 'making our academic schools less academic and our vocational schools less vocational, in other words to provide in all secondary schools a kind of general education which will fit our adolescents for life – as individuals, as citizens, and as workers.'[66] A partial common core of subjects continued into grade 10 with all students taking English, social studies, and health, plus optional subjects from one of four programs: general, industrial arts, household arts, or commercial. Successful completion of these first two years earned an intermediate diploma; thus the student who progressed no further would leave with a sense of accomplishment. The programs for the higher grades had more options, fewer departmental examinations, and more promotion by recommendation. The old junior and senior *matriculation* certificates were replaced by secondary school and honour *graduation* diplomas to emphasize the idea that the high school's *raison d'être* was not primarily preparation for university.

Program changes were accompanied by a relaxation of external examinations. For as long as most teachers could remember, 'departmental' examinations – set and marked by department of education personnel in Toronto – had provided hurdles over which pupils had to jump as they moved up through the grades. These external examinations had been vociferously defended on grounds of preserving standards, providing incentives, measuring objectives, and offering the best indicator of success on the next rung of the educational ladder. During the 1920s, the recommendation system had been partially instituted for the high school entrance and the lower school (end of grade 10) examinations. Thereafter, only the weakest students were compelled to write the departmentals. 'We never got to write our Entrance exam,' recalls Matthew Goderich in *The Swing in the Garden*, Hugh Hood's semi-autobiographical novel of a Toronto boyhood in the 1930s, 'thereby missing out on a scarification rite of early adolescence which had given nightmares to three generations of Ontario children.'[67] By 1932, outstanding students were allowed exemption on the middle school (grade 12) examinations. These moves were motivated partly on economic grounds, since thousands of dollars were spent annually on the setting, distributing, collecting, and marking of papers. Yet there was professional justification as well. 'Teachers who work with pupils and supervise their course,' argued George Rogers, 'are in a position to grant a certificate of standing which would be of more value than any examination.'[68]

In 1935 the Hepburn administration took the boldest move of all – the extension of the recommendation system to the upper school (grade 13) departmental examinations. It was not a move applauded by the universities, but their confidence in McArthur prevented outright opposition. Recommendations were given out sparingly, amounting to just 31 per cent of students in 1939, and the overall percentage of successful candidates (both recommended and writing) remained close to 75 per cent. Once instituted, the new approach met with mixed reaction from university officials. Dean C.H. Mitchell of Toronto's Faculty of Applied Science and Engineering pointed in 1937 to increased failure rates in first-year engineering courses, and suggested that 'it may be partly due to the entrance of students who are not as well prepared in the Secondary Schools.'[69] Yet University of Toronto Registrar A.B. Fennell pointed to *decreased* failure rates in first-year arts and science courses, and concluded that students were 'certainly as well prepared as those who entered previously.'[70] Nevertheless, the grade 13 recommendation system was cancelled in response to university pressure in 1940. The Second World War meant a shorter school-year and a loss of many good teachers to the armed forces and industry. Once again, the traditional arguments for uniform examinations sounded convincing. But in return, the department of education won university concurrence for a total abolition of lower- and middle-school departmentals.

These several changes did not bring an instant revolution to the Ontario high school. People still referrred to lower, middle, and upper school and forms 1 to 5 even though the nomenclature was now grades 9 to 13. And who was going to roll his tongue around the phrase 'secondary school honour graduation diploma' when he really meant 'senior matric'? Often the new grade 9 merely delayed for one year the stampede of pupils towards the matriculation or general program. Universities, normal schools, and other post-secondary colleges continued to demand academic courses that encouraged students to choose the general program. Nor were there many changes in the content and methodology of individual subjects. 'Social studies' enjoyed but a brief existence in departmental terminology; soon history and geography reappeared to reflect the realities of the class-room. But the reform package was significant in introducing more of the social concerns of contemporary North America directly into the high school program. Throughout the 1920s, social purposes had permeated extracurricular activities, but had not penetrated the academic class-room. Now, however, the economic and social dislocations of the 1930s called for another look at this seemingly artificial division of the teenager's school life into water tight academic and social compartments.

8 *Education for Democratic Citizenship*

I

Elementary school program changes of 1937 were even more dramatic than McArthur's high school reforms in that they addressed the methodology of teaching as well as the subjects of the curriculum. The revised *Programme of Studies for ... the Public and Separate Schools* created a new set of demands for the teachers of the first six grades in September 1937, and for their senior class colleagues when it was extended to cover grades 7 and 8 the following year. The teacher was bluntly told that 'the curriculum is to be thought of in terms of activity and experience rather than of knowledge to be acquired and facts to be stored.' Out went rote learning and stimulation through external discipline and fear. Now, the Ontario school 'must follow the method of nature, stimulating the child, through his own interests, into activities guiding him into experiences useful for the satisfaction and development of his needs.' Health, English, social studies – in that order, followed by natural science, arithmetic, music, and art – were the subjects of study or areas of interest around which the teacher would build the curriculum. Course outlines were suggestive rather than prescriptive, book lists replaced single, authorized texts, and teachers were encouraged to use an activity-oriented or 'enterprise' methodology. Even the terminology was altered – history and geography gave way to social studies, forms and books were replaced by grades. The child would advance naturally through the eight grades of the new elementary school, not held back by the artificial barriers of formal examinations. 'The elementary school has no business with uniform standards of attainment,' declared the *Programme of Studies*. 'Its business is to see that children grow in body and mind at their natural rate.'[1]

These 1937 proposals were all the more dramatic given the slow pace of curriculum change since the end of the First World War. The courses of study for the elementary grades had been revised in 1924 'to lighten them and to give them greater elasticity,' but the revisions were extremely mild.[2] From that point on, major innovations had tended to originate at the local rather than the provincial level. The London public school system had its advancement classes, while Windsor public schools were known throughout the province for their 'rotary' plan, which exposed the pupil to several teachers during the course of the school day. Ottawa continued to innovate under its aggressive inspector, J.H. Putman, whose views, according to timid department of education officials 'would require to be carefully weighed.'³ Building on his earlier, pre-war reforms, Putman by the 1920s was moving the Ottawa schools towards an activity-oriented, project-centred learning pattern. Toronto public schools, meanwhile, were experimenting with 'catch-up' classes and differentiated placement according to subject; trial promotions and continuous pupil progress without regard to grading; diagnostic testing, individualized instruction, and the extensive use of audio and visual aids.

But Toronto's eight district inspectors believed that changes of a more fundamental nature were necessary, and they pulled no punches in their 1932 reports. Most class-room teachers talked too much, 'giving the pupils information which they can get for themselves, telling them what they already know, explaining needlessly, and giving unnecessary commands and instructions.' There was an almost universal concern to 'cover the course,' which meant studying the textbook from cover to cover. This had a tendency 'to make the pupils dependent upon book knowledge and to leave them helpless when required to think for themselves in new situations.' This in turn led to the 'memorization method, the key-notes of which are note-taking, repetition, cramming and reproduction of information.' The fruits of such a method were 'mental indigestion, mental laziness and sometimes mental paralysis.'⁴ It seemed that for every innovative class-room, there were another ten or twenty more closely attuned to nineteenth- rather than twentieth-century pedagogical theory. J.G. Althouse, principal of the Ontario College of Education, observed in 1936 that it was almost forty years since John Dewey had enunciated the doctrine of 'the supreme importance of the child in the classrooom.' Yet Althouse found it disturbing that 'even today most of our schools are conducted in a manner which shows that we have a very imperfect understanding of that doctrine.'⁵

Of special concern to a growing number of educators was the gap between school and community, between the focus of the Ontario curriculum and the realities of Ontario society in the early 1930s. It was a criticism applicable to almost every subject, but it was directed most frequently at history, with its emphasis on events of long ago. 'Great movements are not all of the past, but we are in the midst of them to-day,' asserted one inspector, 'and our senior pupils should be encouraged to read of and know them.'⁶ Such views were echoed by C.C. Goldring, who in 1933 at age thirty-three was appointed director of education by the Toronto Board of Education. "We have too often assumed that the school is set apart from society,' Goldring told his principals. 'We should make constant references to the world around ... and try to make our school a miniature of society.' He urged teachers to make greater use of 'real life problems,' both to arouse pupil interest and to prepare children for the future.[7]

Educators like Putman, Althouse, and Goldring were flirting in the early 1930s with what was called 'progressive education.' Although the American-based Progressive Education Association dated only from 1919, the ideas on which it was based went back another twenty years to the pedagogical work and writing of John Dewey in the 1890s. As director of the University of Chicago's laboratory school, Dewey had stressed a child-centred approach to learning. Rather than begin with the traditional disciplinary interests of the adult world, Dewey had used the more intuitive interests of the child as the starting point of instruction. Proceeding from this base, learning was organized around integrated, multidisciplinary themes. The teacher's task was to motivate children to work co-operatively on these activity-oriented projects, and to link the child's immediate interests with the problems and concerns of the larger world.[8]

Toronto supporters of progressive education organized a branch of the New Education Fellowship, the British Empire equivalent of the PEA in the United States. Although the Toronto group never exceeded twenty people and met infrequently,[9] Goldring believed that it influenced 'our schools and educational thinking.'[10] In 1932 its secretary, Marjorie Lord, brought the progressivist message to the Ontario Educational Association. 'Child activities clustering around a centre of interest,' preached Lord, 'promise an enrichment far exceeding the yield that has come from the knowledge loads of traditional education.'[11] Two years later the OEA again heard a loud, clear call for progressive education. President D.A. Morris demanded 'a revision of the curriculum ... that it may specifically be adjusted to growth needs and experiences of the social group for which it is intended.'[12] Before the end of 1934, the OEA joined with the three teachers' federations, the trustees' association, and the Home and School Federation to establish the Ontario Educational Research Committee. With a membership reading like a *Who's Who* of Ontario education at mid-decade, the committee proceeded to rip apart current curriculum and instructional practices. 'Your committee has an ideal,' reported its elementary representatives six months later, 'a school in which the emphasis is placed on child activity not on teacher activity.'[13]

Senior officials within the provincial department of education welcomed such demands for curriculum reform. In the summer of 1934, chief inspector V.K. Greer wrote his new deputy minister, Duncan McArthur, that the courses of study 'should be thoroughly revised and re-written.'[14] In the months ahead, McArthur himself offered constant criticisms of the existing curriculum and hinted at sweeping changes. Teachers had 'failed miserably' by considering that their sole aim was to impart information. 'In all the activities of the school, emphasis should be placed on the development of the creative and social rather than the acquisitive impulses.' Ruthless competition and rugged individualism must give way to 'the promotion of a social consciousness.'[15] In 1936 McArthur chose Thornton Mustard of the Toronto Normal School and Stanley Watson, principal of Toronto's Keele Street Public School, and gave them a year to prepare proposals for curriculum reform. They were instructed to survey other provinces and countries, so that the new Ontario program 'may embrace all that is best and essential in any of the courses which have been issued recently.' A century of provincial pride was not to stand in the way. 'The committee need not feel that it is placed under any limitation so far as the present Ontario course of study and grading are concerned.'[16]

Like many Ontario educators, Mustard and Watson were sympathetic to the American progressive movement, but within certain clear limits. Watson preferred an activity- and experience-oriented class-room, but with the teacher firmly in control and without unlicensed freedom.[17] Mustard's view of class-room freedom was characterized as being 'far removed from the thinking which sees in freedom only absence of restraint and liberation from obligation.'[18] Neither man was comfortable with the ideological radicals who were then nudging American progressive education further left with their call for 'a new social order.' Mustard and Watson were pragmatists, convinced by the realities of the depression that a different approach to class-room learning was necessary to prepare students for an uncertain future. That different approach could come through a careful selection of already proven 'progressive' methodologies. American developments were the major influence, although for political reasons the Hadow reports on curriculum from Great Britain were cited rather than the writings of John Dewey. (The British word 'enterprise,' for example, rather than the American 'project' was used to describe the group activities around which learning would be based.) On paper, the new Ontario curriculum of 1937 looked not unlike recent revisions in other provinces. Alberta's supervisor of schools was delighted when he discovered wholesale plagiarism in program descriptions. 'This is the first time on record,' wrote H.C. Newland, 'that the good old province of Ontario saw fit to import an educational procedure from the West.'[19]

II

What did the new curriculum mean for pupils in Ontario elementary schools in September 1937? 'The focus of attention is shifted from content to child, and from the child in general to the individual child,' declared Mustard. 'The factory system of mass production is replaced by something approaching the care and study of the craftsman and artist.' Mustard saw visions of class-rooms 'that were bright and cheerful, where children could work together grouped around a table, with maybe a rocking chair here and there.' He hoped that the class-room would be 'a place where children could live socially, where it was a joy to go, and where their interests and activities could be fully developed.'[20] Socially-oriented subjects like health and social studies now received more time during the school day, while arithmetic was slightly de-emphasized. In all subjects, the emphasis was to be on activity-oriented learning in a happy, wholesome environment. 'The conditions within which a child lives and learns at school,' declared Inspector V.N. Ames of Hamilton, 'are more imporatnt than the factual knowledge gained.'[21]

The new program meant the end for the old *Ontario Readers*, whose editions of the 1880s and 1910s had served the parents and grandparents of 1937 youngsters. The first crack in the *Ontario Readers'* monopoly had come in 1933 with the publication of a new grade 1 primer – *Mary, John and Peter*. With its clear type, attractive drawings, handsome design, and controlled vocabulary, this little book prepared the way for a new generation of readers. Teachers reported that beginners made more rapid progress and took a greater interest in reading than had been the case with the former, more literary type of reader.[22] By the early 1940s, an entire series of similar readers was in use in the elementary grades: *A Garden of Stories*, *Golden Windows*, and *Gateways to Bookland* for the junior classes, the *Treasury Readers* and the *Life and Literature* series for the older pupils. There was considerably less story material from the 'great' authors of the past, and a much stronger appeal to children's interests. Yet it was still an idealized world that was presented to the children. 'Friendly Village' was pictured in *A Garden of Stories*, the grade 2 reader, as 'a place where most girls and boys would like to live,' with gentle hills and flowing stream, where 'everyone is friendly as friendly can be.' In part, the new readers had transferred the 'good life' from the past to the present, and transplanted it from Great Britain to North America.

Central to the 1937 *Programme of Studies* was the blending of history, geography, and civics into 'social studies' – where the new 'whole' would be greater than the sum of its former 'parts' – and the use of the enterprise or activity approach to teaching and learning in the social studies class-room. Progressive educators argued that traditional approaches to the formal subjects of history and geography – 'the amassing of knowledge in neat lists and summaries' – were inadequate preparation for life in a democratic society where economic hardship and social misery were facts of life. What was needed was a concentration on 'the development of understandings, the growth of interests and the forming of attitudes,' in short a change in pupil behaviour that would manifest itself in socially desirable attitudes and actions. The new social studies courses started with the child and extended into his relationship with society at the neighbourhood, local, national, and international levels, in both historical and contemporary time-frames.

In retrospect, the new program, even in its oft-heard clichés, did not differ much from previous curricula so far as the desired ends of education were concerned. Chief inspector Greer reminded his field inspectors in the spring of 1938 to emphasize 'systematic instruction in essential subjects' and not to neglect 'drill, review and tests.'[23] OCE Principal J.G. Althouse denied that the new curriculum encouraged 'the pupil to do only what he likes to do.'[24] H.J. Clarke, public school inspector in Hastings County, bluntly told the school trustees of Belleville that 'the effort is to interest the child in his work, so that he wants to do what we want him to do.'[25] The elementary schools were still expected to produce graduates who were economically productive, politically stable, socially useful, and morally upright. The crucial differences were in means rather than ends. Preparation for responsible adulthood would now come through the school as social agency as well as academic institution, through socialized group behaviour as well as mental discipline.

The success of the new curriculum depended on both teacher and public support. Mustard maintained that 'the whole programme is founded on the conviction that teachers are honest, intelligent, and genuinely interested in their work, and should be given a great deal of freedom in the selection of content, and in the methods of instruction.' He saw teachers as rising 'from the level of the clerk in a chain-store system to the status of ambassador to the Kingdom of Childhood.'[26] But thousands of Ontario teachers were suddenly asked to abandon the security of traditional philosophies and proven teaching methods in order to venture into the unknown. The anticipated changes were many: wide use of reference materials rather than one basic textbook; no more notes dictated by the teacher; continuous assessment rather than end-of-term examinations; co-operation rather than competition among pupils; noisy chatter of children working together on enterprises, rather than enforced silence. Much greater responsibility was being placed on the elementary teacher.

Teachers might at least have expected a thorough pre-service and in-service training in the new methodology. County inspectors were urged to advise their teachers to familiarize themselves thoroughly with the new course of study, but there were no directives on enterprise learning. The list of departmental summer courses for 1937 was identical to the list for the previous year. Instructors for these six-week courses gave as much or as little attention to the new program as they chose, and often that was precious little. Beginning teachers were no more carefully prepared than were the class-room veterans. Normal-school courses of study and examination papers for the next few years reveal a distinct absence of any focus on instructional reform.

Predictably, the reaction was mixed at the school and class-room level. 'We had been preparing ourselves for some time,' recalled veteran northern Ontario teacher Bertha Shaw, 'not building up our defences against the landslide, but carefully considering how to lop off mouldered branches so that the new ones could be grafted in such a manner as to make for practical continuity.'[27] Inspector H.J. Clarke reported in November 1937 that the Belleville public school teachers were 'adapting themselves well to the new course of study ... The general opinion seems to be that it is a good course.' By February of 1938 he was 'not expecting the full effect of the new course for at least another year.' By March of 1939 he was extremely pessimistic about the staffs of three of the four schools, and was placing all his hopes on Queen Victoria Public School where 'the various teachers and classes are working into the new ideas.'[28] Meanwhile at Dovercourt Public School in Toronto, the minutes of fall 1937 teachers' meetings indicate a concern with everything but the new program. Countless hours were spent discussing fire-drill procedures, daily record books, loitering in the hallways, corporal punishment, and grading on report cards. By 1938 the Dovercourt teachers were fighting back – openly criticizing the new program, demanding more time for the practice of handwriting, shunning co-operation with the manual training teacher in interdisciplinary projects, bemoaning the lack of an authorized textbook in social studies, and falling back on 'note taking.'[29]

Not all was as bleak, however, as the Belleville and Dovercourt experiences indicated. Superintendent C.C. Goldring estimated that 85 per cent of Toronto's 2,200 public school teachers encouraged their classes to undertake enterprises during the 1937-8 school year. Most of these projects were in social studies, with a few in natural science, health, and literature.[30] Meanwhile in Prince Edward County, Inspector C.E. Stothers persuaded trustees of most of his rural schools to move the fixed desks over to one side of the class-room, bring in table tops and trestles for enterprise work on the other side, stress leisure reading and creative writing, and introduce a new report card which emphasized the child's social development. 'On standardized tests,' reported Stothers at the end of the year, 'for the first time in our county the rural pupils excelled the urban pupils.'[31] Across the Bay of Quinte at SS no. 13, Richmond, first-year teacher Walter Wilson took the enterprise approach so much to heart that his class-room was 'transformed into what appears like an artist's studio.'[32]

Nowhere was the new curriculum sold to the public more vigorously than in Hamilton. Leadership came from the Hamilton Teachers' Council, an umbrella organization comprising all the teachers employed by the board of education. During the first week of April 1938, some 60,000 visitors flocked to the city armouries to the HTC-sponsored Hamilton Educational Exposition. 'Never before,' reported one newspaper, 'has the school system of a whole city pooled its efforts to portray to the public the work being done in the schools.' The emphasis was on the new course of studies, with movies and a half-mile of display tables featuring health education, social studies, and citizenship training. The exposition was designed to enlist the co-operation of parents.[33] Later that year the Hamilton Teachers' Council in conjunction with the New Education Fellowship sponsored a conference whose theme was 'Education for Today.'

Keynote speakers included some of the leading lights in the progressive education movement in the United States: Carleton Washburne, school superintendent from Winetka, Illinois, and Harold Rugg of Teachers' College, Columbia University. Rugg's address on 'Building an Education for the Needs of an Individual' was broadcast live by the CBC over a coast-to-coast network of Canadian radio stations.

Laymen's groups reacted to the new curriculum in a manner similar to that of the teachers; vocal support from provincial leaders often changed to apathy and uneasiness at the grass-roots level. Helen Hewson, education convenor of the Home and School Federation, was one of those who welcomed the change. 'This was the stuff,' she proclaimed, 'this was written by someone who really knew children.'[34] The 1937 annual convention of the United Farmers of Ontario recommended that local farm groups study the changes during the coming year, 'with the idea of creating a public opinion which will support them and press on for still greater changes.'[35] The leaders might point the way but the troops frequently balked at the direction chosen. Occasionally the negative public reaction may have been provoked by Thornton Mustard himself through his evangelistic commitment and his flamboyant platform manner. One sympathetic Timmins principal claimed that for two years after a Mustard speech in that community 'the word progressive was taboo.'[36] Moreover, a conservative public was reacting against changes that it perceived as weakening discipline and authority and lessening the emphasis on the three Rs and book learning. Parents and community leaders of the late 1930s – as of any decade – had a strong interest in preserving the status quo in the schools. They had been brought up on a curriculum and through teaching methods that had seemed effective for their generation. Why make a radical change amidst the political and economic uncertainties of the late 1930s? When society wanted stability, the school leaders called for innovation. The wonder is not that the 1937 changes did not sweep the province, but that they gained as much of a foothold as they did.

III

The Second World War affected the daily routine of the schools in a myriad of ways. Teachers and pupils became involved in Red Cross work, Victory Loan concerts, paper and scrap metal drives, air raid drills, and monthly inter-class competitions for the purchase of war savings stamps. Students at Brantford Collegiate organized a 'Bundles for Britain' campaign which sent thousands of articles of clothing overseas. Kincardine High School pupils raised money to help purchase two aeroplanes for the RCAF by selling flowers, washing cars, and donating earnings from part-time jobs. Home economics students at Sarnia Collegiate made dressing gowns, hospital supplies, quilts, socks, and sweaters for the 'boys overseas.'

The normal pattern of high school attendance was severely disrupted, with early spring closings and late fall openings the norm throughout most of the province in order to release teenage labour for farm work. Steady employment in the wartime industrial factories also tempted many pupils. The number of work permits for fourteen- and fifteen-year-olds, for example, jumped from a mere 2,146 in 1939 to 12,792 three years later. Early in 1942 Premier Hepburn toyed with the idea of lowering the school-leaving age to fourteen to encourage more boys to take up apprenticeships since 'winning the war is our first and only important problem.'[37] But strong opposition from labour, Home and School, welfare and educational groups deterred any government action in this area.

The war provided a boost for the school cadet movement, which had languished in the doldrums since the beginning of the 1930s. From a strength of some 44,750 in 1931, the total number of school cadets in Ontario had declined by approximately 5 per cent annually during the remaining years of the decade. Depression dollars were in short supply while isolationism was prevalent. 'There was a feeling on the part of most people,' wrote Toronto's director of education, C.C. Goldring, 'that we would experience a long period of peace and there was not the same enthusiasm for matters pertaining to war and uniforms as there has been at some other times.'[38] But as the European nations began rearming the Toronto Board of Education reintroduced cadet training as a compulsory school activity in the spring of 1939, in the face of Goldring's protest that he was 'entirely opposed to any attempt to make this programme obligatory.'[39] Once established, the momentum for military training was impossible to stop. 'A year ago, I thought we should keep the war out of our schools,' high school inspector S.D. Rendall told the OEA in 1941. 'I do not believe now that we can do that.'[40]

One of the little-known backstage dramas of the Second World War was the battle between the Department of National Defence and the Ontario Department of Education over control of the military preparedness program in the province's schools. On one side were the goliaths of wartime Ottawa, cabinet ministers like J.L. Ralston and Chubby Power, and generals like A.G.L. McNaughton. The educators at Queen's Park held out for five years, aided and abetted in the first instance by Premier Mitchell Hepburn's public row with Prime Minister Mackenzie King over the general question of wartime preparedness. Ontario won the first round in the fall of 1942 with the launching of a new defence training course instead of a compulsory cadet program. Required for all high school students, female as well as male, and referred to as 'the most important new course of recent date,' it was basically a revision of the former health and physical education course. Added emphasis was placed on health habits, diet, and nutrition, and defence topics such as drill, map reading, aircraft recognition, and signalling were introduced.[41] Although the course promised to fulfil the general requirements of any cadet training, its focus and control were in the educational, not the military domain.

The co-existence of this defence training course as a compulsory curricular offering and the traditional cadet corps as an extra-curricular activity produced nothing but trouble. Given their choice (and issued with a khaki uniform) most teen-age boys preferred the 'real' after-hours cadets to the 'pretend' environment of the defence course. Gradually the power of the educational establishment weakened, as the Ottawa military bureaucracy exerted pressure and the manpower situation of the Canadian armed forces through 1943 and 1944 grew steadily more severe. Finally, in September 1944, cadet training under either army or air force auspices became a compulsory part of the high school program, while the health and physical education course reverted to its pre-1942 form. Although the declared emphasis in cadet training remained 'the building of character and citizenship rather than the military aspect,' it was obvious that military requirements had pre-empted educational objectives in the crisis situation of the Second World War.

The fate of Empire Day in the schools of Ontario was linked closely to the cadet movement. Here, too, the previous peak had been reached in 1931, when 15,000 pupils had participated in Toronto's Empire Day parade and open-air festivities. The drift of the 1930s from militarism to appeasement was accompanied by a parallel drift from imperialism to internationalism. 'The time is opportune for the nations to get together and work out world peace,' Mitchell Hepburn told a 1933 Empire Day rally in St Thomas. 'If world peace is to survive it rests with the young people.'[42] But all had changed by the end of the decade. The coronation of King George VI and Queen Elizabeth in the spring of 1937 and their triumphant tour of Canada in 1939 gave to Empire Day celebrations of those years an emotional patriotism as of old. An indication of public feeling came in 1941 when local school-boards rejected a department of education suggestion that Empire Day, St George's Day, and the King's birthday be combined and celebrated on April 23. C.C. Goldring of Toronto might be against compulsory cadets, but he still wanted a 'bang-up Empire Day celebration' that year.[43] By the following year, the spirit of George Ross and 1899 was all-pervasive. The province's 1942 Empire Day pamphlet gave stirring accounts of British and Dominion contributions to the war effort, reproduced 'chins up' messages from King George VI and Winston Churchill, and quoted Education Minister Duncan McArthur on the need to 'remember that our Empire became great, not by reason of material things, but by the dauntless spirit of its people.'[44]

Many Ontario educators hoped that the curricular revisions of 1937 might fulfil these new demands of a society at war. Was not the new social studies course – and particularly the project or enterprise approach – an ideal vehicle for organizing fund-raising projects, for examining the month-by-month progress of the war, for underlining the co-operative endeavours of the Commonwealth and Allied nations? Could students not be led to increased appreciation of the political freedoms of the British Empire and the moral tenets of Christianity? Was not the freer class-room atmosphere a daily example of democracy in action? Such hopes were naïve, given the atmosphere induced by the global conflict. Already buffeted by teacher indifference and public scepticism, progressive education in Ontario was delivered a severe blow with the outbreak of the Second World War.

The School magazine was perfectly correct in the fall of 1940 when it warned that 'the new education, designed to make democracy more effective, will bear the first brunt of the attack.'[45] Toronto high school teacher Isabel Thomas predicted that 'the collapse of the European democracies is going to be ascribed to lack of discipline, and the blame will be given to the schools and particularly to the new "weak" concepts of education.' Her prediction: 'Society will probably require the schools to abandon their efforts to make free citizens, fitted to live happily in a free society ... The public will demand and many teachers will condone a sabotaging of the whole scheme.'[46] The critics of progressive education made up in emotional rhetoric what they lacked in empirical methodology. Did not the lack of basic literary and computational skills among recruits for the armed forces imply a shortcoming of Canadian schools? And did not the abilities of Ontario schoolchildren in verbal and written expression suffer by comparison, once the British 'war orphans' began arriving? It was all very clear to the Middlesex County Trustees' and Ratepayers' Association; that group called for 'more stress on the three Rs and useful subjects rather than playing with paper dolls.'[47]

The 1942 meeting of the Ontario Educational Association demonstrated how quickly the pedagogical pendulum could swing. Throughout the 1930s, the annual OEA Easter session had served as an important forum for arousing interest and mobilizing support for progressivist education. But it was the critics of progressivism who had their innings in 1942. A succession of high school principals pointed out shortcomings of the new grade 8 graduates: they lacked precision in the fundamentals; they were noticeably restless and unaccustomed to discipline; they expected too much entertainment. Of course high school principals were expected to criticize elementary school work; the surprise in 1942 was that the most devastating attacks came from elementary school people. Principal Darcy Davidson of Toronto's Ryerson Public School, for example, began by deploring the absence of examinations and the lack of attention to the basics. Then Davidson summed up an impression of progressive education rapidly gaining aceptance during the war years. 'A feature of the new course that handicaps pupils is the belief that there is a royal road to learning; that pupils need not struggle with problems and master disagreeable tasks if they choose not to do so; that they will develop a better personality by doing only pleasant things or finding easy ways around difficulties.' To Davidson and a growing number of Ontario conservatives, all this was 'only wishful thinking.'[48]

IV

As Davidson demonstrated so well, criticisms of skill attainments could easily be turned into attacks on the intellectual, social, and even political underpinnings of the new curriculum. Many university and high school people – those who thought of themselves as the defenders of the intellectual and cultural heritage of English-speaking Canada – feared that the classical ideal of education had been set aside in the 1937 *Programme of Studies*. More was at stake than the decline of Latin or the replacement of history with social studies. According to the older ideal, there were certain aspects of knowledge with which an educated person was presumed to be acquainted – certain books, certain ideas, certain languages. Few scholars pretended that these ideals became the general property of the entire population; rather they were the intellectual heritage and preserve of an aristocracy of culture. These critics chafed at the replacement of an aristocratic ideal of education with one that claimed to be democratic. They saw the real danger of the new education as a reduction of everyone and everything to the level of the least common denominator. 'It will be disastrous for the advancement of learning and the progress of civilization,' lamented Professor J.S. Thompson of Queen's University, 'if great tracts of culture are left untilled, and the heritage of the past perishes.'[49]

Culturally and politically, the revised program of 1937 implied a partial rejection of absolute values passed on to former generations of pupils through Aesop's fables, Old Testament morality tales, and a focus on the past accomplishments of the British Empire. The new school readers of the late 1930s emphasized the present and future rather than the past, an idyllic world of smiling faces and happy people rather than stories of sorrow, temptation, and death. The search for moral values was now more open-ended, with the correct response in any given situation dependent not so much on Judaeo-Christian absolutes but on what a later generation would call situation ethics. And the search for political values such as patriotism and loyalty did not end with British victories at Blenheim, Trafalgar, Waterloo, and Paardeburg. Toronto Tory W.J. Stewart charged in the legislature in 1942 that the number of patriotic selections had been reduced from fifty-five to eight in the new series of elementary school readers.[50] Despite Duncan McArthur's spirited defence of the 'loyalty' quotient in the new books, it was clear in both the new readers and the social studies reference books that the imperialist mission of the British Empire now had to share the stage with the internationalism of the League of Nations and the continental pull of the United States.

It was not surprising that American themes and ideals had made their way into Canadian school-books in the decade of the 1930s. The period since the end of the First World War had seen a massive Americanization of Canadian popular culture, thanks to the radio, the comic book, the Sunday newspaper, the

Hollywood movie industry, and the cross-border mobility produced by the automobile. A 1932 survey of students in eleven Ontario high schools showed that 62 per cent claimed intimate friendships with Americans, 76 per cent had relatives who were American citizens, and 72 per cent read American magazines almost exclusively.[51] In an attempt to close the gap between the child's classroom and out-of-class-room world, textbook editors and authors turned to American themes. But by the time the books began appearing, the old British imperial ideal was making one last major pull on Canadian loyalties. The coronation of King George VI, the 1939 royal visit, the revival of interest in school cadets, and Empire Day all helped. Most important was the heroic defence of democracy carried single-handedly by Britain and the Empire for eighteen long months after the fall of France in June 1940. By 1941 the north-south cultural orientation of Ontario textbooks was out of harmony with the trans-Atlantic pull occasioned by the war.

In much the same way, the internationalism and the left-wing political orientation of the new readers and social studies books quickly became unfashionable as the 1930s turned into the 1940s. It was unfortunate that the 1937 curriculum change came at the same time as the machinery of the League of Nations was visibly breaking down, when aggression was the order of the day in Europe and the Far East, and when appeasement seemed to encourage even more aggression. At just that point in time, Ontario schools were supposed to be implementing the most significant pedagogical and ideological changes in their history. When society wanted stability, the school leaders called for innovation. At home on the domestic political scene, the 1937 *Programme of Studies* seemed to reflect the idealistic hopes of the CCF party, rather than the hard realities espoused by the older political parties. Joseph McCully, the headmaster who had made Pickering College a beach-head for progressivism in the 1930s, was out of step with the mood of Ontario society when he urged in 1942 that 'education should be inspired, not by a regretful hankering after the extinct beauties of the past, but a shining vision of the society that is to be, of the triumphs that thought will achieve in the time to come, and of the ever-widening horizon of man's survey over the universe.'[52]

The relation between political differences and educational processes was made dramatically apparent at a December 1941 conference on 'Teaching Democratic Citizenship,' symbolically held at McCully's Pickering College. Guest panellist M.J. Coldwell of the CCF believed the schools should stress 'the value of collective security ... based on some form of international law.' That approach, he maintained, was 'the only way to secure a lasting peace for the world.' While a few educational leaders would keep the progressivist spirit alive throughout the war years, its viability as an educational philosophy was by now under consistent attack. Education for peace had been shelved in favour of military preparedness. When one was·no longer supposed to reason why, and when force was again an accepted approach to human affairs, progressive education was doomed. George Drew followed M.J. Coldwell in the panel discussion at Pickering College, and the remarks of the Conservative opposition leader appealed to a different segment of Ontario society. The school's role in preserving democracy, proclaimed Drew, lay through religious education, the cadet movement, and emphasizing 'the closer association of the units within the British Empire.'[53]

Throughout the war years, teachers' magazines and teachers' meetings were preoccupied with the question of how best to teach citizenship and democracy. Should the medium be history, or English, or each and every subject? Should democratic citizenship be formally taught or informally conveyed through teacher behaviour and class-room organization? To rationalize action in this area, ministers of education from several provinces gave financial and moral support to the Canadian Council of Education for Citizenship, whose executive secretary was former Ottawa Normal school master F.S. Rivers. Two conferences in the fall and winter of 1941-2 demonstrated the different ways in which schools could respond. Public school inspectors and normal-school masters meeting in London at a 'Confidential Conference on Teaching of Democracy,' put their faith in the enterprise method, social studies, pupil participation in class-room management, the Junior Red Cross, and the extra-curricular program.[54] Earlier that fall, the biennial meeting of the Canada and Newfoundland Education Association had also focused on 'Citizenship and Democracy.' But here the message had been different. In his keynote address, Principal R.C. Wallace of Queen's University saw the future of democracy depending on 'Protestants putting religion into the education system.'[55]

By 1941, many thoughtful and vocal leaders of Ontario society were ready to support Wallace's views. If the schools could serve to promote the cause of democracy, could they not also be used to buttress Christianity? Indeed, was there not the closest of links between the survival of the political tradition and that of the religious heritage? 'We cannot ensure democracy until we have Bible study in our schools,' inspector J.J. Wilson told the Bruce County Educational Association.[56] Of course opening exercises, including a Bible reading and the Lord's Prayer, were the custom in almost all Ontario class-rooms. A few school-boards also provided direct religious instruction – taught either by the class-room teacher or a visiting clergyman – either before or after regular school hours. Concern over declining Sunday School attendance, the weakening of home influence, and the steady increase in the rate of juvenile delinquency had brought together eight Protestant denominations in 1927 to found the Ontario Religious Education Council. Its goal was compulsory religious education, taught by members of the clergy, during school hours. 'We in Ontario are lagging behind on this point,' Education Minister Simpson told the legislature in 1936. 'It is time we devoted a certain amount of time in our public school curriculum each day to the teaching of religious knowledge.'[57] By 1940-1, some 728 schools or 10 per cent of the provincial total had moved voluntarily in this direction.

The Second World War provided the necessary stimulation for compulsory religious education. With fathers in the armed forces, and mothers flocking to industrial jobs as never before, many children were growing up with a 'lack of parental control' which promoted a 'spirit of unrest and feeling of insecurity' leading in turn to a 'partial breakdown of self-discipline among our young people.'[58] In far too many cases this was seen to promote juvenile delinquency – up from 9,829 court cases in 1938 to 13,802 four years later, and described by Judge G.W. Moberly of Owen Sound as 'the greatest problem before the Provincial authorities in Canada today.'[59] The future might not have seemed troubled if all children had attended Sunday School. But various estimates from the late 1930s and early 1940s put the figure no higher than 50 per cent. 'Half the youth ... never hear the name of Jesus except in anger or profanity,' charged Rev. M.E. Conron of Brantford. 'They choose for their heroes Napoleon Bonaparte, Babe Ruth, John Dillinger or Mae West.'[60] In debates before the OEA and local county educational associations, persuasive speakers like Moberly and Conron could list up to twenty or thirty reasons for religious instruction in the schools. But for many Ontario residents it was very simple: with so many children not attending Sunday School and the home neglecting its responsibility, the school must assume the task of religious instruction.

V

Conservative leader George Drew identified himself and his party with these educational concerns in the 1943 provincial election. While all three political parties stressed the extension of educational opportunity in their official campaign literature, the real difference lay in curricular and philosophic emphases. Two thrusts were plainly evident in a series of 'platform notes' developed by the Conservatives in 1941. First, 'regulations, rigidly enforced, to ensure that pupils in primary schools shall receive a thorough grounding in the Three R's.' Second, 'a definite and planned programme with a view of instilling into young Canadians ... loyalty to King, Country and Empire, respect for the flag, together with a more complete knowledge of British and Canadian history.'[61] In the months that followed, George Drew, UEL descendant, First World War veteran, militia colonel, and author of books on military history, repeated his belief that Empire ties should be stressed as a policy in education. On the eve of the summer 1943 election, he warned that he would not 'allow any school teacher to create doubts in the minds of children of the importance of the great fellowship that was the British Empire.'[62]

Teachers and school administrators were made aware of new directions as the 1943 school year opened. In an address to the Ontario Police Association on 9 September, Premier Drew advocated a return to discipline in the teaching of children 'in order to form a basis for a Christian democracy.' Speaking in Ottawa in October, he stressed formal examinations and cadet training. In a November message to teachers and trustees, 'personal discipline and recognition of constituted authority' were spelled out as the school's role in building a responsible citizenship. During Education Week in December, Toronto teachers were told to 'attach great importance to simply loyalty ... [and] the place of Canada within the Empire.'[63] When the federal government declared May 24, November 11 and the King's birthday to be no longer statutory holidays, Drew amended the necessary legislation to retain them as school holidays. In the months to come, normal-school students were exhorted to 'lay the firm foundations for a strong society based upon those Christian precepts which are the strong foundation of our free democracy.'[64] Drew instructed his departmental officials to 'develop such a system of education as will tend to produce citizens who will conform to the ideal citizen envisaged by the Minister.'[65]

Although the 1943 election had given the Conservatives a narrow minority government victory over the CCF, Drew realized that this was merely the first round in an ideological battle for the hearts and minds of Ontario voters. A second and more decisive confrontation loomed in the near future. Depending on circumstance and tactics, another election could be triggered at any time by either government dissolution of the legislature or a want-of-confidence vote by the combined CCF-Liberal opposition. Education was one area in which Drew out-manoeuvred that opposition in the months ahead, with a strategy that swung many middle-of-the-road voters over to the Conservative camp. Following the lead of his Conservative predecessors of the 1920s and 1930s, Howard Ferguson and George Henry, Drew kept the education portfolio for himself. Quickly a two-fold strategy emerged from the minister and his senior adviser, J.G. Althouse, appointed director of education in 1944. First, a stress on those traditional aspects of education that had been de-emphasized with the progressivist curriculum of 1937: the three Rs, the British Empire, and the Christian religion. Second came a deliberate move to wean Ontario teachers away from left-leaning politics and win their votes for Conservative candidates.

Ontario teachers benefitted financially from the Second World War, in contrast to the situation that had developed during the 1914-18 conflict. Average salaries for high school teachers, for example, rose 22.5 per cent between 1940 and 1945, twice the rise in the consumer price index. This favourable advantage was caused in part by price stabilization induced by the War Time Price Control Board, but was due in greater measure to school-board salary increases in an era of teacher shortage. Yet material improvements brought the teacher no closer to that elusive goal of status and respect within the community. Extolled as the guardian of tomorrow's citizens, he chafed at federal government regulations that froze all teachers in the profession, was expected to volunteer first for any wartime patriotic campaign, and, above all, was forced to be an embodiment of the highest moral standards. 'Lack of status in the public mind was a gnawing irritant,' wrote the historian of the OSSTF. Where the teacher 'had once been recognized as a man of learning in his community, he now felt himself to be a servant.'[66]

It was a mixture of status consciousness and utopian idealism that prompted some Ontario teachers to flirt with the CCF and other left-wing political groups in the early 1940s. Did not this new party promise teachers a role in policy making denied them by the lawyer-businessman-farmer-dominated older parties? Did it not emphasize education as a crucial ingredient in post-war social planning? Joseph Noseworthy, head of the English department at Vaughan Road Collegiate in York Township, showed what could be accomplished. Author of a major study on educational finance in 1935, president of the OSSTF in 1938, Noseworthy achieved a political upset of enormous significance in 1942 by defeating Conservative leader Arthur Meighen in the York South federal by-election. What frightened and annoyed some Ontarians was the fact that almost a hundred of Noseworthy's students campaigned for him.[67] The political situation only worsened in the months ahead. The *Educational Courier* called for continued government control of industry to prevent 'wasteful, competitive, untrammelled methods and fat profits.'[68] The Canadian Association for Adult Education issued a 1943 manifesto calling for democratic social planning, social responsibility ahead of private gain, and 'death to the old individualism.'[69] And in November 1943, some 15,000 citizens attending a rally sponsored by the National Council for Canadian-Soviet Friendship at Toronto's Maple Leaf Gardens heard a call for exchanges of teachers between Canadian and Russian schools.[70] It was time for George Drew to intervene.

Drew and Althouse regarded the important Teaching Profession Act of 1944 as vital to winning teacher support for Conservative policies. Without compromising school-board and provincial government control of educational policy, this act legitimized the teachers' federations, made membership in one of the federations mandatory for anyone teaching in Ontario, and required employing boards to collect the dues. 'Automatic membership' had been a goal of federation members for years, but without government compulsion figures had ranged between 90 per cent of eligible members within OSSTF ranks to only 45 per cent in the FWTAO. Althouse urged Drew to promote the legislation on the grounds that it would 'attract to the teaching ranks a fair proportion of the most intelligent and vigorous of our young people' and give 'higher prestige and greater stability to the teaching profession.'[71] The measure passed the spring session of the legislature with a minimum of trustee opposition and a straw vote showed teachers in favour by a fourteen-to-one majority. The act required the various federations to unite loosely under the umbrella of the Ontaro Teachers' Federation, and meant that these groups could henceforth devote more time to questions of educational policy, professional development, and ethics rather than membership drives and finances. 'No legislative miracle can create a professional attitude in a teacher who is either unable or unwilling to make it a part of his personality,' summed up the OSSTF *Bulletin*. 'But the Act does grant to our present generation the dignity of public recognition of our place in the community.'[72]

The ink on the Teaching Profession Act was hardly dry before members of the two public school federations, the male OPSMTF and the female FWTAO, were called on to institute one of George Drew's most significant educational reforms: religious education as an integral part of the elementary school program. Again, this was an area in which Drew Conservatives capitalized on growing public sentiment to move quickly and decisively. The intent was spelled out in the speech from the throne in February 1944; by September, adaptations of English guide books were available, and the program, taught by class-room teachers, began in grades 1 to 6. Two half-hour periods per week were now devoted to the siudy of the scriptures. The junior grades concentrated on the background of family and community life as Jesus knew it, while the senior classes studied Old Testament stories and the teachings of Jesus. Scriptural interpretations were to be 'non-sectarian,' avoiding the tenets or doctrines of any particular creed. They were to be confined to those expressions of the Christian faith upon which all Christian denominations were in substantial agreement. So strong was the wartime movement for religious education, and so forceful was Drew in his defence of the program, that only forty of Ontario's more than 5,000 school-boards asked for exemption from teaching the course the first year.

According to the 1944 regulations, religious education should do more than teach scriptural facts and biblical text. 'Religious instruction must aim to set up ideals, to build attitudes, and to influence behaviour.'[73] The children of Ontario were to be prepared to live in a democratic society which based its way of life on the Christian ideal. In Drew's mind, a 'Christian society' and a 'democratic society' were closely linked, if not synonymous, and both were central to his vision of post-war society. 'It was a part of the training of the character of the citizens of tomorrow that we expanded religious education in the public schools.'[74] When Jewish leader Abraham Feinberg protested against the narrowly Christian rather than Judaeo-Christian approach, he was reminded that 'this Government is committed to the support of Christianity.'[75] When Mitchell Hepburn, attempting a comeback as Liberal party leader, moved a want-of-confidence motion on the government's handling of the religious education question, Drew saw a ready-made election issue. He entered the 1945 campaign as the defender of Christianity, charging the Liberals would take religion out of the schools, and that the CCF – because of their split vote on the Hepburn motion – had no convictions. So far as Drew was concerned, 'as long as I am Prime Minister it will remain.'[76]

Drew used his educational philosophy and accomplishments to good effect in the campaign. A war-weary public felt comfortable with a party that stressed class-room discipline and factual learning, and had restored Empire Day, the cadet movement, and religious education to their 'rightful' places within Ontario schools. Drew also traded his 1944 Teaching Profession Act for teacher votes. The Conservative party, in an unprecedented two-page advertisement in the May issue of the *Canadian School Journal*, listed fifteen accomplishments of the past two years that helped teachers and fourteen more that benefitted trustees. 'Your government has accomplished much in less than two years. Give us the mandate to go ahead with the job.'[77] Once again, an Ontario premier had used educational issues to excellent political advantage. Drew's landslide victory in the 4 June election marked the death knell of the 1937 curriculum changes. It would have additional important implications for Ontario's post-war educational system.

9 *The Triumph of Conservatism*

I

'People turn to the school after a war,' observed Toronto superintendent Z.S. Phimister in 1947, 'in the faint hope that the school may be able to do something which will make it possible for the next generation to avoid another calamity of the same kind.'[1] Whether one listened to Premier George Drew championing religious education and citizenship training as the 'best bulwarks against Communism,' the National Committee for School Health Research urging the 'need for greater knowledge and understanding of the mental health problems in schools,' or the Home and School Federation criticizing the effects of popular literature and radio on young people, it was obvious that politicians and public groups in the late 1940s were prepared to increase the responsibilities of the school. 'Whatever will enrich the child's mind, develop his personality, or make him more capable of living a successful life is recognized as a legitimate part of the school's work,' declared an Ottawa teacher in an address appropriately entitled 'The School as a Social Agency.'[2] Amid the avalanche of requests for such an extended role, the public scarcely noticed the calm understatement of *The School* magazine that 'they pay the school an embarrassing compliment by assuming that it can do everything.'[3]

Yet Ontario educators were well aware that the province's school system fell short of the mark in several respects. Statistics released in 1945 indicated that, of every 100 Ontario pupils who began school life in the early 1930s, some eighty-four completed grade 8, only fifty-eight entered secondary school, twenty-one completed grade 12, and thirteen graduated from grade 13.[4] A survey commissioned by the Ontario School Trustees' and Ratepayers' Association showed, not surprisingly, that home background influenced success in school. High achievers in grade 8 came predominantly from homes where parents had more education, where books and cultural opportunities were more readily available, family life more stable, and fathers did not 'frequent beer parlours.'[5] Conditions in rural northern Ontario further demonstrated the gap between the theory of equal educational opportunity and the reality. The sixteen northern inspectors reported in 1946 that only 16 per cent of their 583 one-room schools achieved an accommodation grading equal to the provincial average, while 45 per cent employed untrained teachers teaching on special permits.[6] A national survey revealed that while Ontario stood second among the provinces in expenditures on teachers' salaries and third in the proportion of teachers who were university graduates, it ranked last in terms of educational effort based on total provincial wealth.[7]

Clearly, there was much work to be done in improving minimum educational provisions. From 1942 onward, senior educational officials began planning for both a quantitative and a qualitative improvement in schooling in the period of post-war reconstruction. With Ontarians George Rogers and J.G. Althouse playing key roles, the Canada and Newfoundland Education Association established a survey committee to determine the 'outstanding needs' of Canadian schooling. The Ontario Educational Association had its own committee on post-war education, which sponsored four regional conferences during the fall of 1943 and virtually monopolized the program at the 1944 annual convention. These two committees produced similar sets of recommendations: broader curriculum offerings at the high school level; an extension of counselling, library and school health services; higher salaries and improved qualifications for teachers; stronger incentives for larger units of local administrations; and increased provincial funding.

The call for the province to assume a greater share of local school costs had been advocated in the 1938 report of the Committee on the Costs of Education and subsequently endorsed by many urban school-boards forced to cope with swollen enrolments caused by the influx of families through wartime industrial expansion. Initially, the demand had been resisted on two counts: it would be too costly for the provincial treasury and it would discourage local involvement in the schools. But the early 1940s were unusual years, and the 1943 election was atypical. Even before the vote had been called, Conservative leader George Drew, in an attempt to head off the CCF challenge, had talked of a post-war world of economic prosperity and social justice. On 9 July, he set out his election platform, a sweeping twenty-two point program of social and economic development. Included was the specific promise that 'the Provincial Government will assume 50 percent of the school tax now charged against real eatate.' Former Liberal leader and premier, Harry C. Nixon, later called this 'the boldest and most attractive bid for support in any general election in this Province.' With the prospect of his own tax bill of $194 being halved, Nixon declared that 'I almost voted Conservative myself.'[8]

Following the Tory victory at the polls, it fell to provincial treasurer Leslie Frost and department of education officials to work out the details of the new financial arrangements. As one who regarded balanced budgets as a point of honour, and who had not been consulted by Drew in the development of the scheme, Frost was somewhat appalled. It was not surprising, then, that over the ensuing months 50 per cent of local costs (which, added to the existing provincial share, meant more like 58 per cent) was first reduced to 50 per cent of total costs and finally to 50 per cent of a somewhat restricted list of 'approved' costs. When the new policy was implemented in 1945, grants to urban boards varied with population, and ranged from 30 to 60 per cent of approved costs, while rural grants varied with assessment per class-room and ranged from 50 to 90 per cent. As a result, total provincial grants to local school-boards jumped from $1.6 million in 1944 to $9.3 million in 1945; Queen's Park was now financing about 42 per cent of all school expenditures. Now in the closing months of his twenty-year service with the department, chief inspector V.K. Greer finally saw a glimmer of hope in achieving equality of educational opportunity. Greer called the new scheme the most 'momentous change' ever made in school financing. It promised the best of all possible worlds. 'The grants are sufficiently high that the local load of taxation will be greatly lightened,' Greer informed Drew, 'but there will remain a sufficient levy to retain local interest in the schools and a strong local control.'[9]

The increased grants were clearly meant to relieve the burden of school taxation on real property. Departmental calculations forecast possible mill reductions ranging from 2.2 to 5.5 in urban areas, and from 1.8 to 30.6 in rural areas. Obviously, the purpose would be defeated if school-boards or municipal councils increased their expenditures. Frost was adamant that it was 'the duty of the municipalities to pass the great reduction in levies asked for by our school boards on to the people.'[10] The president of the Ontario Association of Real Estate Boards promised to assist Drew 'in retaining for the property taxpayer the benefit of your contribution' and offered to monitor local expenditures.[11] The taxpayers did receive some relief during 1945 but it was only a brief respite. In 1946 public school supporters lost more than what had been gained as their average tax rates increased by 2.3 mills. Nor was there any great relief for separate school supporters, despite the prediction of Toronto Baptist preacher T.T. Shields that 'separate schools will spring up everywhere' under the new arrangements.[12] The separate school portion of the total elementary grant fell from 23 to 14 per cent, despite the fact that these schools enrolled 19 per cent of the pupils. But grants were based on approved costs, and the separate boards – which paid lower salaries – got less.

Without the new provincial grant structure, local boards would have found it even more difficult to cope with the post-war growth in school enrolments. The total number of Ontario pupils attending elementary school rose from 545,000 in 1945 to 612,000 in 1950 to 1,126,000 in 1960 as the full effects of higher post-war birth rates and immigration rates were felt. High school enrolments increased at a similar rate, from 120,000 at the end of the war to 262,000 fifteen years later. In addition to finding class-room places for these new pupils, most Ontario school-boards had a fifteen-year back-log of construction and renovation projects that had been delayed by the depression and the war. Over 900 capital projects were approved between 1945 and 1950 at an estimated cost of $80 million. This expansion, coupled with post-war inflation, boosted per-pupil costs during those years – from $94 to $154 in the public schools and from $167 to $286 in the academic high schools. Total legislative grants for capital and operating expenses jumped from $26 to $41 million, but even so, by 1950 the new schedule of provincial grants accounted for less than 40 per cent of total school-board revenues. Meanwhile, education levies were accounting for 35 per cent of local municipal taxation in Ontario.

Schools were now being built in large numbers for the first time in fifteen years. With their one-storey elevations, larger and more continuous window areas, bilateral lighting, light-coloured chalkboards, tile floors, and movable furniture, they were a welcome change from the commonplace country school-houses and factory-type urban buildings that had long dominated the educational landscape. Encouragement came from the Committee on Planning, Construction and Equipment of Schools, established by Premier Drew in 1944. The showpiece achievement of this committee was the four-room V.K. Greer Memorial School near Utterson in Muskoka District. Completed in 1947 and named after the recently deceased chief inspector, this school was to exibit the latest in exterior and interior design, demonstrate the feasibility of rural central schools, and pave the way for greater flexibility of class-room organization. For the next few years the department of education offered extra financial encouragement for large school sites and landscaping, art and music rooms, gymnasiums and auditoriums, and other amenities. There were cutbacks in the 1950s, when spiralling costs forced the province to reduce its list of approved costs. Yet local boards demanded attractive schools and were willing to raise the extra funds themselves. 'This Department has discouraged needless expense in school-building,' stated Althouse in 1956, 'but the residents of any municipality have shown great reluctance to build anything but the best (i.e., the more expensive) for their school-children.'[13]

The burgeoning areas around Toronto simply could not cope with rising populations and new school construction through an administrative pattern designed for a nineteenth-century agrarian countryside. In 1952, for example, North York Township had one high school board, two township area boards, and three rural school-boards. When Township School Area no. 1 requisitioned funding in 1952 for five new elementary schools, the council approved, but could raise only half the required funds, and the schools erected under these conditions were far below the usual standard. Between 1945 and 1952, provincial grants slipped from 47 to 21 per cent of total revenues in North York. This meant that

55 per cent of the township's local taxes had to go to education, compared with just 34 per cent in the city of Toronto. The creation of Metropolitan Toronto in 1953 was an attempt to provide a measure of fiscal capability by legislating single boards of education for North York and the other suburban municipalities, and establishing the Metropolitan School Board as a co-ordinating agency. As in the 1930s, these suburban developments provided a stimulus for continued rural reorganization. It was a fitting tribute to V.K. Greer, the architect of rural change, that 1945 – the last year of his life – saw the greatest surge to date in the creation of township school areas. That year 149 new areas were created involving 919 former school sections, making a grand total of 397 areas and 2,340 sections since the program had begun in the late 1930s.

Given the trend towards increased provincial funding and larger school districts, it seemed important to some provincial officials to justify the continuing extent of local involvement and control. This task fell largely on the shoulders of J.G. Althouse, who was appointed chief director of education in 1944. 'Forward steps in Ontario education are taken when a number of communities become actively interested in new phases of educational service,' he told a Hamilton audience in 1945. 'Of course the results are mixed. Our reforms march forward on a ragged front ... But when they do march, they seldom have to retreat; and they march with the informed understanding and active support of the people who maintain and patronize the schools.'[14] It is true that Althouse referred to local interest, rather than control, but he certainly implied more of the latter than existed. Firm departmental retraints still prevailed in the important areas of curriculum, textbooks, high school graduation examinations, and the training and certification of teachers.

II

In common with several other provinces in the post-war years, Ontario chose to study its long-range educational future through the vehicle of a royal commission. Such a commission, if representative of many points of view, might provide the schools with a blueprint for the next generation. Throughout much of 1944, Drew, Althouse, and a number of cabinet ministers shared ideas on possible chairmen (even the aged Henry Cody, education minister twenty-five years previously, was suggested) and drew up lists of potential members (including some with CCF 'learnings or sympathies' in order to 'get the youth view').[15] Finally in March 1945, a twenty-member Royal Commission on Education was appointed under the chairmanship of John A. Hope, a justice of the Ontario Supreme Court.

With its encouragement of written briefs and open hearings, the Hope commission provided a forum for the competing philosophies of progressivism and traditionalism. Progressive education was on the defensive, wounded by the pedagogical criticisms of the war years and the political innuendos of the 1943 and 1945 elections. But its advocates within the department of education were still strong enough to influence a thirty-page curriculum statement prepared for the Hope commission. Led by Stanley Watson, co-author of the 1937 reforms, they called for schools to develop inquiring minds, stress experiential learning and co-operative group activities, and use social studies to acquaint pupils with 'the immediate and pressing problems of society.'[16] Traditionalists countered with ringing denunciations of extreme progressivism in the United States which, by implication, seemed ever ready to sweep across the border and engulf Ontario schools. The province's Latin teachers told the commission that progressive education had 'eroded the national leadership,' while the senate of Victoria University charged it with 'sabotaging academic education, thereby jeopardizing much of the democratic ideal in Ontario.'[17]

Ontario waited five-and-a-half years for the commission to finish its work. When finally released in December 1950, the Hope report reflected the social conservatism and political naïvety of the commissioners. While purporting to take a moderate position between the extremes of traditionalism and progressivism, the report demonstrated a consistent underlying preference for a conservative philosophy. Although endorsing 'critical and honest inquiry' in every field, the commissioners laid down 'two virtues about which there can be no question – honesty and Christian love.' Although calling for a smoother transition between elementary and secondary school, they were unwilling to suggest 'any radical departure from the established trend' of the subject-centred high school. 'Mastery of subject-matter is the best present measure of effort and the most promising source of satisfaction in achievement.' School tasks should be challenging, 'because much of life is equally so.' Here was a classical and Calvinistic view of life. 'Efforts should be made to impress on pupils that all who work hard and honestly ... are partners in the good society and warrant social recognition.'[18] It was also, undeniably, a widely shared Ontarian perspective.

The proposed grade reorganization underlined the work-oriented approach of the Hope commission. Alarmed at the amount of repetition in the curriculum, and appalled at the time-consuming nature of progressivist teaching techniques, the commissioners recommended a reduction of elementary and secondary years within a three-tiered system. Six grades of elementary education would be followed by four of secondary education. The third stage would be a junior college, which would offer the equivalent of grade 13, junior university work, and vocational courses. Such a system, argued the report, would ensure that the dividing line between elementary and secondary schooling came at a more appropriate psychological age. Such an approach might also strengthen local school systems, for the report advocated local units large enough to support a junior college and to assume a measure of freedom with respect to curriculum, textbooks, and examinations.

Ironically, in view of their veneration of tradition, the Hope commissioners flew directly in the face of the historical realities of Ontario. Their tri-level organization would have reopened the explosive separate school issue. If Catholic separate schools were restricted to the new elementary grades – as the majority report recommended – Catholics would be deprived of their constitutional and customary rights of from eight to ten years of denominational education. On the other hand, if full separate school rights were granted to the end of the proposed secondary school, then Catholics would be assured of ten years of denominational instruction, where eight was usual. In the first case, Catholics could raise the cry of religious persecution and a denial of rights, as four Catholic members of the commission did in a minority report. In the second, public school supporters opposed extending the school rights of a single religious minority and making further inroads into the common school structure. In either case, it was an explosive issue that faced the Conservative government of Leslie Frost, who succeeded to the premiership in 1949.

Frost later confessed that 'the Hope report left me pretty cold in a good many regards.'[19] His immediate reaction when the report was presented was to declare that 'the Government and the people are not bound by the report, nor are they bound to implement the report in whole or in part.'[20] Presumably acting on the basis of caucus discussions, Marcel Léger, Conservative member for Cochrane North, announced in January 1951 that none of the recommendations 'which could be detrimental to the Catholic religion will be considered, even less enforced, by the present government.'[21] Frost clarified the government's position in a statement to the legislature on February 7. 'There is certainly nothing to indicate that a radical change would now enable us to do better than we are now doing and will continue to do.' In a pointed comment on the explosive separate school issue, he reminded the House that the reforms of the past eight years 'have not created division among our people.'[22]

Mr Justice Hope was understandably annoyed that, for all practical purposes, his report was being shelved. In a lengthy letter to Frost in February 1952 he argued persuasively for his pedagogical and administrative recommendations. 'The lines of division,' he reminded the premier, 'were determined on psychgological and pedagogical grounds alone.' He simply could not understand how political realities could block educational ideals. 'Does it mean that all parts of our educational system must be dragged forever as slaves at the chariot wheels of the Roman catholic Separate Schools and the Roman Catholic Hierarchy?'[23] What Hope failed to realize, however, was that the 1945 revolution in provincial school grants had made his administrative proposals doubly troublesome, while curricular changes announced in 1949 had rendered them partially redundant.

'What the Commission has done,' Frost confided to a political confidant, 'is to advance a theory which, when applied to our tax system, is not practical.'

Apparently the Hope commissioners, when they turned to the financial implications of grade reorganization and the cutback of separate school support to the first six grades, had used the grant and assessment figures of 1942 which were completely outdated by 1950. Frost had in hand a confidential report prepared by department of education officials which detailed the financial impact of the Hope recommendations on representative Ontario municipalities. In most cases, separate school mill rates would fall, whereas public school rates would be significantly increased. 'All of this would create hopeless confusion and misunderstanding with all sorts of bad feelings,' Frost confided. 'I fail to see who it will please ... The recommendation has little relation to the practical realities of the situation.'[24] Frost, of course, had a personal commitment to the reformed grant structure of 1945; but he also feared the impact on the Ontario electorate of direct relief for Catholic taxpayers at the expense of public school supporters.

Hope had also been out-manoeuvred by his long-time rival within the legal profession, Dana Porter. Appointed minister of education following Drew's departure in 1948, Porter and a number of senior departmental officials grew increasingly impatient at the failure of the Hope commission to present its report. Accordingly on 3 November 1949, before a surprised audience of teachers in St Thomas, Porter had announced his own grade re-organization. Curriculum would be organized in four divisions: primary, from grades 1 to 3; junior, from 4 to 6; intermediate, from 7 to 10; and senior, from 11 to 13. Porter forecast even further innovation: multi-age grouping in the primary division; the sharp division between elementary and secondary schooling disappearing with the intermediate grades as a buffer; more options in the senior division; and local responsibility for curriculum development throughout the entire thirteen grades. It was reminiscent of the intermediate-school and progressivist ideas of the mid 1930s. This parallel was not surprising, since the plan was developed by the department's new curriculum branch, headed by Stanley Watson. Watson had first presented his ideas to Hope, but annoyed at the commission's delay, handed the new minister of education a reform proposal that was instantly dubbed 'the Porter Plan.'

Although the Porter plan included no proposals for wholesale administrative reform, its curriculum recommendations ran into teacher opposition and reluctance to innovate. Resurrecting their arguments of the mid-1930s, the Ontario Secondary School Teachers' Federation opposed the new intermediate division. Here was the junior high school or intermediate school again rearing its ugly head. Since there was no provision for specially trained teachers, the new division 'would only attract the ambitious elementary teachers and the unsuccessful high school teachers.'[25] In reality, the OSSTF was reluctant to stoop so low as grade 7, yet not prepared to allow elementary teachers into the 7-to-10 division. Ultimately, the OSSTF relaxed its stand, once it was assured that the department of education regarded grades 7 to 10 as a curriculum division only, not requiring administrative unity within a special-purpose building. Although Chatham and a few suburban Toronto boards introduced the junior high school, most of the public school sector remained with the traditional split after grade 8. But separate school boards used the intermediate division to legitimize their involvement up to the end of grade 10. With financing available for grades 9 and 10 (although at the elementary rather than the secondary rate), Catholic boards no longer had to bootleg these grades as Fifth Book classes.

The promise of local curriculum initiative was only partially fulfilled. Enthusiasm was strong at first, with more than 100 local committees established in the early 1950s, involving an estimated 16 per cent of Ontario's elementary teachers and 18 per cent of the secondary teachers. Almost half the elementary teachers and over two-thirds of the high school teachers later reported local variations in mathematics, social studies, and science. Yet by the end of the decade, no more than half a dozen local committees remained active, and 80 per cent of all teachers had reverted to departmental curriculum guides.[26] In a detailed study of this venture in local curriculum building, Ottawa secondary school superintendent Harry Pullen blamed the collapse on the conservatism of W.J. Dunlop, who became minister of education in 1951; the lack of support from departmental inspectors, jealous of their leadership role; and the haste with which the scheme was presented to teachers who lacked training and background for such work.[27] Nevertheless, this episode was another example of a growing dichotomy in Ontario education: a proposed decentralization of decision making in curriculum combined with a centralization of financing as the province assumed a greater percentage of total costs.

III

In the midst of a 1932 Canadian speaking tour, British professor John Adams sketched for his Toronto audience a vision of the elementary school of the future. 'When Johnnie Jones attends the little old schoolhouse of 1950,' predicted Adams, 'he will have to learn only one-half the amount of arithmetic, spelling and history present-day pupils are required to assimilate.' The classroom of tomorrow, he predicted, 'will echo with the sounds of talking pictures and radios. Pupils may even learn their alphabet on portable typewriters.'[28] But radio and other aspects of Adams's futuristic scenario were slow to penetrate the Ontario elementary school class-room. A 1956 survey identified 38 per cent of elementary teachers as occasional users of school broadcasts, but elicited frequent complaints of programs unrelated to the curriculum and unsuited for the grade level.[29] Likewise, Adams's portable typewriters and 'talking pictures' penetrated only a minority of class-rooms, not as integral parts of the learning

program, but as Friday afternoon treats for the well-behaved class. Most practi-
tioners continued to rely on textbook, blackboard, and the teacher's voice as the
three most effective instructional media.

Knowledgeable educators conceded that the progressivist wave of the 1937
curriculum reforms had been dashed on the rocks of Ontario traditionalism.
'There is no evidence of any tendency toward the Progressivism which has alarmed
our neighbours to the south,' declared Chief Director John Althouse.[30] C.C. Goldring, director of education for the Toronto Board of Education, concluded that
'there is not in Canada today a publicly supported system of education taught
along progressive educational lines for the simple reason that parents and
taxpayers would not approve of it.'[31] Yet by the early 1950s, a 'back-to-the-
basics' movement was in full stride in Ontario education. Typical of the anti-
progressivist venom was a *Maclean's Magazine* article of April 1952 which
castigated the modern educator for his 'dubious campaign to turn us into a
nation of well-adjusted steam fitters.' In an accompanying editorial, *Maclean's*
concluded that 'the revolt of the reactionaries is long overdue, and we wish them
all success and honour.'[32]

Hilda Neatby soon provided the intellectual and inspirational leadership for
such a revolt. A Saskatchewan history professor and former member of the
Massey commission, Neatby's 1953 best-selling book, *So Little for the Mind*, was
a stinging indictment of Canadian schooling. Her leading villain was John
Dewey, the spiritual forefather of twentieth-century progressive education who,
'more than any single person, must be held responsible for the intellectual,
cultural and moral poverty of much modern teaching.' His disciples in Canadian
schools and teachers' colleges, she charged, neglected formal grammar and
written composition, de-emphasized history and the great works of literature,
put too much faith in guidance and extra-curricular activities, and were far too
casual about promotion and graduation standards. The schools must abandon
their 'life adjustment' goals and 'concentrate on the intellectual aspects of
education, on providing children with intellectual preparation for citizenship.'
This approach called for teachers with stronger liberal arts backgrounds and a
curriculum based on the essential values of western civilization. Even though she
conceded that Ontario was 'sufficiently traditional in its progressivism,' her
sweeping generalizations appealed to the conservatism of the 1950s and were
applied by a critical public to schools and teachers across the province.[33]

Ontario teachers might dismiss Professor Neatby as an uninformed outsider,
but they were forced to pay attention when one of their own colleagues publicly
joined the growing campaign against progressivist influences. In a remarkable
presidential address to the OSSTF annual meeting in December 1951, George
Roberts slammed the schools for pandering to the desires of an easy-going
society. 'Education for Juvenility' was his title; his targets were the new report
cards, informal grading procedures, and the neglect of fundamentals and factual

knowledge. These progressive trends, said Roberts, the vice-principal of Oshawa Collegiate, were an 'education for juvenility ... pseudo-psychology gone mad.' If these trends 'are not stopped in their tracks they will be destructive; if they are not rejected they will be lingeringly malignant.'[34] Officials of Ontario teachers' federations rarely spoke publicly on philosophic issues; never had anyone taken such an extreme position before. Some members of the OSSTF executive publicly disassociated themselves from Roberts's remarks. Yet president-elect J.T. Stubbs had to admit that Roberts expressed the views of a vast number of people in the group and predicted that 'the immediate future will no doubt see a greater number publicly take the stand he has taken.'[35] The general conservatism of the period allowed the strong traditionalist sentiments of many teachers to become vocal and respectable.

Education Minister William Dunlop soon gave his unequivocal support to this swing of the pendulum. In writing the introduction to the departmental annual report for 1951, barely three months after taking office, he emphasized that it was increasingly important to make sure that fundamental purposes and values were not overlooked.[36] 'Too many fads are creeping into education these days, to the exclusion of down-to-earth fundamentals,' he told a group of Toronto teachers. These fads encouraged 'self-expression and day-dreaming' and 'were slowly giving the taxpayer the impression that he was contributing to psychological laboratories rather than schools.' The prime purpose of schooling, he emphasized over and over again, was 'to produce loyal, intelligent, right-thinking, religious, and freedom-loving citizens.' But this could not be accomplished 'until the last shreds of this so-called progressive education are gone.'[37] History and geography were reinstated as separate subjects in the intermediate grades; high school options were curtailed; provincial grants for gymnasiums and auditoriums were stopped; local curriculum committees were discouraged.

In the environment of the Cold War, public spokesmen were quick to jump on the anti-progressivist bandwagon. During 1956, for example, the premier of the province, the chairman of Ontario Hydro, and the executive director of the Canadian Industrial Foundation on Education all delivered major addresses in which they compared Ontario's educational accomplishments unfavourably with those of the Soviet Union. Russia's successful launching of its Sputnik satellite in September 1957 served to increase public criticism. Sputnik completely dominated that year's Christmas assembly of the Ontario Secondary School Teachers' Federation. Later, OSSTF *Bulletin* editor T.A. Sanders felt free to chastise those school administrators 'who after attending the pedagogical embalming parlors of Columbia Teachers' College ... return with their veins filled with neo-Deweyism.'[38] As with Neatby, Roberts, and Dunlop, Sanders's reaction to a 'threat' of extreme progressivism was totally uncalled for, given the reality of the typical Ontario class-room of the 1950s.

For the overwhelming majority of post-war children, the school experience was similar to that of their pre-war parents. Most urban youngsters attended classes in buildings constructed in the first three decades of the century. These were substantial two- or three-storey brick or limestone structures, with carefully maintained lawns and flower-beds in front and cinder playgrounds behind. Twice a day, just before nine o'clock in the morning and one-thirty in the afternoon, the principal or a senior teacher would emerge from the building ringing a hand bell. This was the signal to stop playing, line up at the school doors (separate entrances for girls and boys), and march smartly inside to prepare for the serious business of learning. Inside the building, high-ceilinged class-rooms opened in regular order off equally high-ceilinged hallways. Those class-rooms were uniformly predictable: blackboard at the front and down the right-hand wall, a row of six large windows on the pupils' left, bulletin board at the back. There were six straight rows of desks, heavy wooden structures with curly black iron frames, each attached front and back to another desk. At the back of the class-room were cloakrooms with hooks for pupils' coats.

The majority of elementary school teachers were female and single. In most schools, the class-room teacher taught all the basic subjects to her pupils: reading, spelling, grammar, composition, printing and writing, arithmetic, history, and geography. She would sometimes switch with another teacher for such specialized subjects as music, science, and physical training (universally known as PT). Inside the class-room discipline was usually firm, lessons were teacher-directed, and seat work was done individually in an atmosphere of silence. Pupils spent much time with their controlled-vocabulary readers and their arithmetic textbooks. For weekly tests in the senior grades, the teacher distributed foolscap paper by giving it to the pupil at the front of each row who passed it overhead to the person behind, and so all the way down the row. Pupils ruled an inch-wide margin down the left hand side of the paper. They wrote with a straight pen in a penholder, dipping it in the glass inkwells that sat in holes on the upper right corner of each desk and held washable blue ink supplied by the school. It was hard to write with a straight pen; often the nib would scratch, and fuzz from the paper would collect at the tip, making blotches on the work. Pupils blotted everything they wrote with blotters supplied by the school. Mistakes were called errors, and grades came in carefully worked-out percentages. After eight or nine years in such a carefully monitored environment, successful pupils were recommended by their principal for entrance into high school.

IV

Many Ontarians regard the 1950s as the high school's last great decade, a kind of golden twilight before the radical program alterations and student unrest of the 1960s turned the world of secondary education upside down. The tide of rising attendance, first noticeable about 1915, continued through the 1950s; with each passing year more elementary school graduates went on to high school, more stayed longer, and more qualified for graduation diplomas. Of the 46,000 Ontario students who entered grade 9 in 1950, 44 per cent were enrolled in grade 12 three years later and 22 per cent in grade 13 the following year. By 1955, the grade 9 enrolment had jumped to 62,000; 50 per cent reached grade 12 in three years and 25 per cent made it to grade 13 in four. Although grade 13 figures showed an over-representation of students from professional and managerial homes and an under-representation from manual labouring backgrounds, the student body of the first four years more closely reflected the general population mix. 'We get proportionately more people of average or poor quality of brains than was the case formerly,' declared an Ottawa high school administrator in 1956.[39] By the 1950s, high school was the common, shared experience of Ontario teenagers; for three or four or five years the high school was the central focus of teen-age life.

As district high schools replaced continuation schools across the southern Ontario countryside in the 1940s and 1950s, rural teenagers began to share the high school experience of their urban friends. Designed to bring equal opportunity to rural education, the district high schools were 300-to-400 pupil institutions offering a fairly wide range of courses and providing up-to-date facilities in modern buildings. Like the township school areas for elementary education, district high school boards were not made mandatory by the provincial government. But inspectors like Stanley Rendall did not hesitate to praise their virtues to members of county councils, under whose by-laws the new units were established. Essex District High School was the first of the new breed in 1944; within six years some 123 district high schools were serving 75 per cent of the southern portion of the province. With each passing year, the bright yellow school bus became a more familiar sight along county and township roads, picking up its passengers between 7:30 and 8:00 each morning, taking them anywhere from five to twenty-five miles to the district schools, and returning them between 4:30 and 5:00 each afternoon. Between 1945 and 1950, total rural high school attendance grew from 27,000 to 38,000 – a rate of increase more than double that of urban schools, in a period when the rural population was actually declining.

Rural students soon took for granted these daily bus rides, larger schools, wider choice of optional subjects, and the organized athletic and social activities provided by the district high schools. But they showed less enthusiasm for the one subject these schools were expected to emphasize – agriculture. Some schools did make a success of it: Seaforth District High School boasted that 'no students will graduate ... without knowing something about turnips';[40] Blenheim touted its six acres of cultivated fields, its brooder house, machinery shed, and greenhouse; Ridgetown claimed that 80 per cent of its male farm pupils returned to the farm after leaving school. But these schools were in the agricultural heartland of south-western Ontario; elsewhere the record was considerably poorer. In Hastings County, for example, despite the existence of agricultural courses at six high schools, a 1947 survey revealed that only one boy in all of grades 11 through 13 planned to pursue a career in farming – and he was the son of a merchant. Old prejudices died hard. Agricultural courses still were considered second-best; students wanted programs similar to urban schools, and they saw the high school as a means of escape from farm life.[41] The 1950s saw the last concerted attempt at providing agricultural education in rural Ontario; by the next decade all vocational as well as academic courses were virtually interchangeable between city and country schools.

Rural and urban high school students of the 1950s presented almost a distinctive sub-culture with their unique dress and hair styles and tastes in popular music. The male 'uniform' included draped trousers, with V-necked sweaters over white T-shirts, and either a brush cut or ducktail haircut. Girls wore sweaters and skirts, white bobby socks, loafers with pennies or nickles inside the instep of each shoe, topped by pony-tail hairdos. Boys and girls 'went steady,' and dreaded the feeling of being left out. The popular music industry brought in the fox trot, the jitterbug and the jive, idols like Paul Anka and Elvis Presley, and endless songs with lyrics no more inspiring than the 'sh-boom, sh-boom' of the Toronto-based Crewcuts. Television became an all-embracing leisure-time activity; a 1955 survey in London revealed that the average high school student spent fifteen hours a week watching the television screen, the equivalent of six or seven full-length movies.[42] Yet for all their idiosyncrasies, the teenagers of the post-war era were an apathetic and altogether unadventurous generation. As they reached their later teen years, their greatest ambition was to join the economic and social establishment in order to participate in the good life. Protest was out; conformism was in. 'There are no mavericks left,' lamented a psychologist with the Forest Hill Board of Education in 1959. 'Everybody wants to be like everybody else.'[43]

Conformity followed the teenager of the 1950s into the high school classrooms. The high school was even more faithful to tradition and hostile to progressivist elements than its elementary counterpart. Teachers of the decade were highly qualified, with more than half possessing honours degrees. They had all been through a common year of teacher preparation at the Ontario College of Education, and many taught in the same school from the beginning to the end of their careers. Most taught in the traditional manner, taking textbook in hand and proceeding carefully through it, chapter by chapter, from September to June. The teacher would set a page of problems or a chapter to read for the night's homework; next day the work would be taken up, errors corrected, difficulties explained, and another chapter or more problems assigned for that night. Schoolwork was routine, and it meant homework, memorization, and frequent testing. Shakespeare's plays, the causes of the French revolution, irregular verbs, inclined planes, quadratic equations – all seemed to exist in a vacuum, divorced from the outside world. But their importance was continually stressed for students in the general or academic program (approximately 75 per cent of the total student body in 1955) for on their mastery depended success on the grade 13 departmental examinations. Indeed, from the September of his grade 9 year, no student was allowed to forget that the entire academic program was designed to prepare him to write those dreaded 'departmentals.'

The expansion of formal guidance services was one major high school innovation of the post-war years. Group guidance work in the form of a grade 9 'occupations' course became compulsory for all schools in 1944, and individual counselling spread from the vocational schools to the academic high schools and collegiates. The occupations course was designed to orient new students to the complexities of high school life, help them develop proper study habits, introduce them to future employment possibilities, and help channel them into appropriate courses and programs. Personal and vocational counselling plus psychological and aptitude testing were continued throughout the grades. While the official rhetoric talked of assisting students to make their own decisions, the thrust was towards the 'inculcation of right habits of living' and the generating of 'contented workers and happy citizens,' all in the hands of counsellors 'who have a calm, serene philosophy of life based on Christian principles.'[44] Students tended to regard the grade 9 occupations course as a useless exercise; in the senior grades, however, many found the guidance office helpful in finding jobs or selecting post-secondary educational programs.

Post-war affluence and the increasing Americanization of popular culture combined to elevate dances and other social affairs to a higher level of prominence in the high schools of the late 1940s and 1950s. The highlight of the social year in many schools was the annual formal dance, or spring prom. Girls lucky enough to be asked to the dance talked their parents into buying expensive formal dresses, often worn once and then left in the closet to gather dust. Their male escorts donned charcoal grey suits and claimed possession of the family car for the evening. The 1950 spring prom at Fort Erie High school was carefully planned by the students' union: there were corsages waiting at the door for each girl; the gymnasium was decorated with streamers of crepe paper and arranged like a night club with tables placed along the sides of the dance floor; when the imported dance band took its break, the students presented their own floor show of songs and skits; at midnight a buffet supper was served, after which dancing resumed until two o'clock in the morning.[45] But the Fort Erie evening had to be extraordinary if it was to counteract the tendency so prevalent in Ontario border communities – the early exodus of couples from the dance floor to the night clubs of Buffalo or Niagara Falls, Detroit or Port Huron.

London's Sir Adam Beck Collegiate could be regarded as the archetypal Ontario urban high school of the 1950s. Here in Anglo-Saxon, working-class

East London was an institution educating the second generation of children from the district. Here was a principal, an experienced cadre of teachers, and a qualified guidance staff who knew students and parents as individuals. Here was support for and pride in the accomplishments of the school's athletic teams, the Spartans; victorious football and basketball teams took to the field or the court with almost monotonous regularity, culminating in the 1957 provincial basketball championship. Here were yearly productions of Gilbert and Sullivan operattas, with the entire staff and student body combining to make the show an annual success. Here was school spirit at its highest pitch, nurtured by the Friday morning 'singing auditoriums,' where staff and students sat, not by class or grade, but divided into soprano, alto, tenor, and bass sections.No Ontario high school reunion produced a larger turnout of graduates, nor more emotional re-kindlings of old friendships, than did Beck's fiftieth anniversary celebrations in the spring of 1977.

V

Ontario teachers came out of the Second World War extremely pessimistic about their economic position. In 1946, for example, female elementary teachers averaged $23.25 per week, compared to a truck driver's $26.40. That same year the Toronto Board of Education received sixty-five resignations from staff members seeking 'more remunerative positions in other fields.'[46] But between 1947 and 1955, the equivalent real purchasing power of an Ontario secondary school teacher increased by 25 per cent and an elementary teacher by 35 per cent, considerably higher than increases for wage earners and salaried employees in other fields.[47] Records of SS no. 17, Kenyon Township, illustrate this upward spiral of salary increases: in January 1946 the trustees were forced to go $100 beyond their initial $1,300 maximum to secure a teacher; by September 1947 they had to rescind their earlier decision not to offer $1,500.[48] Although the OPSMTF resisted a single salary schedule with the FWTAO until 1951, and the OSSTF continued to oppose parity with the elementary federations until much later, teachers throughout the province increasingly received a fair wage based on qualifications and experience. This improved status was a result of two factors: the improved economic climate and the critical teacher shortage of the period.

The elementary schools of Ontario suffered their gravest crisis in teacher supply during the decade of the 1950s. In demographic terms, there were simply not enough babies born in the depression years of the 1930s to provide the pool of young teachers needed to cope with the post-war baby boom. Between 1951 and 1956, for example, the absolute number of nineteen-to-twenty-one-year-olds increased by only 4 per cent, while the number of six-year-old grade 1 beginners increased by 45 per cent. The shortage was dramatically illustrated in

September 1951 when, for the first time in recent memory, the provincial normal-school enrolment declined by 4 per cent from the previous year. Even though pupil-teacher ratios rose, the elementary schools of 1960 required more than twice the number of teachers they had on staff in 1945. Local boards were forced to relax previous restrictions and employ married women and pensioners in a mad scramble to fill every class-room. There was even a report of the hiring of an eighty-seven-year-old man whose certificate was dated 1897 and who had not taught for thirty years.[49]

During his eight years as minister of education between 1951 and 1959, W.J. Dunlop found no single concern more troublesome than the teacher shortage. It constituted 'the great problem in this Department,' he informed Premier Frost in May 1952. 'It would appear that, under present conditions, this scarcity will continue to increase and will be really acute by 1955.'[50] Dunlop's solution was to implement a series of contingency plans developed by departmental officials over the preceding winter months. Bursaries were made available to teacher candidates, and normal schools were re-named teachers' colleges to provide greater prestige and to attract more grade 13 graduates. More radical were two 'emergency' teacher training plans: a two-year course after grade 12, and an abbreviated six-week crash course in the summer prior to employment, followed two years later by a full year at a teachers' college. The 'six-week wonders' were greeted by the public with considerable alarm, but found no trouble securing jobs during this period of short supply. Generally, they fared not too badly in the class-room. 'Considering the fact that most of them have been hired in schools that have a history of difficulty,' reported Durham county inspector E. Webster in 1955, 'the ones which came to this inspectorate have done very well this year.'[51]

By mid-decade, a comparable shortage had developed among secondary school teachers, resulting in similar emergency summer training programs at OCE prior to September employment. Although the admission requirement of a university degree was maintained, the short duration and unsatisfactory provisions for practice teaching drew criticism similar to that regarding the elementary programs. Not till 1960 (when teachers' college enrolments were four times those of 1950) was the department of education able to report a turning point in the teacher supply situation as far as the elementary schools were concerned.[52] Not till the end of the 1960s could the high school summer programs be terminated. In retrospect, Dunlop had little if any alternative to mounting emergency training programs. He had to provide a teacher for every class-room. Alternative proposals for higher salaries, improved working conditions, day nurseries for the children of teacher-mothers, the employment of teacher aides or assistants – all were premature for Ontario in the 1950s. Dunlop proudly reported that all members of a discussion group at the 1958 Canadian Conference on Education 'came to the conclusion that each of them ... would have done exactly what I have done to solve the situation.'[53]

Despite their concern over lower standards, members of the Ontario teachers' federations might have agreed with the minister had it not been for his attitude during the period of crisis. Dunlop became increasingly sensitive to charges that he and his department were not coping with the problem of teacher supply. He refused persistently to acknowledge the extent of the shortage, except to claim periodically (and prematurely) that it was over. He refused to admit that entrance standards to the profession had been lowered. 'We did not reduce standards at all,' he told the legislature in 1956. 'We readjusted them slightly to give training in another way.'[54] Above all, he stubbornly refused to consult with the profession on ways to improve the situation. Dunlop regarded teacher objections to his summer programs as 'part and parcel of a campaign to transfer to the Federation, from the Minister, the power and responsibility of determining who shall teach in the Province.'[55] By 1955 the press began to feature the strained relations between the federations and the department. In May the Toronto *Telegram* reported that the Ontario Teachers' Federation was preparing 'an all out attack' which would 'ask how the public can be expected to have confidence in Dunlop.'[56] But the minister weathered the storm, retained the support of Premier Frost, and in his patronizing manner kept the teachers in their 'place,' to the satisfaction of small-town Ontario in the 1950s.

Dunlop's attack on teacher power, like his opposition to lavishly-constructed schools and progressivist ideology, was consistent with his fundamental conservatism. He had been a surprise choice to replace Dana Porter in 1951, brought in from outside the legislature and subsequently handed the safe Conservative seat of Toronto Eglinton. On paper Dunlop looked promising. Here was no veteran politician, but rather a professional educator stepping into the portfolio. His background included teaching stints at the University of Toronto Schools and the Ontario College of Education, eight years as editor of *The School* magazine, and thirty years as director of extension for the University of Toronto. This last post had put him in direct contact with thousands of teachers who flocked to the campus each summer in search of degrees and improved salaries. But Dunlop was seventy years old when named minister in September 1951, an age more for reminiscing about the past than for striking out boldly in new directions. And the past did stay with Dunlop: memories of a frugal upbringing in a Baptist parsonage where order, discipline, prudence, and thrift were everything; attendance at a number of small country and village schools where his interests focused narrowly on academic achievement; productive adult years as a Sunday School superintendent and Masonic Lodge grand master.

Throughout this period, Ontario continued to possess one of the most dictatorial and thoroughly state-controlled systems of teacher training in the Western world. Certainly the change in name from normal school to teachers' college did nothing to free the training institutions from the tight bonds of departmental control. There was a rule or regulation for everything. As provincial superintendent of professional training, F.S. Rivers controlled textbooks and examinations, checked budgets and weekly timetables, told staff members which professional conferences they could attend, and even decided how many copies of which books should be purchased for the teachers' college libraries.[57] A 1950 report by a small committee of staff members agreed with public criticisms that, 'instead of mingling their current with the main stream of educational thought and action in the province,' the colleges had 'become tranquil pools along its course.'[58] Yet the committee could recommend nothing more than a doubling of the much-maligned program from one to two years in length. Any suggestion that elementary school teacher training become a university responsibility (which was the trend in western Canada at this time) tended to be rejected outright by Dunlop and departmental officials. They fought to maintain departmental control and to ensure the separation between academic and professional training.

Departmental control, often accompanied by a kind of stultifying conservatism of the mind, was equally strong in the field of secondary school teacher training at the Ontario College of Education. OCE's separation from the mainstream of the University of Toronto was confirmed in 1958 through the method of appointing a successor to retiring dean A.C. Lewis. When acting University of Toronto president Moffat Woodside moved to establish a selection committee to nominate a successor, education minister Dunlop slapped him down. 'Before you have too many meetings,' he lectured Woodside, 'permit me to call to your mind an antiquated, colloquial, but still very valid maxim which reads, "The man who pays the piper calls the tune." '[59] Dunlop proceeded to have his own nominee, B.C. Diltz, appointed to the deanship by order-in-council. As a former English-methods instructor at OCE, Diltz could be counted on to assist Dunlop in what had become the minister's major pedagogical crusade – to snuff out what remained of 'progressive' education in Ontario. Diltz's candidacy was advanced ahead of other, more 'progressive' OCE instructors; his appointment 'took matters out of the hands of a certain school of thought.'[60] In books such as *Pierian Spring* and *The Sense of Wonder*, Diltz had argued against the 'indiscriminate following of the trends of modern socialistic opinion'; there would be no place for 'slithering progressivism' in his institution.[61]

During the twelve years of J.G. Althouse's service as chief director of education (1944 to 1956), departmental leadership in the generation of ideas and the development of policies had continued. And although Althouse steadily moderated his own philosophical stance from slightly left to slightly right-of-centre, a balanced position between progressivism and traditionalism was maintained. His death in 1956, however, gave full rein to the forces of conservatism. Even Dunlop admitted that 'there was no one in sight who can take the place of Dr. Althouse.'[62] New appointments subsequently went to safe bureaucratic figures, whose long years of service in the department made them overly dependent on ministerial approval. Only in the low-status curriculum branch, now headed by

Stanley Watson, was there any sign of imaginative leadership. With no senior person remaining with the stature of Althouse, there was no one to moderate the fixed ideas, the rigidity, and the defensiveness of W.J. Dunlop.

In the years between 1945 and 1960, Ontario proved to be a sober and conventional community which retained established customs. Television, cocktail lounges, affluence, and consumerism were easily incorporated into a society convinced of the worth of its traditional adherence to order and decorum. The 1950s were not a libertarian decade, eager to experience new sensations or determined to break with old conventions. Thus William Dunlop was not at all out of place as the political spokesman for Ontario education during the period. His oft-repeated claims for the virtues of the three Rs and the one-room country schoolhouse struck a sympathetic chord in the hearts of the population. Premier Leslie Frost was equally representative of the traditional virtues of rural and small-town Ontario. While willing to spend millions of dollars annually on school expansion, Frost, who boasted that he saw things from the perspective of 'the barber's chair in Lindsay,' never lost sight of the fact that most Ontarians – as, indeed, most Canadians – regarded the school's primary purpose as the teaching of 'certain basic fundamental subjects which are ... islands of learning.'[63] Voters liked the stability provided by 'Old Man Ontario,' and returned Frost and the Conservatives with solid majorities in the 1951, 1955, and 1959 elections.

During these years the myth of Ontario educational supremacy continued to flourish. 'We do not need to copy the educational systems of any other country,' Dunlop told the legislature in 1959. His firm, oft-quoted conviction was that 'Ontario's educational system is the best in the world.'[64] Such a view was widely held, both at home and abroad, and even within the educational establishment of the Soviet Union. Poet and littérateur John Colombo has related the story of an Ontario educator travelling in Russia in the fall of 1959, visiting Soviet schools in connection with research towards a post-graduate degree. Russian authorities kept greeting her with puzzlement, even suspicion. The Ontarian did not understand why, until the principal of a high school in Kiev blurted out: 'Why are you here? What are you up to? What's behind your visit? Everybody knows the best educational system in the world is in southern Ontario.'[65] Not until the explosive decade of the 1960s, with a new premier and a new education minister in office, would there be a successful challenge to Ontario's educational tradition.

10 The Liberalization of the Big Blue Schoolhouse

I

The initial impetus for Ontario's educational explosion of the 1960s came not from Queen's Park, but through the federal government's Technical and Vocational Training Assistance Act. This federal legislation of 1960, 'designed to undergird the government's programme ... to foster national development,'[1] was the latest and boldest step in Ottawa's fifty-year attempt to stimulate economic activity through shared-cost vocational education programs. Vocational training needed expanding and upgrading at a time of high unemployment among the unskilled and rising occupational requirements in the secondary manufacturing, trade, and service sectors of the economy. Ontario was in no mood to resist the incursion of a federal cost-sharing program into an area traditionally associated with provincial policy. First, the federal initiatives coincided with provincial priorities; more importantly, the additional funds were absolutely necessary, given the relatively narrow provincial tax base. Queen's Park willingly committed itself to long-term expenditure programs that depended in part on the continuation of federal financial support.

The original federal proposal was clearly designed to stimulate expenditures at the provincial, and not at the school-board or municipal level. Ontario's projected $15 million over the six-year life of the act was expected to assist in the construction of provincial institutes of technology and trade schools. But by March of 1961, provincial pressure had persuaded the federal government to finance 75 per cent of provincial grants to local school-boards for the construction of vocational high schools and the vocational components of composite high schools. 'We should do everything possible to further this portion of our program before the same is changed,' Premier Frost confided to his executive assistant. 'Now is the time to do it.'[2] John Robarts, who had succeeded Dunlop as minister of education, saw it as a 'heaven-sent opportunity to get some of those things [school construction] done.'[3] Local school-boards needed little prodding, since all capital costs were picked up by Ottawa and Queen's Park on a 75/25 per cent split. In the first year of the agreement alone, 124 new vocational or composite high schools were approved, as well as fifty-two major additions to existing schools, at a total estimated cost of $230 million. By the time of the act's expiry in 1967, 335 new school facilities and eighty-three additions added up to $806 million.

Some critics charged that the department's reaction to the TVTA Act was the antithesis of careful educational planning. 'Millions of dollars were poured into the provincial system,' claimed NDP education critic Walter Pitman, but 'there was no one who made any philosophic decision as to the effect this would have on the educational experience of the children of the province.' Harry Pullen of the Ottawa Collegiate Board denounced the resulting program as 'hastily conceived and prematurely announced' and charged that 'those who had to live with the plan had nothing to do with its conception.'[4] But as early as July 1960, five months before the federal legislation was passed, and not long after Robarts had assumed the education portfolio, the department of education was planning major changes in high school programs. That summer, Superintendent of Secondary Education S.D. Rendall declined a fall speaking engagement in order to 'conserve my time for a purpose which may become more evident as the year rolls around.' Hinting that 'certain developments' awaited only formal approval by the minister, he promised that 'I shall have more to say next Easter than I would have in November.'[5] Rendall's preliminary announcement of a 'Reorganized Programme' was given to the August 1961 closed conference of the Ontario Secondary School Headmasters' Association. When the public announcement came in the fall, just after Robarts had declared his candidacy for the Conservative party leadership, the press and public immediately dubbed the new program the 'Robarts Plan.'

This Reorganized Programme, scheduled for introduction in September 1962, called for three equal-status branches within the secondary schools – Arts and Science (the former general or academic course); Business and Commerce; and Science, Technology, and Trades. In all three branches, students would be streamed after grade 9 into five-year academically-oriented programs leading to university, four-year programs ending at grade 12 and leading to skilled employment, or two-year occupational programs to prepare for service industries. Wherever population permitted, high schools would become fully composite and offer the entire range of programs, thus making a greater variety of opportunities available to more students than ever before. 'A principal purpose of the reorganization,' stated Robarts, 'is to retain in school until at least the *end* of the Grade 12 year a much higher proportion of the pupils who enrol in Grade 9.'[6] Such pupil retention was imperative in the increasingly complex and technologically-oriented decade of the 1960s, Robarts argued, to ensure 'their better preparation for the duties of citizenship and the particular vocations upon which they will enter.' It would result in the production 'not only of abler individuals but of more useful citizens.'[7]

The need for the schools to upgrade manpower training and diversify their offerings was underscored by Mayor N.S. Grant of Kapuskasing in May 1961. Grant reported that major industries in northern Ontario 'have set standards to employ no one on a permanent basis with less than grade 10 education' whereas '70 percent of those unemployed under age 21 have grade 8 or less.' He blamed the problem on the northern high schools where only the academic program was available, despite the fact that 'less than six percent of high school students ever go on to University and less than 10 percent finish grade 13.' What, asked Grant, 'do we do with the frustrated students and drop outs?'[8] Somewhat greater program diversification and higher retention rates prevailed in the major urban centres of the south, due to the earlier expansion of technical and commercial programs in the 1920s. But all such programs had languished in the 1950s, as Education Minister Dunlop gave high priority to the academic high school. The province-wide result was that only 51 per cent of the 1958 grade 9 class reached grade 12 in September 1962. Despite Dunlop's claims of Ontario superiority, this record was below that of Canada's western provinces.

The Reorganized Programme signalled the temporary triumph of vocational-ism as a central aim of Ontario secondary schooling. Intellectual enhancement initially had seemed to be on the upswing in the early 1960s, surfacing most clearly in the 1962 report of the ad hoc Joint Committee of the Toronto Board of Education and the University of Toronto, entitled *Design for Learning*. 'The aim of whatever is introduced into the school curriculum,' wrote Professor Northrop Frye in his introductory chapter, 'should be educational in the strict and specific sense of that word.'[9] Frye and his supporters slammed the 'fatuous' theories of progressive education, sought inspiration in psychologist Jerome Bruner's the-ories of structured inquiry within the traditional disciplines, and championed the 'new' mathematics and upgraded science courses. But before long depart-mental officials took their cue from the vocational orientation in which John Robarts had cast the Reorganized Programme in 1961. District high school inspector D.W. Scott left nothing to the imagination when he announced later in the decade that 'the basic function of any school is to prepare young people for their life vocation.'[10]

The Reorganized Programme did succeed in boosting retention rates and diversifying the high school program. Between 1960 and 1968 the secondary school enrolment as a proportion of the fifteen-to-nineteen-year age group increased from 67 to 77 per cent. And proportionately more of these students enrolled in the 'non-academic' branches. Science, Technology, and Trades jumped from 15 to 21 per cent of the total student population between 1963 and 1969, Business and Commerce from 20 to 22, while Arts and Science slipped from 65 to 57 per cent. However, the promise of university admission after successful completion of grade 13 in the Science, Technology, and Trades or Business and Commerce branches went largely unfulfilled as university faculties predictably continued to give absolute preference to graduates from Arts and Science. And the new arrangements proved to be far more rigid in practice than had been promised. Students tended to be streamed into a branch and program by the end of grade 9, sometimes even at the end of Grade 8, and then found themselves locked in for the rest of their high school years. They were not always directed into streams on the basis of their occupational goals, but rather on past academic achievement. Low achievers (and often this meant pupils from lower socio-economic backgrounds) found themselves in the vocational branches and in the four-year programs.

The four-year Arts and Science program was a major hope – and ultimately a major disappointment – of the new high school arrangements. It was intended to provide a basic education for the non-university-bound general student, followed by on-the-job training. It did introduce a number of new courses that soon became the envy of students in the five-year program – world politics, theatre arts, speech arts, geology, and an inter-disciplinary social science course entitled 'Man in Society.' But very few students elected the program on their own. Some were 'promoted' into it, others were transferred in because they were 'discipline problems.' The better students tended to reject the program because, in the words of one principal, 'it was a badge of inferiority.' Once in, 'they rationalized failure and seemed almost as though they wished to do badly.'[11] Those who persevered initially found post-secondary opportunities limited. 'I find,' complained one student, 'that the credits I will receive are not respected as sufficient in the entrance requirements to other schools.'[12] Meanwhile, the continual upgrading of occupational requirements closed the doors on many vocational opportunities. The solution was seen in the creation in 1966 of a new type of post-secondary institution with liberal admission requirements – the College of Applied Arts and Technology. The CAATs were launched amidst a fanfare of favourable publicity as the logical culmination of the Reorganized Programme, but in part they were an admission that a central feature of the new scheme had failed.

Grade 13 of the five-year Arts and Science program remained the portal through which all aspirants for university and teachers' college must pass. No year of a student's education was more important in shaping future vocational plans. No month of that year was more critical than June, when thousands of eighteen-year-olds across the province sat down to write their grade 13 departmental examinations. The early 1960s brought increased complaints that the departmentals were neither pedagogically sound nor conducive to good mental health. 'Why should our youngsters be plunged into the agonizing tortures of Grade 13,' one mother asked the minister, 'only to emerge physically worn out, mentally exhausted, and drained of every ounce of energy and ambition?' Aileen Young described the year as 'murder for the kids, and don't ever think it isn't rough on parents too.' To provide 'peace and quiet' for their daughter, the Youngs had to curtail their own social life, cut entertaining to a minimum, and turn down the television and radio. 'In fact you could hardly even cough.' As far as Mrs Young was concerned, it was 'just a whole year out of her life and ours.'[13] Such complaints from parents, universities, teachers, and pupils, coupled with the threat that increasing numbers might cause a breakdown in marking procedures, persuaded William Davis, who had succeeded Robarts as minister of education, to appoint a Grade 13 Study Committee in January 1964. This was not just another committee, for Davis made it clear that all aspects of the year would be questioned, 'including the examinations.'

The committee refused to blame either the universities or the department of education for the unsatisfactory nature of grade 13. 'The real villains are a rising birth rate, a changing economy, the pursuit of social status, and the general proliferation of knowledge,' all of which contributed to a situation in which more facts were crammed into more heads with each passing year.[14] The committee refused to consider band-aid solutions and quickly recommended sweeping changes. The external examinations must go, instruction must be offered at both 'general' and 'advanced' levels in most subjects, and ultimately the thirteen years of Ontario schooling must be reduced to the continent-wide norm of twelve. The last two recommendations were not implemented; advanced level instruction was opposed by the universities, while the thirteen years were too much 'a deeply rooted feature of our system.'[15] But there was near unanimous support for the abolition of the departmental examinations. Pedagogically, they were, in the words of David Tough, Superintendent of North York Secondary Schools, 'a millstone around our necks.'[16] Logistically, the examinations were becoming increasingly impossible to administer and mark, as 234,283 individual papers were written in 1964. Davis immediately announced a gradual phase-out: the teacher's individual assessment would count for 25 per cent in 1965, 35 per cent the following year, and 100 per cent in 1968. Much more than a system of examinations was gone; it was the end of a tribal rite of passage that had confronted over two generations of Ontario teenagers.

II

With the high schools now more in tune with the technological demands of the 1960s, Davis next turned to the century-old problem of the rural elementary schools. Despite the increase in township school areas and central schools during the two previous decades, over 1,500 rural school section boards remained in 1964, each running its own one-room school. A survey by the

Federation of Women Teachers revealed that instructors in these schools felt grossly disadvantaged; compared to their colleagues in graded, urban schools, they taught in inadequate buildings, had little access to teaching aids and instructional materials, offered a very limited curriculum, and felt that community attitudes encroached on their personal freedom and free time.[17] Davis had been persuaded that a large part of his contemplated efforts to modernize the school system would be frustrated without the creation of viable administrative units. Accordingly in February 1964, one month after the announcement of vastly increased provincial grants through the Ontario Tax Foundation Plan, and five months after the Robarts government had been returned to office in a provincial election, Davis introduced legislation which would make every Ontario township a school area as of 1 July 1965. 'The small rural school section has served Ontario well, but the superiority of township school areas has become evident,' he argued. 'They provide for more broadly based financial support through wider assessment, all of which is available to assist in the education of every child in the area.'[18]

Davis's compulsory legislation of 1964 was far stronger than Howard Ferguson's permissive township school-board bill of 1925. The much weaker rural opposition to the Davis plan indicated how much the province had changed over four decades. SS no. 1, Hope Township, went through the ritual of registering a formal complaint, protesting 'the undemocratic method taken in dismissing the section boards and forcing the amalgamation of such sections into township boards.' But the three trustees of SS no. 1, Hope, were quite realistic in their assessment that 'in 1964 the rural vote is of such less consequence' that legislation could be passed 'without consideration or the opportunity to protest by those most affected.'[19] Protesting rural trustees found no support in the legislature; Liberal leader Robert Nixon indicated his party would support the bill, despite the fact that compulsory amalgamation of some of the boards would have to be carried out against the wishes of many of the people concerned. Nor was there any concerted opposition to a further aspect of the legislation – the appointment of county consultative committees to study the feasibility of still larger local school units. Few people in 1964 would have predicted that only five years later, township-sized boards would themselves be replaced by county boards.

Although the legislation for township school-boards called for centralization of administration, rather than centralization of accommodation, Davis correctly predicted that 'there is every reason to believe that ... the trend towards rural central schools will be accelerated.'[20] In a brief two-year period between 1965 and 1967, the number of one-room schools shrank from 1,463 to 530 as the township boards jumped on the bandwagon of central schools. Local newspapers often featured these school closings with nostalgic articles on the end of an era in rural ontario. At SS no. 8, Ekfrid Township, Marion Davie 'bade goodbye to pupils who have known no other teacher, pupils whose parents and even a few grandparents learned their first ABCs under her tutelage.' Pupils at SS no. 9, Mariposa Township, left behind forever their iron water pump and 'pail-a-day type of toilet.' Eight hundred youngsters from the townships of Fullarton, Hibbert, and Logan allegedly jumped from the nineteenth to the twenty-first century with the opening of the 40-room, $1.5 million Upper Thames Centennial School in Mitchell, 'one of Canada's biggest and most streamlined elementary schools.'[21] By 1975, only twenty-one single-room schools remained in Ontario, all in isolated regions of the North.

Changes in teacher training, that perennial backwater of the Ontario educational system, continued the modernizing imperative of the Davis years. A committee chaired by C.R. MacLeod, superintendent of Windsor public schools, recommended in 1966 that elementary school teacher preparation become a university responsibility, with concurrent arts and education programs available in addition to a separate one-year professional course following academic work. So the department of education began the difficult process of phasing out independent teachers' colleges by integrating them with universities, at the same time announcing that all elementary teachers would require a university degree. Five years later, eight Ontario universities were involved, but eight independent teachers' colleges still remained. The integration made sense in theory, but it encountered traditional university aloofness from the schools and from 'education' courses, plus the issue of what to do with the academically underqualified members of teachers' college staffs. Meanwhile, new colleges of education for the training of secondary school teachers were created at Western Ontario and Queen's to ease the enrolment pressures on OCE at Toronto. Despite formal agreements that permitted these new colleges to operate closer to the centre of the university orbit, initial staff continued to be drawn largely from within the Ontario secondary school system. Not till the early 1970s, with York University leading the way, was there any real variety of innovative teacher training programs available in Ontario universities. In the York program, undergraduate academic studies and professional teacher education were more closely integrated than anywhere else in Canada.

The creation of the Ontario Institute for Studies in Education in 1965 provided the initial breakthrough in post-graduate educational studies and research. Advanced training was deemed essential to produce the leadership desired by Davis at the local and provincial levels. Previous OCE efforts in graduate work had not earned high acclaim; instead of studying in Toronto, Ontario teachers had flocked to graduate courses in education at Wayne State, Buffalo, and Syracuse universities across the border. In addition, both pure and applied research, coupled with field development work, were needed to spread the new ideas of the 1960s. Amid great fanfare and lavish funding, OISE was launched in mid-decade under the directorship of R.W.B. Jackson, a veteran of twenty-five years in the field of educational research. Over the next ten years, through its affiliation with the University of Toronto's school of graduate studies, OISE produced 224 doctorates and 3,955 masters' degrees in education. These graduates found positions in university education faculties, local school systems, and the provincial department of education.

But criticism of OISE was quick to develop from the public and the teaching profession. OTF president James McNabb charged in 1970 that the institute spent only one per cent of its $10 million annual budget 'developing and testing classroom materials and does nothing to get new material to classrooms.' One faculty member, referring to his numerous American colleagues, asserted that OISE was staffed by people "who do not know much about Ontario education ... and do not care.'[22] This type of criticism was partially abated in the early 1970s as OISE opened regional centres throughout the province, centres that stressed developmental work in co-operation with local school systems. Yet the academic community remained generally suspicious of this vast educational establishment; by the end of the 1970s the University of Toronto was attempting to cut or reshape its links with OISE.

The Reorganized Programme for the high schools, the end of grade 13 departmental examinations, township school-boards, changes in pre-service and post-graduate teacher education – all were indicative of a more aggressive and innovative approach within the department of education. William Dunlop's retirement from the education portfolio in 1959 had paved the way for the appointment of ministers more sympathetic with the spirit of modernization. Dunlop's immediate successor was John Robarts, a London lawyer, whose most visible contribution to Ontario education during his brief three-year stint was the Reorganized Programme for the high schools. Yet his actual impact went much deeper. He was described as a 'fresh breeze' who dispelled the air of defensiveness within the department, opened lines of communication, and encouraged the flow of new ideas.[23] NDP leader Donald MacDonald credited Robarts with rescuing the department 'from a process of ossification, which was little short of terrifying in its later stages.'[24] Not the least of his contributions was the appointment of Brampton lawyer William Davis as his successor in 1962, a year after Robarts himself succeeded Leslie Frost as premier. The 1962 cabinet shuffle introduced younger and more vigorous leadership into Queen's Park; nowhere was this more evident than in the personality and policies of the thirty-six-year-old Davis.

The careful and pragmatic Davis could hardly be called an unequivocal exponent of any single philosophy of education. Walter Pitman of the NDP later described him as a master tactician, who was 'perceptive of the major directions, rode the mainstream, and convinced his cabinet colleagues that educational expansion should be paramount.' Magazine writer Michelle Landsberg called him the archetypal 'modern liberal Tory – comfortably good-looking, solidly

progressive by instinct, amiably open-minded, and so competent that his department's complex machinery is all but invisible.'[25] Davis told Ontarians that
education in the 1960s had to be a 'flexible process ... operating as it does under a
multitude of changing influences, many of them novel, some revolutionary.'[26]
He broke with Ontario's insular tradition and borrowed ideas from Florida,
New York, and California, although privately boasting that 'in many respects
we seem to be in the vanguard rather than in the rear.'[27] Each year he guided his
departmental estimates so smoothly through the legislature that opposition
members were left virtually speechless. Trustee, teacher, and Home and School
groups praised his work, and begged Premier Robarts to keep him in the
education portfolio.[28] 'Not since Henry VIII or Louis XIV,' observed new NDP
leader Stephen Lewis in 1967, 'has one man accumulated such a retinue of
courtiers, admirers, fawning journalists and a positive harem of sycophants.'[29]

Davis regarded the continuing demographic, physical, and financial expansion of Ontario education as an exciting challenge. Elementary school enrolments increased by 40 per cent during the 1960s from 1,081,000 to 1,456,000,
while secondary school figures ballooned from 237,000 to 530,000, a whopping
120 per cent increase. The construction of new schools and school additions
made the boom of the 1950s pale into insignificance. Between 1960 and 1969,
legislative grants to local school-boards rose from $51 to $227 million annually,
each year consuming a larger proportion of provincial funds. Local taxes
increased almost as much, as municipal councils found school-boards to have
virtually insatiable appetites. Although Davis confessed that the financial
burden was staggering, he assured the Rotary Club of Toronto in 1963 that the
costs were 'well within our power to carry without more than slowing somewhat
the giant strides we are making in all other aspects of our economy.' It was a case
of putting first 'the things of real and lasting worth, which to me means giving
top priority to education.' Five years later Davis was still confident that 'education for years to come has to be the number one priority in government
spending.'[30]

Politicians and public leaders accepted the inevitability of spiralling educational costs because they were convinced that such investment would bring an
economic return. The trend was set early in the decade when federal governments in both Canada and the United States provided funds for educational
programs designed to stimulate the economy. As the 1960s progressed, Ontarians took seriously the various reports of the Economic Council of Canada,
which blamed lower educational attainments for much of the per capita production and income differentials between Canada and the United States. Thus it
became easier for local school-boards and the provincial government to sell high
cost programs and expensive buildings to the public. In 1963 the department of
education spoke of provincial expenditures on education as 'an investment that
will bring invaluable returns in future years.' Three years later education was

declared 'an essential investment of great economic consequence.'[31] So success-ful was the sales campaign that most of the programs introduced by Davis were regarded as money well spent. The political opposition could only attempt to score points on the grounds that not enough was being done.

III

The determination of Robarts and Davis to confront cultural problems of language and religion was consistent with their overall policies of curriculum flexibility and educational modernization. Expanded provisions for French-language education were also part of Robarts's larger plan to ensure a French 'fact' in Canada's future, as exemplified through his harmonious relations with the Quebec government and his hosting of the Confederation of Tomorrow Conference. The acceptance of these changes by English-speaking Ontarians reflected the mood of accommodation that prevailed in the Centennial and Expo year of 1967. By far the easiest change to implement was French-language instruction for English-speaking elementary school pupils. Davis gave official sanction by announcing in 1965 that French would be a recognized option for all English-speaking pupils in grades 7 and 8, and would be allowed on an experi-mental basis below that level. When the 1968 volume of the Royal Commission on Bilingualism and Biculturalism recommended a much earlier start, the Toronto Board of Education reacted the following day by approving a grade 2 beginning. Between 1962 and 1972, the proportion of Anglophone elementary pupils studying French jumped from 7 to 40 per cent of the total. Many of these pupils in Ottawa, Toronto, and other centres were in French 'immersion' classes, where study after study showed no detrimental effects on cognitive learning gains.

Unhappily, in 1967, forty years after Howard Ferguson's shelving of Regula-tion 17, French-language schooling for francophone pupils still left much to be desired. Enrolment in these bilingual elementary schools had doubled from 45,000 to over 90,000 in the twenty years since the end of the Second World War, but statistical comparisons showed these pupils at a continuing disadvantage. In 1963, for example, only 45 per cent of bilingual elementary school teachers held first-class certificates, as compared with 95 per cent in the English-language public school sector. Francophone pupils with inferior elementary instruction encountered further handicaps if they continued on to public high schools. Despite the upgrading of *français* as a subject of instruction, and authorization to teach Latin, history, and geography in French, these pupils still entered a predominantly anglophone milieu in the high schools. Only 38 per cent of the French-speaking students who entered grade 9 in 1959 reached grade 11 and only 3 per cent graduated from grade 13 without losing a year. By contrast, the anglophone survival rates were 52 and 13 per cent. 'No matter how the data were analyzed,' lamented the Royal Commission on Bilingualism and Biculturalism in 1968, 'we were led to the same conclusion – that the attrition rate from Francophone homes is disastrously high.'[32]

To John Robarts, such a situation could no longer be tolerated. He announced a new policy on francophone elementary and secondary schooling to the August 1967 annual convention of l'Association canadienne des éducateurs de langue française. In his view 'the potential contributions of Franco-Ontarians to our society is too great to allow them to dissipate their energies and abilities because they are denied adequate opportunities for furthering their education to the utmost of their abilities.'[33] The details were worked out in departmental committees and provincial legislation over the next few months. Instead of operating almost clandestinely, French would now be permitted as the legal language of instruction for all elementary school subjects, with English becoming an obligatory subject only at the grade 5 level; such schools would clearly be French-language rather than bilingual.

Then on 30 May 1968 Davis introduced permissive legislation he called 'historic not only for Ontario but also for Canada.' With the creation of French-language schools at the secondary level, 'there will be assured to every French-speaking student in the province the opportunity to receive his education from kindergarten through university ... in the language of his choice.'[34] The legislation outlined three possibilities: completely French-language schools; French-language sections within English schools; or classes with various subjects taught in French. Potential opposition was defused with Robarts's announcement that these French high schools would be part of the public rather than the separate system. 'We do not intend to segregate the Franco-Ontarians from the mainstream of life of this province,' he declared. 'Nor do they want to be segregated.'[35]

In September 1968 the Welland Board of Education (which years earlier had been the first public board to operate bilingual elementary schools) opened Ontario's first French-language composite high school, Confederation Secondary School, with some 500 students. Many of these students came from a private school that the Sisters of the Sacred Heart had been forced to close because of financial pressures. And seven of the Roman Catholic teaching nuns came with them, discarding their religious habits for secular dress. 'We just couldn't leave the pupils,' said Antoinette Bisson. 'It would have been an injustice to leave and not continue working with them.'[36] That same month, the Ottawa Collegiate Institute Board assumed responsibility for the city's seven private school that the Sisters of the Sacred Heart had been forced to close costing taxpayers an extra $2 million per year. Within two years, the number of such private Roman Catholic high schools had been reduced from approximately twenty to four; by 1971, French-language public high schools enrolled 28,000 students. Separate school supporters saw this as a blow to their campaign for public support for Catholic high schools, but Robarts was gambling that Ontario would more likely tolerate linguistic diversity than religious pluralism in secondary education.

But the expansion of French-language secondary education did not proceed harmoniously in every Ontario community. In Sturgeon Falls and Cornwall, virtually the entire population divided along linguistic lines as to whether the francophone students should be accommodated in integrated bilingual schools or in segregated French-only environments. English spokesmen feared the latter would hasten the demise of their own traditional control of the community's political and economic life. French spokesmen were equally adamant against bilingual schools, charging that the overall atmosphere would continue to be English and prove to be 'a one-way street to assimilation.'[37] Three years of tension in Sturgeon Falls led to a two-week strike of 1,400 francophone students in September 1971. Ultimately, they attained their goal for a separate high school with 'French ambience'; Sturgeon Falls High School was turned over to them and renamed Franco-Cité, while the 400 anglophone students were removed to a new school, Northern Secondary. A boycott in Cornwall in March 1973 produced similar results; the once-bilingual St Lawrence High School became the unilingual Ecole Secondaire St Laurent. 'They are going to have to see us as a group in the city and respect us for what we are,' declared victorious student leader Luc Bertrand.[38]

By this time it was apparent that bilingual co-existence was giving way to unilingual segregation in the high schools of northern and eastern Ontario. This second phase of development had been tested on the battle lines of Sturgeon Falls and Cornwall, and was confirmed in the 1972 report of the Ministerial Commission on French Language Secondary Education, chaired by T.H.B. Symons, president of Trent University. 'The purpose of establishing French-language schools,' argued Symons, 'is to provide French-speaking students with a means to know and to develop their own language and culture.'[39] He concluded, and subsequent government legislation concurred, that in most cases this implied unilingual French schools, which local boards must establish if demanded. Anglophone resistance persisted, however, and it took a special piece of legislation in the summer of 1977 to force a French-only high school on the Essex County Board of Education. The provincial government's attitude towards francophone Ontario had come full circle in the years since Regulation 17 of 1912.

No similar reversal of government attitude occurred towards Roman Catholic separate schools, although Robarts and Davis scored as many political points in turning back Catholic demands as they had in accommodating French-language requests. Despite the provincial grant scheme of 1945, separate school boards had continued at a financial disadvantage. This was due primarily to low municipal assessments on the property of separate school supporters, plus the continued denial of a share of corporation taxes. In 1957, for example, Toronto separate schools educated 19 per cent of the city's elementary school pupils on four per cent of the assessment; for Cornwall the figures were 60 and 30 per cent, while other Ontario cities fell somewhere in between.[40] In October 1962, the Catholic bishops of Ontario presented Robarts with a brief that called for 'the same advantages, the same rights, and the same opportunity to grow as is enjoyed by our secular counterparts.' Specifically, they demanded a share of corporation taxes plus the extension of full provincial funding to the end of grade 13. When the United Church *Observer* declared that 'the Romans may endanger Ontario's excellent system of public education,' it looked like a revival of nineteenth-century sectarian bitterness.[41] Robarts, however, was able to keep the controversy within bounds by increasing provincial grants for separate elementary schools through the Ontario Tax Foundation Plan of 1964. But he would go no further: there would be no share of local corporation taxes, and no extension of provincial grants beyond grade 10.

Bolstered by a new argument and what they thought was a new climate of tolerance, Catholic educators in late 1967 started yet another campaign to win tax support for the senior high school grades. Now they employed the phrase 'continuous progress' and pointed to recent moves within the provincial department and local school jurisdictions to effect closer elementary-secondary school articulation. Therefore, they concluded, their present tax-supported system, ending at grade 10, discriminated against Catholic children; it broke their schooling into artificial parts at a time when pedagogical thinking called for a unified structure. 'A system that ends at Grade 10 is a truncated system,' declared Archbishop Philip Pocock of Toronto. 'Our major task at the moment [is] to aim for its extension.'[42] English Catholic leaders were spurred on by the realization that the burgeoning costs of secondary education threatened the maintenance of their privately funded high schools, and by the fact that their francophone brethren were opting for secular high schools in exchange for linguistic guarantees. They hoped that their recent rise in numbers to become Ontario's largest religious denomination, plus the Centennial year's favourable disposition towards minority-group aspirations, would result in success after so many decades of failure.

The campaign began in a moderate way under the control of the Ontario Separate School Trustees' Association, with the presentation in early 1968 of a brief entitled 'Equal Opportunity for Continuous Education in the Separate Schools of Ontario.' But the campaign soon became noisier as Catholic teachers, parents, and especially high school students began to participate. Somewhat surprisingly, by the end of 1969 both the Liberal and NDP opposition parties had pledged their support. A year later over 15,000 Catholics jammed Toronto's Maple Leaf Gardens for a partisan rally designed to keep pressure on the government. For month after month William Davis agonized over the issue

– first as minister of education and then in 1971 as premier.[43] Finally, on 31 August 1971, Davis said no. Clearly he genuinely feared that grants to what he termed 'private' Catholic high schools would open the door to similar demands from supporters of Jewish, Christian Reform, and other independent schools. Also, a threatened boycott of Conservative candidates in the forthcoming provincial election promised to deliver him the majority Protestant vote. The Conservative victory in the 1971 election confirmed the political wisdom of Davis's move.

Davis's decision was made easier because of the growing difficulty of defining what a Catholic high school was, and of proving its religious effectiveness. Archbishop Pocock might define a Catholic school as one 'in which God, His truth, His life, are integrated into the entire syllabus, curriculum and life of the school.' And the chairman of the Metropolitan Toronto Separate School Board could claim the central purpose was 'to develop students who will take their place in our pluralistic society, serving both our Creator and our fellow-man.'[44] Yet students who had attended both public and Catholic high school classes claimed in a 1972 interview that 'nothing different really happened' in the Catholic environment.[45] Meanwhile a research study on the religious impact of Catholic high schools demonstrated that the 'effect ... on Catholic commitment was very limited and highly specific' and by itself 'had virtually no effect on Catholicity.'[46] The secular, liberal climate of the late 1960s and early 1970s provided fertile soil for the growth of French-language high schools, but was barren ground for any expansion of Catholic secondary education through state support.

IV

From the vantage point of Canada's 1967 Centennial Year, Premier Robarts and Education Minister Davis could take pride in five years of accomplishments. The Reorganized Programme of Studies and the announced end of the grade 13 departmental examinations had combined to loosen the hold on the high schools of more than a century of academic élitism. The forthcoming integration of teachers' colleges with the universities, plus the launching of OISE, promised improvements in pre-service and post-graduate teacher training. Along with unprecedented university growth, the creation of the Colleges of Applied Arts and Technology provided expanded educational opportunities at the post-secondary level. At the local level, new township size school-boards were functioning smoothly and opening new central schools every week. Within the department, the old split between elementary and secondary education had been lessened, and area offices were being established across the province to better serve local school-boards. Most important of all, J.R. (Jack) McCarthy had taken over as deputy minister of education in 1966. McCarthy was an elementary man, a protégé of Stanley Watson in the old curriculum branch, and the moving force behind the more extensive changes that were still to come at the end of the decade.

The Ontario educational revolution gathered momentum in June 1968 with the publication of *Living and Learning*, the report of the Provincial Committee on Aims and Objectives of Education. For three years this committee, with its open, free-wheeling analysis of Ontario education, had generated a flood of media publicity. The committee was co-chaired by Mr Justice Emmett Hall (who, as recent head of the Royal Commission on Health Care, had shaken up the Canadian medical establishment) and Lloyd Dennis (an unorthodox Toronto elementary school principal). Hall and Dennis did not disappoint those teachers and public critics looking for change in the schools. *Living and Learning* was the most radical and bold document ever to originate from the bureaucratic labyrinth of the provincial department of education.

Living and Learning had nothing but condemnation for traditional approaches to education. 'The school's learning experiences are imposed, involuntary and structured.' The pupil was part of a 'captive audience' from the day of entry, with his hours regulated, his movements controlled, and his freedom of speech curtailed. The report proposed a radical change in the role of the learner, and in phrases reminiscent of John Dewey and the Progressive Education Association, stressed that 'the needs of the child lie at the heart of the educational function, the prime purpose of which is to serve these needs.' The child should not be treated as an isolated entity, but educated for life in a society which respects his individuality. Where conflict occurred between individual and societal needs, the committee tended 'to side with the individual and to ask only for social responsibility that is demonstrably right and essential for the good of all.'[47] 'What we meant,' wrote committee member George Bancroft some years later, 'is that the child is primarily a human being and he is primarily a learner, and it is to these roles that attention should be paid ... We were not advocating a dictatorship of children ... We were for a humane educational system; we were not for soft pedagogy. We were for permissiveness – responsible permissiveness; we were not for laxity.'[48]

Curriculum content and teaching methods would have to change in this child-centred, Hall-Dennis school of the future. Curriculum should no longer emphasize traditional values and ensure social stability, but should prepare youngsters to cope with the accelerated rate of social change expected in the late twentieth- and early twenty-first centuries. Content must be organized around three broad themes – communications, humanities, and environmental studies. 'This approach is intended to free teachers and pupils from the confines of structured, isolated subjects,' declared *Living and Learning*, 'to encourage a wider exploration of knowledge relative to each theme, and to emphasize the embracing nature of the learning experience.' But such an approach must take as its starting point the needs and interests of the learner, rather than prescriptive course outlines. 'One condition becomes increasingly apparent in the learning process, and that is the shift in emphasis from content to experience.' No longer should the child be expected to 'memorize, mimic, regurgitate and duplicate the pearls of wisdom to which he is exposed.' Schools would now emphasize the creative nature of the learning process through methods of discovery, exploration, and inquiry; they would provide learning experiences which were pertinent to the personal needs and interests of the learner. 'The schools that we envisage will give every pupil an opportunity to participate in selecting and planning his own studies.'[49]

Such discovery learning and individual enhancement could only flourish in a positive, supportive class-room atmosphere. The Hall-Dennis Report was against corporal punishment, the writing of lines, after-school detentions, sarcasm, ridicule, and all similar forms of punishment for the un-cooperative learner. 'Punishment is demoralizing because it negates moral responsibility,' concluded *Living and Learning*. 'It fosters cynicism and a belief that the thing to do is simply to avoid being caught by those who have authority to punish.' The warm class-room environment, the emphasis on discovery learning, and the choice in learning activities would combine to eliminate misdemeanours and render irrelevant all forms of punishment. Such devices as class standing, percentage marks, and letter grades would give way to pupil and parent conferences as a method of reporting individual progress. Hall-Dennis advocated as well the elimination of 'lock-step' systems of organizing pupils, such as grades and streams, in favour of continuous progress through the school years. No longer would there be the 'hazards and frustrations of failure.' The pupil would thrive on a curriculum based on his own needs and interests, and 'a system of positive reward.'[50]

Some critics angrily challenged what they regarded as the permissive and libertarian thrust of *Living and Learning*. Historian and former high school teacher James Daly produced a sharp frontal attack in a seventy-nine page booklet entitled *Education or Molasses?* Daly ridiculed the members of the committee for trying to show they were 'with it,' criticized the style of writing in the report ('no cliché is forgotten, no platitude overlooked'), and attacked recommendations that threatened to reduce hard work and competition in the class-room. In a manner similar to Hilda Neatby's 1953 *So Little for the Mind*, he charged that 'the general public would be the eventual victims of what one must regretfully call an assault on civilization as we know it.'[51] Although the OSSTF acknowledged immediate support for 175 of the report's 258 recommendations (flatly opposing only one recommendation – for a single salary schedule), many high school teachers felt it would be a mistake to extend the child-centred school of Hall-Dennis beyond grade 8. 'The early adolescent tends to be introverted and lethargic,' proclaimed OSSTF executive secretary J.R.H. Morgan. 'Left to his own devices, he might very well learn nothing of any real consequence.' Like Professor Daly, Morgan feared that 'we could start a whole generation down a slippery path.'[52] But Daly and Morgan proved to be out of step with the mood of the late 1960s.

Press reaction to *Living and Learning* was overwhelmingly favourable. 'Hall and his crew have set education on its ear,' proclaimed the Toronto *Globe and Mail*, 'exposed the failures of every educational institution in the province, plunged eagerly and creatively into the future, and undoubtedly occasioned the eruption of fountains of cold sweat throughout the educational establishment.'[53] Within four months of publication, the report sold 60,000 copies and had established itself as a national best-seller. It became the most fashionable coffee table decoration in the land – partly because it was too big to fit easily on a bookshelf, and also because it was a lavish book, full of photographs of smiling children. It was widely read because it was easy to read, a popular statement that spoke the layman's language. And it was exceptional among educational reports in that it recognized the impact of rock music, clothing, hair styles, and the sexual revolution – in fact all aspects of the popular culture of the 1960s – on young people and the attitudes they brought into the class-room. It was read as well because it seemed to have the official endorsement of Education Minister Davis. Immediately the government announced the appointment of Lloyd Dennis as a one-man public-relations band to publicize the document. Within a day, Dennis had thirty speaking engagements on his calendar. 'We hate to make statements this early,' he said, 'but it seems that the significance of this report has found acceptance across the board.'[54]

In one sense, the Hall-Dennis Report was less revolutionary than it seemed. Many parts of the new approach spelled out in *Living and Learning* had been talked about and debated for years. The report served to pull the pieces together, give official blessing to change, and encourage cautiously experimental teachers to move further along the road. As early as 1962 the department's curriculum branch had begun moving in the direction of Hall-Dennis's recommendations on curriculum and teaching/learning styles.[55] By 1968 a number of Ontario elementary schools had introduced such innovations as the language-experience approach to reading, the integrated-day curriculum, individualized instruction, pupil choice of learning activities, continuous progress, and non-grading. Changes in architecture had ushered in hexagonal-shaped class-rooms with moveable partitions, carpeted floors, and large open areas with 'learning centres' rather than fixed rows of desks. In 1968, the Toronto Board of Education reported that for the previous five years, three of its junior public schools had 'been developing the kind of learning environments that put the child at the centre of the educational process.' That fall the Toronto board launched its first completely open-plan school (Dewson Street), where the teacher would be 'the person who stimulates and guides, rather than the authority who commands.'[56]

At the end of the decade, there was no doubting the inroads made by *Living and Learning* in the elementary schools of Ontario. Local newspapers ran feature articles and lavish picture layouts on individual schools, emphasizing the number of 'Hall-Dennis' features in operation, and hinting at further changes in the years ahead. Educators had their own lists of favourite Hall-Dennis schools, which they shared with each other at meeting and convention times. In the Hamilton area, for example, a visitor could catch Hall-Dennis in action in schools as diverse as Maple Grove and St Daniel's. Maple Grove was a thirty-five-year-old, two-room rural school near Beamsville, serving kindergarten and primary-grade youngsters. Here, with the volunteer assistance of 95 per cent of the families involved, a language-experience, integrated-curriculum approach to learning was in full swing. Hall-Dennis had combined with community involvement to provide a highly personalized school. Twenty miles west in the city of Hamilton itself was St Daniel's Separate School, a large, recently constructed school serving an urban mixture of Anglo-Saxon and immigrant children. Here, Hall-Dennis had blurred the distinction between children's 'play' and classroom 'work,' and de-emphasized formal grading patterns. A subsequent study of Hamilton-area separate schools showed pupils at St Daniel's matched their traditional school friends in skill development and exceeded them in characteristics of independence, autonomy, and responsibility.[57]

V

The Hall-Dennis Report contributed as well to the second sweeping upheaval in Ontario high schools during the decade. The rigid streaming of the Reorganized Programme of 1962 was incompatible with the emphasis on student choice and flexibility that permeated *Living and Learning*. 'I don't think there was a day when we sat down and said "let's scrap the Robarts plan,"' admitted Emmett Hall, quickly adding that 'it is our idea, however, that the Robarts plan in the main would be displaced.'[58] In actual practice the Reorganized Programme was already being dismantled when the Hall-Dennis Report appeared in June 1968, due to pressures both external and internal to the Ontario high school. By that date, the province had exhausted its quota of federal funds under the Technical and Vocational Training Assistance Act; in addition, technological and occupational changes in society had made the prediction of vocational needs of high school students extremely difficult. Within the secondary schools themselves, the end of grade 13 departmental examinations, the new breed of elementary school graduate, and the influence of such innovative, flexible-program Florida high schools as Melbourne and Nova, had already wrought changes. There were experiments in team teaching and independent study, more elective subjects, and semester programming. And at Queen's park there was Jack McCarthy, the new deputy minister of education, whose elementary experience and progressivist philosophy led away from the rigidities of the Robarts Plan. In an interview at the time of his appointment in December 1966, McCarthy revealed his full support for non-graded high schools and a flexible program that would soon emerge as the 'credit' system.[59]

McCarthy gave his full support to an experimental program introduced in six high schools in September 1967. Each school tried various modifications of the regular program, involving individual timetables, subject promotion, additional optional courses, and a breakdown in the barriers between four-year and five-year programs and among the three branches (Arts and Science, Business and Commerce, and Science, Technology, and Trades). The scheme as worked out in Ottawa's Fisher Park High School involved the use of a credit system. A 'credit' was awarded for the successful completion of work in a subject extending over five periods a week throughout the school year. The grade 12 diploma required twenty-seven credits; thirteen were compulsory and at least six had to be completed at a 'level four' standard. The grade 13 program was defined in terms of seven additional credits at 'level five.' An evaluation of the Fisher Park program after two years of operation demonstrated that a heavy reliance on computer timetabling and individual counselling was needed for an individualized credit system to succeed. But student and teacher reaction was generally favourable, and overall academic achievement had been maintained.[60]

With additional high schools on experimental programs in 1968-69, and still more seeking approval for innovative plans for September 1969, McCarthy believed the time was ripe to formalize the switch from the rigid streaming of the Reorganized Programme to the greater flexibility provided through a credit system. Such a switch seemed inevitable in the social climate of the late 1960s. Still unsettled, however, was the degree of openness that would be permitted. Conservatives within the department of education's supervision section argued for a required core of English, history, and physical education courses which all students should complete. Progressive educators within the curriculum section felt otherwise. 'My argument ... wasn't that such [general] knowledge existed, but over whether or not it could be identified,' stated one of the progressives. 'What was essential for this student was not necessarily essential for the next one.'[61] However McCarthy had already made up his mind: the departmental committee that re-drafted Circular HS 1 (the basic document on high school courses and requirements) in the spring of 1969 contained ten members from the curriculum section and only three from the more conservative, supervision section. The resulting credit system was an extremely flexible one.

The end of the Robarts Plan was announced officially by Education Minister Davis in March 1969, during an address to that most conservative group, the Ontario Secondary School Headmasters' Council. The philosophy of the new

'Davis System' owed much to the Hall-Dennis Report and to Deputy Minister McCarthy; the specific details were close to those worked out at Fisher Park and the five other trial schools during 1967-8. No longer would there be any formal distinction between different types of students; education would progress along a continuum with the choice of experiences and the rate of progress depending on student needs, interests, and rate of maturation. Branch or program classifications gave way to curricular choices based on four broad areas of study – communications, social sciences, pure and applied sciences, and arts. Courses would be offered in up to five levels of difficulty (ranging from 'remedial' to 'advanced'). Course outlines supplied by the department would constitute no more than a framework upon which individual teachers could build. McCarthy actively promoted this decentralization of decision making, since he was convinced that 'the enforcement of departmental standards could only bring about mediocrity.'[62] Students were permitted free choice of subjects, so long as they selected at least three from each of the curriculum areas. Twenty-seven credits secured a grade 12 diploma, while six more earned grade 13 graduation. Attending high school at the beginning of the 1970s was becoming a new kind of experience for Ontario teenagers.

From 1969-70 through 1971-2, Ontario high schools were given the option of offering either the Robarts or the Davis models, or a mixture of both. Ten per cent adopted the new credit system in September 1969, 44 per cent the following year, and by September 1972 every school in the province had been converted. 'The feeling of freedom that was felt in the high schools was perhaps the most significant factor,' reported one principal. 'There arose a willingness to innovate with respect to the total program.'[63] For students, the credit system brought greater freedom and increased self-responsibility. Course choices tended to be influenced by a mixture of post-secondary requirements, parental wishes, advice from guidance counsellors and teachers, and individual whim. Enrolments decreased in history and foreign languages, remained steady in English and mathematics, and increased in the sciences, creative arts, social sciences, and vocational subjects. For teachers, the new approach brought more flexibility in curriculum design and teaching style, together with the feeling that courses had to be 'sold' to students in a competitive market-place. The credit system also doomed the century-old pattern of universities prescribing rigid admission criteria. By the early 1970s, Ontario universities were obliged to rely more than ever before on individual high schools to define readiness for post-secondary study.

Thornlea Secondary School, just east of Thornhill and serving a suburban area north of Metropolitan Toronto, was frequently singled out as the archetypal high school of the late 1960s and early 1970s. Its early adoption of the credit system was merely an extension of many years of innovation on the part of the old York Central and now the York County Board of Education, led by school superintendent Sam Chapman. Thornlea was an open-plan, highly flexible school, run on individual timetabling and a trimester system, and featuring all manner of interdisciplinary, work-study, and independent-learning courses. There was certainly more activity at Thornlea than in most schools: drawings and paintings covering corridor walls, all kinds of music filling the air, seminars and panel discussions held in abundance. There was a sunken student lounge area of brick, carpets, padded benches, and large plants, which the students called 'the jungle.' At any time of the day, students could be seen there studying, playing cards, strumming guitars, or chatting. Highly motivated students dug deeply into their work, while others skipped classes with abandon. Some teachers felt the permissive atmosphere had brought down standards, while other staff members praised the positive student atmosphere. Charles McCaffray, an assistant superintendent of curriculum in the provincial department, was quoted in early 1969 as saying that Thornlea was 'definitely the most advanced high school in Ontario,' and predicted that 'large numbers of other schools' would develop in similar directions.[64]

In addition to the accelerating Hall-Dennis bandwagon and the legitimization of the high school credit system, the year 1969 saw yet another blow to traditional education. In March of that year the provincial committee on religious education – chaired by a pillar of the establishment, former Lieutenant-Governor Keiller Mackay – recommended the total elimination of the 1944 requirements for religious instruction. Prompted by the increasingly secular mood of the decade and by local boards reluctant to expose religiously-mixed pupil populations to Christian indoctrination, the government had established the Mackay Committee three years earlier. Its report was devastating. The existing course was written off as a total failure because it was 'not designed in accordance with modern principles of education.' Its presentation of Bible stories and Christian morals 'does not provide for the objective examination of evidence, nor stimulate the inquiring mind; it does not teach children to think for themselves.'[65] Mackay recommended a switch from religious instruction to informal moral or ethical education, which would permeate the entire curriculum and encourage pupils to make their own value judgments and moral decisions. 'After more than two decades in which Christianity has been the most divisive presence in the public schools,' declared the Toronto *Globe and Mail*, 'reform seems on the way.'[66]

'The days of established order, propriety, virtue and hard work, when schools are institutions of solemn purpose and moral admonition are gone,' observed Lloyd Dennis in 1970.[67] More than anyone else, Dennis had come to be associated in the eyes of the public as the prime instigator in this shift from a Calvinistic to a Rousseauesque approach in the education of the young. Gone was the emphasis on making the student diligent, dutiful, and industrious. Rousseau was now in fashion, and the primary function of the school was to engender independence in each child and to develop his unique intellect and character to the fullest.[68] Many parents and members of the public found it difficult to accept such a sweeping change in the fundamental purpose of schooling. Their apprehension about the increasing permissiveness of society was combined with fears about what the future held for the young generation. But for the moment their voices were drowned in the cry of the 1960s for individual freedom. It was difficult to stem the tide when the new wave received so much reinforcement from the mass media and from the province's political and educational leaders.

11 *As the Pendulum Swings*

I

Little did the liberal educators of the 1960s realize how temporary many of their reforms would be. Even before the end of the decade they were challenged from the left by a small but vocal band of critics, spurred on by the counter-culture movement of the period, who sought to use the schools as beachheads for social and political change. But as the optimistic 1960s were replaced by the more realistic 1970s, such radical criticism was confronted and soon overwhelmed by reaction from both moderates and conservatives. Moderates felt increasingly uncomfortable with what seemed an all-too-rapid change-for-change's-sake approach, and with the imposition of so many innovations without adequate planning time. Meanwhile, ideological conservatives criticized the permissiveness of the 1960s reforms, which, with some exaggeration, they saw as leading Ontario and all of Western society down the slippery path to decadence and destruction.

In ten short years – from about the mid-1960s to the mid-1970s – the educational pendulum swung rapidly from one end of the ideological continuum to the other. Accompanying this philosophical swing was a closely related move from the decentralized and localist tendencies of the 1960s changes back to the stronger central control that had characterized much of the history of Ontario education. If, at the school and class-room level, the 1960s had been years of rapid change, then the following decade brought the equally challenging problems of retrenchment and consolidation of effort. The schools – and their teachers – reeled under the impact of these rapid changes in societal and governmental expectations.

The short-lived radical critique of the 1960s liberalization was first articulated in a number of isolated reactions to the Hall-Dennis Report which went largely unnoticed in the euphoric atmosphere of the report's publication. But philosopher John McMurtry branded *Living and Learning* as a fraud for its failure to transfer power to students and teachers. Historian Michael Katz dismissed it for failing to confront and question such 'basic premises' as compulsory attendance and public control. George Martell criticized its portrayal of a utopian society where people 'experience neither collective roots nor class oppression.'[1] Former high school history teacher Robert Davis argued that a new type of educational community was needed because in the existing situation students had no say in policy making, their minds were fragmented through narrow subject specialization, they were not encouraged to explore their inner selves, and they were discouraged from developing a critical view of society. What was required, concluded Davis, was 'a kind of counter-society, a new kind of family, a place set apart, a way of living more than a way of learning.'[2]

Davis initiated the development of such a learning environment in September 1966. The setting was a quiet farm near the village of Hillsburgh, in the Caledon Hills north-west of Toronto. That year seventeen teenagers became the first students at Everdale Place, one of the earliest and most famous of the 'free schools' that dotted the North American educational landscape in the late 1960s and early 1970s. Through a mixture of small, informal classes, sharing of farm chores, and communal living, students would learn, it was hoped, to accept personal and social responsibility. They were free at all times to do as they wished, as long as they did not infringe on the freedom of others. The founders expected that Everdale would encourage self-knowledge, integrate the intellect with the emotions and senses, practise total participatory democracy, and foster a critical view of society. They hoped their experiment, though designed for a small group of students living collectively, would influence the larger society both as a new kind of learning environment and a model utopian community of the future.

Everdale Place became a magnet for sceptical critics, curious visitors, and committed 'free schoolers' from across the North American continent. It spawned the decade's most radical educational journal, *This Magazine Is About Schools*, and inspired other free schools like Point Blank and Superschool in downtown Toronto. But its enrolment never climbed above thirty students, its high fees excluded all but the upper middle class, and its impact on the larger school system and society proved transitory. Its lack of a fixed curriculum created problems of adjustment for most students and their parents. And its open life-style was too radical and inappropriate a model for Ontario or North American society to adopt *en masse*.

Everdale was an extreme example of the impact on education of the radical culture of the late 1960s. It was a youth subculture or counter-culture that produced a number of challenges for the institutional school. Its most visible characteristics were its distinctive dress and hair styles – jeans and sandals, long hair and beads; its sounds were those of the popular rock-music industry; its moods were often induced by hallucinogenic drugs; its values were individuality, personal liberation, an enhanced self-concept, and personal autonomy. And its Ontario mecca was the Yorkville area of central Toronto, a few square blocks of shops and residences where the culture of youth blossomed in the years between 1965 and 1968. Here some thousands of people in their teens and early twenties, alienated from family, school, and traditional societal norms, lived in a communal setting, and embraced the drug culture and the world of mysticism.

The revolt of the young was attributed to everything from the permissiveness of post-war child-rearing practices publicized by American pediatrician Benjamin Spock, to the example set by civil rights workers in the American South, to the affluence of the decade, and the growing availability of drugs. But to University of Toronto communications scholar Marshall McLuhan, the explanation was found in television. 'The present crop of school kids, who began to watch TV before they learned to read and write,' McLuhan told the Hall-Dennis committee, 'are in a totally different sensory world than their parents and teachers.' Their stimulation was sensual and electronic, rather than intellectual and linear. 'What goes on inside the school is puny and undernourished compared to what goes on the moment the child steps outside.'[3] The youngsters were 'coming out of a highly integrated electronic environment' only to be confronted in school by a 'fragmented, specialist environment of subjects and hours and instructions which baffle them.'[4] They were also confronted by school rules which reflected earlier social and moral patterns, and did not correspond to the new mood of many young people. As late as 1967, most Ontario high schools banned miniskirts, beards and long hair, smoking, holding hands, and participation in school-based radical political clubs.

Faced with such an apparent dichotomy, the articulate, freedom-loving student of the late 1960s might become a psychological drop-out, seek alternatives such as Everdale Place, or actively try to bring about changes in his own school. From 1965, a number of larger, urban high schools were jolted by student protests against alleged curbs on personal freedom and political rights. A controversy over dress styles at Oakville-Trafalgar High School in March 1967 showed how critical of authority once-placid teenagers could be. Here the outburst was prompted by a ban on girls' jumpsuits and flirtskirts (many of which had been made in the school's own home economics classes). One girl termed the ban 'an infringement on their rights by narrow-minded old fogies'; another dismissed the ruling as the product of 'warped minds.'[5] The alleged stifling of political discussion also drove students to protest. In a prohibited 1968 valedictory address that was forwarded to the press, Harold Coldwell criticized his five years of 'non-education' at Mimico High School. During those years, Coldwell claimed, the school had ignored such external events as Vietnam and the drug culture. 'We proceed along in this system as if the outside world does not exist.' The way to succeed in school, Coldwell advised his fellow students, was to 'never think.'[6]

The most highly publicized incident of student protest occurred at Toronto's Forest Hill Collegiate in the spring of 1969. Forest Hill had long been regarded as one of Ontario's most liberal and stable high schools. It was attended by bright and privileged youth, most of them coming from well-to-do Jewish homes where academic achievement was respected. Its principal, H.H. Mosey, was described as a 'sensitive and humane man who has maintained close rapport with students.'[7] Yet for three weeks that spring, classes were disrupted, students bitterly divided, and Mosey pictured as an authoritarian disciplinarian. The focus of attention was a sit-in by three students who claimed they were suspended illegally for demanding freedom of speech. The controversy had been developing for several months, as a small group of students had organized under the name of the Student Guard, and had taken a highly vocal and radical stance on controversial educational and political issues. Claiming the activities of the group had unduly disrupted the operation of the school, Mosey ordered the Guard to disband. Continued provocation by its three leaders, especially the distribution of a newspaper portraying Mosey as a 'paper tiger,' resulted in the suspensions. It was a classic confrontation between radical youth and a liberal school authority that believed in limits on student freedoms.

There were other signs during the 1968-9 school year of organized political action on the part of Ontario high school students. A group called Students Against the War in Vietnam persuaded the Toronto board to allow Vietnam teach-ins in the high schools. In October they organized a march from the board offices to Queen's Park, where they staged a noisy, anti-American rally. Then in December and January came the largest and loudest student protest in Ontario school history. It was triggered by a routine departmental announcement that in June 1969 classes would end five days later than the previous year. A number of student councils labelled the announcement as arbitrary, dictatorial, and showing contempt towards students. A threatened walk-out over the issue by Metro Toronto's 115,000 high school students was only averted by Education Minister Davis in a three-hour session with the chairmen of Metro's six inter-school councils. A new element had been forcefully introduced into the politics of educational decision-making.

The reaction of Ontario's political and educational establishment to student militancy ranged from blindness, to a defence of the status quo, to a willingness to seek accommodation. Blindness best describes the 1967 report of the Ontario legislature's Select Committee on Youth. Appointed three years earlier, and chaired by former hockey star Syl Apps, the committee was charged with 'ascertaining the true needs of youth at this time.' Through a series of open hearings, the members received briefs on recreation and physical fitness, counselling and delinquency, education, and employment opportunities. Most of the petitioners, however – children's-aid societies, school-boards, church and women's clubs – were traditional adult groups who purported to speak for young people. There is little evidence that the committee talked with any young people who were exploring the psychedelic and anarchistic outer limits of the 1960s. Their report failed to acknowledge the existence of Yorkville (about a kilometer from Queen's Park itself). Half a page of the 408-page report was devoted to the increasing use of drugs among young people, with no attempt to probe the causes or explore the significance of this phenomenon. The major recommendation for a provincial department of youth – to co-ordinate programs for the fourteen-to-twenty-four-year age group – would have been appropriate for the 1950s, but the committee failed in 'ascertaining the true needs of youth' in the late 1960s.[8]

By contrast, Education Minister William Davis, confronted with protests in the schools, and sensitive to the public mood of the time, moved with considerable flexibility to accommodate the new orientation of Ontario students. In 1966 he had supported the beleaguered high school principal in his efforts 'to maintain reasonable standards ... of socially acceptable behaviour, as he sees these often controversial matters.' Two years later, however, Davis was more sympathetic to those students pressing for social and educational change. 'By the mid-teen period,' he wrote a correspondent, 'students must begin to relate their own moral code to the wide variety of real-life situations that they see around them and may meet for themselves.'[9]

Executive members of the OSSTF proved less accepting of student behaviour. Their 'Letter of Concern Regarding the Secondary Schools of Ontario' appeared in major daily newspapers in October 1968. 'We believe that the unrest among students in our schools is symptomatic of the revolt against all forms of authority within our society today,' declared the letter signed by the federation's president and general secretary. 'The attempts of our principals to carry out- ... [their] responsibility in an increasingly permissive society are meeting with resistance.' They pleaded for 'the cooperation and support of all citizens in our attempts to educate responsible citizens for a democratic society.'[10]

How Ontario high school teachers reacted to this call-to-arms from their executive may well have depended on two inter-related factors: the extent to which the youth culture and student militancy had permeated their own classrooms, and their own personal identification with the counter culture. Despite the publicity surrounding the Yorkville drug scene, and media attention on the Forest Hill protest, most class-rooms – particularly in rural Ontario – remained relatively serene and unaffected during the late 1960s. Then, too, there were many younger teachers who moved with the thinking of radical students and embraced aspects of the counter culture on their own terms. By the end of the decade, teachers began to appear in beards and turtleneck sweaters, pantsuits and miniskirts, and to support students in their campaigns for more flexible forms of discipline. School-boards dropped dress codes, and school administrators sat down with student councils to begin drafting new rules for student clubs and political action. As the movement peaked in the spring of 1969, confrontation was beginning to give way to accommodation.

II

While free schools and student militancy captured the headlines in 1969, the new decade of the 1970s witnessed brief flowerings of two related, yet less radical attempts at educational change – 'alternative schools' and 'parent power.' Alternative schools, while often as experimental and innovative as the more highly publicized free schools, were usually publicly funded ventures under local boards of education and thus closer to the social and political mainstream. Parent power, while sharing roots with student militancy in the 1960s phenomenon of participatory democracy, tended to confine itself to local educational questions, and rarely took an ideological stance.

SEED – an acronym for 'Shared Experience, Exploration and Discovery' – was the first of several board-sponsored alternative schools of the new decade. Its origins went back to a 1968 summer school for Toronto students. More than 600 teenagers turned up that summer, and formed learning groups according to their own interests, using adult volunteers as resource people or 'catalysts.' The process was repeated the following summer, and continued through the winter, with about ninety students meeting after school hours. The granting of permanent status by the Toronto board in September 1970 was an attempt to meet the needs of articulate, creative students increasingly alienated from regular high schools. SEED students designed their own programs from the credit and 'catalyst' courses offered by the school's small staff and host of volunteers. 'The students tend to be bright, articulate and rather anarchistic,' reported Trustee Fiona Nelson in 1972. Leadership had to be 'of a very high and tactful order' because student 'resistance to structure makes cooperative action and decision-making difficult.'[11] But SEED flourished in the early 1970s. Everdale Place had seen the inspiration for free schools outside the system, and SEED provided the model for alternative schools within the system.

Student success in launching SEED encouraged parent groups to lobby for additional alternative schools within the Toronto system. One such initiative led to the founding of ALPHA (for 'A Lot of Parents Hoping for an Alternative'), a school patronized by middle-class families who believed that Hall-Dennis reforms were not permeating conventional schools quickly enough. Then there were the seven low-income mothers from the Trefann Court public housing project who challenged the board's right to stream their youngsters into dead-end 'opportunity' classes (a polite euphemism for classes for slow learners). Accusing the board of rampant class bias, they charged that 'the school system directly discriminates against children from poor families.'[12] So they began their own school, named Laneway, first as a shoe-string private operation. Within two years Laneway joined SEED and ALPHA as publicly-funded alternatives under the Toronto board. Although alternative schools remained small in size and few in number, and were confined mostly to Ontario's urban centres, they were another new component in what was becoming a pluralistic educational system.

Like student militancy, the push for parent involvement in educational decision making grew out of the emphasis of the 1960s on individual autonomy and participatory action. In earlier periods, when most major decisions in education were made at the provincial level, there was little justification for strong neighbourhood parent groups. The traditional Home and School Association, with its emphasis on fund-raising and meet-the-teacher teas, was sufficient. But by the end of the 1960s the local school was deciding, in large measure, what should be taught, how it should be taught, and how to measure and evaluate pupil progress. With its reluctance to 'interfere' in the work of the principal and staff, the Home and School seemed no longer appropriate. New ad hoc parent groups were dominated by young, articulate fathers and mothers who felt comfortable in the milieu of participatory democracy. They supported local decision making, and they wanted some say in determining the policies for their neighbourhood schools.

The volunteer movement was one manifestation of closer parent-teacher and school-community relations. A February 1970 survey of 100 Niagara Peninsula elementary schools showed that forty-eight were using volunteer assistants – twenty-three directly in the instructional program. Throughout the province, mothers with time, talents, and self-confidence responded to calls for help from schools needing extra adults to individualize and personalize the class-room learning program. But it was in the Niagara region that the phenomenon was most closely observed, studied, and encouraged under the leadership of Henry Hedges, head of OISE's Niagara Centre in St Catharines. Under Hedges's supervision, volunteers were given increased class-room responsibilities in a number of district schools. The results were encouraging: teachers spent more time on the important tasks of curriculum planning, pupil motivation, and the teaching of new concepts and skills; pupils had more contact time with adults and made more rapid learning gains. 'Volunteering represents one of the first innovations in recent times that has no relation to school budgets,' concluded Hedges, 'and yet may have an important bearing on the achievement of the school's objectives.' He predicted it would probably represent in the 1970s the greatest single change of personnel in the schools.[13]

The thrust for greater community use of schools coincided with the parent volunteer movement. As their back-to-school feature in September 1970, the editors of *Chatelaine* magazine gave prominence to a story by Jocelyn Dingman entitled 'Why Can't We All Use the Schools After School?' Dingman found many groups wanting to use school facilities: teenagers with no place to go and nothing to do; elderly people seeking companionship in recreational activities; taxpayers who questioned expensive public facilities standing idle; young apartment dwellers who saw school gymns and auditoriums as starting points for developing community spirit in sterile high-rise developments. She also found good examples of community use. As early as 1966, Flemington Road Elementary School in North York had begun an active partnership with its low-income public-housing neighbourhood: local clubs meeting in the school; home visits by teachers; class field trips into the surrounding streets; offices in the school for local health and community service personnel; and a community advisory council with teacher and parent representatives. Similarly, at Trafalgar Elementary School in London, after-hours recreational programs were based on the Flint, Michigan, model – the North American centre of community education. But these were the exceptions, not the rule. Dingman was discouraged by the constantly recurring problems of school building control, the cost of after-hours programming, and co-operation of multiple funding agencies at the local and provincial levels.

Responding to public pressure, the provincial legislature in 1971 established a Select Committee on the Utilization of Educational Facilities, chaired by Charles McIlveen. Access to schools, the committee argued in a 1973 report, should be the right of every citizen, and therefore after-hours control of facilities should be transferred to local community-action councils. Boards would have first call on the buildings during normal school hours, but the rest of the time they would be true community installations. Schools should be centres of living and learning for all age groups, providing a wide range of community health, recreation, and shopping services. The committee went beyond the issue of utilization of facilities. It called for closer school-community integration through wider use of class-room volunteers and non-certified teachers, granting diploma credits to students engaged in community field-work projects, and allowing more community voice in local curriculum making. McIlveen predicted that implementation of these proposals would give Ontario schools 'much more community involvement than any place in the world – at least any place in the world that we've seen, and we've been halfway around it.'[14]

The spread of publicly-funded alternative schools, the mushrooming of the parent volunteer movement, and new proposals for community schools were indicative of the diversity that permeated social and educational thought at the time. Consistent with the broader range of behaviours and life-styles that the larger society seemed prepared to tolerate, many educators abandoned the search for one solution and accepted the concept that different philosophies, programs, and approaches could be incorporated into the functions of the school. Consistent also with the growth of participatory democracy in the larger society, school administrators were prepared to allow parents, students, and teachers larger roles in planning those different philosophies, programs, and approaches. To citizens who put their trust in institutional conformity imposed from above, alternative and diverse patterns posed a threat. But to those who saw the future as one of increasing divergence and pluralism, with individuals and groups sharing in the decision-making process, alternative choices seemed promising. Momentarily at least, public education in Ontario seemed to be moving a long way from the earlier idea of a monolithic school system providing the same program for every pupil.

The ultimate extension of the student- and parent-power movements would have gone far beyond participation to encompass the more radical concept of parent/teacher/student *control* of the neighbourhood school. Backing this idea was the Community Control Workshop of Toronto, whose leading theoretician was George Martell, an editor of *This Magazine Is About Schools*. Martell argued that the movement must decide for local control, rather than mere involvement in the existing structure, if it were to have any lasting impact.[15] School trustees nudged the Toronto public system in this direction by recommending school-community liaison or advisory councils at the neighbourhood level. But the educational administrators balked at total community control. Toronto's director of education, Ronald Jones, argued that complete local control would be as harmful as complete control by a remote central bureaucracy.

By the mid-1970s the sting had been removed from both the student- and parent-power movements. Student militancy had peaked with the April 1969 sit-in at Forest Hill Collegiate, and focused thereafter on consolidating gains made in liberalized dress codes and wider choice of optional subjects. High school students' councils gave up any dreams of shared control of policy making and settled for membership on school advisory councils. Advocates of increased parental involvement could also point to certain gains: membership on these same advisory councils, widespread and successful volunteer programs, and representation on selection committees that chose new school principals in Toronto. But for the most part, student and parent groups had always been interested in short-term solutions to specific, local issues; participation declined over time. In addition, few could devote the time – or considered themselves competent – to manage the complex school system. Thus the major reason a radical student- or community-control movement failed to take root in Ontario lay with these client or consumer groups themselves. Students and parents proved more reluctant to seize power than were administrators to share it.

III

As in the case of student power, parental involvement, and alternative schools, the continent-wide concern for socio-economic and cultural minorities influenced Ontario schools in those years of commitment from the mid 1960s through the early 1970s. In September 1964 the Toronto *Globe and Mail* head-lined a full-page feature story 'Discovering the Disadvantaged Child.' The writer quoted a number of inner-city elementary school principals who were exceptionally frank in their analysis of the problems faced by poor children. 'They have their own culture,' admitted one principal. 'But some of their values clash with traditional school values. They lack a sound command of formal English, they don't value education for its own sake.' Another principal flatly declared that 'the cards are stacked against the poor.'[16] A research study published six years later confirmed the relationship between poor academic performance of lower-class pupils and middle-class expectations of teachers. Most teachers were found to emphasize those values identified with their own class – orderliness, neatness, punctuality, and 'general respectability.'[17] This was a favourite theme of Liberal party education critic Tim Reid, who charged in 1970 that the 'children of the poor are not being educated.' Despite the massive infusion of public funds into education during the 1960s, Reid claimed, the 'educational participation gap' between rich and poor had not changed.[18]

Innovative programs for economically disadvantaged children frequently proved disappointing. Junior kindergartens for four-year-olds in Ottawa and Toronto provided an initial head start, but the further lower-class children progressed through the grades, the more they fell behind their middle-class rivals in reading and numerical achievement. Experimental efforts such as Hamilton's ENOC program ('Educational Needs of the Older City') or that at Toronto's Duke of York Public School provided extra money for smaller classes, resource materials, remedial teachers, counsellors, and social workers. But these young-sters were still over-represented in 'opportunity' classes in the upper elementary grades and two-year terminal programs in high schools. Toronto's 'Every Student Survey' of 1970 showed that only 24 per cent of grade 8 graduates from low-income Park School went on to five-year programs in high school, compared with 95 per cent from Deer Park School in wealthy North Toronto. Other studies showed that, among Ontario high school students, the desire, expectation, and ultimate attainment of admission to post-secondary institutions diminished as one went down the socio-economic ladder.[19] Once channelled into a special vocational high school, the lower-class student was doomed, according to critic George Martell, 'to accept dead-end jobs, or a life in which there would be no job at all.'[20]

Schools of the period were charged also with discriminating against children of immigrant parents, through their emphasis on assimilation into the mainstream culture rather than preservation of the immigrant culture. In 1968 the Toronto Board of Education reported 3,432 elementary pupils with little or no English, plus a similar number who required special instruction in order to function effectively in the anglophone school environment. The board began pumping extra money into schools with heavy immigrant populations; such schools often coincided with those designated as serving low-income areas. Bilingual teachers and counsellors were appointed; English immersion classes were established to prepare students for the regular grades; General Mercer Public School used Italian as a language of instruction. But children of Greek, Italian, and Portuguese families continued at a disadvantage, as the cultural conflict remained between school and home. As non-white immigration increased in the mid-1970s, moderate criticism of discrimination on ethnic grounds was overwhelmed by charges of outright racism within the schools. The Toronto board's Every Student Survey of 1975 showed that West Indian and Chinese pupils had become the second and fourth largest immigrant blocks, vying with the older Italian and Portuguese groups.

Tension mounted throughout 1975 as reports surfaced of racial incidents between white and black teachers and pupils. By the summer of 1976, board chairman Gordon Cressy admitted that city schools were poised 'on the edge of violence, the verge of racism.' He called for a shift in attitude among parents, teachers, and pupils to prevent a serious confrontation. 'We have to initiate and change things before we start reacting and over-reacting.'[21] New history courses and reading programs were developed to reflect the diverse pupil population, non Anglo-Saxon teachers were appointed, and liaison committees established with immigrant communities. Douglas Barr (Cressy's successor as board chairman) echoed the plight of educators across the province in their attempts to provide equality of educational opportunity to all students. 'It's infuriating when we are blamed for every social problem,' said Barr. 'It's naïve to imagine that we have a magic wand.' But in admitting that 'clearly we do have a role to play in combatting the spread of racism,' he reflected the popular view that the school should be the front-line agency in the amelioration of society's ills.[22]

While large urban boards tried to adjust to immigrant populations, many of Ontario's rural school systems, particularly those in the North, were faced with another multicultural challenge – the native Indian pupil. By 1968 an estimated 50 per cent of the province's Indian children had shifted from federal and mission schools to schools operated by local boards. Here they were confronted by problems similar to those of immigrant groups in major cities – a value conflict between school and home, a curriculum that ignored or distorted their heritage, and a white educational hierarchy. A 1968 study showed that school textbooks most commonly described Indians as 'savage,' 'fierce,' and 'hostile,' portrayed them as semi-naked or in tribal costume, and never showed them in skilled or professional occupations.[23] An initial attempt to overcome these problems came the following year with the designation of Howard-Harwich-Moravian School near Ridgetown as the province's first 'cross-cultural' school. With native children comprising one-eighth of the enrolment, there would be 'official recognition of Indian values and culture in the curriculum.'[24] Over the next few years, Indian trustees were appointed to school-boards enrolling a minimum of 100 native children, and colleges and faculties of education began special programs to encourage more Indians to qualify as teachers.

But the particular interests and claims of Ontario's multicultural communities had to be balanced against demands for more Canadian content in the schools. A.B. Hodgetts, a history teacher at Trinity College School in Port Hope, launched the Canadian Studies movement with the 1968 publication of *What Culture? What Heritage?*, a nation-wide study of history, geography, and civics teaching. Two years of class-room visitations had depressed Hodgetts. He found far too many uncommitted and seemingly uncaring teachers who, lacking any skills or training in Canadian studies, used weak curriculum materials and outdated teaching styles. 'Our kids are being deprived in elementary and secondary school of their own culture and heritage.' Graduates left Canadian classrooms 'without the intellectual skills, the knowledge and the attitudes they should have to play an effective role as citizens.'[25] While Hodgetts consistently stressed the quality of Canadian studies teaching, many of his supporters were equally concerned with quantity – the relatively small attention paid to Canadian history and literature in the total curriculum. One professor predicted a future generation whose lack of knowledge of Canada would produce an epidemic of 'national amnesia.'[26]

The early 1970s saw a number of promising developments in Canadian studies. Following Hodgetts's recommendations, and with financing from both government and the private sector, the Canada Studies Foundation was established in March 1970. Given the decentralized nature of curriculum planning at that time, the foundation did not strive for a unified history curriculum that would be used across the country. It hoped to enrich or supplement existing curricula by developing and testing new teaching units and learning materials. Groups of Ontario teachers joined with colleagues from Quebec in the Laurentian Project, which focused on past and present cultural differences between Canadians. By 1975 the foundation had poured three million dollars into this developmental work. In common with earlier external attempts to influence school programs, the Canada Studies Foundation enjoyed limited success. Teachers and curriculum consultants who had not been included in the projects were often unenthusiastic about implementing them. Students found the social science, inquiry-oriented approaches to Canadian topics no more exciting than traditional constitutional-history approaches.

The move to stimulate interest in Canadian literature in the schools was more successful, in part because it could draw on the talents of a new and vibrant generation of Canadian writers. Its catalyst was James Foley, an English teacher at Port Colborne High School. A working-class, industrial city in the Niagara Peninsula, Port Colborne seemed an unlikely centre for what became the CanLit movement. Yet its apparent handicaps – a polyglot population drawn from nearly every European country, and a location near the border that produced an all-pervasive American cultural environment – were the challenges on which the energetic Foley thrived. Beginning in 1971, he organized an annual Canada Day, with Canadian novelists and poets invited to share ideas with students. Delighted to find such an interest in the national literature, writers from across the province paid their own travel expenses and showed up in large numbers. Canada Day at Port Colborne High School soon expanded to Canada Week and became the largest annual gathering of the Canadian literary élite. The desired results were forthcoming: publishers, curriculum consultants, and classroom teachers embraced Canadian authors, and Ontario students were exposed to their national literary heritage.

IV

While the respective claims of traditionalism and progressivism, multiculturalism and nationalism, were debated in Ontario education in the late 1960s and early 1970s, the major developments of the new decade were pronounced shifts towards fiscal retrenchment and pedagogical conservatism in school affairs. These moves were prompted by unrest among taxpayers over increased school costs, and unease among many laymen at the changes of the Davis years. With its remarkable capacity for judging the political mood of the electorate, the Conservative government began to tighten the screws on the flow of money and to introduce more structure into the provincial curriculum.

The first specific manifestation of the new order came in response to provincial moves towards further centralization of local school-board administration. In November 1967 – one month after a provincial election – Premier Robarts announced that legislation to abolish township school-boards and establish county boards would be introduced to take effect in January 1969. Department of education officials argued that the township boards – introduced with so much fanfare in 1965 – were still too small to raise enough funds or generate enough pupils to provide the expanded services and diversified programs demanded by the technological world of the late twentieth century. Queen's Park officials also argued that the new county boards would enable the province to transfer still more aspects of educational decision making to these larger, stronger local authorities.

But opponents in small towns saw the move as the antithesis of localism. A Jarvis clergyman branded it 'a triumph of bureaucracy over democracy'; a Stoney Creek lawyer mourned 'the passing of the small unit in which people feel a sense of belonging and involvement'; a Tavistock doctor predicted that close teacher-pupil and teacher-parent relations would be lost in the impersonal contacts of the larger county control.[27] One study found trustees who opposed county organization were those with deep roots in their local communities, whose values were particularistic, and who were oriented 'not to the scientific establishment but away from what they perceived as a cold, impersonal bureaucracy of experts.'[28] Such a group of 108 trustees and councillors, organized by the stubborn Tavistock Public School Board and drawn from across south-western Ontario, travelled to Queen's Park to fight the legislation in early 1968. 'We saw such things happen in Germany in the 1930s in the name of progress,' warned their spokesman. But Deputy Minister Jack McCarthy – as committed to administrative reorganization as he had been to program change – gave not an inch. 'We have to move ahead,' he replied. 'We can't stand still on this.'[29]

The deposed rural and small-village trustees were often correct in their prediction that the new county boards would embrace the central planning concept at the expense of local community control. This was repeatedly demonstrated in the early 1970s as county boards closed many of the small, economically inefficient high schools they had inherited. An example was Pelham District High School in the village of Fenwick, which had passed under the jurisdiction of the new Niagara South Board of Education. Pelham's declining enrolment and limited academic program invited closure. County education director R.A. McLeod argued that a small secondary school was not viable under current conditions. While sympathizing with local concern, McLeod maintained that 'the re-arrangement of operations to meet new circumstances is a common occurrence in today's society.'[30] Equality of opportunity and of expenditure across the region must prevail over entrenched localism.

The Niagara South administrators and trustees were confronted by intense opposition from Pelham students, parents, and alumni. Since its origins as a continuation school in 1927, through its upgrading to district high school in the 1940s, and throughout the turbulent 1960s, Pelham had been a central feature of the village of Fenwick and its surrounding fruit-orchard and farming region. For forty-five years it had transferred to the next generation the bedrock values of responsibility, respectability, and pride in work well done. Villagers united against what they perceived as a distant, alien board. 'They don't know a thing about the school and they don't want to know anything about it,' complained one resident. 'They just want to close it.'[31] Mass meetings, media publicity, and court cases, however, failed to halt the centralization thrust, and Pelham District High School closed its doors for the last time in June 1974.

Yet even the closing of dozens of Pelhams failed to halt spiralling education costs. Establishment of the new county boards confronted many rural municipalities with dramatic increases in mill rates for school purposes. In part, increased school-board budgets were the result of the rapid increase in the number of high-salaried administrative personnel required to operate the larger, complex educational systems. More important was the cost of extending much needed, and much demanded, educational services to rural areas – special education services, learning assistance programs, and psychological and medical support services. This meant increases in professional staff which, when combined with general moves towards smaller classes and high teacher salaries, greatly increased the personnel budgets of the county boards. For the most part these challenges were met – the large boards functioned well, given the century-old tradition of localism in Ontario education – but the financial strains were obvious.

Equally important, however, in explaining higher mill rates in rural areas was the nature of the tax base for the new county boards. Rural municipalities could no longer maintain relatively low rates of taxation through a combination of low expenditures and special protective features in the school-grant plan. Now they were faced with a tax rate based on expenditures across an entire county, often with one or more cities included, and the new grant structure removed virtually all of the protective provisions formerly available from the province. The village of Shelburne, for example, was asked by the Dufferin County Board of Education to raise $155,000 in 1969, more than double the previous year's levy. The warden of that traditionally Conservative county was reported to have suggested the possibility of a tax strike on the part of farmers unwilling or unable to pay the taxes demanded.[32] They could legally have withheld tax payments for up to three years before confiscatory action could be taken.

With its antennae picking up rumblings of unrest throughout rural Ontario, the Robarts government moved to put a lid on local budget and tax increases. On 16 March 1969 Provincial Treasurer Charles MacNaughton 'fired the first shots in what was eventually to emerge as the Tory war on its own education system.'[33] Forecasting increased fiscal difficulties in the years ahead, MacNaughton proposed firm restraints on social spending. He urged municipalities to exercise 'voluntary restraint in spending programmes, particularly in the field of education,' and hinted at provincial compulsion if local efforts failed.[34]

As a temporary relief measure for rural areas, amendments to grant regulations in July 1969 provided increased provincial money for boards able to limit their tax increase to one mill for elementary purposes and one for secondary, provided their total expenditure per pupil was no greater than 115 per cent of the previous year's figure. In a further move to pacify rural supporters, the government later announced a rebate of 25 per cent of all farmers' property taxes. But these were interim measures. The government eventually committed itself to raising provincial grants over three years until they reached an average of 60 per cent of total school-board expenditures. Not surprisingly, this was accompanied by the assertion of greater provincial control over all school costs.

The key piece of legislation was Bill 228, introduced in November 1969. Regulations under Section 4(1) could fix the amount a board might raise through a local levy. Previously, boards could raise property taxes as much as they judged to be politically feasible; now they were forced to accept specified annual budget increases and tax rises. The next few years saw considerable bitterness and acrimony between provincial and local authorities. Boards now faced fixed ceilings but were provided with few guidelines for trimming costs and reducing programs. A barrage of parental and community criticism resulted. Meanwhile the government, with the editorial support of most of the province's leading newspapers, led a vigorous and popular campaign to bring 'sky-rocketing' costs under control.

On 20 October 1970, under the authority of Bill 228, Education Minister Davis announced the first budget ceilings to take effect in 1971. From an educational point of view the timing was atrocious, coming two months before the beginning of the new provincial fiscal year and long after local boards had made commitments for the 1970-71 school year. Politically, however, the timing was most astute. With John Robarts's impending retirement, Davis was about to enter the race for party leadership and the premiership of the province. He had to reverse his image as the big-spending cabinet minister of the 1960s and project himself as an advocate of restraint. Not surprisingly, school finance became an important issue in the 1971 leadership campaign. Allan Lawrence, Davis's main rival, accused Davis of allowing education costs to spiral out of control, and promised to cut school spending from 43 to 33 per cent of the provincial budget. Davis ultimately eked out a narrow victory in the leadership race. His subsequent rejection of Catholic demands for separate high school support temporarily diverted attention and helped the new premier score a landslide victory in the fall 1971 provincial election. Succeeding ministers of education – Robert Welch and Thomas Wells – would have to deal with the retrenchment policies of the new decade.

The crisis of this new decade signalled more than a turning point in the history of school finance. It heralded the beginning of public disillusion with the effectiveness of education. In 1962 the Economic Council of Canada had called education the nation's best long-term investment. But now the 'pay-off' seemed non-existent, with the economy in a slump, and school costs exceeding the 8.5 per cent increase in productivity the council had predicted. A survey of 360 high schools led the council to conclude that family factors had more to do with student performance than elaborate equipment, teacher quality, and class size. 'Our secondary school systems may, in general, have reached a certain level of maturity in which significant improvements in the performance or aspirations of students may not be best obtained by further buildup of resources.'[35] The OSSTF responded in a realistic fashion. 'Too much magic was expected,' declared the federation. 'The great boom in education ... [had] ended.'[36]

Implementing such a retrenchment policy meant reversing the trend towards local autonomy in Ontario education. County boards of education were visible manifestations of reckless spending on new programs. The new order for the new decade – for both financial and program matters – would have to be centralization of decision making. Any doubts about the location of control were resolved at a 1972 provincial conference on the politics of education. A ministry of education spokesman announced that local boards, 'while they effect postures of sovereignty ... can never be sovereign.' A Toronto trustee complained that 'we do the dirty work while they make the decisions.' Lincoln County education director Roger Allen called it 'centralized control and de-centralized blame.'[37]

V

By 1970 there were 94,000 teachers in the province of Ontario, almost double the number ten years previously. From the always powerful OSSTF to the perennially weak FWTAO, the federations were prepared to demonstrate their new strength. The average age of their membership – and particularly of their more vocal leaders – was much lower than ever, as thousands of new university and teachers' college graduates were recruited in the expansion years of the 1960s. Most of these new professionals had known nothing but the relative affluence of the post-war years and the optimism of the 1960s. When contentious issues arose, as they were now bound to in a period of retrenchment, the federations were prepared to resist. Elsewhere in North America, teachers' groups provided examples of a new militancy for their Ontario counterparts: Quebec teachers in the vanguard of the separatist movement; American teachers exhibiting charac-teristics of trade unionists. Before long, the provincial government would dis-cover that unsatisfied teachers were more difficult to pacify than farmers threatening a tax strike on the back concessions.

Economic welfare was one factor that fueled teacher unrest in the early 1970s. Salary increases had kept pace with the rising cost of living for most of the previous decade, but began to slip in 1969. In the next few years many teachers took a hard look at public-sector wage trends and began to resist school-board and provincial attempts to hold the line on salary increases. But it was just at this time that ceilings on local board spending reduced the flexibility of the county jurisdictions to respond to teacher demands.

There was more to teacher unrest than money, however. At least as important was the question of quality instruction within the class-room. Many elementary teachers felt uncomfortable with the pressures arising from the implementation of the Hall-Dennis Report. Their high school colleagues were even more troubled by what they perceived to be the negative effects of the open credit system on their own teaching and on pupil achievement. The credit system – in-troduced in many schools without regard to staff support – was seen as the cause of reduced instructional time in English and mathematics, the perpetrator of inflexible uniformity in timetabling, and the end of the security provided to pupils in a 'home room' setting. Then as financial ceilings were imposed, class sizes were increased and such valuable adjuncts as guidance and library service were cut back. From the perspective of many high school teachers, the credit system had produced rigidity rather than flexibility, and student uncertainty rather than security.

A further concern – at first most apparent among elementary teachers – was declining pupil enrolment. A result of lower birth and immigration rates of the 1960s, declining enrolment hit Ontario elementary schools in September 1971. In that month almost 1,000 fewer elementary teachers were needed than in the previous year. Studies predicted an overall 10 per cent drop in elementary positions before the bottom would be reached in 1986, and a 15 per cent drop in secondary school jobs by the mid 1990s. Per pupil grants fell and the number of teaching positions was reduced as declining enrolment worked its way up through the grades in the early 1970s. At first, positions were dropped through natural attrition – retirements and resignations. Soon, it was the turn of teachers on temporary contracts, lacking permanent certification. Before long, most teachers felt threatened. With job security at stake, it was not difficult for teachers to become more conservative in the curriculum area and more vociferous in the economic arena.

Then too, the creation of the county boards helped transform annual trustee-teacher negotiating sessions into confrontation situations. Where once there had been a high trustee-to-teacher ratio with relatively simple and frequent communication, the new administrative units widened the gap between public authority and class-room practitioner. The move to county boards created stronger management groups at the local level, and the 1968 amalgamation of four independent trustee groups into the Ontario Public School Trustees Association created a stronger provincial body. But the teachers' federations had also grown in membership, economic strength, and political acumen. In two respects, at least, teacher groups seemed stronger than their trustee counterparts. First, federation membership was mandatory for all teachers, whereas trustee association membership remained optional. Second, while a federation like OSSTF could bargain for all high school teachers employed by public boards, the OPSTA never spoke for all public jurisdictions; splinter groups in northern Ontario, and later among the larger urban boards, undermined trustee unanimity. With the OSSTF in the lead, teachers' groups possessed certain advantages.

Signs of trouble appeared as early as the spring of 1969. During a legislative debate in March, Education Minister Davis announced that pupil-teacher ratios would have to be tightened the following September 'in some areas.' The OSSTF's response was immediate and negative. 'The secondary school teaching profession,' declared a federation spokesman, 'finds itself in the inevitable position of being squeezed between a bandwagon mandate to launch new programs and a swing towards greater workloads that can only hinder quality teaching.'[38] The sense of urgency about that year's salary negotiations reflected a realization among leaders of all the federations that their bargaining position was becoming unfavourable. Supply and demand were about in balance, and the possibility of a teacher surplus loomed. Meanwhile the newly formed county boards turned to professional staffing as the only area where substantial cost savings could be effected. The federations responded by insisting that class sizes, teaching loads, and other working conditions must be negotiable.

In ensuing years, teacher-trustee salary negotiations became increasingly acrimonious, finally escalating into a major political issue in the fall of 1973. That school year began with the OSSTF threatening a province-wide boycott of extra-curricular activities as its answer to proposed 1974 ceilings on school-board expenditures. No sooner was that issue resolved than 90 per cent of Metro Toronto's high school teachers voted to resign on 31 December unless they secured higher salaries and smaller classes. Although the financially pressed Metro boards finally presented an acceptable offer, the issue ignited sparks across the province. By 30 November, some 7,500 teachers in seventeen Ontario boards submitted mass resignations dated 31 December. The issues were salaries and working conditions; mass resignations were a tactic to avoid the illegality of a teacher strike. Confident that public opinion was running against the teachers, the government in early December introduced Bills 274 and 275, to invalidate mass resignations and to enforce compulsory arbitration.

But William Davis, now premier, and his education minister, Thomas Wells, had underestimated the strength and solidarity of the teachers' federations. Teachers responded to Bill 274 by walking out of every school in the province on December 18; some 30,000 converged on Queen's park for the largest protest demonstration in Ontario's history. The federations denounced the bill as an invasion of civil rights; organized labour and the two opposition parties supported the teachers. Wells accused the teachers of attempting mob rule and charged them with intimidation.[39] But the government gave in the following day, agreeing to the teachers' request that local arbitrators not be instructed to keep contract awards within provincial ceilings. Davis recessed the legislature without the bill receiving final reading, and the federations advised teachers to postpone their resignations. For the moment the crisis was over. The government claimed a victory because it had kept the schools open, but it had failed to hold down school costs and restrain teacher militancy.

The December 1973 confrontation was a taste of things to come. The following year saw mass resignations by Catholic teachers in seven separate-school jurisdictions, and prolonged illegal strikes by Windsor and Ottawa high school teachers. These strikes resulted in unprecedented salary increases and, at Windsor, in teachers being granted the right to negotiate class sizes and teaching loads – once the jealously held prerogatives of management. Wells again charged 'public blackmail' and described teachers' tactics as 'holding a gun to the province's head.' Davis announced that the government 'cannot tolerate requests of this kind if they are translated province-wide.'[40] Rumours that the government was preparing again to prohibit strikes were met by the federations through suggestions that a political-action fund would be established, and by the threat to 'enter the political arena in a partisan fashion and ... retire the present government.'[41]

Finally, after both the NDP and Liberal parties committed themselves to supporting the right to strike, the Conservative government in June 1975 introduced Bill 100: The School Boards and Teachers Collective Negotiations Act. This gave teachers the right to negotiate 'any term or condition of employment' as well as the sought-after right to strike. But it also established elaborate procedures to ensure that every bargaining expedient was exhausted before this right could be exercised. The legislation created an independent body, the Education Relations Commission, to 'monitor and assist' all local negotiations between teachers and school-boards. 'This legislation,' claimed Wells, 'is based on a second set of 3 R's for the 1970s – rights, reason and responsibility.'[42]

These new procedures did not prevent the largest and longest disruption of educational services in the province's history. On 12 November 1975 Metro Toronto's 8,800 secondary school teachers struck to back demands for a 43.9 per cent salary increase over a two-year period. For the next two months, 140,000 students in 135 schools were without classes, until teachers were ordered back to work by legislation on 18 January 1976. The happy-go-lucky atmosphere among students at the start of the strike soon turned to disillusionment, resentment, and bewilderment, and fear of losing the opportunity to move from grade 13 to university. Some students established their own independent classes, others enrolled in high schools elsewhere in the province, while many were confronted with a choice between prolonged idleness or joining the labour force. Teacher enthusiasm also waned as strike pay fell short of regular income, and especially as media publicity became increasingly negative.

Initially it appeared that the high-water mark of teacher militancy had been reached with Bill 100 and the Toronto strike. Certainly the number of strikes and lockouts dropped from twenty-seven in the three years up to 1975 to nineteen in the three years after the passage of Bill 100. Yet both teacher and trustee groups considered the new machinery for resolving differences to be cumbersome, time-consuming, and generally unsatisfactory, and the Education Relations Committee drew criticism from both sides. Although the inclusion of teachers within the mandate of the federal government's 1976 Anti-Inflation Board put a temporary limit on salary increases, the thorny issues of class-room size and instructional hours remained unresolved at mid-decade. And these were the factors, along with declining enrolments, that bore directly on the number of jobs.

VI

In November 1976 the Kingston *Whig-Standard* sent education reporter Mike Sykes into Helen McCormach's grade 2 class-room at Linklater Public School in nearby Gananoque. Sykes was to examine the state of the schools after eight years of life with the Hall-Dennis Report. What he discovered delighted Lloyd Dennis, but failed to satisfy the growing number of critics of Ontario schools. Sykes began his written account with the bold assertion that 'the three R's are alive and well.' But that was only the beginning of a glowing portrayal of McCormach's class-room. The children were 'learning more today than my teachers could impart in twice as many school years.' They read voraciously, knew geometric shapes, grasped the abstract concept of Remembrance Day, were co-operative, eager, and enthusiastic. 'Those kids are learning without fear; they seem self-confident,' observed Sykes. That self-confidence generated a feeling of co-operation and consideration for other pupils. Sykes constructed his story as a personal letter to Lloyd Dennis, now McCormach's superior as director of education for the Leeds and Grenville Board of Education. 'If the foregoing is your idea of permissiveness, Lloyd, then I'm all for it.'[43] It was one layman's vote of confidence for the Hall-Dennis-inspired reforms that had influenced Ontario elementary schools in the years since *Living and Learning*.

Studies of pupil achievement in the early 1970s confirmed Sykes's intuitive reaction. Donald Hastings found forty years of steady improvement in reading comprehension among grade 6 pupils in St Catharines; the median grade score had climbed from 6.1 in 1938 to 6.5 in 1953 to 6.8 in 1971. A Toronto Board of Education study revealed that, immigrant children excepted, pupils were achieving reading scores according to their grade level and consistent with norms established over several years of measurement in Ontario. An OISE study of elementary school mathematics showed that pupils of the 1970s possessed computational skills that equalled and often bettered those of students a decade previous. And a 1972 Environics Research opinion study showed that 72 per cent of elementary school parents thought schools had improved over the past five years.[44]

Yet for every study cited by supporters of Hall-Dennis, there was another set of figures that fed the growing number of education critics. Between 1971 and 1976, for example, while enrolments declined in publicly supported school systems, Ontario's private school enrolment jumped by 32 per cent to 58,000. One Statistics Canada official suggested publicly that dissatisfaction with public school education was the major factor in the increase in private school enrolment.[45] And by 1975 the Gallup Poll did show a change in public attitude, particularly among adults removed from the immediate school environment. Whereas 52 per cent of Canadian parents with three or more youngsters at school believed children were being taught reading and writing as well as they had been, only 33 per cent of adults with no youngsters at school agreed. Across Ontario as a whole, 50 per cent of the public believed the teaching of reading and writing had declined.

If the elementary schools were judged by the three R's, the high schools stood or fell on their grade 13 examination results. Under the old system of departmental exams, with passing levels controlled by the province, the proportion of successful papers had hovered around 80 per cent annually for more than two generations. But in 1968, the first year without departmentals, more than 92 per cent of the locally set and graded exam papers were passed. With higher marks came an increase in the number of Ontario Scholars – those grade 13 graduates with averages of 80 per cent or more – from 5 per cent of the 1965 class to 11 per cent in 1968 and 17 per cent in 1973. The Environics opinion study of 1972 showed that 69 per cent of secondary school parents believed the quality of high school education had improved over the previous five years.[46] But a growing number of veteran school and university officials disagreed; they saw a steady decline in achievement standards throughout the province's high schools.

In early 1973 the Ontario Teachers' Federation singled out the credit system as the major cause of trouble within the new-look Ontario high school. All secondary schools in the province were now operating on this new system which, with numerous choices and few restrictions, allowed students to put together any twenty-seven courses or credits for a grade 12 diploma, with a further six required for grade 13. In a brief to Education Minister Wells, the OTF charged that the credit system 'simply isn't working.' It had reduced the face value of a high school diploma, put intolerable demands on overburdened guidance coun- sellors, intensified the loneliness and alienation of students, increased teacher insecurity, and had failed to improve the curriculum. Lindsay principal Stewart Howard complained that the new freedom of choice downgraded the role of high school principal from that of educational leader to 'being manager of a supermarket.'[47] The OTF called for a return to some degree of compulsory courses.

Sensing support on the hustings from a concerned public, Liberal leader Robert Nixon joined this call for a 'compulsory core curriculum.' Such demands could not be ignored by the Conservative government. Education Minister Wells, who had lost ground with teachers over the strike question, soon gained a measure of teacher respect with his stand on curriculum. Wells began the reverse swing of the curriculum pendulum in November 1973 by reinstating six compul- sory credits, four in English and two in Canadian studies. This, claimed the minister, was in response to a wide public consensus that wanted assurance that students acquired a deeper understanding of the English language and of Canada.[48]

The question of standards inevitably emerged as an issue in the September 1975 provincial election. For the Liberals, Robert Nixon criticized the 'elimina- tion of standards' as well as 'sharp increases in costs.' Wells continued to boast that the Ontario school system was the envy of others and the model school system in North America.[49] But he also continued the back-to-the-basics move. When the ministry released a document entitled 'The Formative Years,' a policy statement on goals and curriculum for the primary and junior divisions, it contained none of the flowery rhetoric and promised freedoms of the Hall-Dennis Report. It stressed 'the basic skills that are such an essential part of a child's education, especially in these early years of formal schooling.'[50] Although the Conservatives squeezed out a narrow victory in that year's election, their loss of a majority helped convince them that educational retrenchment was the order of the day.

By the fall of 1976 the pendulum of public opinion was gathering momentum in its swing towards a more traditional conception of education. 'Bitching about education has become a staple of cocktail-and-dinner-party conversation,' declared *Maclean's Magazine* in its annual September back-to-school story.[51] Critics were making daily 'discoveries' of student illiteracy, supposedly resulting from a lack of attention to the three Rs in the elementary grades and a smorgasbord of unchallenging courses in high school. Results of an English test given to 6,200 freshmen students led the Council of Ontario Universities to conclude that more than 46 per cent needed remedial English assistance. The Ontario Economic Council, the Canadian Chamber of Commerce, and various trustee and parent groups joined the call for a core curriculum. So did the OSSTF in *At What Cost?*, the published analysis of a survey of 19,000 high school teachers. This study reported teacher morale at an all-time low; the root cause was seen to lie in the 'Hall-Dennis theory' which had spawned the 'happy school' of the 1970s. Such a high school, with its emphasis on freedom and individualization, failed to meet the new social goals of the 1970s. 'The present demand for a core curriculum can no longer be denied,' stated the OSSTF. 'There are subject disciplines that are keys to the preservation of our civilization and these should be studied in some depth.'[52]

How would the government react? A series of studies commissioned by the ministry at a cost of approximately half a million dollars concluded that 'exaggerated charges of illiteracy' were unfounded, that 'marking standards ... are not in the state of chaos which some people believe,' and that the public was of the opinion that schools were doing a good job in promoting positive attitudes to learning and in developing individual and social responsibility. Yet the same studies revealed a general criticism of the lack of external testing and evaluation, a belief that overall academic achievement had declined in the high schools, and that the public wanted more emphasis on basic, academic skills.[53] For Wells and his cabinet colleagues in a minority government situation, such perceptions were extremely important. 'If we don't act on public perceptions and frustrations,' he admitted, 'the credibility gap will remain largely unbridged.'[54] On 6 October 1976 Wells made a long-expected announcement. All grade 9 and 10 students would be required to study English, mathematics, science, and Canadian history or geography. Eventually the ministry would produce new guidelines dictating a core content in every subject at every grade level, with the exception of some optional high school courses. Further, Wells asked the Ontario Secondary

School Headmasters' Association to produce a plan for uniformity in marking, and he urged the universities to introduce entrance examinations.[55]

Such changes were consistent with the growing conservative trend in society and education that was evident by the mid 1970s. The optimism of the previous decade had ended. The brave new world promised by critics of traditional approaches had not arrived. This utopia had been replaced by the realities of economic recession and unemployment, galloping inflation; and a widespread crisis of confidence. Education was one area where the promises had noticeably failed. Facilities had been expanded to meet the enrolment explosion; suddenly, because of declining birth rates and student disillusion, there were empty places in schools and universities. Teachers' salaries had been raised to competitive levels; now the federations seemed to be acting like militant trade unions. Administrative systems had been reorganized in the name of economy and efficiency; now they loomed like impenetrable bureaucracies, inaccessible to local pressures. Pedagogical and curricular reforms had been implemented in wholesale quantities; yet students seemed less satisfied than ever. Given the social and economic anxieties of the 1970s, it was not surprising that politicians and the public should re-examine educational priorities. The widespread call for a reversion to the seeming security of older norms was inevitable.

Many critics of the 1970s saw the school not as a benign mirror of social change, but as the malignant cause of an unhealthy situation. The conservative view was that society had become far too permissive. The old self-reliant individualism had disappeared, and people were becoming too pampered, looking for more, but contributing less. Examples of moral slippage were not difficult to find: a de-emphasis on the work ethic and an increasing dependence on the state; preoccupation with rights at the expense of responsibilities; the sexual revolution and the decline of family stability. And the school was seen as a major contributor to this general malaise. During the 1960s, educators had been too concerned with the needs of the individual child as opposed to the needs of society, and had de-emphasized punitive and structured approaches. In the interests of the development of the individual they had sacrificed academic standards. By 1976 it seemed time to return to the basic subjects and the more rigorous pedagogy that had characterized Ontario education for most of the previous century.

Epilogue

The city of Philadelphia did not stage a repeat performance of the 1876 Centennial Exposition when the American bicentennial occurred 100 years later. Philadelphia's more than 300 smaller commemorative events and projects in 1976 reflected the decentralized nature of America's two-hundredth-birthday festivities, with each state and countless cities planning their own ventures. Even if a world's fair had been planned, it is doubtful that the Ontario Ministry of Education would have been represented, let alone have occupied more space or captured more major awards than any other Canadian exhibit. By 1976, a full century after Egerton Ryerson's retirement and the creation of the Ontario Department, later Ministry of Education, the wheel had come full circle for public education as it had for grandiose international exhibitions. Public pride in the quantitative achievements of public education, so obvious in the last quarter of the nineteenth century, had markedly receded. In its place were diversity, dissent, and uncertain educational futures. So the absence of an Ontario educational display in the United States in 1976 went completely unnoticed.

The *Report of the Minister of Education* for 1975-6 made brief reference to the fact that 'the Ministry marked its one hundredth anniversary in February 1976.' There followed a summary history of the administrative development of the department. Except for a curious three-paragraph reference to the Northern Ontario railway car schools of the 1920s – described as 'one of the most romantic eras of education in Ontario' – there was little attention to past accomplishments in extending educational opportunity and improving its quality.[1] Rather, the emphasis in the 1975-6 annual report was on recent changes in policy and problem areas currently under study. By 1976 developments in Ontario education were no longer viewed as inching a province-wide school system ever closer to that point of perfection that Ryerson's supporters and heirs seemed to believe 100 years previously was within their reach. By the last quarter of the twentieth century, educators were more pragmatic and realistic in their assessment of the role and the accomplishments of the public school.

Yet there were impressive accomplishments of the previous 100 years that could have been catalogued in the 1975-6 annual report: the delivery of highly acclaimed and generally well received educational services to the people of Canada's most populous province. As demands increased through the late nineteenth and twentieth centuries, so did the services: vertical extension of public education downwards to what had once been considered the pre-school years of early childhood, and upwards to the tertiary level of post-secondary education; lateral or horizontal extension through diversified program offerings to an almost infinite variety of special learners; and geographic extension to the most remote areas of the province, so that the urban-rural discrepancies of 1876 were close to being eliminated.

Yet many of the concerns of 100 years earlier still plagued Ontario educators in 1976. Cultural problems that had troubled early education ministers such as Adam Crooks and George Ross had been dealt with repeatedly, yet in some ways seemed no closer to resolution. Separate school rights and privileges had been steadily increased, yet were still an issue in the 1971 provincial election; five years later Ontario's Roman Catholics still chafed at the denial of public funding for their three senior high school grades. French language rights had been increased even more dramatically – no return to the repression of Regulation 17 was possible – yet linguistic conflicts in education could still tear apart Ontario communities. And by 1976 additional ethnic and racial minorities were vocal in demanding 'fair treatment' from a multicultural school system. Finally, what was the responsibility of a provincial school system in the area of cultural nationalism? Thomas Wells grappled with the issue of Canadian content in the 1970s just as George Ross had in the 1890s.

Economic and vocational objectives of the schools remained a concern and, like cultural objectives, gave every indication of continuing as priority agenda items into the second century of the ministry of education. Granted, the rural school problem of the late nineteenth and early twentieth centuries had disappeared, since rural Ontario as it once existed had vanished in the technological changes and urbanizing trends of the post-Second-World-War period. But the responsibility still rested with the school – whether in Toronto or Timmins or Teeswater – to graduate young people who could take their place as productive members of the economic order and responsible citizens of the socio-political sphere. This implied constant adjustments between school programs and the changing tastes and demands of the larger provincial society.

The curriculum changes announced by Education Minister Thomas Wells in the fall of 1976 illustrate this necessarily close relationship between schooling and society. If Ontario society and its schools in the 1960s had flirted briefly with an ethos which declared that education should take place in an atmosphere free of the pressure of conforming to a standard of behaviour and scholastic attainment common to all schools in the province, by the mid 1970s both the life-style and the prerequisites were tightening. Now the new core curriculum requirements for grades 9 and 10 were justified on 'the need for a greater amount of direction and guidance in these early years of secondary school.'[2] Likewise, a major revision of the English courses for the senior high school grades reflected 'the Ministry's firm commitment to provide detailed direction and assistance in teaching the essential skills and abilities of language use and communication.'[3]

Yet these changes were more than a swing of the curriculum pendulum. They also demonstrated a shift from decentralized or local to more centralized or provincial control over school programs. Wells admitted that in the heady years of the late 1960s and early 1970s, 'we may have gone too far in decentralizing the responsibility for the preparation of courses of study.' The idea 'was great in theory but it just isn't working.'[4] Accordingly, in November 1976 a second phase in changed curriculum policy was announced. Now, the ministry would 'take a firmer grip on the content of the programs in elementary and secondary schools.' This would be achieved by making the ministry's curriculum guidelines 'more comprehensive and of greater assistance and direction to classroom teachers.' All such guidelines, of course, would be 'more prescriptive, and descriptive, than previous guidelines.'[5]

Only through a reassertion of provincial power could the public demands for higher, more uniform standards be met. Such a move seemed to confirm the historic relationship that had always characterized the history of Ontario education. Diversity of offerings tended to prevail during those periods when local power had asserted itself. This could be illustrated in the early years of the nineteenth century, prior to the transfer of education from the private to the public sector. But it was also evident during the 1895-1910 years of the New Education movement, the 1937-45 period of Progressive Education reforms, and the 1968-73 era of Hall-Dennis and the high school credit system. But the reverse trend towards program uniformity manifested itself in those periods when the central authority grew more dominant, as in the ministries of George Ross in the 1880s, William Dunlop in the 1950s and Thomas Wells in the 1970s.

The shift from the free-wheeling 1960s to the more structured 1970s demonstrates one further lesson to students of Ontario educational history. Before his retirement as chief superintendent of schools in 1876, Egerton Ryerson had established a successful formula for policy change – proceed only as quickly as the conservative nature of provincial society will permit. Ministers of education who enjoyed the greatest political success over the next century were those who respected this lesson. George Ross had hesitated to extend the role of the elementary school in the 1880s because he sensed public resistance. Howard Ferguson pulled back on the township school-board plan in the 1920s because of rural opposition. Meanwhile those ministers concentrated on adapting the school to changing conditions in areas where the public seemed most supportive. Ross strengthened the high schools at a time when large numbers of middle- and lower-middle-class youngsters began to consider remaining beyond the entrance class. Ferguson promoted technical and commercial education when the academic orientation of the collegiate institute proved too limiting.

When change came too quickly, or was too expensive or too extreme, the more conservative elements of society exerted counter-pressures on local school-boards, the education department, and the politicians. Thus James Hughes, Adelaide Hoodless, and James Robertson had pushed the New Education reforms to the limit of acceptance by about 1904. The progressivist movement of the 1930s was slowed down by the harsh realities of the Second World War. In a similar manner, the reforms of Jack McCarthy, Lloyd Dennis, and their supporters were acceptable in the late 1960s; but the conservative restoration of the 1970s found the ideals of *Living and Learning* too radical, too expensive, or just plain silly.

By 1976 it was time once again for the schools of Ontario to do what the dominant and pragmatic majority of the provincial population always wanted them to do – teach the children to read, write, and do their arithmetic; pursue class-room goals and school objectives in a linear, structured manner; and prepare graduates for careers and occupations within the established economic, social, and political order. Schools were to follow, not to lead. By and large, societal needs and not individual preference shaped the Ontario educational system. Yet the changes of the 1960s in attitude and structure were not swept away entirely. The clock could not be set back, and as the system continues to evolve in the 1980s it will take with it many of the faults and merits of both progressive and conservative paradigms. It is this dynamic interaction which continues to shape the values of the Ontario educational experience.

Notes

CHAPTER 1: *The Illusion and the Reality: Ontario Schools in the 1870s*

1 J. George Hodgins, ed., *Historical and Other Papers and Documents Illustrative of the Educational System of Ontario, 1858-1876* (Toronto: King's Printer, 1911), IV, 320, 311, 323
2 J. George Hodgins, *Special Report to the Hon. the Minister of Education on the Ontario Educational Exhibit and the Educational Features of the International Exhibition at Philadelphia, 1876* (Toronto: Hunter, Rose and Co., 1877), 25, 38-9
3 J. George Hodgins, ed., *Documentary History of Education in Upper Canada, 1791-1876* (Toronto: King's Printer, 1910), xxviii, 60
4 William Pearce Randell, *Centennial: American Life in 1876* (Philadelphia, 1969), 400-1
5 Hodgins, *Special Report*, 15-16
6 Hodgins, *Documentary History*, xxviii, 60
7 PAO, RG2, Hodgins to Adam Crooks, 17 June 1876
8 Ibid., S.P. May to Hodgins, 30 June 1876
9 Hodgins, *Documentary History*, xxviii, 219-20
10 For a more detailed study of the immediate and long-range effects, see Robert M. Stamp, 'Ontario at Philadelphia: The Centennial Exposition of 1876,' in Neil McDonald and Alf Chaiton, eds, *Egerton Ryerson and His Times* (Toronto: Macmillan, 1978).
11 Toronto *Globe*, 22 Jan. 1876
12 George W. Ross, *Getting Into Parliament and After* (Toronto: William Briggs, 1913), 200
13 Toronto *Mail*, 17 Dec. 1889
14 C.B. Sissons, ed., *My Dearest Sophie: Letters from Egerton Ryerson to His Daughter* (Toronto: Ryerson, 1955), 287, 291, 292
15 Dianna S. Cameron, 'John George Hodgins and Ontario Education, 1844-1912' (MA thesis, University of Guelph, 1976), 96-9. Hodgins remained as deputy minister until 1890 (despite a salary reduction from $3,000 to $2,000 annually) and then functioned as departmental historian until 1912.
16 A.J. Donly, 'Education and its Machinery in Ontario,' *Canada Educational Monthly*, March 1880, 142
17 Hodgins, *Documentary History*, xxiii, 83
18 Ibid., xxiii, 109
19 PAO, RG2, report of Inspector J.A. McLellan on Brantford Collegiate, 10 March 1877
20 Ibid., report of Inspector S.A. Marling on Fonthill High School, 18 May 1877
21 AR, 1880-1,92, and 1879, 103
22 AR, 1880-1, 247
23 Sir William Peterson, 'National Education,' OEA *Proceedings*, 1904, 74-6
24 James G. Hume, 'Moral Training in Public Schools,' ibid., 1898, 233-4

25 Peterson, 'National Education,' 76

26 *Canada Educational Monthly*, January 1879, 95

27 AR, 1880-1, 247-8

28 Toronto *Globe*, 18 Oct. 1886

29 Hodgins, *Documentary History*, xxviii, 92

30 AR, 1882, 119

31 Egerton Ryerson, *First Lessons in Christian Morals* (Toronto, 1871), 35, 38, 86-93

32 *Canada School Journal*, September 1878, 95

33 AR, 1876, 7

34 Ibid., 1885, 123

35 G. Mercer Adam and W.J. Robertson, *Public School History of England and Canada* (Toronto: Copp Clark, 1886), iii

36 Royal readers, *Second Book of Reading Lessons* (Toronto: James Campbell and Son, 1882), 153, 50

37 Ontario readers, *Second Reader* (Toronto: Copp Clark, 1884), 24

38 TBE, Jesse Ketchum Public School, principal's diary, 25 Oct. to 9 Nov. 1888

39 OTA, *Proceedings*, 1873, 9

40 *Canada School Journal*, March 1878, 94

41 London *Free Press*, 4 Feb. 1967, citing Boyle's annual report for 1876.

42 Kingston *Daily News*, 16 Nov. 1887

43 AR, 1889, 120

44 E.C. Drury, *Farmer Premier, The Memoirs of E.C. Drury* (Toronto: McClelland and Stewart, 1966), 39

45 PAO, RG2, inspector's report on SS no. 9, Sunnidale, 1879

46 Watson Kirkconnell, *A Canadian Headmaster: A Brief Biography of Thomas Allison Kirkconnell, 1862-1934* (Toronto: Clarke Irwin, 1935), 13

47 AR, 1876, 85

48 J.H. Putman, *Fifty Years at School: An Educationist Looks at Life* (Toronto: Clarke Irwin, 1938), 10

49 AR, 1877, 19

50 Toronto *Globe*, 5 Dec. 1883

51 AR, 1877, 26

52 PAO, RG2, inspector's reports on SS no. 3, Nottawasaga, and SS no. 2, Nottawasaga, 1876

53 AR, 1878, 124

54 Ibid., 1879, 67

55 Howard Campbell, *A History of Oro Schools, 1836 to 1966* (Barrie, Ont., 1967), 16-53; PAO, general education collection, 'Minute Book of SS no. 1, Hope Township'

56 AR, 1880-1, 33

57 Ibid., 1885, 117

58 *Canada Educational Monthly*, March 1880, 139

59 PAO, RG2, J.J. Wadsworth to G.W. Ross, 15 Feb. 1894

60 Putman, *Fifty Years at School*, 10

61 PAO, RG2, Ottawa Normal School petitioners to the minister of education, 1886

62 Ibid., Hodgins to Crooks, 9 May 1876

63 Ibid., contract of Joseph Rowan with SS no. 19, York, 16 Nov. 1878

64 Ibid., 'Minute Book of SS no. 1, Hope Township'

65 AR, 1888, 107-8, and 1879, 64

66 W.T. Allison, 'The Pioneer Teacher,' *Canadian Magazine*, December 1911, 199

67 AR, 1877, 26, and 1890, 99

68 John S. Martin, 'Rural Education,' OEA *Proceedings, 1924*, 263-8

69 J.G. Bourinot, *The Intellectual Development of the Canadian People* (Toronto, 1881), 43

70 AR, 1882, 116

71 J.G. Althouse, *The Ontario Teacher, 1800-1910* (Toronto: Ontario Teachers' Federation 1967), 108; A.R. Cummings, *The City of Ottawa Public Schools: A Brief History* (Ottawa: Ottawa Public School Board, 1971), 41

72 AR, 1899, xviii
73 Toronto *Globe*, 25 Feb. 1882
74 For an analysis of the feminization of the teaching force, see Alison Prentice, 'The Feminization of Teaching in British North America and Canada, 1845-1875,' *Histoire sociale/-Social History*, VIII (no. 15), mai/May 1975, 5-20, and Wendy Bryans, 'Virtuous Women at Half the Price: The Feminization of the Teaching Force and Early Women Teacher Organizations in Ontario' (MA thesis, University of Toronto, 1974).
75 E.W. Bruce, 'Elevation of the Status of the Teacher,' OEA *Proceedings, 1899*, 337
76 *Canada Educational Monthly*, February 1880, 100-1
77 Hodgins, *Special Report*, 15
78 AR, 1886, 58
79 Kitchener Public Library, 'Annual Report of the Inspector of Public Schools of the County of Waterloo, 1872,' 2
80 PAO, RG2, 'Diagrams, Specifications, Conditions and Comments on Township School Houses in Simcoe County,' n.d. (c. 1876)
81 R.J. Bolton, *History of Central Public School, Peterborough, 1860-1960* (Peterborough, 1960), 11
82 PAO, RG2, inspector's special reports on Barrie Public School and Orillia Public School, December 1876
83 'Our Public Schools,' Toronto *Globe*, 22, 28 and 30 Nov. and 5 Dec. 1883
84 Ian E. Davey, 'Educational Reform and the Working Class: School Attendance in Hamilton, Ontario, 1851-1891' (PHD thesis, University of Toronto, 1975), 209
85 TBE, *Annual Report of the Inspector of Public Schools, 1875*, 16
86 Honora M. Cochrane, ed., *Centennial Story: The Board of Education for the City of Toronto 1850-1950* (Toronto: Thomas Nelson, 1950), 69
87 AR, 1889, 122. For an extensive discussion of local-provincial relations, see D.A. Lawr and R.D. Gidney, 'Who Ran the Schools? Local Influence on Educational Policy in Nineteenth-Century Ontario,' *Ontario History*, 72 (3), September 1980, 131-43.
88 Hodgins, *Documentary History*, xxviii, 90-1
89 AR, 1872, 31; 1875, 17; 1871, 52
90 Ontario, order-in-council, 31 July 1882
91 Department of education, 'General Circular,' 2 Aug. 1882
92 AR, 1876, 13
93 Adam Crooks, *Speeches of the Hon. Adam Crooks* (Toronto: C. Blackett Robinson, 1879), 16-17
94 Cameron, 'Hodgins and Ontario Education,' 39-41
95 Toronto *Mail*, 1 Oct. 1883; UTA, Sir Daniel Wilson diary, 28 Feb. 1883
96 PAC, George Munro Grant papers, Grant to Mowat (draft copy), n.d., probably November 1883
97 Toronto *Mail*, 29 Nov. 1883
98 PAO, Col. Charles Clarke papers, Mowat to Clarke, 15 Nov. 1883
99 Margaret Ross, *Sir George W. Ross, A Biographical Study* (Toronto: Ryerson, 1923), 73
100 Toronto *Globe*, 24 Nov. 1883
101 PAO, RG2, J.M. Gibson to Ross, 27 Dec. 1883

CHAPTER 2: *'The Nooks and Crannies of Dr. Ryerson's Den'*

1 PAO, RG2, separate school records 1882-1909, reports of Inspector James White, December 1883
2 Adam Crooks, *Speeches of the Hon. Adam Crooks* (Toronto: C. Blackett Robinson, 1879), 11
3 Toronto *Globe*, 12 Oct. 1886
4 AR, 1885, xvi
5 UTA, Wilson diary, 17 Oct. 1882
6 Toronto *Mail*, 18 and 30 Oct. 1882

7 *Speech of the Hon. George W. Ross, Minister of Education, at His Nomination, October 11, 1886; The Progress of Our Schools, Textbooks, and Religious Instruction* (Toronto, 1886), 19
8 Toronto *Mail*, 5 June 1884
9 *Speech of the Hon. George W. Ross*, 20
10 Toronto *Mail*, 2 Jan. and 17 April 1888
11 Oliver Mowat, *Protestantism Not in Danger* (Toronto, 1886), and *The Separate School Question: The No Popery Cry* (Toronto, 1886)
12 PAO, RG2, separate school records 1882-1909, report of Inspector James White, 23 Nov. 1883
13 Toronto *Mail*, 24 Nov. 1886
14 J.R. Miller, ' "Equal Rights for All": The ERA and the Ontario Election of 1890,' *Ontario History*, 65 (4), December 1973, 215
15 *Speech Delivered by Hon. George W. Ross on the Occasion of the Annual Demonstration of the Toronto Reform Association, June 29, 1889* (Toronto: Hunter, Rose and Co., 1889), 11
16 AR, 1887, lix-lxi
17 Toronto *Mail*, 9 March 1889
18 Ontario Department of Education, *Regulations and Correspondence Relating to French and German Schools in the Province of Ontario* (Toronto, 1889), 62-4
19 *Ordinances and By-Laws of the Equal Rights Association for the province of Ontario* (Toronto, 1889), 5-6
20 Louis H. Tacke, ed., *Men of the Day: A Canadian Portrait Gallery* (Montreal, 1894), 213-16
21 Toronto *Mail*, 17 Dec. 1889
22 Oliver Mowat, *The Sectarian Issue, History of the Separate School System in Ontario and Quebec, and Proposed Amendments to the Act Relating to Separate Schools* (Toronto, 1890)
23 Toronto *Weekly Empire*, 17 March 1892
24 George Ross, 'Presidential Address,' OTA *Proceedings*, 1884, 33
25 J. Castell Hopkins, *The Origins of Empire Day* (Toronto, 1910), 7-8
26 George Ross, 'Address of Welcome,' DEA *Proceedings*, 1892, 52
27 W.H.P. Clement, *The History of the Dominion of Canada* (Toronto: Copp Clark, 1897), vi, 341
28 OEA *Proceedings*, 1894, 168-75
29 Toronto *Empire*, 2 Dec. 1893
30 George Ross, 'Address,' DEA *Proceedings*, 1898, xxxvii-xxxviii
31 R.J.D. Page, 'The Impact of the Boer War on the Canadian General Election of 1900 in Ontario' (MA thesis, Queen's University, 1964), 149
32 George Ross, 'The Future of Canada,' in J. Robert Long, ed., *Canadian Politics* (St Catharines, Ont.: The Journal of St Catharines, 1903), 284
33 PAO, RG2, William Spankie to John Millar, 29 May 1899 and 9 June 1900
34 R.J.D. Page, 'Canada and the Imperial Idea in the Boer War Years,' *Journal of Canadian Studies*, 6 (1), February 1970, 33, 47. For a more detailed account of Empire Day, see Robert M. Stamp, 'Empire Day in the Schools of Ontario: The Training of Young Imperialists,' *Journal of Canadian Studies*, 8 (3), August 1973, 32-42
35 AR, 1882, 31
36 Ibid., 1899, xxiv, and 1880-1, 13
37 David Boyle, 'The Natural Sciences in the Public Schools,' OTA *Proceedings*, 1880, 36-45
38 AR, 1889, 130
39 Canada, Royal Commission on the Relations of Labour and Capital in Canada, *Evidence – Ontario* (Ottawa, 1889), 163
40 AR, 1889, 120
41 Toronto *Globe*, 22 Jan. 1888
42 Douglas A. Lawr, 'Development of Agricultural Education in Ontario, 1870-1910.' (PHD thesis, University of Toronto, 1972), 148
43 Thomas Shaw, 'Agriculture in Our Rural Schools,' OTA *Proceedings*, 1888, 75
44 PAO, RG2, F.L. Michell to Ross, 8 Feb. 1892; D.A. Maxwell to Ross, 4 Feb. 1889; John Macdonald to Richard Harcourt, 10 April 1901
45 Ibid., Ross to D.A. Maxwell, 8 Feb. 1889

46 AR, 1885, xiv
47 Ibid., 1887, xiv
48 Ontario, *Sessional Papers*, 1882, no. 9, 42
49 Ontario, *Annual Report of the Inspector of Factories, 1892*, 25
50 AR, 1891, 140
51 Toronto *Globe*, 20 Dec. 1886
52 AR, 1896, xxix
53 George Ross, 'Citizenship and Higher Education,' OEA *Proceedings*, 1897, 81
54 George Ross, 'Presidential Address,' DEA *Proceedings*, 1892, 98
55 George Ross, 'Education in Ontario since Confederation,' in J. Castell Hopkins, ed., *Canada: An Encyclopedia of the Country* (Toronto: Linscott Publishing Co., 1898), III, 174-5
56 *The School*, May 1919, 572
57 Strathroy *Age*, 22 Jan. 1891
58 Watson Kirkconnell, *A Canadian Headmaster: A Brief Biography of Thomas Allison Kirkconnell, 1862-1934* (Toronto: Clarke Irwin, 1935), 36
59 J.D. Purdy, 'The English Public School Tradition in Nineteenth Century Ontario,' in Frederick H. Armstrong et al., eds, *Aspects of Nineteenth Century Ontario: Essays Presented to James J. Talman* (Toronto: University of Toronto Press, 1974), 239
60 Carolyn Gossage, *A Question of Privilege: Canada's Independent Schools* (Toronto: Peter Martin Associates, 1977), 60
61 AR, 1880-1, 390
62 Gossage, *A Question of Privilege*, 43
63 G. Dickson and G.M. Adam, eds, *A History of Upper Canada College, 1829-1892* (Toronto: Rowsell and Hutchison, 1893), 156
64 AR, 1899, xxi
65 *Canada School Journal*, August 1878, 56; *Canada Educational Monthly*, April 1881, 186-7
66 AR, 1895, xx
67 Toronto *Globe*, 19 Jan. 1877; AR, 1894, xxiv
68 AR, 1886, 21
69 Ibid., 326
70 *Palladium of Labor*, 22 Dec. 1883
71 Royal Commission on the Relations of Labour and Capital, *Report*, 12, 119
72 AR, 1884, 207
73 Alexander Steele, 'The Relation of Education to Our National Development,' OEA *Proceedings*, 1894, 95
74 Toronto Trades and Labour Council, 'Minutes,' 6 Oct. 1893
75 For a more detailed account of the technical education movement, see Robert M. Stamp, 'The Campaign for Technical Education in Ontario, 1876-1914' (PHD thesis, University of Western Ontario, 1970)
76 AR, 1880-1, 23
77 C.F. Lavell, 'Queen's Faculty of Education,' *Queen's Quarterly* 15 (2), 1907, 134-7
78 George W. Ross, *The Universities of Canada: Their History and Organization* (Toronto: Warwick and Rutter, 1896), v-vi
79 AR, 1887, xxv
80 Ross, 'Education in Ontario since Confederation,' 176-7
81 Ontario, *Report of the Ontario Commissioner to the World's Columbian Exposition* (Toronto, 1893)
82 E.B. Biggar, *Canada: A Memorial Volume* (Montreal: E.B. Biggar, 1889), vi, 12; J.G. Bourinot, *The Intellectual Development of the Canadian People* (Toronto, 1881), 41; *Educational Weekly*, 5 Feb. 1885, 88
83 Toronto *Empire*, 17 Dec. 1889
84 J.H. Putman, *Fifty Years at School: An Educationist Looks at Life* (Toronto: Clarke Irwin, 1938), 13; J.B. Calkin, *School Geography of the World* (Halifax: A. and W. MacKinlay, 1869), 46
85 AR, 1894, xiv

86 *Canada Educational Monthly*, February 1880, 125

87 J.E. Bryant, 'Education in the Twentieth Century: A Criticism and a Forecast,' OTA *Proceedings*, 1892, 67-8

88 John Dearness, 'Examining Other School Systems to Improve Your Own,' OEA *Proceedings*, 1897, 73

89 H.A. Morrison, 'Education vs. Cram,' *Canadian Magazine*, May 1893, 169

90 John Herbert Sangster, *Progress in Education: The System of Today Compared with that in Vogue Half a Century Ago; Dr. Sangster's Able Address at the Normal School Jubilee Celebration* (Toronto, 1897), 9

91 Lyman C. Smith, 'The Trend of Education in Our High Schools,' OEA *Proceedings*, 1910, 159

92 PAO, James Pliny Whitney papers, Cephas Guillet to Whitney, 6 Feb. 1899

93 AR, 1894, xxv

94 W.N. Bell, 'The Ontario High School – Past and Future,' OEA *Proceedings*, 1920, 392-409

95 George M. Grant, 'What We Lack,' OEA *Proceedings*, 1900, 86

96 James Loudon, *Convocation Address, University of Toronto, October 1st, 1900* (Toronto: Rowsell and Hutchison, 1900)

97 Toronto *Globe*, 18 April 1897

98 Toronto *Mail and Empire*, 13 Nov. 1897

99 George Ross, *Speech of the Hon. G.W. Ross, Minister of Education, on the Policy of the Education Department; Delivered in the Legislative Assembly, 1897* (Toronto: Warwick Bros. and Rutter, 1897)

100 George Ross, *Great Speech by the Hon. Geo. W. Ross, Premier of Ontario; Delivered at Whitby, November, 1899; Government's Policy* (Toronto, 1899), 24-5

CHAPTER 3: *The New Education Movement – Those 'Yankee Frills'*

1 J.E. Wetherell, 'Conservatism and Reform in Education Methods,' OTA *Proceedings*, 1886, 86-8. John Dewey credited Francis W. Parker with christening and launching the New Education movement in 1882 (see Timothy L. Smith, 'Progressivism in American Education, 1880-1900,' *Harvard Educational Review*, 31 [2], Spring 1961, 168-93), although President Charles Eliot of Harvard had first used the term in the title of an *Atlantic Monthly* article as early as 1869. (See Edward A. Krug, *The Shaping of the American High School, 1880-1920* [Madison: University of Wisconsin Press, 1964], I, 121.)

2 James L. Hughes and L.R. Klemm, *Progress of Education in the Century* (London and Edinburgh: W. and R. Chambers Ltd., 1900), 1

3 Nina Vandewalker, *The Kindergarten in American Education* (New York: Arno Press, 1908, 1971), 171

4 PAO, RG2, Frederick Merchant to George Ross, 4 Oct. 1899

5 Frederick Tracy, 'The Practical Results of Child Study,' OEA *Proceedings*, 1897, 338-44

6 Hughes and Klemm, *Progress of Education in the Century*, 1

7 Ada Hughes, 'Presidential Address,' OEA *Proceedings*, 1901, 81-5

8 Lorne Pierce, *Fifty Years of Public Service: The Life of James L. Hughes* (Toronto: Oxford, 1926), 90, 93

9 Agnes MacKenzie, 'Kindergarten Extension,' OEA *Proceedings*, 1894, 176

10 AR, 1886, 82

11 Ibid., 1889, 139

12 PAO, RG2, Ross to Arthur Brown (copy), 5 March 1895

13 Alexander Jackson, 'Importance of Kindergarten Training to the Nation,' OEA *Proceedings*, 1896, 402

14 J.J. Kelso, 'Neglected and Friendless Children,' *Canadian Magazine*, January 1894, 215

15 TBE, *Annual Report of the Inspector of Public Schools*, 1893, 30

16 James L. Hughes, 'Influence of the Kindergarten Spirit on Higher Education,' OEA *Proceedings*, 1896, 103-8

17 PAO, RG2, Ross to R.H. Biggar (copy), 13 Oct. 1896

18 James L. Hughes, 'The Future Evolution of the Kindergarten,' *Education*, April 1902, 459
19 James L. Hughes, 'The Influence of the Kindergarten Spirit on Higher Education,' OEA *Proceedings*, 1896, 98
20 James L. Hughes, 'European Schools,' OEA *Proceedings*, 1908, 244
21 Toronto *Globe*, 14 Jan. 1901
22 Pierce, *Life of James L. Hughes*, 27
23 TBE, *Annual Report of the Inspector of Public Schools*, 1886, 29-36
24 James L. Hughes, 'Manual Training,' OEA *Proceedings*, 1897, 352-7
25 TBE, Wellesley Public School, *Minutes of Teachers' Meetings*, 17 June 1895
26 Trades and Labour Congress of Canada, *Proceedings*, 1888, 25
27 W.H. Huston, 'Manual Training,' OTA *Proceedings*, 1890, 86; J.H. Putman, 'Country Schools,' OEA *Proceedings*, 1895, 310
28 James Robertson, 'The Macdonald College Movement,' *Proceedings of the National Education Association of the United States*, 1904, 92
29 James Robertson, 'Manual Training,' *Canadian Magazine*, April 1901, 524
30 Adelaide Hoodless, 'The Labour Question and Women's Work and Its Relation to Home Life,' NCWC *Proceedings*, 1898, 257-8
31 Adelaide Hoodless, 'Domestic Science,' DEA *Proceedings*, 1907, 192
32 Ruth Howes, *Adelaide Hoodless: Woman With A Vision* (Ottawa: Federated Women's Institutes of Canada, 1965), 17
33 Adelaide Hoodless, 'Domestic Science,' NCWC *Proceedings*, 1902, 118
34 Hoodless, 'The Labour Question and Women's Work,' 258
35 Adelaide Hoodless, *Report to the Minister of Education, Ontario, on Trade Schools in Relation to Elementary Education* (Toronto: L.K. Cameron, 1909), 3
36 Adelaide Hoodless, 'Domestic Science,' NCWC *Proceedings*, 1894, 117
37 Adelaide Hoodless, 'Domestic Science,' NCWC *Proceedings*, 1902, 119
38 Howes, *Adelaide Hoodless*, 12
39 Adelaide Hoodless, 'Domestic Science,' NCWC *Proceedings*, 1894, 118-19
40 PAO, RG2, Hoodless to Richard Harcourt, 8 June 1903
41 Adelaide Hoodless, 'A New Education for Women,' *Farmers' Advocate*, 15 Dec. 1902
42 Adelaide Hoodless, 'Domestic Science,' NCWC *Proceedings*, 1905, 38
43 PAO, RG2, Hoodless to John Millar, 1 Sept. 1900. For a more detailed account of the home economics movement, see Robert M. Stamp, 'Teaching Girls Their "God-Given Place in Life" – the Introduction of Home Economics in the Schools,' *Atlantis*, 2 (2), Spring 1977, 18-34
44 W.R. Parkinson, 'The Centralization of Rural Public Schools,' OEA *Proceedings*, 1903, 391
45 Harvey M. Gayman, *Rittenhouse School and Gardens* (Toronto: William Briggs, 1911); see also, AR, 1905, ix
46 'Unusual System of Classes in Carleton County,' Toronto *Daily Star*, 27 Feb. 1906
47 Robert Stothers, *A Biographical Memorial to Robert Henry Cowley, 1859-1927* (Toronto: Thomas Nelson and Sons, 1935), 29
48 AR, 1899, xix
49 PAO, RG3, George W. Ross file, 'Memorandum of a Plan Proposed for the Improvement of Education at Rural Schools,' 6 Jan. 1902
50 James Robertson, 'The Macdonald College Movement,' 92
51 Ibid.
52 AR, 1903, xxxiii
53 R.H. Cowley, 'The Macdonald School Gardens,' *Queen's Quarterly*, April 1905, 415-18
54 A.J. Madill, *A History of Agricultural Education in Ontario* (Toronto: University of Toronto Press, 1930), 185
55 'Memorandum of a Plan Proposed for the Improvement of Education at Rural Schools'
56 Toronto *Globe*, 16 Dec. 1902
57 Parkinson, 'The Centralization of Rural Public Schools,' 391
58 PAO, RG2, Harcourt to Macdonald (copy), 7 Jan. 1902
59 AR, 1899, xxi

60 Richard Harcourt, 'Address,' OEA *Proceedings*, 1903, 95
61 AR, 1899, xviii
62 PAO, RG2, Harcourt to J.C. Harstone (copy), 17 Oct. 1901; Harcourt to A.O. Beatty (copy), 2 May 1901; Harcourt to T.H. Preston (copy), 15 Oct. 1901; Harcourt to D.Z. Morris (copy), 28 April 1904
63 Richard Harcourt, 'Address,' OEA *Proceedings*, 1902, 61
64 John Seath, 'Some Needed Educational Reforms,' OEA *Proceedings*, 1903, 85
65 AR, 1880-1, 247. For a more detailed analysis of the school health movement in Ontario, see Neil Sutherland, ' "To Create a Strong and Healthy Race": School Children in the Public Health Movement, 1880-1914,' *History of Education Quarterly*, 12 (3), fall 1972, 304-33
66 Ontario Board of Health, *Report*, 1883, xlvi
67 Charles E. Phillips, *The Development of Education in Canada* (Toronto: W.J. Gage, 1957), 366
68 Ontario Board of Health, *Report*, 1883, 242-3
69 James L. Hughes, 'Address of Welcome,' OTA *Proceedings*, 1892, 114
70 Ontario Board of Health, *Report*, 1899, 72-4, and 1901, 6
71 Edward Miller Steven, *Medical Supervision in Schools: Being An Account of the Systems at Work in Great Britain, Canada, the United States, Germany, and Switzerland* (London, 1910), 182-3
72 PAO, RG2, J.G. Adams to George Ross, 1 March 1901
73 Ibid., John Thomson to Richard Harcourt, 4 April 1900
74 Neil S. MacDonald, *Open-Air Schools* (Toronto: McClelland, Goodchild and Stewart, 1918), 54
75 W.E. Struthers, 'The Open Air School,' OEA *Proceedings*, 1914, 282-7
76 Toronto Playgrounds Association, *Account of Its Stewardship* (Toronto: TPA, 1910), 3
77 TBE, *Annual Report*, 1913, 22
78 Ibid., 1914, 17
79 J. Castell Hopkins, ed., *The Canadian Annual Review for 1911* (Toronto: Annual Review Publishing Co., 1912), 442
80 PAO, RG2, J.H. Putman to A.H.U. Colquhoun, 20 Jan. 1914. For an analysis of the work of Arthur Beall and early sex education in Ontario, see Michael Bliss, ' "Pure Books on Avoided Subjects": Pre-Freudian Sexual Ideas in Canada,' Canadian Historical Association, *Historical Papers, 1970*, 89-108
81 Gerald T. Hackett, 'The History of Public Education for Mentally Retarded Children in the Province of Ontario, 1867-1964' (PHD thesis, University of Toronto, 1969), 86
82 Ibid., 88
83 PAO, George Howard Ferguson papers, Hughes to Ferguson, 28 Sept. 1927
84 Ottawa *Journal*, 21 Nov. 1939
85 Ottawa Public School Board, *Inspector's Annual Report*, 1913, 12
86 TBE, Givens Public School, diary of teachers' meetings, 1890-1913, and Dovercourt Public School, minutes of teachers' meetings, 1890-1941
87 Ibid., *Annual Report*, 1913, 54
88 *Saturday Night*, 20 March 1920, 1
89 Vincent Massey, 'Primary Education in Ontario,' *University Magazine*, October 1911, 495-6
90 William Linton, 'A Retrospect,' OEA *Proceedings*, 1911, 233
91 John Henderson, 'Reminiscences of Education in Ontario,' OEA *Proceedings*, 1911, 172
92 AR, 1889, 108
93 PAO, RG2, Mary McIntyre to Robert Pyne, 6 Nov. 1905
94 I.J. Birchard, 'Some Educational Fallacies,' OEA *Proceedings*, 1902, 252
95 TBE, *Annual Report*, 1913, 49
96 Albert Leake, 'Manual Training in the School,' *The School*, March 1914, 438
97 Lyman C. Smith, 'The Trend of Education in Our High Schools,' OEA *Proceedings*, 1910, 163

98 Vincent Massey, 'Primary Education in Ontario,' 498
99 AR, 1903, 155
100 PAO, RG2, John Laughton to R.A. Pyne, 29 Nov. 1905
101 Smith, 'The Trend of Education,' 155-63
102 PAO, RG2, H. Gibbard to Richard Harcourt, 25 April 1904; R.H. Cowley to Harcourt, 5 Jan. 1903
103 Terrence Robert Morrison, 'The Child and Urban Social Reform in Late Nineteenth Century Ontario, 1875-1900' (PHD thesis, University of Toronto, 1971), 429-30
104 Civic Improvement League of Canada, Report of Conference, 1916, 31-2
105 Ontario Teachers' Manuals, History of Education (Toronto: Copp Clark, 1915), 177-81

CHAPTER 4: Industry, Efficiency, and Imperialism

1 Toronto Globe, 18 Dec. 1897
2 James Whitney, The Educational Question and the School Book Outrage (Toronto, 1902), 6, 9
3 The Educational Policy of the Whitney Government: Three Years of Progressive Legislation and Administration, 1905-1908 (Toronto, 1908), 3
4 PAO, James Pliny Whitney papers, Whitney to Henry Eiler (copy), 27 Nov. 1906
5 'John Seath,' OEA Proceedings, 1919, 512
6 PAO, Whitney papers, C.C. Hodgins to Whitney, 13 Dec. 1906, and Whitney to Hodgins (copy), 14 Dec. 1906
7 Educational Policy of the Whitney Government, 4
8 R.A. Pyne, 'Address,' OEA Proceedings, 1906, 97-102
9 Doris French, High Button Bootstraps: Federation of Women Teachers' Associations of Ontario, 1918-1968 (Toronto: Ryerson Press, 1968), 21
10 AR, 1906, 176
11 Howard Campbell, A History of Oro Schools, 1836 to 1966 (Barrie, 1967), 16-53
12 Ontario Department of Education, Regulations of Continuation Schools (Toronto, 1908)
13 Ibid., Accommodation and Equipment of Rural Public and Separate Schools (Toronto, 1907)
14 PAO, RG18, W.J. Hanna file, Moshier to Hanna, 1 Oct. 1906, and 15 Jan. 1907
15 PAO, RG2, Harcourt to H.J. Talbot (copy), 15 Nov. 1901
16 Ibid., various briefs and petitions to R.A. Pyne, February and March 1906
17 Toronto Globe, 14 July 1906
18 PAO, RG3, Hearst file, 'Memorandum re Normal Schools'
19 Toronto Globe, 1 March 1912
20 AR, 1907, viii
21 'Holidaying,' The School, October 1913, 62
22 James Collins Miller, Rural Schools in Canada: Their Organization, Administration, and Supervision (New York: Columbia University Teachers College, 1913), 60
23 Margaret Moffat, 'Some Suggestions for the Beginner,' The School, March 1914, 399-403
24 AR, 1905, xxvii
25 Educational Policy of the Whitney Government, 12
26 Miller, Rural Schools in Canada, 78
27 Harold W. Foght, The School System of Ontario, With Special Reference to Rural Schools (Washington: Government Printing Office, 1915), 5, 18, 21, 41, 73
28 'A Consolidated School,' The School, May 1914, 531
29 S.B. Dyde, 'Should There Be a Faculty of Education in the University?' Queen's Quarterly, October 1904, 176
30 J.F. Macdonald, 'Salaries in Ontario High Schools,' Queen's Quarterly, October 1909, 132, 135-6
31 J.F. Macdonald, 'Men in Ontario High Schools,' Queen's Quarterly, October 1918, 229
32 London Board of Education, Annual Report, 1908, 9
33 John Henderson, 'Some Defects in the High School Curriculum,' OEA Proceedings, 1901, 107-8

34 Charles E. Phillips, *The Development of Education in Canada* (Toronto: W.J. Gage, 1957), 447
35 John Watson, 'The University and the Schools,' *Queen's Quarterly*, April 1901, 324-9
36 N.F. Dupuis, 'The Conservative and the Liberal in Education,' *Queen's Quarterly*, October 1901, 121-2, and January 1902, 164-6
37 James Cappon, 'Is Ontario to Abandon Classical Education?' *Queen's Quarterly*, October 1904, 190-3
38 PAO, RG2, Seath to Richard Harcourt, 12 Dec. 1904
39 AR, 1907, 155
40 Miller, *Rural Schools in Canada*, 122
41 Douglas Lawr, 'Development of Agricultural Education in Ontario, 1870-1910' (PHD thesis, University of Toronto, 1972)
42 PAO, RG3, Whitney file, R.H. Knight to Whitney, 9 Jan. 1906
43 *Industrial Canada*, July 1900, 12
44 *The Tribune* (Hamilton), 16 June 1906
45 *Industrial Canada*, November 1911, 435; Toronto *Mail and Empire*, 1 March 1911
46 *Industrial Canada*, November 1911, 437
47 Walter N. Bell, *The Development of the Ontario High School* (Toronto: University of Toronto Press, 1918), 8-9
48 Charles Humphries, 'The Sources of Ontario Progressive Conservatism,' Canadian Historical Association, *Historical Papers*, 1967, 118
49 Canada, Royal Commission on Industrial Training and Technical Education, *Report* (Ottawa, 1913), I, 22
50 Albert Leake, *Industrial Education: Its Problems, Methods and Dangers* (Boston: Houghton, Mifflin Co., 1913), 136
51 PAO, Whitney papers, Whitney to Lord Grey (copy), 17 Jan. 1910
52 Ibid., Whitney to Archbishop F.P. McEvay (copy), 9 March 1910
53 'Education for Efficiency,' Ottawa *Citizen*, 24 Oct. 1912
54 F.W. Merchant, *Report on English-French Schools in the Ottawa Valley* (Toronto: L.K. Cameron, 1909)
55 J.H. Putman, 'Secondary Education III,' Ottawa *Evening Journal*, 4 July 1907
56 *Sentinel*, 6 Jan. 1910 and 3 Feb. 1910
57 PAO, Whitney papers, J.A.C. Evans to Whitney, 29 Jan. 1910
58 Toronto *Daily Star*, 8 March 1912
59 C.B. Sissons, *Church and State in Canadian Education* (Toronto: Ryerson Press, 1959), 81
60 R.C. Brown and G.R. Cook, *Canada, 1896-1921: A Nation Transformed* (Toronto: McClelland and Stewart, 1974), 254
61 Michael Joseph Fitzpatrick, 'The Role of Bishop Michael Francis Fallon and the Conflict between the French Catholics and the Irish Catholics in the Ontario Bilingual Schools Question, 1910-1920' (MA thesis, University of Western Ontario, 1969), 16
62 PAO, Whitney papers, Hanna to R.A. Pyne, 23 May 1910
63 Toronto Archdiocesan Archives, F.P. McEvay papers, Fallon to Archbishop C.H. Gauthier, 18 Aug. 1910
64 Toronto *Mail and Empire*, 17 Oct. 1910
65 Toronto *Daily Star*, 15 Oct. 1910
66 PAO, Whitney papers, Whitney to N.A. Belcourt (copy), 12 Aug. 1910
67 Toronto *Globe*, 26 Jan. 1911
68 Peter N. Oliver, 'George Howard Ferguson: The Making of a Provincial Premier' (PHD thesis, University of Toronto, 1970), 132
69 Kemptville *Advance*, 7 Dec. 1911
70 F.W. Merchant, *Report on the Condition of English-French Schools in the Province of Ontario* (Toronto: L.K. Cameron, 1912), 69, 74
71 'Bilingualism,' *The School*, November 1913, 125
72 PAC, John S. Willison papers, memorandum to the minister of education from the superintendent, 18 April 1912

73 PAO, G. Howard Ferguson papers, Ferguson to Ernie McQuatt (copy), 1 Feb. 1928. It is quite likely that Ferguson was speaking in a general rather than a specific way.
74 UTA, papers on French-language schools, Fallon to Pyne, 2 Jan. 1912
75 Toronto *Daily Star*, 12 Sept. 1912
76 PAO, Ferguson papers, J.S. Crate to Ferguson, 22 Feb. 1916
77 UTA, papers on French-language schools, Summerby to John Waugh (copy), 6 Oct. 1913
78 PAO, RG2, St Jacques to John Waugh, 27 Sept. and 18 Oct. 1913
79 Kingston Archdiocesan Archives, memorandum on Regulation XVII, undated
80 J. Castell Hopkins, *Canadian Annual Review for 1916* (Toronto: Annual Review Publishing Co., 1917), 532
81 AR, 1913, 318
82 Hopkins, *Canadian Annual Review for 1916*, 532
83 PAO, Ferguson papers, memorandum to the minister of education, c. 1916
84 PAO, RG2, Waugh to A.H.U. Colquhoun, 19 Sept. 1917
85 Ibid., Waugh to Henry J. Cody, 8 March 1919
86 AR, 1915, 34
87 Letter to the editor, Toronto *Globe*, n.d., cited by Robert Choquette, *Language and Religion: A History of English-French Conflict in Ontario* (Ottawa: University of Ottawa Press, 1975), 215
88 PAO, Ferguson papers, Ferguson to Albert R. Cameron (copy), 19 July 1927
89 David M. Duncan, *The Story of the Canadian People* (Toronto, 1904), 379-82
90 J.H. Putman, *Britain and the Empire* (Toronto, 1906), 395; *Ontario Public School History of England* (Toronto: Macmillan, 1910), 297
91 *Ontario Public School Geography* (Toronto: Educational Book Co., 1910), 60-1, 187-98
92 PAC, Frederick Borden papers, Strathcona to Borden, 8 March 1909
93 Archives of Saskatchewan, Walter Scott papers, Borden to Scott, 22 Jan. 1909
94 Sam Hughes, 'The Defence of the Empire,' *Empire Club Speeches, 1904-05* (Toronto: Empire Club of Canada, 1906), 183
95 Sam Hughes, 'The Relationship between the School and the Empire,' OEA *Proceedings*, 1911, 301-2
96 Hopkins, *Canadian Annual Review for 1912* (Toronto: Annual Review Publishing Co., 1913), 284
97 Toronto *Globe*, 22 May 1909
98 J.R. Lumby, 'The Stranger Within Our Gates,' OEA *Proceedings*, 1912, 355
99 AR, 1914, 558-9
100 Hamilton Board of Education, minutes, 15 May 1915
101 Hopkins, *Canadian Annual Review for 1917* (Toronto: Annual Review Publishing Co., 1918), 426
102 Arthur Lower, *Canadians In the Making* (Toronto: Longmans, 1958), 352-3

CHAPTER 5: *Post-war Change and the Education of the Adolescent*

1 Toronto *Mail and Empire*, 18 April 1919, and 10 April 1920
2 W.L. Grant, 'The Education of the Workingman,' *Queen's Quarterly*, 27 (2), October 1919, 161
3 AR, 1919, 8
4 J.H. Scott, 'Presidential Address,' OEA *Proceedings*, 1922, 166-72
5 Sir Robert Falconer, *Idealism in National Character: Essays and Addresses* (London: Hodder and Stoughton, 1920), 35
6 C.V. Corliss, *Educational Reform: Its Relation to the Industrial Deadlock* (Toronto: University of Toronto Press, 1918), 45
7 *The School*, June 1920, 615-18
8 Margaret Evans, 'The Home and School Club,' *The School*, December 1922, 262
9 S.B. McCready, 'A School Progress Club in Junior Red Cross Service,' *Canadian School Board Journal*, August 1923, 27-8

10 Ontario Department of Education, *The Thrift Campaign in the Schools of Ontario, with a Brief Sketch of What Ontario Has Done in the War* (Toronto: Ontario Dept. of Education, 1919), ii

11 PAC, Sir John Willison papers, pamphlet issued by the Canadian Industrial Reconstruction Association, c. 1917

12 C.E. Phillips, *The Development of Education in Canada* (Toronto: W.J. Gage, 1957), 350

13 AR, 1918, 12

14 'The Schoolmaster as a Citizen,' *The School*, February 1914, 323

15 Canadian Teachers' Federation, *Trends in the Economic Status of Teachers, 1910-1955* (Ottawa: Canadian Teachers' Federation, 1957), 58-60

16 PAO, Henry J. Cody papers, May Robson to Cody, 3 Dec. 1918

17 PAO, RG2, Jennie Stead to Cody, 21 May 1919

18 Toronto *Globe*, 4 April 1918

19 OSSTF *Bulletin*, June 1922, 18; April 1922, 9

20 J.H. Hardy, *Teachers' Federations in Ontario* (Toronto, 1938), 128

21 Doris French, *High Button Bootstraps: Federation of Women Teachers' Associations of Ontario, 1918-1968* (Toronto: Ryerson Press, 1968), 31

22 Wendy Bryans, 'Virtuous Women at Half the Price: The Feminization of the Teaching Force and Early Teachers' Organizations in Ontario' (MA thesis, University of Toronto, 1974), 4

23 PAO, Cody papers, Hearst to Cody, 26 April and 1 May 1918

24 Henry J. Cody, 'The Test of Progress,' *Proceedings of the Ontario Educational Association, 1920*, 140-57

25 Henry J. Cody, 'The Growth and Genius of the British Empire,' *Empire Club of Toronto Addresses, 1922*, 64

26 PAO, Cody papers, scrapbook, vol. II, 25 Feb. 1917

27 Toronto *Globe*, 29 Aug. 1919

28 PAO, Cody papers, scrapbook, vol. III, 9 Nov. 1918

29 *Farmers' Sun*, 2 April and 5 Nov. 1919

30 Toronto *Daily News*, 25 Nov. 1916

31 Henry J. Cody, 'The Teacher in Relation to the National Spirit,' *Proceedings of the Ontario Educational Association, 1912*, 92

32 Toronto *Globe*, 24 May 1921

33 Ibid., 24 May 1919

34 AR, 1918, 10

35 PAO, RG2, Cowles to Colquhoun, 31 Dec. 1921

36 AR, 1923, ix

37 Ontario Department of Education, *Part Time Courses to be Established in Accordance with the Provisions of the Adolescent School Attendance Act* (Toronto: Ontario Dept. of Education, 1922), n.p.

38 PAO, RG2, James Simpson to Howard Ferguson, 3 Jan. 1924

39 AR, 1921, 32

40 Toronto *Globe*, 22 March 1923

41 PAO, RG3, William Hearst file, 'Speech at Lennox Picnic, 16 July 1919'

42 PAO, Cody papers, Cody to John Robinson (copy), 6 Nov. 1919, and Cody to Katherine McDonald (copy), 6 Nov. 1919

43 PAO, RG18, Ottawa Collegiate Institute inquiry, 1927, 'Report,' 1-5

44 Ibid., 'Evidence,' 6-30

45 Ibid., 'Report,' 18-19

46 *Canadian School Journal*, January 1929, 3

47 PAO, RG18, Ottawa Collegiate Institute inquiry, 'Evidence,' 60

48 P.F. Gavin, 'Some Tendencies in Secondary Education,' OEA *Proceedings*, 1927, 278

49 'Vocational Guidance,' *The School*, June 1920, 600

50 John Wanless, 'Value of Matriculation to a Business Man,' OEA *Proceedings*, 1924, 197-201

51 Alice Vincent Massey, *Occupation for Trained Women in Canada* (London: Dent, 1920), 11; Ellen M. Knox, *The Girl of the New Day* (Toronto: McClelland and Stewart, 1919), 99

52 E.A. Hardy, *Talks on Education* (Toronto: Macmillan, 1923), 60
53 AR, 1920, 56
54 W.F. Dyde, *Public Secondary Education in Canada* (New York: Columbia University Teachers College, 1929), 67
55 Elizabeth Serson, *Glebe: The First Twenty-Five Years* (Ottawa: Glebe Collegiate Institute, 1947), 8
56 J.G. Althouse, *Addresses* (Toronto: W.J. Gage, 1956), 53
57 TBE, Secondary School Principals' Association, minutes, 1925-9
58 A.M. Overholt, 'The Schoolmaster and His Job,' *The School*, April 1927, 746
59 *The School*, January 1923, 338; AR, 1924, 25; *The Daily British Whig* (Kingston), 1922; *Canadian School Board Journal*, January 1928, 13
60 AR, 1920, 22-34
61 A.W. Crawford, 'The Progress and Development of Secondary Vocational Education in Canada,' CEA *Proceedings*, 1927, 61-2
62 PAO, Cody papers, scrapbook, vol. III, 18 Nov. 1918
63 AR, 1918, 22
64 D.A. Campbell, 'Cultural Vocational Schools,' OEA *Proceedings*, 1927, 354-5
65 Tom Moore, 'Attitude of Organized Labour towards Technical Secondary Education,' ibid., 1928, 131-4
66 H.B. Beal, 'President's Address,' ibid., 1928, 125-6
67 AR, 1914, 11; 1918, 10
68 PAO, George Henry papers, unsigned memorandum from departmental officials, 13 Nov. 1931
69 'The Composite High School,' *The School*, June 1923, 726-32
70 C.L. Burton, 'Radical Reforms Needed in Our Educational System,' *Canadian School Board Journal*, February 1926, 17
71 H.B. Beal, 'Vocational and Industrial Classes,' OEA *Proceedings*, 1924, 294-5
72 G.M. Jones, 'Student Newspapers,' *The School*, September 1922, 35-7
73 Phillips, *The Development of Education in Canada*, 540
74 AR, 1929, 15
75 A.W. Burt, 'School Sports,' *The School*,May 1914, 565
76 PAO, RG2, Inspector's report on Shelburne High School, 22 Oct. 1929
77 Dyde, *Public Secondary Education in Canada*, 124
78 TBE, *Annual Report, 1930*, 18
79 PAO, RG2, Inspector's report on Jarvis Collegiate Institute, 14 Feb. 1930
80 W.H. Tuke, 'President's Address, 1929,' OSSTF *Bulletin*, February 1930, 43
81 TBE, *Annual Report, 1926*, 13
82 A.W. Overholt, 'On Getting in a Rut,' *The School*, September 1921, 9-12
83 Ibid.
84 PAO, Cody papers, Seath to W.H. Hearst (copy), 25 March 1918
85 UTA, Falconer to R.B. Taylor (copy), 12 May 1920
86 PAO, RG2, minutes of a Special Committee on the Organization and Administration of the University of Toronto, 17 Jan. 1923
87 UTA, Taylor to Falconer, 5 May 1920
88 F.W. Merchant, 'Some Practical Problems in Canadian Education,' CEA *Proceedings*, 1922, 27
89 E.A. Hardy, 'Some Impressions of American High Schools,' OEA *Proceedings*, 1922, 112-22
90 Fred Clarke, 'Some Issues of Modern Secondary Education,' ibid., 1931, 35
91 Fred Clarke, 'Secondary Education in Canada: Past and Present,' in E. Percy, ed., *The Year Book of Education, 1934* (London: Evans Brothers, 1934), 569

CHAPTER 6: *Equality of Educational Opportunity*

1 Ontario Department of Education, *Regulations of the Public and Separate Schools* (Toronto: Ontario Dept. of Education, 1922), 11

2 PAO, RG2, E.W. Jennings to A.H.U. Colquhoun, 28 Dec. 1927; W.J. Dallas to Colquhoun, 11 March 1923
3 John Kenneth Galbraith, *The Scotch* (Boston: Houghton, Mifflin, 1964), 88
4 PAO, RG2, Hazel Bell to D.T. Walkom, 10 Aug. 1929
5 *Canadian School Journal*, April 1938, 107
6 AR, 1919, 24
7 E.G. Savage, *Secondary Education in Ontario* (London: HM Stationery Office, 1928), 65
8 AR, 1921, 34
9 George McMillan, *The Agricultural High School in Ontario* (Toronto: University of Toronto Press, 1924), 23
10 *Canadian School Board Journal*, July-August 1926, 7
11 Ontario Department of Education, *The Consolidation of Rural Schools in Ontario* (Toronto: Ontario Dept. of Education, 1922), 6
12 V.K. Greer, 'Question Drawer,' OEA *Proceedings*, 1927, 312-13
13 *Ontario School Board Journal*, November 1922, 6
14 PAO, RG2, unsigned memorandum to Grant, 29 April 1920
15 W.J. Goodfellow, 'President's Address,' OEA *Proceedings*, 1923, 474-5
16 'Debate on Consolidation,' *Canadian School Board Journal*, May 1924, 16-17
17 AR, 1920, xiii
18 *The School*, March 1922, 386, and March 1919, 423-4
19 Galbraith, *The Scotch*, 90
20 J. Castell Hopkins, *The Canadian Annual Review, 1919*, 400, and *1920* (Toronto: Canadian Annual Review Ltd., 1920), 521
21 *Canadian Forum*, July 1922, 679
22 PAC, C.B. Sissons papers, Sissons to John Godfrey (copy), 26 Dec. 1924; Peter Oliver, 'The Ontario Bilingual Schools Crisis, 1919-1929,' *Journal of Canadian Studies*, 7 (1), February 1972, 33-4
23 PAO, G.S. Henry papers, Ferguson to Henry, 8 May 1931
24 G.H. Ferguson, 'Address,' OEA *Proceedings*, 1924, 18
25 AR, 1925, ix
26 Toronto *Globe*, 2 April 1925
27 G.H. Ferguson, 'Address,' OEA *Proceedings*, 1925, 13
28 PAO, RG3, Ferguson file, Ethel Robson to Ferguson, 26 April 1925
29 Ibid., Colquhoun to Ferguson, 22 Sept: 1925
30 CEA, *Proceedings*, 1925, 127
31 Ontario Department of Education, *The Bill to Establish Township Boards of Trustees, A Letter from the Hon. G.H. Ferguson* (Toronto: Ontario Dept. of Education, 1925)
32 Sydney Williams, 'The Attitude of the People Towards the Proposed School Boards Bill,' *Canadian School Board Journal*, March 1926, 3
33 J.H. Putman, 'The Larger Unit of Administration,' *Canadian School Board Journal*, December 1927, 8-12
34 PAO, Ferguson papers, Ferguson to W.A. Boys (copy), 8 March 1926
35 G.H. Ferguson, 'Address,' OEA *Proceedings*, 1924, 16
36 Toronto *Globe*, 27 March 1929
37 PAO, Ferguson papers, Ferguson to Sir Joseph Flavelle (copy), 12 Jan. 1926
38 UTA, Sir Robert Falconer papers, Ferguson to Falconer, 20 Jan. 1925
39 K.P.R. Neville, 'University Training in Secondary Schools,' OEA *Proceedings*, 1927, 363
40 UTA, Falconer papers, Falconer to Sir James Whitney (copy), 9 July 1908
41 J. Castell Hopkins, *The Canadian Annual Review, 1925-26* (Toronto: Canadian Review Co. Ltd., 1926), 361
42 PAO, Ferguson papers, memorandum from the Council of the Faculty of Arts to Premier G. Howard Ferguson, undated
43 W.J. Alexander, 'The Case Against the Proposed Change,' *University of Toronto Monthly*, April 1926, 315-17
44 UTA, Falconer papers, Ferguson to Falconer, 22 Dec. 1926, and reply (copy), 23 Dec. 1926

45 PAO, RG2, J.C. Walsh to A.H.U. Colquhoun, 20 Dec. 1922
46 PAO, Ferguson papers, Ferguson to F.M. Robinson (copy), 15 Nov. 1927
47 C.B. Sissons, *Nil Alienum, The Memoirs of C.B. Sissons* (Toronto: University of Toronto Press, 1964), 234
48 Ibid., 235
49 PAC, Sissons papers, diary; comments added November 1952 following excerpt of 30 July 1920
50 3 July 1923
51 Oliver, 'The Ontario Bilingual Schools Crisis, 1919-1929,' 33
52 PAO, Ferguson papers, Ferguson to John Godfrey (copy), 24 April 1924
53 PAC, Sissons papers, John Godfrey to Kirwan Martin (copy), 14 Nov. 1924
54 Toronto *Globe*, 7 April 1925
55 PAO, RG2, inspector's reports on Cochrane and Hearst separate schools, 1 and 7 Dec. 1925
56 Ontario, Legislative Assembly, *Report of the Committee Appointed to Enquire into the Conditions of the Schools Attended by French-Speaking Pupils* (Toronto: King's Printer, 1927)
57 Toronto *Globe*, 23 Sept. 1927
58 PAO, RG3, Ferguson file, Ferguson to C.D. Gourlie (copy), 30 Aug. 1929
59 PAO, George S. Henry papers, Henry to Edmond Cloutier (copy), 10 Nov. 1933
60 Ibid., Merchant to Henry, 28 June 1932
61 *The School*, March 1937, 553
62 AR, 1922, 5
63 PAO, Ferguson papers, Ferguson to James Patterson (copy), 15 Nov. 1926
64 For a more detailed account of this venture, see Robert M. Stamp, 'Schools on Wheels: The Railway Car Schools of Northern Ontario,' *Canada: An Historical Magazine*, 1 (3), Spring 1974, 34-42
65 PAO, RG3, Mitchell Hepburn file, Neil McDougall to Hepburn, 11 Sept. 1937
66 Ibid.
67 *The School*, June 1920, 554
68 Ontario, Legislative Assembly, *Report on the Care and Control of the Mentally Defectives and Feeble Minded in Ontario* (Toronto: L.K. Cameron, 1919); 'Survey of Guelph Public Schools,' *Canadian Journal of Mental Health*, January 1920, 342-6
69 Ruth Hooper and Edna Lancaster, 'Classes for More Intelligent Pupils,' *The School* (elementary edition), December 1940, 353
70 PAO, Ferguson papers, 'Speech to Ward 8 Conservative Association,' St John's Parish Hall, Toronto, 2 Feb. 1928
71 Ibid., Ferguson to Sir Robert Borden (copy), 3 Jan. 1929
72 Ontario Department of Education, *Empire Day in the Schools of Ontario, May 23, 1926* (Toronto: Ontario Dept. of Education, 1926), n.p.
73 AR, 1928, ix, and 1929, xi
74 Fred Clarke, 'Impressions of Canadian Education,' *Canadian Forum*, December 1932, 96
75 W.L. Grant, 'The Education of the Brilliant Child,' OEA *Proceedings*, 1928, 210
76 PAO, Henry papers, Ferguson to Henry, 8 May 1931
77 Ibid., Ferguson to Henry, 12 March 1931
78 PAO, Ferguson papers, Scott to Ferguson, 10 Dec. 1930
79 *Educational Courier*, April 1931, 1; PAO, RG2, George Rogers to J.H. Scott (copy), 16 Dec. 1930
80 Toronto *Mail and Empire*, 11 May 1929

CHAPTER 7: *The Ontario Taxpayer and the Depression*

1 PAO, Henry papers, Henry to C. Gordonsmith (copy), 14 May 1931
2 PAO, RG3, Hepburn file, McArthur to Hepburn, 23 Feb. 1933
3 PAO, Henry papers, William J. Hicks to Henry, 8 March 1933, and T. Mountford to Henry, 25 May 1933

4 PAO, RG2, Greer to public and separate school inspectors, memorandum, 8 April 1931
5 J. Ferris David, 'Secondary Schools and Their Relation to Business,' *Canadian School Journal*, April 1933, 128
6 Edwin C. Guillet, *In the Cause of Education: Centennial History of the Ontario Educational Association, 1861-1960* (Toronto: University of Toronto Press, 1960), 238
7 *Canadian School Journal*, January 1935, 23
8 PAO, Henry papers, Rogers to Henry, undated memorandum, c. spring 1932
9 Ibid., Colquhoun to Henry, 20 May 1932
10 Ibid., H.L. Cummings to Henry, 22 Feb. 1933
11 Ibid., J.E. Robertson to Henry, 22 Feb. 1933
12 Toronto *Globe*, 23 April 1935
13 OSSTF *Bulletin*, December 1932, 310; December 1931, 35; February 1936, 53
14 Dormer Ellis, *Seven Thousand Men Who Are Members of the OPSMTF* (Toronto: OPSMTF, 1971), 15
15 Canadian Teachers' Federation, *Trends in the Economic Status of Teachers, 1910-1955* (Ottawa: Canadian Teachers' Federation, 1957), 58
16 Toronto *Globe*, 23 May 1932
17 McGregor Easson, *The Intermediate School in Ottawa* (Toronto: University of Toronto Press, 1934), 39, 95-7
18 *Canadian School Journal*, August 1930, 18
19 PAO, Henry papers, Merchant to Henry, 5 April 1932
20 George Rogers, 'Intermediate Schools,' *Proceedings of the Ontario Educational Association, 1934*, 101-5; 'The Intermediate School,' *The School*, April 1932, 104-6
21 PAO, Henry papers, H.L. Cummings to Henry, 14 March 1934
22 Ibid., unsigned memorandum on department of education stationery, 2 March 1934
23 Ibid., Loftus Reid to Henry, 10 March 1934
24 Ibid., Henry to C.G. Mikel (copy), 24 July 1933
25 Ibid., Scott to Henry, 10 Dec. 1932; see also Scott to Henry, 10 March 1934
26 J. McQueen, 'Relations of Intermediate Schools and Technical Schools,' OSSTF *Bulletin*, June 1934, 187
27 TBE, Secondary School Principals' Association minutes, 17 Jan. 1940
28 L.J. Flynn, *At School in Kingston, 1850-1973: The Story of Catholic Education in Kingston and District* (Kingston: Frontenac, Lennox and Addington Counties Roman Catholic Separate School Board, 1973), 67
29 M.A. Cameron, *The Financing of Education in Ontario* (Toronto: University of Toronto Press, 1936), 108
30 PAO, Ferguson papers, Ferguson to Fallon (copy), 19 June 1924
31 PAO, Henry papers, Ferguson to Henry, 24 Oct. 1933
32 Ibid., Henry to S.L. Squire (copy), 25 June 1934
33 Toronto *Mail and Empire*, 23 Jan. 1925
34 Toronto *Globe*, 12 April 1935
35 *Maclean's Magazine*, 15 Sept. 1936, 46
36 Toronto *Telegram*, 9 April 1936
37 PAO, RG3, Hepburn file, Emmett Sheehy to Hepburn, 10 Nov. 1936
38 Toronto *Telegram*, 6 April 1936
39 PAO, RG3, Hepburn file, Hepburn to McArthur (copy), 21 March 1933
40 Toronto *Globe*, 5 and 12 June 1934
41 J. Castell Hopkins, ed., *The Canadian Annual Review for 1933* (Toronto: Canadian Review Co. Ltd., 1934), 144
42 Toronto *Globe*, 22 Oct. 1934
43 *Saturday Night*, 28 July 1934
44 Toronto *Globe*, 25 April 1935
45 PAO, RG2, E.C. Desormeaux to Simpson, 2 July 1935
46 Ontario, Legislative Assembly, *Budget Address Delivered by the Honourable Mitchell F. Hepburn, March 18, 1938* (Toronto: King's Printer, 1938), 41
47 Toronto *Daily Star*, 5 April 1938

48 *Canadian School Journal*, May 1933, 154
49 PAO, RG2, Greer to McArthur, 3 Jan. 1936
50 J.A. Partridge, 'A Township School Area and Its Accomplishments,' *The School* (elementary edition), February 1941, 517-20
51 Toronto *Globe and Mail*, 29 March 1940
52 *Canadian School Journal*, May 1939, 189
53 F.P. Gavin, 'President's Address,' OEA *Proceedings*, 1935, 11
54 OSSTF *Bulletin*, February 1933, 15
55 Ibid., June 1936, 216
56 Ibid., February 1934, 16
57 Ibid., December 1941, 349-51, and February 1935, 12
58 Ibid., February 1933, 21
59 *Canadian School Journal*, February 1939, 60
60 Orillia *Packet and Times*, 18 Oct. 1934
61 *Canadian School Journal*, April 1937, 126
62 PAO, RG3, George Drew file, Althouse to Drew, 27 March 1945
63 *Canadian School Journal*, February 1939, 63
64 PAO, RG2, McArthur to G.A. Wheable (copy), 18 Dec. 1937
65 Ibid., J. Cuthell to McArthur, 4 Nov. 1937
66 *Canadian School Journal*, June 1937, 235
67 Hugh Hood, *The Swing in the Garden* (Ottawa: Oberon, 1975), 52
68 Toronto *Daily Star*, 1 Oct. 1932
69 PAO, RG2, Mitchell to McArthur, 17 Feb. 1937
70 Ibid., A.B. Fennell to McArthur, 18 Feb. 1937

CHAPTER 8: *Education for Democratic Citizenship*

1 Ontario Department of Education, *Programme of Studies for Grades I to VI of the Public and Separate Schools* (Toronto: Ontario Dept. of Education, 1937), 5-9
2 AR, 1924, 4
3 PAO, RG2, John Waugh to Henry Cody, 4 June 1918
4 TBE, *Annual Report, 1932*, 103-4, 116-19
5 J.G. Althouse, *Addresses* (Toronto: W.J. Gage, 1956), 174
6 TBE, *Annual Report, 1931*, 96
7 C.C. Goldring, 'The Work of a Principal,' *Educational Courier*, June 1933, 8
8 The essence of Dewey's approach, and the basis of twentieth-century 'progressivism' in education, is found in John Dewey, *The School and Society* (Chicago: University of Chicago Press, 1965)
9 McCully to J.W. Rule, 11 Aug. 1974. J.W. Rule, 'Innovation and Experimentation in Ontario's Public and Secondary Schools, 1919-1940' (MA thesis, University of Western Ontario, 1975), 77
10 TBE, C.C. Goldring papers, Goldring to Gordon Ferguson (copy), 15 Oct. 1954
11 Marjorie Lord, 'The New Education,' OEA *Proceedings*, 1932, 46
12 D.A. Morris, 'Obstacles of Progress in Education,' ibid., *1934*, 10
13 *Educational Courier*, June 1935, 6-7
14 PAO, RG2, Greer to McArthur, 20 Aug. 1934
15 Duncan McArthur, 'Message from the Deputy Minister,' *Educational Courier*, October 1934, 2; 'Education for Citizenship,' *Canadian School Journal*, October 1935, 299-302
16 PAO, RG2, McArthur to Watson, 17 Dec. 1936
17 Stanley Watson, 'Is the Role of the Teacher Changing?' *Understanding the Child*, April 1936, 28
18 Althouse, *Addresses*, 196
19 Alberta Department of Education Archives, Calgary public school district file, Newland to Mrs. W.O. Hurlburt (copy), 30 Sept. 1940
20 Thornton Mustard, 'The New Programme of Studies,' *Educational Courier*, October 1937, 8-10; Orillia *Packet and Times*, 25 Nov. 1937

21 V.N. Ames, 'Some Observations on Interpretations of the New Programme of Studies,' *Educational Courier*, September 1938, 6
22 Viola Parvin, *Authorization of Textbooks for the Schools of Ontario, 1846-1950* (Toronto: University of Toronto Press, 1965), 99
23 *Educational Courier*, June 1938, 34-5
24 Althouse, *Addresses*, 9
25 PAO, RG2, Clarke to Belleville Board of Education (copy), 14 Feb. 1938
26 Mustard, 'The New Programme of Studies,' 8-10
27 Bertha Shaw, *Broken Threads: Memories of a Northern Ontario School Teacher* (New York: Exposition Press, 1955), 127
28 PAO, RG2, Clarke to Belleville Board of Education (copies), 8 Nov. 1937, 24 Feb. 1938, 22 March 1939
29 TBE, Dovercourt Public School, minutes of teachers' meetings, 28 Oct. 1937, 21 March 1938
30 Ibid., *Annual Report, 1938*, 16
31 *Canadian School Journal*, December 1938, 169
32 'New Life in a Country School,' *Canadian School Journal*, June 1939, 234
33 Toronto *Globe and Mail*, 1 April 1938
34 Helen Hewson, 'Parents Are Teachers Too,' *The School* (elementary edition), October 1940, 121
35 PAO, RG2, 'Resolution from United Farmers of Ontario Convention,' 23 Nov. 1937
36 Ibid., Ernest Transom to McArthur, 19 Aug. 1942
37 PAO, RG3, Hepburn file, Hepburn to John P. MacKay (copy), 15 Jan. 1942
38 TBE, Goldring papers, Goldring to chairman of management committee (copy), 23 Jan. 1939
39 PAO, RG2, Goldring to McArthur, 17 March 1939
40 *Canadian School Journal*, June 1941, 199
41 PAO, RG2, George Rogers to Margaret Pelisser (copy), 5 Nov. 1942
42 Toronto *Globe*, 24 May 1933
43 *Canadian School Journal*, May 1941, 170
44 Ontario Department of Education, *Empire Day in the Schools of Ontario, May 22, 1942* (Toronto: Ontario Dept. of Education, 1942), n.p.
45 *The School* (elementary edition), October 1940, 93
46 Isabel Thomas, 'Mobilizing the Teachers,' *Canadian Forum*, September 1940, 174
47 *Canadian School Journal*, March 1944, 105
48 Darcy Davidson, 'Does the Present Elementary Course Adequately Prepare Pupils for High School?' OEA *Proceedings*, 1942, 39
49 J.S. Thompson, 'New Education Has Come to Canada,' *Dalhousie Review*, July 1941, 230
50 Toronto *Telegram*, 16 April 1942
51 A.A. Hauck, *Some Educational Factors Affecting the Relations between Canada and the United States* (Easton, Pa.: 1932), 12ff.
52 Toronto *Globe and Mail*, 27 April 1942
53 'Democracy at Pickering,' OSSTF *Bulletin*, February 1942, 41-6
54 PAO, RG2, conference of inspectors and the staffs of the London and Stratford normal schools, 29 and 30 Jan. 1942
55 *Canadian School Journal*, September 1941, 277
56 Ibid., June 1942, 196
57 Toronto *Globe*, 7 April 1936
58 PAO, RG3, Hepburn file, C.H.R. Fuller to Hepburn, 20 April 1942; TBE, Secondary School Principals' Association, minutes, 11 December 1942
59 G.W. Moberley, 'Juvenile Delinquency,' *Canadian School Journal*, June 1943, 182
60 M.E. Conron, 'Brantford Does Something,' ibid., October 1934, 347
61 PAO, RG3, George Drew file, 'Notes for Platform: Ontario General Election,' 29 Sept. 1941
62 Toronto *Globe and Mail*, 12 July 1943
63 Ibid., 10 Sept. 1943; *The School* (secondary edition), November 1943, 267-8; *Canadian School Journal*, November 1943, 339, and December 1943, 359-60

64 PAO, RG3, Drew file, 'Message from the Minister of Education for Use in Normal School Year Books,' 23 March 1946
65 Ontario Department of Education, 'Memo re Duties, Power and Responsibilities of the Chief Director and the Deputy Minister of Education,' 27 Nov. 1944
66 S.G.B. Robinson, *Do Not Erase: The Story of the OSSTF* (Toronto: OSSTF, 1971), 293
67 Gerald L. Caplan, *The Dilemma of Canadian Socialism: The CCF in Ontario* (Toronto: McClelland and Stewart, 1973), 93
68 *Educational Courier*, February 1943, 7
69 Ron Faris, *The Passionate Educators: Voluntary Associations and the Struggle for Control of Adult Educational Broadcasting in Canada* (Toronto: Peter Martin Associates, 1975), 156
70 *Canadian School Journal*, January 1944, 27
71 PAO, RG3, Drew files, Althouse to Drew, 3 April 1944
72 OSSTF *Bulletin*, June 1944, 163
73 Ontario Department of Education, *Regulations and Programmes for Religious Education in the Public Schools* (Toronto: Ontario Dept. of Education, 1944), 8
74 Toronto *Globe and Mail*, 23 March 1945
75 PAO, RG2, Althouse to Drew, 9 Aug. 1944
76 Toronto *Globe and Mail*, 23 March 1945
77 *Canadian School Journal*, May 1945, 196-7

CHAPTER 9: *The Triumph of Conservatism*

1 Z.S. Phimister, 'The Principal and His School,' *The School* (elementary edition), November 1947, 103
2 P.J. Kennedy, 'The School as a Social Agency,' *Canadian School Journal*, April 1945, 147-9
3 *The School* (secondary edition), December 1943, 279
4 AR, 1945, 106
5 *Canadian School Journal*, November 1945, 431
6 PAO, Royal Commission on Education, brief no. 189
7 *Canadian School Journal*, January 1944, 33
8 Cited by David M. Cameron, *Schools for Ontario: Policy-making, Administration and Finance in the 1960s* (Toronto: University of Toronto Press, 1972), 46
9 PAO, RG3, Drew file, Greer to Drew, 17 Dec. 1944
10 Ibid., 'Remarks Made by L.M. Frost at Lindsay, December 22, 1944,' (copy)
11 Ibid., Roy H. Rice to Drew, 29 Nov. 1944
12 Toronto *Telegram*, 25 Feb. 1944
13 PAO, RG2, Althouse to W.J. Dunlop, 11 Jan. 1956
14 J.G. Althouse, *Addresses 1936-1956* (Toronto: W.J. Gage, 1958), 117-18
15 PAO, RG3, Frost file, Dana Porter to Frost, 25 Feb. 1944, and Althouse to Frost, 29 Nov. 1944
16 Ibid., Stanley Watson to R.W.B. Jackson (copy), 2 Sept. 1947, 'Special Report on Curriculum'
17 PAO, Royal Commission on Education, briefs no. 125 and 126
18 Ontario, *Report of the Royal Commission on Education in Ontario* (Toronto: King's Printer, 1950), 23-40
19 PAO, RG3, Frost file, Frost to W.E. Phillips (copy), 4 Sept. 1958
20 Ibid., 'Re Report on Education, Press Release,' 21 Dec. 1950
21 *Le Droit*, 20 Jan. 1951
22 Toronto *Globe and Mail*, 8 Feb. 1951
23 PAO, RG3, Hope to Frost, 25 Feb. 1952
24 Ibid., Frost to Reginald Soward, 22 Feb. 1951 and Althouse to Frost, 22 Feb. 1951
25 OSSTF *Bulletin*, June 1950, 123
26 Canadian Teachers' Federation, *Trends in the Economic Status of Teachers, 1910-1955* (Ottawa: Canadian Teachers Federation, 1957), 20, 26

27 H. Pullen, 'A Study of Secondary School Curriculum Change in Canada with Special Emphasis on an Ontario Experiment' (EDD thesis, University of Toronto, 1955), 212

28 *Canadian School Journal*, April 1932, 164

29 W.G. Fleming, *Ontario's Educative Society: V Supporting Institutions and Services* (Toronto: University of Toronto Press, 1972), 388

30 Althouse, *Addresses*, 48

31 TBE, Goldring papers, Goldring to Gordon Ferguson (copy), 15 Oct. 1954

32 William Hume, 'Schools are for Schooling,' *Maclean's Magazine*, 1 April 1952, 2

33 Hilda Neatby, *So Little for the Mind* (Toronto: Clarke Irwin, 1953)

34 George Roberts, 'Education for Juvenility,' OSSTF *Bulletin*, January 1952, 5-6, 27

35 J.T. Stubbs, 'Remarks of President-Elect,' OSSTF *Bulletin*, January 1952, 10. For the opposite philosophy, see remarks of the next OSSTF president, Claire Coughlin, 'Secondary School – An Experiment in Living,' OSSTF *Bulletin*, May 1953, 85

36 AR, 1951, 1

37 OSSTF *Bulletin*, March 1953, 63; AR, 1952, 2; Toronto *Globe and Mail* 16 April 1958

38 OSSTF *Bulletin*, May 1959, 160

39 Frank Patten, 'Achieving Standards,' OSSTF *Bulletin*, May 1956, 115

40 J.W. Morriss, 'Rural is the Fourth "R" at Seaforth High School,' OSSTF *Bulletin*, October 1950, 179

41 See Arthur J. Rennie, *Some Aspects of Rural and Agricultural Education in Canada* (Toronto, 1950), 78; and PAO, RG2, 'Report of the Regional Agricultural Teachers' Conference at Saltfleet High School, October 28, 1950'

42 Kingsley Vogan, 'London Television Survey,' OSSTF *Bulletin*, March 1956, 71-2

43 Cited by Alexander Ross, *The Booming Fifties: 1950-1960* (Toronto: Natural Science of Canada, 1977), 40

44 See H.R. Beattie, 'General Principles of a School Guidance Programme,' *Canadian School Journal*, April 1945, 137; AR, 1945, 88; Honora Cochrane, ed., *Centennial Story: The Board of Education for the City of Toronto, 1850-1950* (Toronto: Nelson, 1950), 284

45 OSSTF *Bulletin*, June 1950, 127

46 *Educational Courier*, December 1946, 26; Doris French, *High Button Bootstraps: Federation of Women Teachers' Associations of Ontario, 1918-1968* (Toronto: Ryerson Press, 1968), 123

47 Canadian Teachers' Federation, *Trends in the Economic Status of Teachers*, 57-60

48 PAO, 'Minute Book of SS no. 17, Kenyon, 1885-1948'

49 Sidney Katz, 'The Teachers,' *Maclean's Magazine*, March 1953, 9

50 PAO, RG3, Frost file, Dunlop to Frost, 15 May 1952

51 PAO, RG2, Webster to R.S. Rivers, n.d. (c. June 1955)

52 AR, 1960, iii

53 Ontario, Legislative Assembly, *Debates*, 12 March 1958, 775

54 Ibid., 14 March 1956, 1035

55 PAO, RG3, Frost file, Dunlop to E.J. Young (copy), 31 March 1955

56 Toronto *Telegram*, 11 May 1955

57 PAO, RG2, F.S. Rivers, 'Memorandum to Teacher College Principals, August 4, 1955'

58 Fleming, *Ontario's Educative Society*, V, 22

59 PAO, RG3, Frost file, Dunlop to Woodside (copy), 18 Dec. 1957

60 Ibid., Dunlop to Frost, 29 Aug. 1957; Frost to W.E. Phillips (copy), 4 Sept. 1958; Frost to Diltz (copy), 26 Feb. 1959

61 Bert Case Diltz, *Pierian Spring: Reflections on Education and the Teaching of English* (Toronto, 1946), vii; *The Sense of Wonder: Observations on Education and the Teaching of English* (Toronto: McClelland and Stewart, 1953), vii-ix, 3

62 PAO, RG2, Dunlop to W.M. McIntyre (copy), 27 Aug. 1956

63 PAO, RG3, Frost file, Frost to Dunlop (copy), 23 Sept. 1957

64 Toronto *Globe and Mail*, 3 Feb. 1961

65 Cited by Hugh Hood, *The Governor's Bridge is Closed* (Ottawa: Oberon, 1973), 63, and verified by correspondence from John Colombo to the author, 11 July 1977.

CHAPTER 10: *The Liberalization of the Big Blue Schoolhouse*

1 Canada, House of Commons, *Debates and Proceedings*, 25 Nov. 1960, 231-2
2 PAO, RG3, Frost file, Frost to Ray Farrell (copy), 3 May 1961
3 Ontario, Legislative Assembly, *Debates*, 15 April 1961, 1310
4 Ibid., 18 July 1968, 5953 and 29 Nov. 1961, 82
5 PAO, RG2, Rendall to A.D.G. Billingsley (copy), 13 July 1960
6 Ibid., Robarts to E.D. Kyle (copy), 19 Dec. 1961
7 AR, 1962, 4
8 PAO, RG2, Grant to Robarts, 5 May 1961
9 Northrop Frye, ed., *Design for Learning* (Toronto: University of Toronto Press, 1962), 7
10 London *Free Press*, 11 Dec. 1968
11 V.K. Gilbert, *Let Each Become: An Account of the Implementation of the Credit Diploma in the Secondary Schools of Ontario* (Toronto: Ontario Institute for Studies in Education, 1972), 7ff.
12 PAO, RG2, Robert Yurchuk to Robarts (copy), 15 Nov. 1965
13 Ibid., Young to Davis, 16 Aug. 1965
14 Ontario Department of Education, *Report of the Grade 13 Study Committee* (Toronto: Ontario Dept. of Education, 1964), 16
15 PAO, RG2, Davis to Kenneth Brueton (copy), 17 Oct. 1966
16 Toronto *Globe and Mail*, 1 April 1966
17 FWTAO, 'A Survey of the Problems of Female Rural Elementary School Teachers in Ontario, 1960-61' (Toronto, 1961)
18 AR, 1964, 3
19 PAO, 'Minute Book of SS no. 1 Hope,' 20 Dec. 1964
20 AR, 1964, 3
21 London *Free Press*, 22 March 1969; Toronto *Globe and Mail* 1 July 1972; *Canadian Magazine*, 14 Aug. 1969
22 Martin O'Malley, 'Just Ask OISE,' *Globe Magazine*, 11 April 1970
23 W.G. Fleming, *Ontario's Educative Society: II The Administrative Structure* (Toronto: University of Toronto Press, 1971), 12
24 Ontario, Legislative Assembly, *Debates*, 28 April 1964, 2557
25 Walter Pitman, 'The Big Blue Schoolhouse,' *Canadian Forum*, October-November 1972, 65; and Michelle Landsberg, 'At Queen's Park,' *This Magazine is About Schools*, April 1966, 119
26 AR, 1964, xiii
27 PAO, RG3, Robarts file, Davis to Robarts, 17 July 1964
28 Ibid., P.M. Muir to Robarts, 17 Feb. 1964; Nora Hodgins to Robarts, 19 Feb. 1964; Mrs T. St Lawrence to Robarts, 30 Nov. 1965
29 Toronto *Globe and Mail*, 25 May 1967
30 Cited by Loren Lind, *The Learning Machine: A Hard Look at Toronto Schools* (Toronto: Anansi, 1974), 134; Toronto *Globe and Mail*, 10 Jan. 1968
31 AR 1963, ii, and 1966, iii ·
32 Canada, parliament, *Report of the Royal Commission on Bilingualism and Biculturalism* (Ottawa, 1968), II, 87-8
33 Cited by T.H.B. Symons, 'Ontario's Quiet Revolution: A Study of Change in the Position of the Franco-Ontarian Community,' in Robin Burns, ed., *One Country or Two?* (Montreal: McGill-Queen's University-Press, 1971), 182
34 Toronto *Globe and Mail*, 30 May 1968
35 PAO, RG2, Robarts to Kathleen Peters (copy), 5 Oct. 1967
36 Toronto *Globe and Mail*, 4 Oct. 1968
37 Ibid., 28 March 1970
38 Calgary *Albertan*, 21 April 1973
39 Ontario, *Report of the Ministerial Commission on French Language Secondary Education* (Toronto: Ontario Dept. of Education, 1972), 15-16

40 PAO, RG2, John Middleweek to W.J. Dunlop, 17 Jan. 1957
41 John T. Saywell, ed., *The Canadian Annual Review of Politics and Public Affairs for 1962* (Toronto: University of Toronto Press, 1963), 309
42 Toronto *Globe and Mail*, 27 Oct. 1967
43 PAO, RG2, Davis to Rose Marie Gross (copy), 23 Oct. 1967; PAO, RG3, Robarts file, Davis to Robert Welch (copy), 25 Feb 1969
44 *The Catholic Trustee*, March 1972, 16-18; Toronto *Star*, 10 June 1972
45 United Church *Observer*, February 1972, 20
46 Jozef Denys, 'Commitment through Education; A Study of Religious Socializing in Separate Schooling,' in Richard Carlton et al., eds, *Education, Change and Society: A Sociology of Canadian Education* (Toronto: Gage, 1977), 211-24
47 Ontario Department of Education, *Living and Learning: The Report of the Provincial Committee on Aims and Objectives of Education in the Schools of Ontario* (Toronto: Ontario Dept. of Education, 1968), 54, 67, 147
48 *Canadian and International Education*, 3 (1), June 1974, 102-3
49 *Living and Learning*, 77, 49, 54, 169
50 Ibid., 96, 180-1, 14
51 James Daly, *Education or Molasses? A Critical Look at the Hall-Dennis Report* (Ancaster, Ont.: Cromlech Press, 1969), 1-5
52 Toronto *Globe and Mail*, 13 Jan. 1969
53 Toronto *Globe and Mail*, 13 June 1968; see also Toronto *Telegram*, 14 June 1968
54 *Globe Magazine*, 29 June 1968
55 Fleming, *Ontario's Educative Society: III Schools, Pupils, and Teachers*, 151–4
56 TBE, *Annual Report, 1968*, 5, 7
57 Ross Traub et al., *Openness in Schools: An Evaluation Study* (Toronto, 1976), 50
58 London *Free Press*, 13 June 1968
59 Toronto *Telegram*, 20 Dec. 1966
60 Gilbert, *Let Each Become*, 57-8
61 Cited by John J. Stapleton, 'The Politics of Educational Innovations: A Case Study of the Credit System in Ontario' (unpublished PHD thesis, University of Toronto, 1975), 186
62 Ibid., 100
63 Gilbert, *Let Each Become*, 79
64 Toronto *Star*, 15 Feb. 1969
65 Ontario Department of Education, *Religious Information and Moral Development: The Report of the Committee on Religious Education in the Public Schools of the Province of Ontario* (Toronto, 1969), 27
66 Toronto *Globe and Mail*, 15 March 1969
67 *Maclean's Magazine*, September 1970, 6
68 See Niall Byrne, 'Innovation and the Teacher,' in Niall Byrne and Jack Quarter, eds, *Must Schools Fail? The Growing Debate in Canadian Education* (Toronto: McClelland and Stewart, 1972), 90-2

CHAPTER 11: *As the Pendulum Swings*

1 John McMurtry, 'The Iconoclast,' *Monday Morning*, November 1968, 28; Michael Katz, 'The Present Moment in Educational Reform,' in Terrence Morrison and Anthony Burton, eds, *Options: Reforms and Alternatives for Canadian Education* (Toronto: Holt, Rinehart and Winston, 1973), 20; George Martell, *The Politics of the Canadian Public School* (Toronto: James Lewis and Samuel, 1974), 15
2 'Newsletter from Everdale Place,' *This Magazine Is About Schools* winter 1967, 79
3 Marshall McLuhan, 'Education in the Electronic Age,' in Hugh A. Stevenson et al., eds, *The Best of Times/The Worst of Times: Contemporary Issues in Canadian Education* (Toronto: Holt, Rinehart and Winston, 1972), 515-31; and McLuhan, 'Electronics and the

Psychic Drop-Out,' in Satu Repo, ed., *This Book Is About Schools* (New York: Pantheon Books, 1970), 383-9

4 Toronto *Globe and Mail*, 25 May 1967

5 Toronto *Telegram*, 23 March 1967

6 Ibid., 16 Nov. 1968

7 Toronto *Star*, 3 May 1969

8 Ontario legislature, Select Committee on Youth, *Report* (Kingston, 1967)

9 PAO, RG2, Davis to C.D. Cutmore (copy), 1 Nov. 1966; Davis to L.C. Maule (copy), 21 Nov. 1968

10 Toronto *Globe and Mail*, 15 Oct. 1968

11 Fiona Nelson, 'Community Schools in Toronto: A Sign of Hope,' *Canadian Forum*, October-November 1972, 56

12 Toronto *Star*, 4 April 1970

13 Henry G. Hedges, 'Volunteer Assistance in Schools: Help or Hindrance?' unpublished address, Calgary, Alberta, March 1973

14 Ontario, legislature, Select Committee on the Utilization of Educational Facilities, *Interim Report Number One* (Toronto, 1973); Toronto *Globe and Mail*, 20 June 1973

15 George Martell, 'Notes to the Blake Street Community Council,' *This Magazine Is About Schools*, Spring 1971, 74-84

16 Toronto *Globe and Mail*, 14 Sept. 1964

17 Frank Jones and John Selby, 'School Performance and Social Class,' in Thomas J. Ryan, ed., *Poverty and the Child: A Canadian Study* (Toronto: McGraw-Hill Ryerson, 1972), 115-38

18 Timothy E. Reid, 'Education and Social Intervention in the Cycle of Canadian Poverty,' in Allen M. Linden, ed., *Living in the Seventies* (Toronto, 1970), 115-21

19 See John Buttrick, 'Who Goes to University in Ontario?,' *This Magazine is About Schools*, Summer 1972, 81-100; Edmund Clark, 'Socialization, Family Background and Secondary School,' in Robert Pike and Elia Zureik, eds, *Socialization and Values in Canadian Society* (Toronto: McClelland and Stewart, 1975), 77-103; P.M. George and H.Y. Kim, 'Social Factors and Educational Aspirations of Canadian High School Students,' in J.E. Gallagher and R.D. Lambert, eds, *Social Process and Institution: The Canadian Case* (Toronto: Holt, Rinehart and Winston, 1971), 352-63

20 Martell, *Politics of the Canadian Public School*, 8

21 Toronto *Star*, 27 July 1976

22 TBE, 'Chairman's Letter,' 4 May 1977

23 Garnet McDiarmid and David Pratt, *Teaching Prejudice: A Content Analysis of Social Studies Textbooks Authorized for Use in Ontario* (Toronto: Ontario Institute for Studies in Education, 1971), 41, 52

24 London *Free Press*, 25 Oct. 1969

25 A.B. Hodgetts, *What Culture? What Heritage? A Study of Civic Education in Canada* (Toronto: OISE, 1968); Toronto *Globe and Mail*, 18 Jan. 1969

26 Patricia Wellbourne, 'The Yanks are Coming,' *Weekend Magazine*, 22 March 1969, 3

27 PAO, RG2, Kenneth Brueton to Davis, 25 June 1968; Ronald Coombs to Davis, 19 Dec. 1968; G.D. Pritchard to Robarts (copy), 20 Nov. 1967

28 Sondra Thorson, 'Attitudes Towards School District Reorganization,' unpublished paper, OISE, 1968, 33-4

29 Toronto *Star*, 30 Jan. 1968

30 David Charles Walker, 'Public Policy and Community: The Impact of Regional Government on Pelham, Ontario' (PHD thesis, McMaster University, 1975), 308

31 Toronto *Globe and Mail*, 23 Nov. 1972

32 W.G. Fleming, *Ontario's Educative Society: II The Administrative Structure* (Toronto: University of Toronto Press, 1971), 149

33 Howard Fluxgold, 'Fool's Gold: The Politics of Education in Ontario,' *Canadian Forum*, January 1975, 22

34 Toronto *Globe and Mail*, 5 March 1969

35   Cited by Loren Lind, *The Learning Machine: A Hard Look at Toronto Schools* (Toronto: Anansi, 1974), 133
36   OSSTF, *Report of the Educational Finance Committee* (Toronto: OSSTF, 1973), 6-7
37   Lind, *The Learning Machine*, 198-9
38   Jack Hutton, 'First Hall-Dennis – And Now the Crunch,' *OSSTF Intercom*, March 1969, 1
39   Peter Oliver, 'Ontario,' in John T. Saywell, ed., *Canadian Annual Review, 1973* (Toronto: University of Toronto Press, 1974), 119
40   Toronto *Globe and Mail*, 4 and 8 March 1975
41   Toronto *Star*, 29 March 1975
42   Peter Oliver, 'Ontario,' in Saywell, ed., *Canadian Annual Review, 1975* (Toronto: University of Toronto Press, 1976), 132
43   Mike Sykes, 'Dear Mr. Dennis,' *CEA Newsletter*, January 1977, 5
44   Ronald Duhamel, 'Standards in Education: What Are the Issues?' *OCLEA News*, June 1977, 10-11
45   Toronto *Globe and Mail*, 20 Aug. 1977
46   Duhamel, 'Standards in Education,' 10
47   Toronto *Star*, 23 Feb. 1973
48   *Educational Dimensions*, January 1974, 1
49   Toronto *Globe and Mail*, 22 and 30 Aug. 1975
50   AR, 1974-5, 2
51   'Are Canadians Getting Their $12 Billion Worth?' *Maclean's Magazine*, 6 Sept. 1976, 38
52   OSSTF, *At What Cost? A Study of the Role of the Secondary School in Ontario* (Toronto: OSSTF, 1976), 34, 47
53   Ontario Ministry of Colleges and Universities, 'News Release,' 20 Jan. 1977
54   Cited by Barbara Amiel, 'Let's Learn (Again) How to Produce an Elite,' *Saturday Night*, October 1976, 25
55   Toronto *Globe and Mail*, 7 Oct. 1976

EPILOGUE

1   AR, 1975-6, 4
2   AR, 1976-7, 5
3   Ibid., 6
4   Toronto *Globe and Mail*, 13 November 1976
5   AR, 1976-7, 5

Appendix 1

PREMIERS, MINISTERS OF EDUCATION, DEPUTY MINISTERS OF EDUCATION, AND CHIEF DIRECTORS OF EDUCATION, 1876-1976

Premiers	Ministers	Deputy Ministers	Chief Directors
Oliver Mowat 1872–96	Adam Crooks 1876–83 George W. Ross 1883–99	John G. Hodgins 1876–90 Alexander Marling 1890 John Millar 1890–1905	
Arthur S. Hardy 1896–99			
George W. Ross 1899–1905	Richard Harcourt 1899–1905		
James P. Whitney 1905–14	R.A. Pyne 1905–18	Arthur H. Colquhoun 1906–34	John Seath* 1906–19
William H. Hearst 1914–19	H:J. Cody 1918–19		
E.C. Drury 1919–23	R.H. Grant 1919–23		
G. Howard Ferguson 1923–30	G. Howard Ferguson 1923–30		Francis W. Merchant 1923–30
George S. Henry 1930–34	George S. Henry 1930–34		George F. Rogers 1930–34

* Superintendent of Education (forerunner of Chief Director of Education)

APPENDIX 1 (cont'd)

Premiers	Ministers	Deputy Ministers	Chief Directors
Mitchell F. Hepburn 1934–42	Leo J. Simpson 1934–40 Duncan McArthur 1940–43	Duncan McArthur 1934–40 George F. Rogers 1940–45	Duncan McArthur 1934–43
Gordon Conant 1942–43			
H.C. Nixon 1943			
George A. Drew 1943–48	George A. Drew 1943–48	John P. Cowles 1945–46 Frank S. Rutherford 1946–51	John G. Althouse 1944–56
T.L. Kennedy 1948–49	Dana Porter 1948–51		
Leslie M. Frost 1949–61	William J. Dunlop 1951–59 John P. Robarts 1959–62	Cecil F. Cannon 1951–56 Charles W. Booth 1956–63 Floyd S. Rivers 1956–61	Cecil F. Cannon 1956–61
John P. Robarts 1961–71	William G. Davis 1962–71	Harold E. Elborn 1961–65 William R. Stewart 1963–65 Zachary S. Phimister 1965–66 John R. McCarthy 1967–71	Floyd S. Rivers 1961–65**
William G. Davis 1971–	Robert S. Welch Mar. 1971–Feb. 1972 Thomas Wells 1972–78	Edward E. Stewart 1971–73 George H. Waldrum 1973–79	

NOTE: From November 1956 to January 1965 there were two deputy ministers, one for elementary, the other for secondary education. For many years also, there were chief directors of education who were responsible for the academic side of the department's work.
** Position abolished with departmental reorganization in 1965.

Appendix 2

AVERAGE SALARIES OF TEACHERS IN ONTARIO

| | Public Schools | | | | | | | | | | Secondary Schools (High Schools & Collegiate Institutes) |
| | Male | | | | | Female | | | | | |
Year	Prov-ince	City	Town	Urban	Rural	Prov-ince	City	Town	Urban	Rural	Province
1877	$ 398	$735	$583	$ –	$379	$264	$307	$269	$ –	$251	$ 756
1887	425	832	619	–	398	292	382	289	–	271	823
1897	391	892	621	–	347	294	425	306	–	254	920
1907	596	1157	800	907	458	420	592	406	453	379	1039
1917	1038	1637	1166	1425	686	650	795	628	731	580	1448
1926	1644	2287	1775	2097	1136	1203	1470	1094	1340	963	2376
1935	1376	2180	1390	1922	848	1035	1531	951	1348	710	2191
1944	1930	2527	1756	2268	1224	1295	1625	1174	1469	1063	2396
1956	4289	4963	4009	4686	3101	3504	4159	3427	3948	2774	5249
1965	5261					4515					7220
1974	11862					9501					13333
1975–6	14578*										18415
1976–7	16668										20629
1977–8	18467										22487
1978–9	20030										24357

* No separation of male and female after 1974
In 1975–6 public school teachers' average salaries rose 23%; secondary school teachers' salaries, 38%.
SOURCES: Annual Reports of the Minister of Education of Ontario and of the Ontario Education Relations Commission

Appendix 3

SCHOOL ENROLMENTS

Public Schools					High Schools and Collegiate Institutes			
	No. of Teachers		No. of	Pupil / Teacher		No. of	No. of	Pupil / Teach
Year	Male	Female	Students	Ratio	Year	Teachers	Students	Ratio
1877	3,020	3,448	465,908	72:1	1877	280	9,229	33:1
1882	3,362	3,660	445,364	63:1				
					1887	398	17,459	44:1
1892	2,635	5,183	458,553	59:1				
					1897	579	24,390	42:1
1902	2,202	6,297	420,094	49:1				
					1907	750	30,331	40:1
1912	1,415	8,105	429,030	45:1				
1917	1,219	10,055	458,436	41:1	1917	1,051	29,097	28:1
1927	2,101	11,857	535,691	38:1	1927	1,875	59,692	32:1
1934	2,804	11,652	465,171	32:1	1934	2,361	70,283	30:1
1941–2	4,391	17,002	433,597	20:1				
1945	2,891	15,079	436,709	24:1	1945	4,751	119,773	25:1
1955	5,214	16,804	676,246	31:1	1955	8,036	174,562	22:1
1960	7,107	20,963	843,737	30:1				
					1962–3	14,923	331,578	22:1
1965	9,479	23,304	949,374	29:1	1965	21,659	418,738	19:1
1970	8,151	34,300	1,047,055	25:1	1970	32,342	556,913	17:1
1975	8,192	32,519	961,625	24:1				
1976	6,679	33,785	937,292	23:1	1976	35,352	613,055	17:1
1977	5,606	33,789	907,777	23:1	1977	35,454	613,830	17:1
					1978	35,068	611,668	17:1

SOURCE: Annual Reports of the Minister of Education of Ontario and of the Federation of Women Teachers' Associations of Ontario; *Education Statistics*, Ontario, 1980

Index